THE MOSAIC MIND

Empowering the Tormented Selves
of Child Abuse Survivors

Other books by Richard C. Schwartz

Internal Family Systems Therapy

Family Therapy: Concepts and Methods (3rd ed.)
(with M. P. Nichols)

Metaframeworks: Transcending the Models of Family Therapy
(with D. C. Breunlin and B. Mac Kune-Karrer)

Handbook of Family Therapy Training and Supervision
(edited, with D. C. Breunlin and H. Liddle)

A NORTON PROFESSIONAL BOOK

THE MOSAIC MIND

Empowering the Tormented Selves
of Child Abuse Survivors

Regina A. Goulding
Richard C. Schwartz

W. W. NORTON & COMPANY • NEW YORK • LONDON

CREDITS
Selected excerpts and three excerpts used as chapter epigraphs from
Trauma and Recovery by Judith Lewis Herman, M.D. Copyright © 1992
by BasicBooks, a division of HarperCollins Publishers, Inc. Reprinted by
permission of BasicBooks, a division of HarperCollins Publishers, Inc.
Excerpts from **You Don't Love Yourself** by Nathalie Sarraute. Copyright
© 1990, English translation by George Braziller, Inc. Reprinted by permission of George Braziller, Inc.
Excerpts from **Unity and Multiplicity** by John Beahrs. Copyright ©
1982 by John Beahrs. Reprinted by permission of Brunner/Mazel, Inc.

Printed in the United States of America

First Edition

Composition by Bytheway Typesetting Services, Inc.
Manufacturing by Haddon Craftsmen, Inc.

Library of Congress Cataloging-in-Publication Data
Goulding, Regina A.
    The mosaic mind : empowering the tormented selves of child abuse
survivors / Regina A. Goulding, Richard C. Schwartz.
      p.   cm.
    "A Norton professional book".
    Includes bibliographical references and index.
    ISBN 0-393-70178-6
    1. Adult child sexual abuse victims—Rehabilitation. 2. Multiple
personality. 3. Psychosynthesis. I. Schwartz, Richard C.
II. Title.
RC569.5.A28G68   1995
616.85'83690651—dc20   94-48407 CIP

W.W. Norton & Company, Inc., 500 Fifth Avenue, New York, NY 10110
W.W. Norton & Company, Ltd., 10 Coptic Street, London WC1A 1PU

1 2 3 4 5 6 7 8 9 0

To my daughter Elizabeth for sharing her vision of a world filled with beauty and love. To Maurice, a man with great courage and compassion; I have always been proud to call him my son. And to Emily and Sophie Elizabeth for the joy they have brought to our family.

—RAG

To Lorene and the many other survivors who have acted as my mentors.

—RCS

Contents

PART IV: SURVIVOR-THERAPIST RELATIONSHIP ISSUES

Acknowledgments

This book would not exist were it not for Dick Schwartz's rare compassion and commitment to both the discovery and the safe application of the principles underlying his Internal Family Systems treatment model. He continually opens his mind to new ideas without bias, re-examines old ideas with fervor and freshness, examines mistakes with engaging candor, and spiritedly debates complex and troubling issues.

—RAG

The contributions of the people who helped develop the Internal Family Systems model have been acknowledged elsewhere (Schwartz, 1995). A few of those people have made major contributions to the model's application to adult survivors of childhood sexual abuse. Deborah Gorman-Smith's insights regarding the therapist/client relationships and many other aspects of this work have been invaluable, as have Ann Womack's ideas. I am also indebted to Mary Jo Barrett, David Calof and Susan Hoke. Finally, this book is a tribute to Regina Goulding's amazing mind and soul.

—RCS

We both thank Lorene, for everything she has given us, and other survivors who have shared so much with us in both our personal and professional lives. We received able assistance from numerous people; we especially thank Janet Grossman for reading portions of the book and exploring ideas with us, and Nancy Hobbie-Lowe for hours of painstaking reading and perceptive editing. And we thank Susan Barrows Munro for her enthusiasm, her guidance, and her considerable talent at turning ideas and verbiage into a living, breathing book. A special thanks to Kate Boyle and staff of the Suburban Library System Photocopy Services, and Cris Sakalas at Suburban Library System Reference Services; without their professional research assistance, this book would be barren.

—RAG & RCS

Preface

Because the issue once touched my family, I feel great empathy for people who were sexually abused as children. As an attorney, much of my pro bono work has been with child abuse victims—both children and adult survivors. I have often felt particularly troubled that the fields of mental health and law have so little to offer in terms of reparation or healing. I was intrigued, therefore, when, after becoming friends with a legal client whom I'll call Lorene, I heard her often speak enthusiastically about her exhilarating and healing "parts" therapy with Richard Schwartz. She explained how she had learned to identify and explore the subtle but autonomous subpersonalities within her personality, such as her "sad part," "angry part," and "hurt part." Lorene was most excited about discovering her "Self," an inner core of enormous strength which could comfort and lead the various parts of her personality.

Thus I encountered the Internal Family Systems (IFS) model, which Richard Schwartz began developing in the early 1980s. Lorene introduced me to Dick, and a new friendship began to develop. Over the next few years, Dick and I vigorously poked at the model's underlying concepts, oftentimes brave enough to explore our own inner families as our odyssey pulled us forward. In addition, Dick introduced me to therapists he had trained in the IFS model; they provided me with invaluable information and reported finding the IFS model to be highly effective with extraordinary consistency.

In my work as an attorney, I continued to encounter mental health professionals who used the IFS model. I found their understanding of the effects of child abuse and survivors' capacity to heal outdistanced many other clinicians I encountered. I began to regret that the IFS model was not more readily available to a greater number of professionals, adult survivors, parents of victimized children, offenders, and attorneys who sought to grasp the relevant psychological issues. And so this book was born.

One of the greatest gifts I received during these years of exploration was from Lorene. She provided extraordinary audiotapes of her sessions with Dick, in addition to journals where she recorded her inner conversations. These documented conversations proved invaluable in my learning process and, with her permission and support, I have excerpted many of them to illustrate aspects of the survivor's world and IFS therapy. Thus, in addition to a comprehensive description of the IFS model, this book provides a unique window into the inner world of one survivor of childhood sexual abuse. Because of this, I think that survivors will find this book very helpful; however, because some of the material is quite intense and heart-rending, it may be advisable for survivors to take it in small doses and share their reactions with a therapist.

The first half of this book presents the theoretical underpinnings of the IFS model. It explores differences and similarities between IFS and other multiplicity-oriented theories which may be found in both the general literature of multiplicity and dissociation and the literature pertaining directly to child abuse. The remainder of the book focuses on practical treatment issues in working with adult survivors of child sexual abuse. The book also provides ways for therapists to understand and change their own personal reactions to survivors in this most provoking and difficult of therapies.

Finally, having come to grips with our understanding of the complexities and subtleties of the psyche of traumatized people, we were left to face the nemesis of every writer using the English language — gender pronouns — how to avoid offending anyone without destroying the flow of the sentence by awkwardly inserting a her-or-him, he-or-she, he/she, s/he, or a plural where there should be a singular. Great linguists have not solved the problem, and quite honestly we have not tried. We chose to write much the way people talk — somewhat arbitrarily in our scattered use of he and she. (Because the majority of victims are female, however, one might find, in counting the hers and hims, that we more often refer to abuse victims with female pronouns.) We hope the pronouns are not distracting, and we look forward to a linguistic solution.

                                                                    —RAG

This book is concerned with the turbulent and tortured inner worlds of people who were severely abused as children. It presents a framework, the internal family systems (IFS) model, for understanding and safely changing delicate ecologies of the psyche. It is thoroughly researched and generously sprinkled with quotes from the literature on treating sexual abuse survivors. The remarkable journal of one courageous survivor, Lorene (a pseudonym), gives us a window for observing a polarized inner society in action. Her private internal conversations illuminate the myriad issues with which survivors struggle.

Yet this book is much more than that. It is an expansion and enrichment of the IFS model, rendering it clearer and yet more sophisticated. The first book on the model (Schwartz, 1995) had room for only a few chapters describing the operation of internal systems. In contrast, the topic of internal families is the focus of this entire book. As a result, we are able to elaborate on our understanding of the Self, and to add ideas of quantum physics to describe how the whole internal system can be both a particle and a wave—both multiple and unitary. It also advances the notion of a continuum of inner polarization and enmeshment, which aids us in assessing and conceptualizing internal families. We also are able to carefully examine parts of therapists who are activated in this work, as well as the key elements of the therapist/client relationship. Most importantly, Lorene's journal entries bring the parts to life. The personality and predicament of each part, as well as the intricate web of relationships among them and how these are affected by abuse, are dramatically revealed such that readers will be left with renewed respect for the multiplicity phenomenon. In addition, readers will gain a heightened appreciation of the struggles of a client's Self to earn the trust of her terrified parts and their struggle to trust the therapist. For all these reasons, this book is a major advance in the evolution of the IFS model and should be read not only by those who work with survivors but also by anyone interested in the intrapsychic process.

This book owes its existence to an odd and serendipitous collaboration which begs for explanation. Lorene, the heroine, was a client with whom I had been working for three years by the time she met Regina Goulding. My work with Lorene was at once the most thrilling and frustrating of my career to that point. Together we explored her amazing internal landscape, searching through caves and abysses and meeting all manner of strange, scary, and stubborn inhabitants. Together we experimented with new concepts and methods for helping her change all that. Much of what I learned from helping Lorene wrestle with her parts became significant advances in the IFS model.

Four years ago, Lorene was referred to Reg for a legal consultation, and the two quickly became friends. Historically, Lorene had kept a safe distance from family and friends but, as evidence of her increased trust in her Self, she gradually opened the door to Reg and began describing the work we were doing. Ultimately, Lorene shared her journal with its documentation of her fascinating inner dialogues and, as different parts interacted, its dramatic shifts in handwriting. Reg became intrigued with the process and called me to see how she could learn more. After attending workshops and seminars, Reg declared that I was not writing enough about the IFS model as it applied to survivors of childhood sexual abuse, a topic that was increasingly consuming my interest and energy. She proposed a collaboration—if I would teach her the IFS model and what I was learning from my survivor clients, she would do much of the research and writing. I accepted this proposal reluctantly, and we began what evolved into regular meetings over the past two years. My initial skepticism changed to delight as I gradually realized what a quick and powerful mind I was engaged with. We quickly became good friends.

These meetings not only produced this book but also spurred me to clarify, expand and improve the IFS model so as to satisfy Reg's sharp curiosity. She proved to be an amazing researcher, quickly digesting nearly everything written about treating survivors and comparing that literature to my ideas and methods.

Midway through this project, Lorene decided that we should use her journal to illustrate the book. She and I had terminated therapy over a year before (she returned only twice in the following year to order to clarify specific issues), but she remained close friends with Reg and was advising her on the book. After several conversations with Lorene, reassuring me that she and all her parts were aware and approving of this decision, we began inserting appropriate entries into the manuscript. These additions brought the book to life and, in my mind, are a large part of what makes this book so valuable. Lorene's journal richly demonstrates the full-personality nature of parts, their common patterns and reactions, their ability to transform, and the courage and wisdom of the Self. After reading these entries, it is hard to deny that within Lorene lives an internal family.

I am enormously grateful to Reg and to Lorene for this remarkable book.

—RCS

"I must go, but my soul lies helpless
beside your bed."

—D.H. Lawrence, 1913

PART I
Theory and Principles

CHAPTER 1

A Systems Model
of Multiplicity

*The chronically abused person's apparent helplessness
and passivity, her entrapment in the past, her intractable
depression and somatic complaints, and her smoldering
anger often frustrate the people closest to her.*

—*Judith Herman, 1992*

MANY CLINICIANS TREATING survivors of severe sexual abuse report that the treatment process remains a long, confusing, frustrating, and often unsuccessful ordeal. The literature is replete with statements by clinicians attesting to the formidable challenge presented by unresolved childhood sexual victimization (Sgroi & Bunk, 1988). Briere (1989b) reports that many survivors seem as if they are "not home" emotionally and he acknowledges that "the drama of a psychologically absent person may prove overwhelming to some clinicians" (p. 120). Steele (1988) describes a common clinical reaction of fear: "As her history unfolded before me, I became witness to the shattering of her soul. I became afraid at times that nothing good was left" (p. 77).

Lorene, a 28-year-old client of Schwartz, is typical of many survivors of severe sexual abuse who seek therapy as adults. She describes memories of her father slipping into her childhood bed. She insists that she is evil, worthless, and deserving of punishment (which she often inflicts on herself). Session after session, she continues to talk about herself in disparaging ways, despite her therapist's best efforts to assure her that she is not bad. The therapist knows that powerful feelings resulting from the abuse lurk beneath this veil of self-loathing, but Lorene resists every attempt to access those feelings. She maintains that her abusive father (now dead) loved her; she "spaces out" every time she is asked for any details of the abuse; she drops out of therapy for weeks or months at a time following any session in which she shows sadness or rage; and she insists that her self-mutilation, drug abuse, sexual compulsions, and depression are evidence of her inherent craziness and have nothing to do with her past. Clients like Lorene test the limits of even the most compassionate and accepting therapists, who eventually feel exasperated at the apparent lack of significant change, frustrated and unappreciated at being blocked by the client at every turn, and scared by the client's self-destructive behavior. These feelings of the therapist are invariably, if unintentionally, transmitted to the client, causing her to feel that, once again, she is a failure and will be abandoned soon — thus increasing her reluctance to trust the therapist.

Without a comprehensive treatment model to show us otherwise, therapists are left to believe that these early traumas have damaged some of their clients severely and permanently, destroying any internal resources that might have permitted a full recovery. The extreme protectiveness and desperation that survivors typically exhibit in therapy only reinforce these beliefs. "As caregivers tire of these chronically unhappy people who do not seem to improve, the temptation to apply pejorative diagnostic labels becomes overwhelming" (Herman, 1992, p. 119). While the therapist's responses are understandable, the consequences for treatment are far more devastating than might be commonly recognized. The client and therapist share a growing sense of despair over what they perceive to be the client's psychological defectiveness induced by the childhood abuse. The therapeutic relationship sinks into a heavy dependency which, in turn, perpetuates the client's basic assumption that she is broken beyond repair. They both believe the client cannot be fixed, and that in order to function well the client must remain forever dependent on a mental health professional, like a kidney patient and her dialysis machine.

For survivors, the initial abuse triggers a nightmarish life permeated by denial, betrayal, and further abuse. The child initially adapts to the sexual abuse by isolating from conscious awareness those "parts" of her that hold the memories, physical sensations, aloneness, sense of betrayal, and vulnerability. Other parts, who hold the terror, rage, and shame, clash with parts who want to act "good," socially acceptable, and successful. These internal polarizations lead the victim to behave in extreme ways throughout childhood and into adult life. The adult survivor entering therapy may complain that those around her often misunderstand her and push her away. Rejection, in turn, reinforces her belief that she is unlovable, flawed, tainted, or evil. And, in truth, some people *do* sense her vulnerability and exploit and reabuse her. Still others might try to help, but later join the survivor in feeling overwhelmed and frustrated by the contradictory behavior she exhibits, one moment appearing cooperative and the next resisting any attempt at friendship or help.

As if these external factors were not enough, a host of inner critics, terrorists, and tricksters chronically torment the survivor. She alternates between the limbo of numbness and the chaos of excruciating sensations and emotions. She desperately craves love, yet feels vile and unlovable. All manner of physical pains and illnesses, as well as dreadful flashbacks and images, plague her. She feels uncontrollably driven toward secretive and destructive activities such as bingeing on alcohol, drugs, food, sex, or self-mutilation. Throughout this torturous haze, the survivor may both fear and long for the day she finally kills herself. Often a mask of calmness, competence, and courtesy hides this nightmarish life that she wanders alone.

THE NEED FOR A NEW TREATMENT MODEL

Despite the daunting challenges, many therapists working with survivors continue the struggle to learn how to safely enter, and bring harmony to, their clients' internal lives, but they seek a new treatment model to help in that struggle. Rieker and Carmen (1986) contend that therapists "need a schema to help them recognize the behavior and the subtle clues" presented by adult victims of childhood abuse (p. 368). Kilgore (1988) notes the absence of a "theoretical framework for understanding the descriptive findings and for predicting and applying [the] findings to clinical practice" (p. 224) with sexual abuse victims, perpetrators, and their families. Similarly, Ellenson (1989) decries the lack of a theoretical framework and criticizes the use of orthodox analytic theory to treat incest survivors. Blake-White and Kline (1985) maintain that it "has become increasingly necessary for clinicians to develop a method of treatment" (p. 394). Siegel and Romig (1988) point to the "less than adequate" literature addressing the overall needs of adult survivors of child sexual assault, and "even fewer references pertaining to treatment" (p. 229). We believe that both clinicians and survivors would struggle far less if they were certain that the survivor still held healthy internal resources that could be located and used.

An abuse-oriented philosophy views a victim's extreme beliefs and behavior as responses that were initially healthy and adaptive defenses—not signs of pathology—but are now outdated, unhelpful, or destructive. But we need more than this philosophy. We need a treatment model that thoroughly familiarizes survivors with their already existing internal resources, which can once again be used to benefit the survivors. These resources need only be reorganized and freed from abuse-related beliefs learned in childhood. This book presents a treatment model that attempts to address these needs.

HEALTHY INTERNAL DEFENSES

The mental health field has taken an important first step by recognizing the shocking prevalence of childhood sexual abuse. Reports of sexual abuse (defined as ranging from fondling to penetration of a child by an older person) are increasing rapidly, despite the fact that it is still considered one of the most *under*reported crimes being committed today. In 1993 the National Committee for the Prevention of Child Abuse and Neglect reported that there are about 200,000 *substantiated* cases of sexual abuse annually, and the number increases by about 10% each year. Clinicians have also taken the next important step by recognizing the devastating sequelae of childhood sexual abuse, which remains one of the most severe types of trauma suffered by human beings (Herman, 1992).

A movement now occurring in the mental health profession offers yet another source of hope for survivors of childhood abuse. Previously, many therapists offered clients a diagnosis, assigning them a pathological label. A significant number of clinicians now recognize that labels of psychosis, schizophrenia, bipolar disorder, depression, borderline personality, alcoholism, multiple personality disorder, phobia, anorexia, and bulimia bring little relief to clients and, in fact, downplay or deny the healthy internal defenses that sexual abuse victim so capably organized as children in order to survive. In addition to diagnostic labels, the over-simplified explanations of bad genes, bad parenting, current family interactions, sociocultural attitudes, or biochemical imbalances are no longer accepted as accounting fully for why many people become trapped in cycles of severe depression and self-destructive behavior. Instead, we know that for many of these victims the explanation lies in the betrayal, deception, and torture of childhood sexual abuse that shattered their natural instincts to trust themselves, the safety of their environment, and the honesty and caring of those around them. Because of this knowledge, increasing numbers of therapists strive to create safe environments where clients can reveal and liberate themselves from their abusive histories. This knowledge establishes a new basis of support for clinicians to treat clients with care, patience, and empathy rather than with medication, pathologizing diagnoses, and hospitals. They can avoid imposing unnecessary psychiatric nomenclature on clients, instead sharing with them a more positive, empowering language and philosophy.

THE INTERNAL FAMILY
SYSTEMS MODEL

The Internal Family Systems (IFS) treatment model, developed by Richard Schwartz in the early 1980s, combines the recognition of the initially adaptive and healthy responses to child abuse and the growing understanding of the natural and healthy multiplicity of the personality. Under this view, the normal psyche consists of various subpersonalities or "parts." The number of theorists who recognize the multiplicity of the mind has mushroomed in the past decade, such that this previously nontraditional view is no longer perceived as esoteric or radical. Jung's ground-breaking concepts, followed by Assagioli's (1965) theory of psychosynthesis, have been joined by the explorations of numerous theorists (Beahrs, 1982; Hillman, 1975; Johnson, 1986; Putnam, 1989; Redfearn, 1985; Stone & Winkelman, 1985; Watanabe, 1986; Watkins & Watkins, 1981, 1988; M. Watkins, 1986). In addition, there are more mainstream theories such as object relations, self psychology, transactional analysis, and Gestalt therapy, all of which describe subminds of some sort.

The IFS model is unique in its synthesis of two conceptual frameworks: *multiplicity of the mind* and *systems thinking*. Certain principles and techniques in other models that recognize the natural multiplicity of the mind bear some similarity to IFS, but the underlying assumptions differ at key points; these include views on the origin of the parts, their status in the personality, and the ultimate goal of therapy. Some theorists contend that parts exist in "normal," healthy individuals, but they differ as to the origin of parts in the absence of trauma. Almost all theorists conclude that trauma triggers some type of increased division or dissociation within the personality, but some believe that the division of subpersonalities appears *only* in traumatized individuals. Many theorists respect multiplicity but do not use systemic principles to understand the inner relationships. While some see the logical necessity for an internal leader of the various subpersonalities, they differ as to what the leader is like, how the leader is selected, and how long that leader reigns. Others find that internal leadership, if any, simply passes to the most powerful or aggressive part of the moment. Some clinicians agree theoretically with many of the principles underlying the IFS model, yet struggle to apply them within the psychotherapy relationship, particularly when challenged by the powerful defenses of survivors of severe childhood abuse. Despite the many differences in these therapeutic approaches, however, they all recognize the essential need to address the multiple nature of the personality.

MULTIPLICITY AND DISSOCIATION

We shall see that, because we are naturally multiple, it is healthy to *differentiate* our multiple parts from each other. But this separateness becomes unhealthy — *dissociation* — when the separateness between parts is extreme. We are particularly interested in the extreme dissociation of survivors' parts because it acts as a magnifying glass, permitting us to more easily view the natural multiplicity in all people. While trauma does not cause the innate separateness within the psyche, the trauma heightens or intensifies the separateness until it becomes unhealthy or destructive. Survivors of abuse become adept at pushing their parts further away from each other into dark isolation, so that memories, sensations, and intense emotions resulting from the abuse will remain buried. One part can keep the survivor functioning, while others hold frightening memories and bodily sensations.

Victims of abuse effectively use their natural multiplicity, along with extreme dissociation, to adapt to severe trauma. Putnam (1989) remarks that the dissociative process is "receiving attention . . . as a model for understanding the impact of trauma on such crucial developmental tasks as the consolidation of a sense of self" (p. 1). In the IFS model, the multiplicity inherent in dissociation is viewed as neither abnormal nor unhealthy. Rather, it is the extremeness of the dissociation or polarization between parts and the loss of trust in any natural internal leader that cause the crippling difficulties experienced by survivors.

As with multiplicity, "most authorities recognize that dissociation occurs in both minor non-pathological and major or pathological forms. Many authors conceptualize these different forms of dissociation as lying on a continuum from the minor dissociations of everyday life, such as daydreaming, to the major pathological forms, such as multiple personality" (Putnam, 1989, p. 6). Therefore, the extreme multiplicity we see through defensive and protective dissociation lies on the same continuum (depicted in chapter 3) as the less extreme multiplicity we each experience in our daily lives.

Accepting the premise that we all contain a number of discrete, relatively autonomous subpersonalities changes our understanding of labels like multiple personality disorder (MPD). In clients such as Lorene, the existence of different subpersonalities, with various values and viewpoints, is not an indication that survivors differ drastically from the rest of us. Instead of branding a person as having an intimidating disorder, the multiplicity view places multiple personality disorder on a continuum, noting it as one of the ways in which the naturally-occurring internal family of subpersonalities adapts to sadistic and chronic abuse. The difference between non-abused people and MPD clients is that the latter suffer from the lack of communication between their parts and from the absence of any continuity in the leadership of their internal system.

ORIGIN OF PARTS

The literature on sexual abuse survivors indicates that virtually every clinician has encountered subpersonalities. For example, Briere (1989b) states that "[s]ome survivors of severe sexual abuse . . . appear to operate from multiple, coexisting developmental states that variously influence . . . her adult behavior" (p. 107). In treating adult survivors of childhood abuse, many clinicians have described working with a client's "inner child" and other internal parts (Agosta & Loring, 1989; Courtois, 1988; Dolan, 1991; Ellis, 1990; Gannon, 1989; Hoffman, 1987). In attempting to describe this multiplicity phenomenon, various terms are used (coexisting developmental states, ego states, internal objects, subpersonalities, alters, sub-selves). The IFS model uses the word "parts" because it is user-friendly; clients are generally very comfortable using it ("a part of me wants to take this new job, but another part of me is afraid").

Most theorists writing about sexual abuse survivors attribute the existence of the inner subpersonalities to the trauma of the abuse, which they assume caused a splitting of the normally unitary personality into fragments. This is the same view commonly held by MPD theorists. Typical of this position, Courtois (1988) describes the "splitting off of dimensions of the personality into partial or whole alter personalities, each with a different degree of consciousness or lack of consciousness" (p. 154). Courtois goes on to say that "survivors who have used dissociation extensively, some to the point of developing multiple personalities, present the most extreme form of splitting and the greatest challenge in the integration process" (p. 174).

The clinician's belief regarding the origin of subpersonalities or parts dramatically impacts the course of treatment. If the clinician believes a part originated from trauma—a splitting off—then the goal will be to fuse the split. The effectiveness of the therapeutic work with parts suffers when parts realize that their individual existence is not respected. In contrast, we believe that the existence of parts is normal, and that parts exist from birth in potential. They emerge as distinct parts as we pass through significant points in our life. Many theories have been proposed regarding the origin of parts. Redfearn (1985) suggests the following list of possible origins of the many selves within us: (1) archetypes, (2) complexes, (3) introjected objects, (4) introjected part objects, (5) parts of the body-image, or bodily functions, functioning as subpersonalities, (6) part-brain functions, and (7) deities, social values and ideals. Johnson (1986) reasons that archetypes are the "pre-existing 'first patterns' that form the basic blueprint for the major dynamic components of the human personality. . . . They are inborn within us as part of our inheritance as members of the human race" (p. 29). Watkins and Watkins (1979) speculate that, "Some ego states probably are demarcated as part of normal human development. Others split off during times of stress to function as defenses" (p. 6).

The IFS principles concur with Samuels' (1989) belief that, "Once formed, each sense of self remains fully functioning and active throughout life. All continue to grow and coexist" (p. 23). The IFS model is grounded on the belief that parts are natural, an innate resource we have from birth. In his recent book on the IFS model, Schwartz (1995) explains his understanding of the developmental process of a healthy internal system:

> Human systems come fully equipped in that they have all the resources they need at the outset for a healthy, harmonious existence, [however] they need time within a sustaining environment to develop those resources. The

members of the system need time to discover their visions and preferred roles; to harmonize their relationships; and to balance influence, resources, responsibilities, and boundaries. The system's leader also needs time to establish credibility, trust and a shared vision. If the system exists in a sustaining, nurturing environment during its development, this healthy state will unfold naturally and at its proper pace. Indeed, central to the IFS model is the belief that systems have a wisdom about that pace, which needs to be respected. (p. 135)

Sexual abuse robs the child of this healthy developmental process. The IFS model describes a process in which trauma causes parts' development to become frozen in time. Trauma changes each part's perception of the world and role in the person's life. Trauma does not *create* an entity which did not exist previously. Even a part who absorbs the impact of trauma existed before the trauma occurred. (Sometimes a part will say it was born at the time of the trauma, but what it usually means is that it was forced into an extreme role at that point.)

Thus, the IFS model concludes that the differentiation process is inherent in the nature of the mind rather than being the result of trauma or introjection of external phenomena. Our disagreement with a trauma-only view of the origin of multiplicity is that it unnecessarily imbues survivors with an odor of pathology and defectiveness (Schwartz, 1995). This tone changes drastically if one respects natural multiplicity. The client is given the message that she is not damaged so much as parts of her are scared and continue to base their actions on outdated beliefs which are related to the early sexual abuse. As we shall see, severe and chronic abuse polarizes internal families. Many of the survivor's subpersonalities come to fear, hate, and avoid each other such that when one takes over, others have to leave.

The IFS model fosters a treatment philosophy, language, and process which creates a collaborative atmosphere, not only between the therapist and client, but also among the client's inner parts and between the client's Self and parts. The model offers a fresh, systemic look at the internal process which takes place within victims of severe sexual abuse. As the client's inner resources surface, the foundation of empowerment and hope becomes solidified.

AN OVERVIEW OF IFS PRINCIPLES

We briefly outline the major assumptions of the IFS model, which are explored in detail in later chapters.

Multiplicity

The human mind is naturally divided into parts. The parts of one person demonstrate different temperaments, talents, desires, ages, and gender. Together they form an internal family, which organizes in the same way as other human systems. Each part, in its non-extreme state, wants what is best for the internal system. Use of the IFS multiplicity perspective teaches the survivor that she differs from people who were not abused only in the degree to which her internal parts have become isolated from each other and have lost their trust in her ability to protect them. Clinicians using the IFS approach no longer characterize the client's personality as "splintered" or "fragmented," or cite the goal of wholeness and unity that is supposedly experienced by "normal" people. Rather, multiplicity itself is viewed as a normal, healthy state.

Parts are forced into extreme states by their environment. Survivors of childhood sexual abuse, for example, learn to be hyper-vigilant, looking for danger around every corner. Extreme or isolated parts will use a variety of strategies to gain influence within the internal system in order to have their goals met, often becoming polarized with other parts who have conflicting goals. The goal is not to fuse all these personalities. Instead, the IFS therapist seeks to restore leadership, balance, and harmony in the internal system such that each part can take its preferred, valuable role. The parts will only relinquish their protective or extreme roles, however, when they believe it is safe to do so. Once internal and external constraints are removed, a part always reveals an innate drive toward balance and health.

Polarization

The abuse results in near-impermeable boundaries between the parts. Polarizations leave parts isolated in their opposing positions. For example, one part of a survivor may wish to disclose secrets of the abuse, while other parts prohibit such disclosure for fear the person will drown in feelings of betrayal, rage, and despair.

Blending

The opposite of polarization is what we call blending, a process resulting in blurred or non-existent boundaries between parts. For example, if a frightened child-part successfully blends with other parts, the survivor feels overwhelmed by fear. The child-part must learn that by not keeping his emotions within his own boundaries, he is preventing the survivor from actively helping or caring for him.

Self Leadership

In addition to parts, people contain a "Self," an innate core of the psyche that differs significantly from parts due to its meta-perspective and its many leadership qualities, like compassion, curiosity, and courage. The unconstrained Self leads the internal system by caring for and depolarizing parts in an equitable, firm, and compassionate way. It leads discussions with the parts regarding major decisions in the person's life. The Self does not need to be strengthened, nor is it merely a passive observer. Child abuse victims become particularly adept at hiding and protecting the Self, so that it will not be damaged by the childhood trauma. Various parts take over leadership in the Self's absence, but they have neither the meta-perspective nor the stamina to lead the entire system effectively. Until the key parts learn to trust the Self, it typically cannot take an active role in leading the system. Later we will describe more about how it is possible that all people have a Self, regardless of the severity of trauma they may have suffered.

The goal of IFS therapy is to work with the survivor's parts and help them learn to trust the Self in their midst and enable it to return to its natural leadership position. Once Self leadership is achieved, the parts do not disappear. They remain to advise the Self, help resolve problems, or lend talents and emotions. Each part plays a different, valuable role according to its interests and abilities. In this type of harmonious system, the parts generally cooperate with each other; but when conflicts arise, the Self mediates.

LORENE: OUR WINDOW TO AN ABUSE SURVIVOR'S INTERNAL SYSTEM

This book provides a unique window to the inner world of one survivor of childhood sexual abuse. When she began therapy with Schwartz, Lorene,* a 28-year-old white female, had been married briefly at age 20 and had one child, a seven-year-old son. She worked as a public accountant and had earned both a CPA and a graduate degree in economics. As a teenager and during her early twenties, Lorene had been in therapy with four different clinicians but never for longer than six months. She had been diagnosed as having borderline personality disorder. Throughout her teens she had self-mutilated, been hospitalized four times for depression and suicidal ideology, shoplifted, consumed various illegal drugs, experienced deep depression and intense rage, and engaged in promiscuous behavior.

When therapy began, Lorene reported that her father started abusing her when she was three years old; the abuse continued until she was 13 years old. Her younger sister also reported having been molested. Lorene's

---

*Her name and any other identifying factors have been changed. Even her parts were renamed to prevent any possibility of identification.

father had used both psychological and physical terror to secure his daughters' submission and silence. He had involved the girls in child pornography and had shared them with other men. Lorene's mother, an alcoholic, was aware of the abuse, but had remained passive throughout Lorene's childhood. Lorene's father died when she was 20 years old; since her father's death, Lorene has had little contact with her mother.

The main characters of this book are Lorene's parts. Some would say that because she has distinct parts, Lorene suffers from multiple personality disorder (MPD). This diagnosis, however, does not fit Lorene; for example, she has never experienced "losing time"—periods of amnesia when certain parts would take over. Moreover, as mentioned earlier, this label has a different meaning in the IFS framework, which sees MPD as only one way that inner families organize after severe and chronic abuse. The IFS model recognizes that the internal "families" of abuse victims like Lorene's have become highly protective and volatile, whereas non-abused people are able to maintain a more harmonious level of communication among their internal parts. We introduce Lorene's internal family here— but only very briefly, since the reader will have the opportunity to become more familiar with their names and personalities in later chapters. We group Lorene's parts in three categories (more about categorizing parts in chapter 6) which describe how Lorene perceived their place in the internal family a few months after she entered therapy with Schwartz.*

The High-Functioning Managers

Super-She is a 20-year-old young woman who generally organizes Lorene's daily life and permits her to function quite well at work. This part is extremely intelligent, articulate, and energetic. Her main function is to block contact between external people and Lorene's "true" feelings and thoughts—especially feelings of shame and terror held by the younger parts. Super-She permits Lorene to maintain an appearance of normalcy, success, and independence.

Dashiell is about 20 years old. He allows Lorene to function socially as an adult, but at great cost to himself. Dashiell feels anguish and desolation penetrating him, and describes the "agony of his spirit." He feels deep shame for sexual conduct he encouraged Lorene to participate in during her teen years.

Vincent is in his mid twenties. He likes to act as the "Internal Self Helper," the inner guide. While he is quite astute and offers much wisdom about the inner family, he is also withdrawn, ashamed, stubborn, and

---

*Other parts of Lorene emerged during therapy but did not play a major role in the abuse-related work and therefore are not listed here.

reluctant to change. He often pretends to be Lorene's Self. What gives him away is his refusal to actively seek out things which would benefit either him or other parts; he remains quite passive unless Lorene approaches him and asks for help. Other parts follow Vincent's lead frequently but also become quite angry with him for his passivity. He appears to sacrifice immense amounts of energy to passively conceal and protect younger parts.

Bridgette is a young woman who seems to have had little contact with the abusive episodes. She emerges occasionally to advise Lorene about the way to explore her spirituality, her connectedness to other people and to the universe. While she is very serene, she carries a deep element of sadness, too.

The Energetic Rescuers

Destiny is a young woman (perhaps 17 or 18 years old) who holds many of the memories related to the more severe, torturous incidents of sexual abuse. She suffers intensely, but other parts prevent her from expressing rage or pain directly. Nonetheless, Destiny is first to jump in and rescue other parts or people from feeling any degree of sadness, hopelessness, or despair.

Alexandra ("Alex") is a 15- or 16-year-old girl who is very promiscuous, lively, and volatile. She has a rather flirtatious, playful manner which disguises an overpowering intensity. She acts mature for her age and appears confident and courageous. Alex feels extreme confusion about her place in the internal system and in the world. She often feels compelled to numb Lorene's feelings or hide herself in what she calls her "other-world." She is very busy, very angry, and very manipulative, taking the most expedient means to secure whatever she perceives to be safety. (To Alex, chaos often means safety.) Alex often blends with Jennifer (who is described below), making Lorene feel engulfed in sensations of fear, hopelessness, and abandonment.

Nicholas is a 12-year-old boy who yearns to be older and not so scrawny. He has fought long and hard to protect some of the younger parts, but often with a roughness that does them little good; indeed, often he chooses punitive means directed against Lorene or other people. He has previously encouraged Lorene's use of drugs, sex, stealing, and self-mutilation as distractors. He often projects terrifying scenes and images of Lorene's father "inside" her. (This ability to project images initially made him seem like more than a single part.)

Victor is a 14-year-old boy quite inflated by his own negative powers. He is rambunctious and destructive. No one ever knows what he is going to do next. While he purports to be a protector, those he protects would often prefer to be on their own because he is so destructive.

The Child-Parts

Bonnie is a 10- or 12-year-old girl who played a key role in helping Lorene bridge the gap between her abuse-filled childhood and her teenage years. She learned at this age how to offer herself to young men as a "sacrifice" to keep them away from younger parts. She is closely connected to any physical sensations Lorene experiences — whether numbness or pain. Bonnie calls herself the "Body-Guard" because she is in charge of the body's safety. She insists that she wants to be a boy, since a girl might not have enough physical power to protect Lorene's body.

The "seven-year-old" part is the most secretive of the young parts. She is even unwilling to give her name to the therapist and refuses to reveal any of her secret memories. She hides behind Vincent, who valiantly conceals her from the therapy process.

Andy is a five- or six-year-old boy who holds many abuse memories. Both Victor and Nicholas repeatedly convince Andy that he should remain frozen in the past, and consequently Andy believes the abuse is still occurring. All parts are afraid of Andy's vulnerability.

Jennifer, the first part Lorene encountered in therapy, is a four-year-old girl who initially appeared to be panic-stricken, terrified, bleeding, and barely breathing. She has revealed many abuse memories. She believes that she is worthless and she often expresses hope that Lorene's father will return and redeem her. Jenny is able to draw in other parts and the Self to blend with her, filling the others with her terror and pain. Every other part willingly acts as a protector, although some parts are rough on her, sometimes insisting she needs to be "toughened up," and other times disciplining her for participating in the original abuse.

The next several chapters explore underlying theoretical assumptions of the IFS model, including multiplicity, the systemic organization of parts, and the release of the Self as the natural leader of the parts within the internal system. The later chapters address treatment techniques, unique treatment problems in working with survivors, and the therapist-survivor relationship. We expand on and draw from ideas and techniques presented in Schwartz' *Internal Family Systems Therapy* (1995), and apply them specifically to survivors of sexual abuse — especially severe, chronic abuse. Finally, we discuss what therapists can do when their own parts react to working with adult survivors of sexual abuse.

CHAPTER 2

A Mosaic Consciousness

I am Large, I Contain Multitudes.

> —*Walt Whitman, 1892*

I multiplied myself, by going deeply into myself.

> —*Fernando Pessoa, 1991*

WE HAVE ALL EXPERIENCED simultaneous, contradictory feelings. For example, when one part feels scared about getting married, another part is excited; one part feels relieved about quitting a job, while another part is sad. The IFS model rests upon the assumption, supported by such divergent fields as physics, psychology, neurobiology, artificial intelligence, philosophy, and literature, that these internal fluctuations and contradictions result from individual subpersonalities or parts comprising the psyche of all healthy persons. Each part consists of a discrete and autonomous mental system that has an idiosyncratic range of emotion, style of communication, and set of abilities, intentions, and functions. Schwartz explains (Breunlin, Schwartz, & Mac Kune-Karrer, 1992):

> To give a common example, most people can identify an assertive part that tells them to stand up for themselves and go after what they want. This part is organized around the premise that it is best to confront problems and people directly. Most people are also aware of a cautious part that tells them to be careful, so as to not get hurt emotionally or physically. This cautious part's organizing premise is that the world holds dangers that must be considered. (p. 66)

Another typical example of the multiplicity phenomenon experienced in the course of a normal day:

> Consider a time in your life when you were facing a difficult decision. You probably experienced internal debates among conflicted thoughts or feelings regarding the right move to make. If you had focused exclusively on one of those thoughts or feelings and asked it questions, you might find that it was more than just a transient thought or feeling. You might find that it had a lot to say, that it had been saying similar things to you all of your life, and that it commonly fought with the same parts it was fighting with at that point. . . . [In other words,] people habitually favor and listen to some parts while disliking and shutting out others. (Breunlin et al., 1992, p. 502)

In the parts of a person who suffered early abuse, the evidence of multiplicity is readily apparent in the sudden shifts from a relaxed conversation to a bout of self-mutilation, from confidence to terror in a sexual relationship, from a polite friend to a raging enemy. For example, in a matter of minutes Lorene passed quickly from one voice to another (in a journal entry made prior to her father's death), as she thought about an upcoming holiday dinner with her parents:

I'm scared to see my father at Thanksgiving next week. Part of me freezes, afraid he'll force me into his bed, like when I was little. Another part of me wants to kill him, stab him with the butcher knife after he carves the turkey. And I want to just ignore him, tell jokes, watch the football game on TV, pretend everything is normal. Or I can just numb myself to his staring and sexual comments by drinking too much, or by eating so much that I get sick after dinner. Most of all, I hope that if he scares me, my mom will step in and protect me.

Many practitioners who treat abuse survivors have recognized, in varying degrees, the existence of multiplicity in their clients. For example, Courtois (1988) works with a survivor's "helpless child" and her inner "nurturing adult" by promoting communication and cooperation between "each part of [the] personality," each of whom craves "legitimacy and acknowledgment for the function it serves" (pp. 174–75). Briere (1989b) speaks about a survivor's "multiple, coexisting developmental states," urging the client to "interact with different parts of herself," particularly the "various warring (or at least isolated) components of her psyche" (pp. 90–91). Spiegel (1989) helps clients with the "part of themselves that attempted to provide protection, maintain dignity, or protect others, during the attack" (p. 301).

Similarly, Swink and Leveille (1986) treat incest survivors by working with their inner personalities, including rational parts, rebel parts, compliant parts, and preverbal parts, by giving them "the freedom to let these personalities express what they need to express," and by establishing communication among them (p. 137). Malmo (1990) strives to develop increasing cooperation among a survivor's "ego states," which must be "equally responsible and equally respected" (p. 298). She explains how she began using ego-state therapy: "I began to understand that I was working with different states of mind that were dissociated from each other and that needed to be explored fully so that they could either learn to work together cooperatively or become integrated.... Each part is worked with as an individual but as if it were in family therapy, having to encounter, relate to, and deal with the feelings, desires and behaviors of the others" (pp. 296–97).

Ellis (1990) works with a victim's inner "divine child," "guardian spirit," and "hidden friend," noting the "running inner dialogue" among them (p. 252). Utain (Utain & Oliver, 1989) works with various subpersonalities of her clients, combining family systems approaches from Virginia Satir with gestalt and psychodrama techniques. Hoffman (Sisk & Hoffman, 1987) describes the personality of her client and co-author, Sisk, as "a collection of many separate personalities," including "parts that owned her critical-parent messages and her frightened-little-girl feelings" along with her "perfectionist, compulsive adult-self" (pp. 133–34). Hoffman adds that her client "clearly did not have a multiple personality disorder ... and she was quite coherent and amazingly aware of the transitions from one aspect of her personality to another" (p. 133). D. Miller (1994) writes that a survivor exists as "more than one person," with various selves who are "not in harmony with each other and [who] actively collude in the patterns of self-harm" (p. 31). She views the survivor's personality as a "Triadic Self," similar to MPD "but much less extreme" (p. 113), which includes the Victim ("wounded child"), the Abuser (internalized representation of the abusive adult), and the Nonprotecting Bystander (the adult figure who was unable or unwilling to protect the child victim) (p. 31). Often a survivor "is aware and partially in control of the separate parts of herself, but is unable to understand or accept how these often conflicting parts fit together" (p. 106). Arnold Miller (1986) describes working with one incest survivor's parts on the issue of abandonment:

> As Jean spoke about her fear of abandonment, I was struck with how disparate this part of her was from a part of her personality which was resourceful and competent and had been given additional responsibility at work. If she possessed this other self-aspect, might not the more sturdy part of her help the part which was overwhelmed at the prospect of losing her special relationship with her father? This general notion and its elaboration guided work with Jean over the last year of her treatment. (p. 20)

Like therapists, survivors have written about experiencing various parts of themselves. Many survivors, including Lorene, enter therapy experiencing chaos and turmoil as they try to force the discordant inner emotions into a single, unitary self with consistent feelings and behavior. Lorene wrote:

I'm so confused. I bounce from hate to anger to vulnerability to loneliness to despair with a blink of the eye. It makes me dizzy. I can't keep a fix on anything—my feelings flip in and out of focus, nothing is within my immediate reach. I jump from one "reality" to another. The slightest event whirls me off in another direction.

Even in the earliest sessions, Lorene immediately felt comforted by the discovery that it is normal to experience simultaneous and conflicting feelings or thoughts. Instead of believing that hate consumed her entire being, she learned that only one part of her felt paralyzed with hate. She learned to acknowledge and respect each part's individual feelings, opinions, and desires. Not feeling a consistent and unified identity no longer bewildered and frightened her. The day after a particularly difficult session, several months into therapy, Lorene wrote in her journal:

I feel much better today. When I was falling asleep last night, I comforted the parts and they comforted each other. It sounds silly, but I did it just by touching my arm softly, like a hug, I guess. I put the energy of my healthiest parts (Super-She, Dashiell, and Vincent) into my hand and touched my arm. They could feel my arm and each other's arms.

I realized that even if I never went back to therapy, I would always have the parts. They can never be taken away from me. Even if I misunderstand them, get angry with them, miscommunicate with them—they'll always be mine. It is reassuring for them to remember that each of them exists within me and I will take care of their needs and listen to them.

Other survivors have also described how the acknowledgment of these inner voices served as a foundation for their healing work. Newall (1992) describes working with her inner voices which include the observer, the liar, the grave-seed self, and the psychic self, along with various parts she labels abandoned. Wisechild (1988, 1994) offers stirring reports of the dialogues and relationships among her inner parts as she heals from incest. Williams (1991), both a therapist and a survivor, speaks of the internal abuser, the internal terrorizer, the wounded child within, and the courageous lion within. Bierman (1992) reports that she identified five internal voices, including an inner child voice, a healing voice, an adult public voice, a protective but critical voice, and a protective but angry voice. Bird (1992) labels her inner voices "emotion goddesses": Fear, the goddess of courage; Shame, the goddess of self-love; Rage, the goddess of personal power; Sadness, the goddess of change; and Moon, who contains her wisdom, compassion and higher power. Oksana (1994) writes about her own and other survivors' work with various parts of themselves after suffering ritual abuse. Bass and Davis (1988) report that survivors often experience themselves as "interconnected parts of a whole" (p. 164). They quote one survivor who saw herself as a Russian nesting doll: "And each Susan inside me has other little Susans inside her, and I am, at this moment, inside a wiser gray-haired Susan that is yet to be. Like the Russian doll, I am round—and complete" (pp. 164–165). D. Miller (1994) quotes one survivor: "Am I a multiple personality? I don't think so, but I do feel like there is more than one me. . . . [T]here's a war going on between different parts of my mind, the part that feels murderous, the part that wants to do the right thing, the part that keeps telling me to drink or to vomit my lunch" (p. 12).

MULTIPLICITY ACROSS FIELDS

The recognition of multiplicity among clinicians and sexual abuse victims reflects an awareness that is decades old within the broader fields of philosophy and psychology. Williams James (1890) wrote: "It must be admitted, therefore, that in certain persons at least, the total possible consciousness may be split into parts which coexist but mutually ignore each other, and share the objects of knowledge between them. More remarkable still, they are complementary" (p. 206).

Later, C.G. Jung (1934/1969) discussed the "extreme dissociability of consciousness," and noted that his concept of a "complex" was similar to Janet's "fragmentary personality," which was supported by the evidence from split personality experiments: "It turned out that each fragment of personality had its own peculiar character and its own separate memory. These fragments subsist relatively independently of one another and can take one another's place at any time, which means that each fragment possesses a high degree of autonomy" (par. 202). Jung (1939/1968) was convinced that evidence existed of "much less fragmentary and more complete personalities, even though they are hidden" (par. 509). Jung (1921/1971) noted that "even in normal individuals character-splitting is by no means an impossibility. We are, therefore, fully justified in treating personality dissociation as a problem of normal psychology" (pars. 797–811). Jung (1939/1968) later added:

> Nor can we assume that the unconscious is capable of becoming autonomous only in certain people, namely in those predisposed to insanity. It is very much more likely that the tendency to autonomy is a more or less general peculiarity of the unconscious. . . . This tendency to autonomy shows itself above all in affective states, including those of normal people. When in a state of violent affect one says or does things which exceed the ordinary. Not much is needed: love and hate, joy and grief, are often enough to make the ego and the unconscious change places. Very strange ideas

indeed can take possession of otherwise healthy people on such occasions. Groups, communities, and even whole nations can be seized in this way by psychic epidemics. (par. 496)

More recently, Johnson (1986) describes the inner world in terms reminiscent of Jung: "The unconscious is a marvelous universe of unseen energies, forces, forms of intelligence—even distinct personalities—that live within us. It is a much larger realm than most of us realize, one that has a complete life of its own running parallel to the ordinary life we live day to day" (p. 3).

Beahrs (1982) boldly notes that "we are all actual multiple personalities in perhaps a more meaningful sense than the way the term is used psychiatrically. Every individual has many internal subparts, each with its own conscious experience, even if unperceived by his executive self and therefore relegated to the unconscious" (p. 80). Hilgard (1986) also emphasizes the normality of multiplicity: "Divided consciousness is familiar in ordinary waking life; the division permits fantasy to continue even while the person is performing the obligations of the work life or satisfying the proprieties of social interactions and communications" (p. 185). Putnam (1989) writes that "at birth, our behavior is organized into a series of discrete states" (p. 51). Redfearn (1985) agrees: "[W]e are not one person but many" (p. 115). Watkins and Watkins (1988) take the same position: "[M]ore practitioners are beginning to think of divisions within a personality as being quite common, but with differing degrees of severity" (p. 67).

Lancaster (1991), a British researcher in the fields of brain science and psychology, finds that "each of us in fact harbours a multiplicity of 'I'" (p. 17). DeBerry (1989) also adds a scientific perspective of consciousness:

Current thinking in neuropsychology indicates that the notion of linear consciousness is in error and that the brain tends to organize itself in a *modular* fashion. That is, instead of a group of separate organizational structures connected in series, there are *independent functioning units* that operate in a parallel fashion and can be totally separate from our conscious verbal self. (p. 85)

Ornstein (1987) likewise views the intrinsic organization of the mind as a group of semi-autonomous subminds: "There are quite separate selves, with differing priorities, that move in and out of their own accord, sometimes under the governing self's control, sometimes on their own" (p. 144). Zohar (1990) writes from the viewpoint of quantum physics: "Most of us have had the common experience of having selves within ourselves, or having pockets of awareness that seem temporarily split off from the mainstream of consciousness, or even whole sides of ourselves that we seldom get a look into" (p. 112). Gazzaniga (1985) points to neurobiological brain studies:

But what of the idea that the self is not a unified being, that there may exist within us several realms of consciousness? It is precisely the idea of the unity of conscious awareness, of self as it is commonly understood, that comes under direct challenge from split brain studies. From these studies the new idea that emerges is that there are literally several selves in man, and they do not necessarily "converse" with each other internally. (p. 356)

Poetry, plays, fiction, and prose all contain depictions of the psyche as multiple. For example, Fernando Pessoa, who lived from 1888 to 1935 and was Portugal's most renowned modernist poet, saw each person as a multiple being, which allowed him to access a multiplicity of poets within himself. Each inner poet had a unique view, writing style and personality. Pessoa (1991) wrote the following in his diary:

Each of us is various, many people, a prolixity of selves. Which is why the person who disdains his world is not the same as the person who rejoices or suffers because of his world. In the vast colony of our being there are many species of people, thinking and feeling differently. Now at the very moment when I am writing these few impressions. . . . I am the one who attentively writes them, I am the one who is happy not to have to work now, it is I who see the sky out there, invisible in here, it is I who think all this, I am the one who feels his body to be happy and his hands to be still vaguely cold. And like a diverse but compact multitude, this world of different people that I am projects a unique shadow. (p. 15)

In *Aristoi*, Walter Jon Williams (1992) creates a science-fiction world where great value is placed on the development of subpersonalities whom he calls "daimones" ("the godlets of the liberated mind"). The term *daimon** is further defined: "Daimones are Limited Personalities. They aren't well rounded, they're just component aspects of a larger psyche" (p. 166). These daimones or subpersonalities greatly enrich the perception of the individual:

Once only saints or madmen could speak to the daimones, could hear whispering the personalities that dwelt within their own minds. The condition could be caused by an imbalance in brain chemistry, a history of abuse in early childhood so severe that the personality fragmented, a deliberately induced ordeal, a spiritual agony. . . . The voices were mislabeled: *angels, past lives, dead spirits, demons.*

All self. Personalities with their own thoughts, their own capabilities, their own glories, wrapped in the primary personality like swaddled children, ready to come out and play in the fields of the mind. . . . The ancients had consistently underestimated the glories of their own psyches, preferred to consider these aspects of their own psyches as manifestations of invisible forces, forces divine or demonic. (pp. 40–41)

---

*"Daimon" is the singular version of "daimones."

The children in *Aristoi* are taught to expend great efforts of concentration in seeking out their subpersonalities. One young man, Yaritomo, speaks with his mentor about having encountered a part he calls "Burning Tiger":

> "Have you brought [Burning Tiger] out . . . ?"
> "Yes." Yaritomo licked his lips. "Twice now. I've found that being here in the cloister helps."
> "Yes. It would."
> "I've felt someone else, though. Another." Yaritomo hesitated. "A kind of pressure in my mind."
> "How have you tried to bring him out?"
> "I've tried the Sutra of Captain Yuan. Posture exercises. Directed meditation. I even tried just talking to it." He shook his head. "I don't think the other is ready."
> "Continue what you've been doing for another four or five days," Gabriel said. "If it doesn't manifest, simply return to your duties. Try to see what states of mind or activity bring on the intuition that the daimon is there. And then try to duplicate those conditions deliberately." (p. 111)

An extraordinary piece of fiction entitled *You Don't Love Yourself*, written by 90-year-old Frenchwoman Nathalie Sarraute (1990), whom Jean-Paul Sartre named the founder of the nouveau roman literary movement, is told through dialogue between the many subparts of the narrator. One part comments that people would laugh if they saw each other's inner subpersonalities: "[T]he people who observe us from outside, if they could see what we see in ourselves at times... so many [inner] lively young people and adolescents gathered together in 'old fogeys,' and so many [inner] old men in young people... and everywhere so many [inner] children..." (p. 26). Another part remarks that the selves are "as many... as there are stars in the sky... others are always appearing whose existence no one expected... So you see, I've given up, I am the entire universe, all its virtualities, all its potentialities... the eye can't perceive it, it extends to infinity..." (p. 10). And with a few words Sarraute demonstrates the multitude of attitudes within:

> All the objections we raise make [the narrator's friend] think of paper screens that he tears as he makes his way through them one subpersonality's voice after the other.
>> Yes, but if it were me, I wouldn't attach any importance to...
>> If it were me, in spite of that I'd find room for...
>> If it were me, I wouldn't hesitate to dismiss...
>> If it were me, I'd hand out...
>> If it were me, I'd keep...
>> If it were me, I'd be on my guard...
>> If it were me, I'd keep quiet...
>> If it were me, I'd admit....
>> If it were me... If it were me... If it were me... (p. 150)

Sarraute also beautifully uses the part-selves' inner conversation to show how even they struggle with the language of multiplicity.

"Yes, we here, among ourselves... we don't use those words, "me," "I"...

Or rather let's say we don't use them any longer. . . . We realized more clearly than ever that we had broken up into a multitude of disparate "I's"... whom could we love in all that? For a time, several "I's," "me's," "you's" were still questioning each other within us: "How could you have done that?"...

And then these "I's," these "me's," these "you's" disappeared...

When, exactly?

We didn't really notice... it was as if they became naturally diluted into shapeless masses... several "we's," several "you's"... made up of many similar elements...

Like banks of fish of the same species, flights of birds moving as one, groups whose members have the same tendencies... To talk about them in the singular... no, we couldn't do that any more... we needed a "we," a collective "you."

It's only the spokesmen we still send to the outside world who go on using those "I's," those "me's."

But they have to, otherwise how would they manage to make themselves heard? (pp. 85–86)

LORENE'S MULTIPLICITY

Within a relatively short period of time, Lorene became adept at identifying the simultaneous feelings and thoughts of various parts within her internal family. Her internal conversations vividly reveal to us a system of subpersonalities, each of whom experiences ongoing thoughts and feelings. For example, in one session she focused on sorting out the various feelings and views of her parts on the topic of dating. Lorene was able to identify many simultaneous but often conflicting opinions, each of which seemed consistent with the particular part's history and personality. Both the teenage part she called Alexandra (or "Alex") and the young adult, Dashiell, wanted adventure and sex; the tough sentry Nicholas was looking for a man who could guard Lorene's safety so that he could rest; the very young parts, Jennifer and Andy, wanted safety and love; the older, more spiritual parts, Destiny and Bridgette, wanted intimacy and exploration; 12-year-old Bonnie wanted affectionate touching and comfort; the great organizer and manager, Super-She, wanted order and security; and even the cautious, contemplative Vincent hoped for companionship and intellectual stimulation. Lorene recorded statements from some of these parts:

Jennifer *[4 years old, timid, craving affection]: I'll ask the man Lorene dates to please not hate me; just tell me it'll be fine, no one will hurt me, he'll protect me, and that I can hide behind him.*

Nicholas *[12 years old, rageful]: Fine, let men touch you again. I've had* enough guard duty. I quit! Maybe you can even find someone man enough to take my job as your heroic protector-against-rapists.

Alexandra [16 years old, promiscuous, lively]: I can't wait! She's finally going to stop being a wimp and let me get back into the action again. Men! This'll be fun!

Super-She [20 years old, organizer, manager]: I can't imagine how we will squeeze in dating along with the dissertation, the extra classes I'm teaching, and the article I need to finish. Well, I'll just have to reorganize everything.

Vincent [mid-twenties, contemplative, stuffy, quiet, passive]: It sounds like an interesting possibility, but one must remember that men tend to trigger all sorts of extreme reactions in you, and perhaps it would be wiser to avoid them for the time being.

Victor [a 14-year-old "Rambo"]: That damn therapist should systematically be cut out of your life. He's destroyed any trust I had in him. It's his fault you're discussing dating. If he weren't a man, he wouldn't be encouraging you to see men. I shall remain in charge here! Any man who tries to interject himself into your life will be in my way, and I will destroy him.

These concurrent feelings experienced by Lorene typify the experience of parts in all of us. Lorene's parts were simply more extreme, particularly around issues that triggered feelings relating to sexuality or intimacy. The IFS model values the skills and interests of each part and finds that such diversity enriches our lives. But for abuse survivors, the value of the parts goes beyond mere enrichment. The multiplicity empowers these victims and fosters what D. L. Miller (1974) calls "survival power."

> The person experiences himself as many selves each of which is felt to have autonomous power, a life of its own, coming and going on its own and without regard to the centered will of a single ego. Yet surprisingly this experience is not sensed as a pathology. One gets along quite well in reality; in fact the very disparateness of the multifaceted self seems to have *survival power* [italics added]. (p. 5)

In abuse victims, the survival power created by the multifaceted nature of the personality repeatedly surfaces as they continue to reflexively draw upon creative defense mechanisms that were once necessary to their physical and psychological survival. Lorene's various parts often served as a poignant demonstration that the "very disparateness of [her] multifaceted self" produced survival power. Like viewing a videotape in slow motion, in therapy, Lorene learned to listen.

Lorene: When I was little, what was it like when you were waiting to be hurt again?

Dashiell: I was petrified. But when it didn't come for so long, I almost missed it—*I actually looked for it. Now that you say it's really over, I sit and shake. I'm too exhausted to cry, too scared to move. I was so tired of waiting.*

Lorene: *Did anyone ever help you?*

Dashiell: *No one could help. I wanted someone to hold me.*

Lorene: *I can do that now.*

Dashiell: *But the center of my body feels torn.*

Lorene: *I don't care. I know you won't hurt me. I am here for you and all the parts.*

Dashiell: *No, wait. I changed my mind. Leave me alone, please.*

Super-She: *Leave him alone! Don't you know he's there to absorb pain and terror for you? He must remain strong enough to do it alone. That's his job.*

Lorene: *No, he doesn't need to do that now. There's no reason for it. Nothing here is putting me in danger. Dash, I won't hold you if you'd rather not—but imagine yourself resting by the stream in the woods. This blanket will hold you.*

Dashiell: *I feel the warm blanket and warm sun, and I hear the water next to me and the leaves rustling above me. Why is the middle of me so weak and damaged? So torn and scarred? I'm so frightened of the images in my mind—the secret of the blood and ripping holes in skin to pour in the urine and feces; the pain of the knife that purifies the body. I was just a little boy, but I am ashamed of my presence there, watching Dad with other little kids, with me. I can't stay alive!*

Lorene: *Explain what you mean.*

Dashiell: *I'm better off dead because then I won't spread poison to those around me.*

Lorene: *Dash, you spread nothing but life! You make my life so much more full and complete. I'd be so much less of a person without your humor, your thrills, your pangs of love and yearnings and joy. But I know you also hold pain, and I'm sorry.*

Dashiell: *Will anyone hurt me now?*

Lorene: *I will always try to prevent you from getting hurt. I need you to heal. I need Super-She to stop trying to hurt my body.*

Dashiell: *I want to hide and cry for my mother. She won't come. Someone told her not to come, told her they'd hurt me again, maybe. I don't want anyone to know I have an abdomen filled with fresh juices and meat for burning. What horrible images I have. I am so tainted, ruined.*

Lorene: *You are wrong. Work slowly on healing the middle of your body. You are strong and you have courage, too. I love you. Look at me—I am an adult now and we are safe here in my own home. You can help by telling me how to heal you. I don't know what to put in place of the scars in the center of your body.*

Dashiell: *I don't know.*

Lorene: Dashiell, when I touch your arm like this it doesn't hurt. It is warm and reassuring and leaves no mark on your skin. It is like the wind on your arm. It gives you trust and caring and you can hold those things like a bank holds money, and I will keep giving you more. I touch your arm again and add to the healing reservoir.

Vincent: Don't force it or hurry it. The key is to continue to help Dash express his fear and sadness. He no longer has to be the impenetrable sentry, watching for danger. When he lets go of the armor of scars protecting the center of his body, you will have begun to be successful.

Lorene: I can wait.

Lorene's multifaceted self brought her strength and experiential richness. Indeed, it is our illusion of a *unitary* self that robs many of us of survival power. Without conscious access to her various parts, Lorene would have experienced an overwhelming hodgepodge of conflicting emotions: *toughness* (the old Dashiell, as sentry), then *fear* (the new Dashiell, wondering if he could stop acting as guard), intermittent *impatience* (Super-She wanting things to function in the most efficient manner, which means that Dashiell must absorb pain and act as guard), and *tolerance* (Vincent, encouraging a slow pace).

After understanding the natural separateness of these clashing voices, Lorene was able to proceed directly to the part who was petrified (Dashiell), identify possible opponents to the notion of relieving Dashiell of guard duty (Super-She), and obtain advice from other parts (Vincent). As long as Lorene clung to the illusion of being a single unitary entity ("*I* am completely terrified," or "*I* am always to be unloved," or "*I* am all-powerful"), none of this complex processing was possible.

WHAT EXACTLY IS A PART?

The IFS model defines a part as an aspect of the personality that possesses the following seven qualities*:

1. *A persistent sense of its own singularity or selfhood, autonomous and discrete from other parts within the same person.* For example, Lorene might say, "part of me (Alex) feels excited about going to the party tonight, but another part of me (Vincent) would much rather stay home and read a book." Neither Vincent nor Alex gets confused with the other. Alex knows she exists as an entity separate from Vincent and vice versa.

---

*Adapted from Beahrs' (1982) definition of "co-consciousness" and Putnam's (1989) definition of "alter-personality."

2. A *range of functions*. It is incorrect to say that one part functions as the creative part and another as the protector part. Each part is capable of functioning in more than one capacity. For example, the four-year-old part named Jenny often functions as a resource for Lorene's creativity. However, she has also proved to be a mighty protector for a still younger child-part named Brittany and has also served as a release for rageful fury when she perceives an injustice.

3. A *range of emotional responses*. Each part is capable of many emotions. No single part can be labelled simply the angry part, the sexual part, or the terrified part. A part can feel angry about some things but calm and happy about others. While Nicholas could easily earn the label of angry or malevolent part, he is also the part of Lorene who displays the most zest and passion for living. Sixteen-year-old Alexandra could be called the sexual part, but her flirtations and promiscuity may have very little to do with sexual feelings. (If a part exhibits only one or two emotions, it is probably because the part is trapped in an extreme role.)

4. A *range of behavior*. No single part is solely responsible for categories of behavior such as self-mutilation, alcohol abuse, promiscuity, intellectual pursuits, creativity, or parenting activities. Each part behaves in various ways, even mimicking behavior of other parts. For example, it would be easy (but erroneous) to assume that Lorene's self-mutilation could always be blamed on Nicholas, an adolescent "Rambo." The behavior might instead originate in 16-year-old Alexandra, who might cut herself so that she can bandage the wound and pretend she is being cared for by someone who loves her. Similarly, it would be wrong to assume that continual sobbing and feelings of abandonment can be traced only to four-year-old Jenny; it may very well be that the ferocious Nicholas has momentarily unveiled his deep sadness.

5. A *significant life history of its own existence*. Most parts are able to identify either when they came into existence or when life circumstances forced them into extreme roles. In an abuse victim, it is usually possible to discover what each part experienced during the abusive incidents or other significant events in the person's life.

6. A *separate experience of continued functioning, simultaneously with other parts in the same person*. Parts do not necessarily stop functioning merely because the person is not consciously focusing on them. For example, when Lorene is conducting a business meeting, it does not mean that Nicholas has stopped searching for danger among the meeting's participants. Unlike an infant who thinks his mother disappears when she is out of his vision, each

part knows that it continues to exist even when it is not near the surface of the person's conscious awareness.

7. A *characteristic and consistent pattern of behavior and feelings in response to given stimuli.* Although each part is unique and has a full range of possible emotional responses and functions, characteristic patterns do evolve and serve to differentiate one part from another. (See chapter 6 for further exploration of three particular patterns.) For example, if Lorene considers making a change in her life, typically Alexandra gleefully votes yes, and Vincent takes a more conservative, passive stance and votes no. While they are capable of many other responses, a pattern of behavior begins to emerge that can be tied to each part.

Through the seven characteristics described above, we see that each part is a complex sub-organism vital to the whole psyche, where parts function like a family or a tribe of people living together, where some members share certain values and ideas, and some other members disagree and squabble.

OUR ILLUSORY SENSE OF UNITY

Along with the growing recognition of our innate multiplicity is a concurrent recognition that on a day-to-day basis we typically function under the illusion that the self is a unified entity. "The notion that 'I' is a multiple entity and that our sense of being a single, unitary self is illusory could be described as an idea whose time has come" (Lancaster, 1991, p. 83). He adds: "The publication of articles and books from biologists, psychologists and philosophers arguing [that unity is an illusion] has recently developed avalanche proportions" (p. 83). The fact that we experience a "unified sense of 'I' is only a superficial feature of the human mind" (Lancaster, 1991, p. 17). Similarly, Hilgard (1986) plainly announces, "The unity of consciousness is illusory" (p. 1). Jung (1957/1964) wrote of mankind's "comfortable belief that a unitary God had created man in his own image, as a little unity" (par. 576). He earlier wrote that, "the existence of complexes throws serious doubt on the naive assumption of the unity of consciousness, which is equated with 'psyche,' and on the supremacy of the will" (1934/1969, par. 200).

In *You Don't Love Yourself* (Sarraute, 1990), one part (#1) chastises another part (#2) for creating the illusion of unity:

Part #1: You... The one who showed yourself to them [external people], the one who volunteered, you wanted to be the one on duty... you went up to them... as if you were not merely one of our possible personifications, one of our virtualities... you broke away from us, you put yourself forward as our sole representative... you said "I"...

Part #2: We all do that all the time. What else can we do? Every time one of us shows himself to the outside world he designates himself as "I," as "me"... as if he were the only one, as if you didn't exist... (pp. 1–2)

At one point, a part explains that an illusion of unity was necessary because "the outside pressure was so great, we tried to get together and show a splendid 'I' that was presentable, really solid . . . " (p. 32). Later, another part realizes: "So *that* was the construction she had seen before her, which had prevented her from seeing our tumultuous mass . . . " (p. 77).

Zohar (1990) offers the physicist's point of view:

The self is not an eternal indivisible whole as Descartes argues, any more than particles are the tiny, solid, and indivisible billiard balls that Newton's physics supposed. Both [sub]selves and particles are more fluid than that, both a little more "shifty." They flow into and out of existence, now standing alone, now wedding themselves to other selves or particles, now disappearing altogether — teasing us with their dancing forms and shadows. (p. 112)

Theorists ask why our internal systems maintain this pretense of unity. Lancaster (1991) writes that the unified "I" makes "retrospective sense of mental events" (p. 79). M. Watkins (1986) points out that recognizing multiplicity would require a "breach with a unitary concept of the self that relies on a stable identity and does not look closely at shifts of mood, tone, or attitude that might, if examined, suggest a multiplicity of the self" (p. 43). Focusing on the practical aspects of the illusion of unity, Samuels (1989) writes: "On an experiential level, we have to reconcile our many internal voices so that we can, when we need, speak with one voice" (p. xi).

We believe that a person experiences the mind as unitary when the internal system functions well, when all parts of the psyche are in sync, functioning as one unit. Yet the individual components still exist as distinct, autonomous units. It is their harmonious coordination that creates an illusion of unity. Or, there are times in highly polarized systems where one part or a coalition of parts dominates to the point of conveying an illusion of oneness by shutting out all other parts.

Some parts work hard to maintain the illusion of a unified personality. For example, a protective part guarding vulnerable inner children might find it useful to project a unified tone to avoid the trespassing of a clumsy therapist. This protective part might be acting on a general rule that blocks access to all vulnerable parts, or it might be worried that one particular younger part is preparing to disclose a secret. Lorene has a protective part, Nicholas, who likes to distract both the therapist and Lorene by making singularly unified proclamations such as: "No one else is here! I'm in charge!" Or:

Therapist: We were working with the scared little girl—what happened?
Nicholas: I'm just tired of these goofy role-playing games, that's all. I'm supposed to conjure up images of a scared little girl just to please you. The truth is—and you know this—there is only me! I'm Lorene. That's it—just me. Now let's talk about something else.

Still another part may find it beneficial to maintain an illusion of unity because such an illusion brings much power: "I am the ruler of Lorene's actions. I control the body, I control the thoughts, I control the emotions, I control the behavior." The part may announce, "Nothing exists but pain and despair, and suicide is my only hope for peace." Or, "Nothing exists but numbness; sadness, rage and terror have been banished forever." The part who experiences the despair or numbness gains power and confidence if it can get other parts to experience the same feeling. Sometimes a part is so overwhelmed by emotions that he, intentionally or not, leaks the emotions to other parts, creating an illusion of unity by forcing other parts to blend with those emotions, instead of retaining the feelings within his own boundaries. For example:

Lorene [blended with 16-year-old part, Alex]: Things are getting worse and worse. The nightmares every night are horrible, chipping away even at my best defenses. Nothing is working. I feel disoriented and scared. I feel like crying. I couldn't even go to work today or answer my phone. I can't escape from this hole of despair.

In this example, Lorene blends to the point where she feels as if she *is* Alex. If a person describes a complete sense of unity—of feeling only one way—it may be that the client is experiencing blending. According to the IFS view of blending, one part temporarily overwhelms the person, as Alex did with Lorene, blocking her ability to experience other aspects of her personality and embracing her in a false or illusory sense of unity. The illusion of unity serves different needs; nonetheless it remains an illusion, cloaking an underlying reality: the multiplicity continuum.

CHAPTER 3

The Multiplicity Continuum

*The dividing of the personality lies on a continuum,
ranging from normal adaptive differentiation at one end
to pathological maladaptive dissociation at the other.*

—John Beahrs, 1982

I F I AM NOT a unified being, but instead a multiple being, just *how much*
of a multiple am I? After all, I can't go around telling people that I hear
voices conversing inside my head. According to the IFS model, the degree
of inner dividedness falls along a continuum. A healthy differentiation
between inner selves permits us to enjoy psychological and emotional
richness and adapt to the demands of everyday life. We can daydream and
still bathe the children. We can feel angry at a friend and still give a
presentation to the board of directors at work. Watkins and Watkins (1988)
cite coping with stresses as a benefit of our natural multiplicity, noting
that the term dissociation implies dysfunction, while the closely related
term differentiation suggests healthy boundaries. Each person calls upon
different inner resources as he or she encounters various experiences in
life: a passion for literature or art evokes one type of inner resource; exercising logic and reasoning evokes another type; and playing with children
still another.

The continuum of multiplicity (see figure 3.1) begins with the typical,
healthy fluctuations in multiplicity that we each experience during the
day. Moving down the continuum (toward the right side of figure 3.1), we
find more extreme states. At each level of extremeness, the person can
alternate between too much differentiation or too little differentiation.
Thus, multiple personality disorder is viewed as only one extreme of a full
range of multiplicity. "One of the distinguishing characteristics of people
diagnosed with multiple personality disorder is that the degree of this
isolation and polarization among their subpersonalities is so extreme that
they lack any sense of integration, of an 'I-ness' connecting the elements

of their experience" (Schwartz, 1988, p. 29). Apart from the degree of polarization and isolation, the MPD's inner family is no different from that in people who are less traumatized.

Where an individual falls on the continuum at a given moment depends on the circumstances in which he finds himself and what external and internal resources are available to him. For a young child trapped in an abusive setting, at times he must use either very little differentiation or extensive dissociation (both located at the same point on the extreme right end of the continuum depicted in figure 3.1) so that he can either *blend* with the abuser in order to anticipate the abuser's demands or *block out* terrifying experiences by building walls within his inner fortress. Either extreme choice lessens the detrimental impact on the child's body and psyche.

If Lorene had never suffered child abuse, as an adult she might easily call upon her orderly, business-type part, Super-She, to help her finish a difficult report to be presented the next day to the board of directors; impermeable walls would not be needed and she could function at the least extreme (left) end of the continuum. Her other parts would be aware of what she was doing and could still communicate with each other (perhaps quietly remarking that if Super-She would give up the project, Lorene could get some extra shut-eye, or treat herself to some ice cream). As an abuse survivor, however, Lorene more typically functions away from the non-extreme (left) end of the continuum, and closer to the extreme (right) end. Lorene is likely to have difficulty keeping the business-type part differentiated and functioning. The other parts might perceive danger in her presenting the report to the board of directors the next day; they will use every tactic available to stop her work. By focusing on the feeling that she should stop working on the report, Lorene could track this inner conversation:

Nicholas: *You're crazy if you think you can turn in that report tomorrow. Don't you remember that the board is almost all men? They'll stare at you, sending you messages about sexual atrocities you deserve to have inflicted on you. They'll refuse to agree with your report unless you take your clothes off. You better just hurt your body now—cut it up—to ward off any pain they want to inflict tomorrow.*
Super-She: *Leave me alone, let me write—*
Nicholas: *Shut up! No one can hear you! Now* cut, *now* drip blood on the report, *now* cut again, *now you must go to bed because you've been hurt and you can't possibly finish a report while you're bleeding all over the desk.*

The boundaries created by Nicholas' dramatic techniques are almost impermeable. Super-She makes an attempt to break through, but Nicholas successfully blocks any communication from other parts. If Nicholas

Figure 3.1. Multiplicity Continuum.

⟶ multiplicity becomes less adaptive, more extreme	⟶ more extreme ⟶	
MULTIPLICITY BALANCED	**INCREASED RIGIDITY OF BOUNDARIES** ⟵ either ⟶ **INCREASED BLURRING OF BOUNDARIES**	
	Too much differentiation	Too little differentiation
Characteristics: • Self leads • respectful communication between parts • parts receive appropriate portions of responsibility, resources • parts recognize that they exist within a system; they respect other parts' needs and views	*Shared characteristics:* • Self often leads; even when it does not lead, it is easy to find • parts are extreme only regarding one or two volatile issues, e.g., disciplining of teenage child • Self mediates internal disagreements and finds fair resolutions	
(Self cares for young parts who need connection to other people)	*Behavior (either):* • parts create walls to block communication on volatile issues	• parts hide behind, or blend with, other parts to avoid confrontations or to pretend that no problems exist
Example: (directed within) • calm the playful parts, promising to go to a movie after the report for work is done	(other-directed) • person thinks about what her boss asked for and makes independent judgment of best method to reach boss's goal	*Example:* • person repels inner voices telling her not to finish a report for work. She demands they be quiet and refuses to discuss the matter or listen to them.	• person focuses excessively on anticipating boss's precise wishes as to the report. She loses the ability to independently think through report-related issues, or offer any recommendations based on her own viewpoint
"Good idea! Let's go to a movie—but later."	"I can best accomplish his goal by _____."	"No! Not right now. I can't listen!"	"I think he would prefer _____. If he'd just tell me what he wants, I'd do it."

→ more extreme	→ more extreme →

MALADAPTIVE DISSOCIATION *either* ←→ BLENDING	EXCESSIVE DISSOCIATION OR MPD *either* ←→ SYMBIOSIS
Too much differentiation	Too little differentiation	Too much differentiation	Too little differentiation
Shared characteristics:		**Shared characteristics:**	

Left panel — Shared characteristics:
- Self rarely leads, is difficult to locate, and is often hidden away by protective parts; parts are very reluctant to trust Self
- leadership role shifts from part to part
- parts are extreme regarding many issues
- longstanding polarizations between parts or groups of parts
- intensity and frequency of extreme behavior increases, occurs in inappropriate contexts
- leads to dangerous or destructive situations
- severely limits person's ability to act or make choices
- initially adaptive skills are now "symptoms"

Right panel — Shared characteristics:
- Self does not lead and is very difficult to find
- parts very extreme
- boundary violations (too rigid or too diffuse)
- polarizations are longstanding

Behavior (either): [left]

• parts have established semi-permanent walls prohibiting communication of change as to a variety of issues	• parts' view of the volatile issues is clouded by blending with more intense extreme parts' views • very difficult to stay separate from extreme ʿmotions and viewpoints

Behavior (either): [right]

• rigid and impermeable boundaries • some parts unaware that other parts exist, or unaware of what other parts are doing	• no sense of self as a separate person • no boundaries between parts, or between the person and other people • person clings to symbiotic relationships between parts, or between the person and other people, as the only safe way she can experience reality

Example: [left]

• child walls off experience of several assaults because it is too overwhelming and terrifying	• child blends with abuser in order to anticipate his demands

Example: [right]

• person allocates specific tasks (e.g., driving, parenting, participating in therapy) to certain parts, while other parts have no idea the person performed any of the tasks	• a woman mirrors her husband's wishes and views (e.g., dress like X, code like Y, buy car Z, vote for W, read book XX, keep up on current events regarding YY)

"I am not really here."	"I am you."	"I never called you yesterday; you're mistaken."	"Steven doesn't like it when _____; Steven says _____; Steven believes _____; Steven would rather that I _____."

blocked all communication, and even believed that no other parts existed—that he alone constituted the entire being called Lorene—then Lorene would be trapped even further toward the extreme right end of the multiplicity continuum.

Children suffering severe and repeated abuse almost universally discover that dissociation—setting up impermeable walls to restrict internal communication—is a particularly useful tool. They "develop a kind of dissociative virtuosity" (Herman, 1992, p. 102). Dissociation acted as a "life-saving solution for [an] otherwise powerless child" (Putnam, 1989, p. 54). Putnam lists four survival benefits of dissociation, which several of Lorene's parts exemplify:

1. *Escape from the constraints of reality.* Jennifer: "It doesn't matter what Dad does to me, because it isn't real. It's just a dream. It doesn't matter."
2. *Containment of traumatic memories and affects outside of normal conscious awareness.* Nicholas: "I insist that the seven-year-old part hide the memories. No other parts have access to them. No one has the power or ability to force me to release those memories."
3. *Alteration or detachment of sense of self (so that the trauma happens to someone else or to a depersonalized self).* Jennifer: "I am no longer here. I've gone into the light on the ceiling. I don't exist anymore. There is a body on Dad's bed that looks like me, but it isn't me."
4. *Analgesia.* Andy: "I know I'm supposed to feel something, but everything is so numb. I can't tell where he's putting his fingers. My body is all blurry. Sometimes I see blood come out of it, but I don't feel pain."

Thus, parts often adapt to abuse by heightening the separation and creating rigid boundaries between themselves and other people, other parts, memories, or emotions. Or they create the opposite—the annihilation of all boundaries. The differentiation becomes "maladaptive, however, in an adult world that stresses continuity of memory, behavior, and sense of self" (Putnam, 1989, p. 54). It is like the common experience of waking up in the morning to discover you cannot remember the dream that you just finished moments ago. The difference is that not remembering the dream won't interfere with your functioning that day, while extreme, long-lasting, pervasive dissociation will.

Most theorists agree that a continuum of dissociation or multiplicity exists. Hilgard (1986), "with his 'neodissociative' theory of the mind, has probably been the most instrumental modern figure advocating the concept of a continuum of dissociation from the normal to the pathological" (Putnam, 1989, p. 9). Watkins and Watkins (1988) report having "gathered increasing evidence that the dividing of the personality lies on a continuum, ranging from normal adaptive differentiation at one end to pathological maladaptive dissociation at the other, where the true multiple personality disorder occurs" (p. 67). IFS envisions the continuum more like Beahrs' (1982) view which includes "blending" or "symbiosis" so that "one extreme is the multiple personality. . . . [and] the other is the 'symbiotic psychosis,' where the person has such difficulty distinguishing 'self' from 'beyond' as to render reality-testing difficult" (p. 4). Thus there is either too much differentiation or an absence of any healthy differentiation. Beahrs (1982) also points out that "in a very real sense we are all multiple personalties, and we also have some element of symbiotic psychosis. What is relevant to these syndromes is then relevant to all of us" (p. 13).

At what point does a healthy differentiation move down the continuum and become an unhealthy dissociation? Putnam (1989) answers the question by pointing to the time when the increased division or separation of parts stops being useful or adaptive: "Central to the concept of the adaptive functions of dissociation is the idea that dissociative phenomena . . . become maladaptive only when they exceed certain limits in intensity or frequency, or occur in inappropriate contexts" (p. 9). Similarly, Beahrs (1982) defines dissociative disorder as "personality splitting that is dysfunctional, not useful or maladaptive, limiting instead of enhancing the organism's power for action, or leading to behavior dangerous to self and others" (p. 81). The IFS model similarly cautions against the elimination of all differentiation between parts because in healthy humans, the ability to differentiate and dissociate actually "enhance[s] health when properly used. . . . [The] goal is not to be 'rid' of a psychological process, but to shift it from the harmful or maladaptive ('pathological') dimension to where it is useful in its effect, so that what was once a symptom can truly become a skill" (Beahrs, 1982, p. 82).

In working with survivors, this concept of a multiplicity continuum plays a key role. Healthy individuals readily differentiate various aspects of their personalities. Multiplicity should be viewed "not as a fragmentation or splitting of a unity—as in psychoanalysis—but as a process of differentiation" (M. Watkins, 1986, p. 106).

Most survivors of sexual abuse continue to hold archaic beliefs that were once useful as defense mechanisms but are now maladaptive. For example, at the beginning of therapy Lorene still held childhood terror about a myriad of potential dangers threatening her. Her antedated beliefs in this area severely limited her parts' ability to recognize trustworthiness and safety.

Nicholas sees danger everywhere. If I think it'll be safe to go to a baseball game, he goes nuts, listing all the possible dangers. All his senses become distorted. My eyes feel like they don't belong to me; they're burning through my skull. I hear things either in muffled or as loud, crashing noises. Everything is magnified. I can taste sperm, even after all these years. Sensory memories ripping up my body are Nicholas' warnings to me that impending danger looms around every corner.

Nicholas' warning that a man might molest Lorene was appropriate in the context of a four-year-old who goes to bed at night not knowing if her father will invade her sleep; it was an adaptive response designed to protect Lorene by preparing her for danger. However, in a completely different context, Nicholas' present attempts, such as trying to convince the adult Lorene that exposure to thousands of strangers makes going to a baseball game dangerous, or that the board of directors might rape her if they don't like her report, are no longer useful, adaptive responses.

When does permeable become impermeable? It is sometimes helpful to be able to say, "I'll worry about that later." Tucking away one's concern about an exam grade, or the cost of car repairs, or the calories in chocolate cake does not create an impermeable boundary as long as the worry is easily accessible so that it can be addressed at an appropriate time. But when parts are not aware of each other's existence or cannot communicate with each other, the boundaries become rigid and impermeable. Similarly, boundaries become *too* permeable when, instead of trying to imagine what your father wants for Christmas, you can no longer say what you want for *yourself.*

The problems experienced by survivors of severe abuse occur when the natural division between parts are transformed into impermeable (or the opposite — excessively permeable) boundaries. The more distorted the boundaries become, the less communication and cooperation. However, once the boundaries return to their natural state, recognition and respectful communication among all parts become possible. (Later we explore how parts simultaneously remain both separate and connected.) Why would parts be motivated to move to the non-extreme end of the continuum? The answer requires us to examine whether parts prefer to be extreme or actually hold more positive intentions.

POSITIVE INTENTIONS OF ALL PARTS

Lorene was afraid to look too closely at some of her parts — they seemed so ferocious and evil. They raged and spit fire, often embarrassing her greatly. If she could not get rid of them — exorcism was not the goal — could she at least hide or bury these unattractive parts? Both therapist and client may lose confidence in the possibility of change when faced with a seemingly malevolent, rageful, manipulative, or extraordinarily resistant part. Without exception, however, therapists and clients using the IFS model have discovered that each part sincerely wishes something good for the client, and for himself, and contains potentially useful resources for the survivor. Schwartz (1995) explains this fundamental tenet of IFS:

> A basic premise of IFS is that people have an innate drive toward and wisdom about their own health. They not only try to maintain steady states and react to feedback; they also strive toward creativity and intimacy. They come fully equipped to lead harmonious internal and external lives. From that basic premise, it follows that when people have chronic problems, these inner resources and wisdom are not being fully accessed. Elements in the systems in which they are embedded or that are embedded within them are constraining their access to these resources. IFS therapy is designed to help people find and release these constraints. (p. 19)

Johnson (1986) espouses a similarly respectful approach to all parts: "You should go to the unconscious and find the one who is causing the paralysis, the resistance, or the depression, and find out *why*. If you do this, you are often surprised to find out that the unconscious has very good reasons for disagreeing with your project or your goals" (p. 186). Parts instinctively strive towards health and balance when they develop in a sustaining environment. Due to the abusive environment in which she was raised, Lorene's good-girl parts (Jennifer, Destiny, and Bonnie) feared misbehavior by the rageful parts (Victor and Nicholas). Gradually, however, the good-girl parts learned that even the seemingly malevolent parts could play a productive role in Lorene's internal ecology.

Uncovering a part's good intentions does not necessarily mean insisting that the part act happy, lighthearted, or jovial. Often a part correctly instructs the therapist and client that the healthiest choice is to permit that part (or another part) to experience and express pain, sadness, or fear. Lorene had parts (Super-She, Vincent) who wanted her to maintain a calm, wise, harmonious equilibrium. A tasteful tear was preferred over a messy, sobbing scene. A quiet tone ("Yes, I've overcome all childhood problems") was preferred over a painful howl ("I'm terrified of ev-er-y-thing!"). Yet some parts need to express their pain by sobbing or shouting. While openly expressing pain might feel distressing to the managers, it may be just what is needed before change can occur, and it may be exactly what the client or the protective parts have denied the abused parts for many years. "Given permission to be," even persecutor parts will express the desire to act as "a constructive part of a whole person" (Beahrs, 1982, p. 146). M. Watkins (1986) poignantly describes how "the characters we meet implore us to listen to them for a change. . . . Oftentimes the figures are angry; tired of being cast out, they break into our houses in dreams, rape and murder us, attempt to drive the dream ego to madness" (p. ix). Lorene's extreme part, Nicholas, offered a brutal but honest explanation for his disruptive behavior:

Lorene: *Why did you encourage me to get drunk at the Christmas party and yell at people?*

Nicholas: *Because I hate you! I don't want you laughing and pretending you're normal.*

Lorene: *Nicholas, I recognize your ferocious voice, but I need you to be more direct. Just tell me what's really bothering you.*

Nicholas: *I can't handle all these holiday parties and family events. I want someone to come and hold me at night time. No one ever holds me. I'm tired of guarding scared parts.*

Lorene: *You've carried a lot of adult responsibilities by yourself for a long time.*

Nicholas: *You bet I have! I'm very tired and lonely.*

Lorene: *That's a big admission for you.*

The underlying dynamics often seen in adult survivors appear quite extreme and invite traditional psychotherapists to impose a variety of pathological diagnoses. These diagnoses ignore the fact that parts learned extreme reactions while in extremely toxic contexts. This is especially true for sexual abuse victims. For example, Lorene's part, Nicholas, can be very aggressive and abusive to Lorene and other people as well—behavior learned during the molestations. But in judging Nicholas' behavior, consider one of the memories he lives with:

I keep thinking about the baby, the baby inside. Dad does things to my body, then to Mom who has the baby inside. She is very, very pregnant, and I can see the baby moving inside of her. How can he do those sexual things to her body when the baby is trapped inside? It scares me the most, because the baby can't get help from anyone. The baby can't even get sick and be taken to the doctor for a fever or vomiting. He's just trapped inside. I can't stop watching and I can't stop him from doing it. So it's like I'm participating in hurting that little baby inside. It's my fault.

Nicholas, terrified of the molestations, took on the burden of being responsible for doing *anything* to prevent them. If bad things were going to happen, at least he'd be in control of them. The extreme behavior (often labeled "acting out") of a part like Nicholas derives from the part's experiences in the original abuse experience. Once each part understands that the environment has changed, or that the adult is now able to avoid or remove herself from abusive relationships, the part feels free to—and wants to—renegotiate its role to help the internal system function better. In therapy, this type of part should be reminded that its destructive behavior was originally courageous and useful to the child, allowing him or her to survive physically and psychologically. Persecutor parts are "full of life energy . . . usually willing and able to become positive parts of a greater whole once their own existences were validated and their needs met" (Beahrs, 1982, p. 152). The therapist will find that such parts (not just the parts who have won the label "hidden friend" or "spirit guide") are eager to provide the therapist with information about the system and they often know the quickest, most effective means of change.

In therapy, Lorene quickly learned that each part had valuable qualities and wanted what was best for her. Nicholas' aggressive skills were useful when Lorene needed to assert herself during debates at her job in a large public accounting firm; but the same ferocity was not useful when triggered simply by a man's walking into a room where Lorene was alone. Nicholas had to discover his current role in Lorene's life:

Nicholas was the part who braced me against total collapse during the terrifying invasions of my body. I could always count on him to get angry and cold and protect me from sinking into the quicksand of despair. Now Nicholas thinks he's useless. It's true that I don't need his cold fury in the same way, but I keep reminding him of the tremendous value of his strength. He committed himself to my very survival! So now I ask him to help me be strong and to help me through this healing process. There are so many times when I want to give up, to block out those memories and pretend I'm "normal." Nicholas says that doesn't sound like suitable work for a great warrior. I remind him that his cold, steel-like determination is definitely what I need. He says okay, he'll give it a try.

Nicholas' continued use of his "steel-like determination" had become a destructive force in Lorene's life; the reapplication of his strength to other tasks was vital. While other parts who held archaic beliefs were not necessarily as destructive as Nicholas, they also could contribute little to her adult life until they released the old abuse-related beliefs and feelings — what we call "burdens" (Schwartz, 1995). The part named Destiny, for example, did not emerge until later in therapy because she had remained hidden behind her chosen protector, Nicholas. While the camouflage of Destiny caused no apparent destruction or unhappiness, the discovery of her existence released an entirely new life-energy in Lorene.

Destiny: My unique ability is to flow throughout an entire body. But Dad's physical invasion made me hide behind Nicholas-the-warrior. I lost my sense of independence, of boundaries. I felt like I was locked up inside of the abdomen. When Nicholas began working in therapy, and he calmed down, I could peek out and see that Dad was gone. The invasion was over! Now I can almost fly — spreading energy throughout Lorene's entire adult body. It feels incredibly light and colorful.

Parts learn ideas from those around them and respond in the best way they know. A valuable premise that IFS borrows from family therapy is that extreme behavior in people is often not caused by personal idiopathic pathology, but instead reflects the individual's family context. Similarly, therapists of abuse survivors should not take extreme parts at face value, but learn instead how the part became extreme in the context of the survivor's internal system. Parts, like children in troubled families, are often neglected, hurt, and depended upon beyond their capabilities. In response, they grasp at primitive, expedient means of survival. The internal system, in turn, responds to these rampant parts; the accompanying polarizations leave the person feeling increasingly turbulent, chaotic, and fragmented. Parts labeled "malevolent" always prove to be valuable assets to an internal system, just as the designated "problem child" has many valuable qualities to offer the family. Initially Lorene's part, Victor, repeatedly disrupted therapy as he frantically tried to turn the therapist and Lorene away from long-buried feelings of sexuality, shame, and anger. Soon Lorene learned, however, that Victor hated his role as protector of these buried emotions, and longed to play a more fulfilling role in her life:

Victor: *I had an extraordinary therapy session today. If I could experience and believe that Bonnie's sexual feelings were safe, then I could actually give up my job of guarding her. (Of course, I'm concerned about Alex's and Bridgette's sexuality, too, but I have no power over them.) This change would mean Lorene could have her body back. She wouldn't be evil; she wouldn't be in danger of being overwhelmed by her sexual feelings. She could learn to feel sexual without arbitrarily acting on those feelings with any man she can find. Such freedom has seemed unimaginable to me until today. Last week I was furious when Dick said he knows that Lorene experiences sexual feelings! I thought I was the only one who knew that. But now, I wonder. If Dick knows she is truly a sexual being, and he isn't disgusted, maybe — just maybe — there's a chance that it's okay. It would have such a tremendous effect. Bonnie and other parts won't be afraid that remembering sexual things done to Lorene as a child will make some part feel aroused — a feeling I'm always supposed to suppress. Lorene could feel her full sexuality now — she could actually own it and enjoy it. Her sexuality would no longer be a mysterious blur, something I'm suppose to help hide and, if necessary, destroy with punishments.*

It is also important to remember that often the label of "malevolent" or "persecutor" was given by another part. If the survivor expresses a wish to eliminate this undesirable part, that wish actually belongs to another part who perhaps believes that internal homicide is possible and necessary. For a long time, even after Lorene acknowledged that Victor wanted a different role, he continued to disrupt therapy. Lorene finally realized why. Faced with contempt and scorn from other key parts, it was no wonder that Victor remained locked into a menacing role.

Lorene: *Super-She and Vincent, both of whom I like very much, highly disapprove of Victor. They see little value in the havoc and destructive isolation he creates—like today when he adamantly refused to make a therapy appointment for next week—and they rarely converse with him in a civil tone.*

When approached with respect, however, Victor explained how other parts' insistence that he was or should be "bad" triggered even more self-punishment:

Victor: *I tried to sleep, but I started crying and shaking. I tried to drill my arm but I couldn't figure out how to get the drill bit to stay in the drill. I tried to pour hot oil on my arm, but it wasn't hot enough. I cried a lot. I'll try again later.*
Lorene: *Sounds like you don't really want to hurt me.*
Victor: *I'm so tired. I'm tired of being ready for danger, scanning constantly for power-threats and sexual danger and, most of all, for betrayal. I'm exhausted. Somewhere I lost the "me" I was born with and just became the "point man" in a dangerous war. I can't answer the door; I'm scared to open the mail or answer the phone; I'm scared to go to the bathroom, scared to take a shower. I do anything to stay away from people—turn down invitations, avoid taking public transportation. I always say that the fear belongs to other parts and I'm strong, but that isn't true. After being Mr. Hypervigilant for so many years, the fear became mine, too.*

I wish I could just trust someone, feel safe, be liked for something besides my ability to be aggressive and cold. Today while I was crying, I was afraid the worst things would start happening to Destiny and Jenny again. I knew then I would be called upon to protect them. I can't stand it anymore. I'd rather die.

Finally, the frightening images projected by a "malevolent" part may be nothing more than a dramatic device to gain attention (Johnson, 1986, p. 70). After a child has muttered eight times, "Mom, Joey took my cookies," he finally gets immediate attention by screaming: "Joey is the worst most horrible brother in the world! I hate him! I wish he were dead!" After a wife has repeatedly suggested to her husband, "I think it would be nice to go to see my parents on Sunday," and gotten no response, she is sure to get his attention by yelling: "You've *always* hated my parents; you've *never*

thanked them for the loans they've given us; you'll *never* treat them nicely."
When parts (like Nicholas or Victor) repeatedly scream at a survivor
("You're evil, you must die, I'll burn off your skin, you poison everything
around you"), they need to be assured that they have secured the survivor's
attention. The parts who were frightened by the screaming need to be
comforted, and then the so-called malevolent parts should be asked to
explain more directly what they want.

THE QUESTION OF MEMORIES

The mental health and legal fields are in the throes of a bitter debate
regarding the validity of delayed memories of sexual abuse that emerge in
the context of therapy (Begley & Brant, 1994; Calof, 1994b; Horn, 1993).
This debate has taken on all the qualities of polarization that this book
describes regarding parts and that characterize other emotion-charged conflicts in our culture, such as the abortion, welfare, or death penalty debates. Each side views the other monolithically instead of acknowledging
the multiple aspects of the issue. Each side huddles in its extreme position
and discounts or minimizes any of the potentially valid or useful points of
the other. In a debate, extreme parts of each person jump in. This issue is
too important to be subjected to a polarized analysis. While a healthy
debate benefits everyone — clients, clinicians, researchers, accused offenders, judges, and juries — a bitter war harms all. It is our position that both
sides have some concerns that are legitimate and others that are not helpful. Both sides need to find a common ground where communication can
begin and work to avoid having extreme parts give advice to clients and
their families.

The Opposing Positions

Those who take the "false memory syndrome" position claim that repression over many years of repeated episodes of abuse is not possible
(Dawes, 1992; Loftus, 1993; Loftus & Ketcham, 1994; Nash, 1992; Nathan,
1992; Ofshe & Watters, 1994; Wakefield & Underwager, 1992; Yapko,
1994.) The "false memory syndrome" crusade sometimes offers unsup-
ported assertions that memory recall is nothing more than a fad (Yapko,
1994; C. McHugh, 1993*). One psychiatrist writes that memory recovery

---

*The journalist quotes Dr. Paul McHugh, director of Department of Psychiatry
and Behavioral Sciences at Johns Hopkins Medical Institution, who describes the
diagnosis of repressed memory of sexual abuse as a "big fad" within the psychiatric
community.

therapy is "based on pseudoscientific notions," is "pop psychology," and that "memory therapists urge their patients to believe that their 'recovered memories' are the only proof needed that long-trusted friends and family are actually perverted perpetrators whom one can never trust again (and probably never will talk to again)" (Hochman, 1994). Many in this camp believe that "recovered memories" are the product of therapists who unwittingly suggest and implant these memories. A defense attorney writes: "We will always have disturbed individuals making false claims for one reason or another. Bringing cases based on them, however, is the mistake of the professional listener, whose duty is to be alert for error factors" (Sheridan, 1994). They also blame these "disturbed individuals" for trying to shift responsibility for their problems from themselves to some putative abuser—just because they prefer the label "victim" rather than to view themselves as a "failure." The result is lawsuits like those filed against *Courage to Heal* authors Laura Davis and Ellen Bass alleging that they promised healing but failed to heal. One journalist applauded these suits, claiming that Davis and Bass "prompt[ed] some desperate people to conjure up false memories, with tragic consequences" and concluded that "Victimology has gone full circle; America has devolved from a country of pioneers to a nation of plaintiffs" (Saunders, 1994).

The false memory group also contends (without documenting evidence) that there are legions of therapists around the country who are jumping to the abuse conclusion as soon as a client mentions certain symptom patterns. "There are paranoid therapists. There are therapists who are intent on finding abuse no matter what someone comes in for, including acne" (Yapko, 1994, reported in Wright, 1994). As is common within polarizations, some advocates of this position see a conspiracy at work. They insinuate that there are large numbers of therapists making great sums of money or otherwise profiting by pushing their clients toward victimhood and exploiting the resulting dependence. They view the resistance of therapists to their position as self-serving attempts to maintain the survivor industry. And they encourage the accused to sue these therapists.

On the other side are the therapists who work with abused clients. The extreme positions from this camp include dismissing concerns regarding the influence of therapist suggestion by contending that clients could never construct elaborate mental images based merely on hints from a therapist. This, despite the fact that decades of research into possible bias resulting from hypnotic suggestion—however subtle—reveal almost identical problems. Some also minimize the practice of jumping to the abuse conclusion, suggesting that such therapists are few, if they exist at all. Yet the problem still faces those clients who find themselves working with the few hard-to-identify therapists who try to fit clients into a peg hole marked "sex abuse." Some advocates support the validity of delayed memories by citing the fact that many clients do not want to believe them and would be relieved to discover the memories were false. While this is logical and often true, there are individuals who have extreme parts that need to create chaos, seek revenge for a perceived wrong, or keep their therapist interested.

Some "believers" escalate the extreme sides of the polarization by encouraging clients to confront or even sue family members based only on vague recovered memories with little corroboration, and by paying little attention to the consequences of such a suit. Many of these therapists argue that the other side represents only another in a long series of inevitable backlashes in our culture designed to deny or minimize the prevalence of abuse. They accuse the false memory advocates of aiding and abetting perpetrators and have conspiracy theories of their own.

Thus, just as when parts, people, or countries begin to polarize, each sees the other through a distorted lens. The other is evil, selfish, or ignorant, and anything he has to say is biased. If one concedes any of the other's points, then one feels vulnerable to being totally dismissed. For example, we believe that the false memory crusade has been helpful in its forcing therapists to be aware of undue influence they may bring to the therapy session (Ernsdorff & Loftus, 1993; Loftus & Ketcham, 1994). But victim advocates who hug the extreme end of their position feel that admitting that the FMS camp's work has resulted in anything positive would constitute a betrayal of their position. As the polarization escalates, the positions on each side become increasingly extreme and distanced from the available data, and the goal of seeking additional reliable data is further impeded.

It may be that the false memory movement is part of another cultural backlash and that some are using it to supress news of abuse. Yet there are people and positions associated with the movement that have validity and need to be addressed by those who help survivors. Similarly, there are too many therapists who lead clients to abuse conclusions. Yet there are far more who do not and whose clients are retrieving powerful memories that have been dissociated. The false memory people are wrong to discount all delayed memories because some may be false. In other words, we need more self-leadership on both sides in which the other is viewed multiply rather than monolithically.

Many Delayed Memories are Real

We wholeheartedly believe in the reality of many delayed memories. One of us is a therapist who works extensively with survivors of childhood sexual abuse, some of whom only realized they were abused—or (like Lorene) realized the extent of the abuse—after entering therapy. Schwartz has been with a number of clients as they remembered or relived vivid scenes of abuse, humiliation, and betrayal. Sometimes these images are crystal clear and accompanied by appropriate emotions and sensations. Other times they are hazy, inchoate. The idea that all of these memories are totally fantasized is as preposterous as the claim that they are all perfectly accurate and valid. Similarly, the idea that they have all been induced by Schwartz's behavior is as preposterous as the claim that his presence has had no effect.

One of us is an attorney who daily confronts issues of truth, credibility questions, evidentiary burdens, compensation and justice for victims, and punishment and blaming of offenders. Some cases are bursting with strong corroboration, while others rest only on the credibility of the complainant. Either type of case can be successful, and rightfully so. The variables in types of evidence and factual scenarios are endless. It is impossible to announce a clear-cut, general rule regarding suggestibility of the alleged victim, involvement of therapists in uncovering dissociated memories, or the type of evidence an accused must bring forward in a civil case to defend against corroborated accusations.

Distortions in Memories

Notwithstanding our belief that many delayed memories are real, we have no illusions about the possibility that memories can be distorted, contain inaccuracies, or be influenced by others. As Terr (1994) explains:

> Because defenses come into play in true memories, these memories often sound fragmented—especially if the abuses or other traumas went on time after time. On the other hand, true memories cannot ordinarily be distinguished from the false by the amount of detail that comes out in the telling. People who have dissociated away their terrible childhood memories can pick up false details from TV, the print media, or suggestive therapists. Moreover, a memory coming from a person who massively dissociates, be it true or false, will probably sound peculiar. You can't tell from a story alone whether a memory is true or false. Every case must be individually evaluated for corroborations. (p. 172)

Protective parts of a person work diligently to dissociate traumatic memories for decades. The person should be given every chance to uncover and articulate those memories. This view is supported by the fact that many state legislatures have recently amended their statutes of limitations to permit adults to bring charges of childhood sexual abuse following the delayed recovery of memories. This does not rubber-stamp the allegations as being true—it merely opens the door to the courthouse so the person can make the allegations regarding the circumstances in which the memories surfaced. Time and careful attention to what "facts" parts are reporting permit the client and therapist to sort out consistent, credible aspects of the information.

Extreme Parts Neither Confirm nor Negate the
Reality of the Abuse

In verifying which aspects of memories are credible, we believe it is *vital* that judges, prosecutors, police officers, clinicians investigating the case, and those expressing "public opinion" realize that the presence of extreme parts in any person involved in the case cannot determine the validity of the charges. An extreme vindictive part of the client does not *negate* the client's position that the accused is guilty; nor does an extreme bullying part of the accused negate the accused's position that he never molested the client. Any one of us might have extreme parts that react to an avid crusader for either side—those who cry "false memories" or those who support victims taking action based on newly recovered memories. We all have stories to tell of clients, friends, or family members who were adversely affected by people in one camp or the other; we all bring our own histories with us (e.g., "I was once falsely accused of something," or "I suffered horrendous emotional abuse that someone should have recognized"); and we all have parts who strive to play various roles around the issue (protector, rescuer, victim, fellow-sufferer, truth-finder).

The therapist plays a crucial role. The point where the client chooses to *act* on the delayed memories is the point where the external realities of life come into play. A statute of limitations or currently abusing perpetrator might force one client to announce her allegations sooner than another. Therapists, then, must be familiar with their own parts and try to keep their Self in charge as they explore with clients what position each of the client's parts takes and where the client's Self stands on this issue. Many of us might recognize some of our own parts supporting either the accused or the accuser:

- Imagine what would have happened to my life if a false accusation had been made against me (or my teenage son, my husband, my minister). It would break my heart. The destruction to my family's life would be immense. (I could lose my job; I might have to visit my son in jail; the other children would be taken from me and put in foster care unless I made my husband move out.) Just being accused would be horrible; even if the charges were later dropped, my life would never be the same. Whether the accused (me, my son, whoever) is innocent or guilty—and usually the facts are such that we will probably never know—how will it help to have my family destroyed, my livelihood destroyed, have my son locked up in jail or a juvenile home, or my children moved to a foster home? Can't this be handled with a family therapist and no public accusations?

- But part of me says that this woman has suffered for decades — all for something that was not her fault. She has the right to "break silence." It will be healing for her, and it will make the public aware of the issue, and perhaps keep it from happening to other children.
- At a minimum, the victim has right to compensation; she's spent thousands of dollars in therapy, and has been unable to work for months at a time due to abuse-related symptoms.
- The abuser made all the choices when he molested his daughter as a toddler. Now it's time for the adult daughter to take control and make her own choices. She shouldn't have to protect the abuser from the consequences of her accusations. She's already spent enough years protecting him with her coerced silence.

And therapists will recognize some of these parts in themselves:

- I can't believe courts let these people sue *me* just because one of my clients accused her father of sexual abuse. It certainly isn't my fault she uncovered these memories. I'm being punished for doing my job well — working hard so that she'll trust me and feel safe enough to reveal secrets she's walled off for so long.
- I feel wonderful knowing that I can bring my client the type of relief she's sought for years. I'm *sure* that all of her problems and improper diagnoses over the years were caused by some terrible childhood trauma. Everything she says points to sexual abuse, and it's my responsibility to give her that information.

You'll also recognize some of the parts of clients:

- I just want him to apologize.
- If he'd only admit abusing me, I wouldn't have to make the accusation public. I just want him to tell me that it was a horrible mistake — a temporary aberration in his personality — and that now he loves me a great deal and would never think of hurting me.
- It feels good to get attention from fellow victims in my survivor support group; I finally *belong* somewhere.
- It feels so wonderful to finally have an answer to explain my years of depression, self-mutilation, and promiscuity. I always knew it had something to do with my father, but I never knew someone I trusted and felt safe enough to look at scary memories with.
- It may sound mean, but I truly believe that he should be punished for what he did. After all, I've been punished for years with the consequences of his depraved acts. I know him — he'll never apolo-

gize. So the only way to make him realize what he did was wrong is to force him to serve some jail time. All my friends agree with me—he deserves the worst the courts can hand out.

All of these parts should be acknowledged and worked with—hopefully before *any* decision is made by the therapist, the client, or any professional involved after the suspicions are raised or the allegations announced. It is the *Self* of each of these people—not the extreme parts—who should make decisions.

The therapist should tell the client, "Convince me as your Self that confrontation with the abuser or making public your accusations is important and why you want to do it. I'll support you, but I'm not going to let parts make this decision. It must be a Self decision." A majority of the client's parts might actually disagree with the Self's final decision to publicly announce her childhood victimization; nevertheless, the Self's decision should be supported by the therapist. Or vice versa, a majority of the client's parts might *insist* on a public announcement, while the Self holds firmly against it; again, the Self's decision must be supported.

Delay Acting on Delayed Memories

In many cases, where external circumstances permit, clients should be encouraged to *not* immediately bring the accusations out of therapy and into the client's external world. The decision to confront, to sue, or to cut off relations with one's family need not be made quickly. The most helpful thing the therapist can offer a client is exploration of the inner family members' influence on this decision. Ask which parts want the confrontation and what they hope to gain from it; ask which parts are against the confrontation, either because they fear the results or simply believe it would not be helpful. Locate the survivor's Self and determine the best decision for the entire inner family. The therapist should make sure that his or her Self is in charge, particularly if the therapist is also a survivor.

Therapy is not a court of law. A therapist is not a judge, jury, or executioner. The therapist should not urge the client into an intense search for "the truth." Unlike raising allegations in the legal system, exploring memories in therapy has no time limit and no trier of fact to vote on the credibility of the client. In therapy, then, it is better not to attack the uncovering of memories as an intense, time-oriented project to be accomplished as soon as possible.

Inaccuracies

Early in his career, Schwartz made the mistake of suggesting to a client that perhaps she had been abused. Shortly afterwards, while working with her parts, she came forth with a series of horrific images involving her family. Fortunately, some sessions later and before the client acted on these images, a part confessed to having generated the images to maintain the therapist's interest and to scare other parts. Other parts believed in these pictures because the purported memories *fit* the intense pain and sense of betrayal they had lived with for years, or because the images were too powerful to ignore, or because they trusted the client and the therapist to uncover the truth, whatever it might be.

After a year of parts work, this client's other exiled parts showed abuse scenes involving a neighbor that were qualitatively different—factually detailed, emotion-laden, and later corroborated by a sister who had never lost her memories of also being abused. Schwartz learned from this experience that, indeed, clients have parts that can generate "false memories."

Initially false — or *partially* false — memories should not rule out the existence of genuine ones. When a person's parts feel safe with the therapist, and the stage is properly set, they will show the truth but only as they know it. A survivor who reports a detailed vision of her father standing over her bed, screaming obscenities at her while holding an axe, does not mean that is precisely what happened. The content might be accurate in all details, or it might be a metaphoric representation of what actually happened. Some of the details may be colored by the small child's perceptions, decades of repression, or other distorting factors. Terr (1994) explores these concepts in *Unchained Memories*:

> Even if a person remembers a horror consistently for years, as this man did, the attendant perceptions are not necessarily accurate. The principal events, however, are generally accurately remembered. It would be highly unlikely for a man who had been orally attacked to remember it as an anal attack, for instance. It would be highly unlikely for him to remember being taken from his father or from a friend rather than from his mother. And it would be unlikely for him to believe that his attacker was a woman. The gist of the memory stays true, but the details sometimes go "off." That's why the extreme polarization of the false-memory controversy does not make sense to me. People who say that their accusers are completely fabricating may be missing the essence of how traumatic memories manifest themselves. Parts are true—often the gist. Parts are false—sometimes details in the descriptions of the perpetrators. (p. 168)

Thus, a mistake in time ("Dad could not have abused you the summer of 1962, since he was in Europe that whole time"), a mistake in describing the physical setting ("No one raped you on a brown couch in our basement, because we never owned a brown couch"), or a mistake in description of the offender ("Uncle Bob never had a beard") does not necessarily negate the rest of the memories.

Often an incomplete picture emerges because different parts hold different pieces of traumatic memories. Lancaster (1991) discusses the theory that the "nature of memory . . . [is] multiple systems of memory" and thus memory is stored "in the brain in diverse sites" (p. 49). Similarly, Putnam (1989) describes techniques for assembling whole memories from fragments, where each alter contains a fragment of the event, or one alter contains the details while others hold the affects generated by the event. Schwartz explains the significant role which the survivor's managerial parts play in pacing memory retrieval:

> The [managers] have some control over the way information is released within the inner system, especially if the [exiled part] who holds the memories or sensations is willing to cooperate. That is, the memories can be released in flashbacks or in dreams. . . . They can release just the images without the feelings or sensations, or just the sensations without any image or feeling, etc. They can control the clarity of the images and the pace at with each memory is released. All of this can be overtly negotiated with whichever managers have most control over this area so that the memory-release is done in a safe way and at a safe pace. Just knowing that they will have some control over the pace will help managers relax. (Schwartz, 1995, p. 211)

A therapist might also find it helpful, in "verifying" memories, to determine whether the internal family is in conflict about memories reported by some parts. Do all parts agree the memories are true, or do they disagree about the source or content of the memories? Recovering memories is not an easy task. Yates and Pawley (1987) describe one survivor's multiple reactions to the possibility of uncovering incest-related memories through hypnosis. She "simultaneously experienced the desire to know and understand, the need to withhold information from her conscious awareness, and the fear of knowing what she had repressed in her unconscious" (p. 37). While part of her was determined to know the truth about her past, another part was equally activated "to restrain the memories and feelings with forceful determination." She experienced an "internal conflict: the will to remember against the terror of remembering." Each time the patient "recalled new memories of the sexual abuse during psychotherapy, she experienced the sensation of spinning, and relived the intense emotional conflict" (p. 39). Lorene's parts are typical of those who fight memory retrieval:

Nicholas: *I refuse to work with Dick anymore. All the stuff he says is a trick to make me expose more and more of myself until he can finally laugh at me and leave me raw, exposed meat for vultures to feed off. He strips me of everything familiar and leaves me nothing safe.*

I can't even sleep anymore. my nightmares blend with the daytime and I don't know what is real. Can I kill Andy? I hate his vulnerability. I want to end the screaming pain. My head is going to explode.

Cuts all over my stomach. Covered with blood. Every cut—I scream "I hate you" at Lorene. Kill the abdomen. It is the enemy. Hateful horrible body is the enemy. It betrays me by feeling. Forces me to be alive when I want to be dead. More, more cuts. I scream "I won't talk to you, I won't talk to you, I won't, I won't." I will never talk to Dick. Never tell him things.

Andy: I need to feel nothing. Please.

Victor: Nicholas and Bridgette are screaming. Jenny is bleeding. Andy isn't here anymore. He's not real, I guess. Vincent left. Super-She wants to take over if the others will let her. It's ok with me. Super-She can work-work-work and ignore everything else. Dash is pissed. Catherine hides in garage with Jenny. Alex is furious and crazy. I've screwed up everything by talking to Dick and telling him my feelings.

Alex: Look at what's happening. Andy is just becoming catatonic. All curled up on the floor. No one can reach him. Maybe that's better. Maybe the others will calm down. But he's not totally gone. I can feel his tears waiting. He's so frightened. I don't want to be alone. I wish Andy would die. We'd be better off. The infant inside is crying, cold, not safe. Nothing comforts her. She will die crying and abandoned. Let her curl up under a blanket with Andy. Maybe just being near each other will help. Like animals curled up in a den, waiting for their mother to bring them food. So weak that they can't nurture each other.

Swink and Leveille (1986) note that when survivors begin to remember and face the abuse, most of them experience

> dreams, nightmares and/or flashbacks of the abuse. If these had been totally blocked previously, they can be very frightening and confusing as they seem to be coming out of nowhere. . . . It feels as if she is being further victimized as she relives these experiences, but this time from within her own mind rather than from someone outside. (p. 123)

Similarly, Putnam (1989) writes that the patient, with her "timeless unmetabolized trauma," may believe the abuser can harm her if she retrieves memories in therapy (p. 173). Many parts, therefore, will fight with everything they have to block memory retrieval because it feels like the abuse is recurring simultaneously with the memory.

Victor: After Destiny opened her big mouth and told more secrets, Lorene had to go to work. At work, I was flipping out, crying, physically disintegrating, cells exploding. Inside I hear screaming, moaning, begging Mom to come get me. It's happening now; she's coming to touch me now; I'm far away, in the basement; I'm so little without my new adult body to protect me; everything's happening so fast I can't even scream.

This demonstrates why we believe that, if possible, it is best to delay confrontations with the accused until the therapist and client can work through the most polarized and extreme internal conflicts or not confront at all. Contrary to a myth in the survivor movement, it is not necessary for the abuser to acknowledge or apologize for the client to heal.

Memories and the Law

It is important for those filing civil lawsuits or bringing criminal charges to realize that the courts are in a state of flux around the crucial issue of memories (Barall, 1994; Ernsdorff & Loftus, 1993; Kanovitz, 1992). Some courts refuse to allow a survivor to delay bringing a lawsuit until her dream-like images become concrete "memories."* Other courts have convicted the accused based on recovered dissociated memories (Maclean, 1993).

Some courts artfully dodge the question of whether decades-old memories are of any value in the courtroom. In a recent Pennsylvania case,** the judge's reasoning probably had Freud turning over in his grave: "Is there any reason to suppose that courts are better equipped to determine these questions than Sigmund Freud?" Incredibly, the judge went on to portray psychological opinions about childhood events as always falling outside the realm of the law:

> Psychology has, since the time of Freud, been in the business of exploring and finding subjective reality. Courts, on the other hand, are in the business of trying to find objective reality. In cases like this, these two enterprises necessarily clash. Indeed, reasonable people could well wonder whether courts are suited at all to deal with problems like these. To the extent, however, that courts are required to determine these questions, there is no doubt in our mind that the objective enterprise is far better served by receiving fresher evidence than recollections of events that occurred eighteen to twenty-four years ago.†

In a landmark case that has shocked the mental health community, a California jury awarded $500,000 to a father suing his daughter's therapists for implanting or reinforcing false memories of incest.‡ It has been viewed by some as a "significant broadening of exposure of health care providers to non-patients" (McKee, 1994). And at least one federal appellate judge has endorsed the Ernsdorff and Loftus (1993) requirements for strong

---

*Roe v. Doe, 28 F.3d 404 (4th Cir. 1994).
**Messina v. Bonner, 813 F. Supp. 346, 350 (E.D. Penn. 1993).
†813 F. Supp. at 351.
‡Ramona v. Ramona, No. 61898 (Napa, California) (jury awarded entered May 13, 1994).

strong corroboration.* Courts will remain cautious in basing judgments on previously dissociated memories, much as they have overwhelmingly rejected posthypnotic recollections due to the absence of a reliable method for determining whether undue suggestions has interfered with the accuracy of the recollections (Barall, 1994).**

Role of Therapists as Memory Detectives

Clearly it is imperative that therapists never suggest what clients will find when they work with their parts or hypothesize about the hidden roots of a problem. Along these lines, we would also encourage therapists to work with their own parts to empty them of any presumptions regarding a client's past so they can be genuinely curious and not lead clients subtly and unconsciously in any one direction.

As one works with a client's exiled parts and asks them where they are stuck in the past, the client may suddenly see a scene of abuse for which he or she had no former, conscious memory. To answer the question of how a therapist is to understand such an experience and what kind of response the therapist can give to the client, we note a few basic principles about memory work.

Craving Memories

Survivors often crave the recovery of memories. Some parts desperately want to reveal the memories, sometimes in the belief that they can convince other parts the abuse occurred, and was not the survivor's fault. ("If I could remember exactly what Dad did, maybe I could finally identify him as the perpetrator and me as the victim.") Putnam (1989) notes that victims of severe trauma will ask "what really happened?" because they have difficulty "in determining the origin of the dreamlike images that flood their inner awareness at times" (p. 123). Lancaster (1991) explains that the "relevant memories have not been lost; it is the patient's control over them that has suffered" (p. 71). But how accurate are these "memories," once retrieved? Does the retrieval process itself taint the validity of the memories?

It is normal for survivors to want "proof" of their abuse, much like a patient wanting an x-ray or blood test firmly establishing that disease does

---

*Roe v. Doe, 28 F.3d 404, 411 n.7 (4th Cir. 1994) (J. Hall, concurring).
**See a recent federal decision in Illinois, *Sullivan v. Cheshier*, 846 F. Supp. 654 (N.D. Ill. 1994), where the court held that the plaintiffs/parents' suit against their daughter's therapist could proceed to trial because a trier of fact could reasonably find that the therapist implanted the sexual abuse memories since the daughter made no allegations until *after* she had been hypnotized.

or does not exist. It is often a tremendous relief to hang a tag on something; the survivor feels she is not crazy and has an explanation for the years of depression and pain she has suffered.

But such proof is not necessary in order to work with clients who come to therapy complaining of overwhelming feelings of terror, fear of sexual or intimate relationships, self-mutilation, certain addictions, or other symptoms fitting the typical sexual abuse victim. Some parts of survivors who monitor the release of memories do not care about filing criminal charges against the offender, or bringing civil suits for compensation, or confronting family members about past deeds. These parts only care that it is *safe* for the survivor to become consciously aware of horrors that have been long buried. The survivor and therapist may need to work with other parts, those who want absolute proof, retribution or revenge, or a purging confrontation or a declaration to the world that the molestation occurred, encouraging them to not rush through the survivor's past and present lives like a bull in a china shop.

Therapists should reassure these parts of clients that *proving* whether childhood abuse occurred is not the only—or the main—goal. In most cases, whether each detail remembered actually occurred is *not relevant* to the pathway taken towards, or the ultimate goal of, healing the survivor.

The Right to "Break Silence"

This is not to say that survivors should not be able to exercise their right to make public the atrocities they suffered as children.

> The adult survivor community has fought hard for the right to bring delayed childhood sexual abuse suits that psychological impairments disabled them from bringing on time. . . . This will be a hollow and bitter victory if courts now exclude their testimony because the psychotherapy treatments that helped them remember were legally unacceptable. (Kanovitz, 1992, p. 1260)

Therapists may find that parts of them, parts of the client, or the realities of life (an abuser who is still actively molesting children, a statute of limitations that will soon run out, being called as an expert witness for litigation purposes) require them to act as psychological detectives and proclaim, at the end of the investigation, whether the client was or was not molested as a child. But how can the detective determine whether emerging memories are accurate?

Corroboration

In or out of a courtroom, corroboration is the most helpful means of verifying the accuracy of abuse-related memories. In litigation, of course, that corroboration must take the form of admissible evidence.* But it is important to remember that the legal process can actually distort the accuracy of what occurred, instead of bringing the true facts to light and ensuring that justice prevails (Summit, 1994). The legal question of culpability is very narrow and adversarial (Summit, 1994, p. 13); pursuing it often has a devastating effect on the victim and the accused, with little relief or justice for either.

When memories of repeated events are repressed, dissociated, split off, or displaced, they are not necessarily more inaccurate when they return than are single-event memories that were always remembered. They tend to be more fragmentary, however, and they tend to be more condensed.

But our purpose here is to focus on the use of memories *outside* of the courtroom. The following factors are relevant in gauging the validity of previously dissociated information. The therapist will find the factors of interest, but none of them is a crystal ball. No single factor determines whether the abuse is "true" — but balancing and weighing these factors may offer some insight into the veracity of the memories:

- The emotions accompanying the memories are intense, or there is a total absence of affect.
- Similar memories have been revealed by siblings, or there is some other type of confirmation by family members.
- The selective fragments of memories, while perhaps out of sequence, combine to form a consistent picture of abuse.
- The memories have returned at a significant time (death of offender, survivor's child has reached age at which survivor was molested, first time survivor returns to childhood home or town).
- The offender has admitted some or all of the abuse (even in a private, informal conversation).
- The survivor has found pornographic pictures of herself as a child or of other children.
- The repression is explained by relevant factors (young age at time of abuse, accompanying violence or threats, number of times it occurred, the offender being a close family friend or member of the family).

---

*We disagree with Terr's (1994) statement that "what juries use and what psychiatrists use to ascertain the 'truth' of a memory are basically the same" (p. 171). But as we stated earlier, we will embark on that journey at a different time. In this book, we do not attempt to advise therapists on how to interview, on behalf of the plaintiff or the defense, individuals who have made allegations of sexual abuse, or how to interview alleged perpetrators for litigation purposes. We leave that subject for another time.

- The offender has been accused of, or found guilty of, molesting other children.
- There is no apparent reason why the client might *choose* to remember horrible things and plunge herself or her families into the pain of facing such trauma.
- The client's symptoms, particularly those that surfaced in childhood or adolescence (such as various types of repeated reenactments, suggestive physical sensations, or specific fears), are extensive, longstanding, and severe.

Other factors might also come into play.

It is not the therapist's role to put their "patients' stories . . . to rigorous tests of internal and external confirmations" (Terr, 1994, p. 160). Whether or not treatment "succeeds" does not depend on therapists' presiding over mini-trials and evidentiary hearings held in therapy sessions.

Uncovering dissociated information and counteracting the intense reactions to bringing dissociated abuse-related memories into the conscious awareness of the client require the therapist and survivor to perform the painstaking work of disarming managers, disarming firefighters, and retrieving exiled parts. Both therapists and survivors must remember that their goal is not always precise, measurable, accurate memory. It is not necessary for an adult to recover full, detailed memories in order to achieve relief in therapy.

And what of the survivor who has *no* specific memories, yet believes she was abused? This is not uncommon. Sometimes parts of the survivor will do *anything* to keep memories hidden, because they believe the survivor will be overwhelmed by, perhaps even annihilated by, these memories. Consequently, many, many survivors cannot access clear pictures of their childhood (not just the abuse incidents—they often wipe out the entire childhood) or have nothing more than a few fragments released by parts who are not under the collective thumb of the over-protective managers.

There will be much more said about the accurate retrieval of traumatic memories before this debate is over. The fields of mental health and law overlap somewhat, but take diverging paths on many points. Before the delayed memory controversy is resolved, more research must take place, particularly into the ability to interview a hidden observer part or the Self, either of whom might hold accurate memories. We agree with Terr's recommendation and conclusion:

> Only a series of strong clinical studies on adult memories of confirmed incidents of childhood abuse will resolve the false-memory controversy. We will need long-term follow-ups of children with proven abuse in their backgrounds. Until these definitive studies are accomplished, each case must speak for itself. The facts of a case will settle the debate on an individual level. Each case must be assessed and diagnosed for its particular truth. Each

patient must be checked for specific symptoms and signs. Adult patients must be willing to look not only for internal but for external confirmation of newly returned memories. Lack of external confirmation does not negate a memory. But many more memories lend themselves to such confirmation than one might think. (1994, p. 165)

Once accusations have been made, the secretiveness surrounding the process greatly complicates matters and makes it more difficult for people to remain them Selves. In keeping with IFS principles, we believe that a skilled therapist and legal representatives (whether prosecutors, police, or private attorneys representing the parties) can be quite successful in bringing all the concerned people together to review situation, available facts, and their present positions, and to clarify what each side wants.

CHAPTER 4

A Systemic View of the Multiple Psyche: A Moving Mosaic

Impact at one point of the psychic system leads to ripples through the whole apparatus.

—*Andrew Samuels, 1989*

WHEN ONE MEMBER OF a family throws a tantrum, others invariably react—whether it be with counter-tantrums, or with fear, or maybe with cold indifference. When one member of a family allies with another on an issue—perhaps a teen daughter's pregnancy, an impending divorce, or selling the family home—others typically respond with a counter-alliance as they vie for control over the final decision.

Similarly, parts—as internal family members—form relationships with each other that can significantly impact the whole system. "Just like people in a family or countries in international politics, parts cannot and will not change unilaterally" (Schwartz, 1995, p. 43). The relational context of all parts within the system helps to define the nature of each part. Zohar (1990) quotes the renowned quantum physicist David Bohm:

> Thought processes and quantum systems are analogous in that they cannot be analyzed too much in terms of distinct elements, because the "intrinsic" nature of each element is not a property existing separately from and independently of other elements but is, instead, a property that arises partially from its relation with other elements. (p. 77)

The parts or subpersonalities who inhabit our inner world relate to, and react to, each other. Instead of living as disconnected parts of a balanced but sterile system (figure 4.1), they live as both interconnected and autonomous beings (figure 4.2). These parts, like members of an external family,

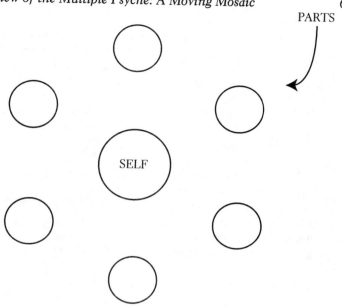

PARTS

SELF

Figure 4.1. All components of the system are balanced,
but relationships are ignored

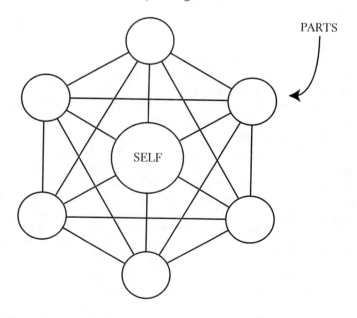

PARTS

SELF

Figure 4.2. A balanced system with the addition
of connections and relationships

vie for control, interact sequentially, organize into alliances, and at times go to war with each other. "Just as what goes on in a community of humans or animals affects each member of that community, so what goes on in one part of an organism affects what goes on in each part of it" (Redfearn, 1985, p. 60).

Identifying and communicating with individual parts may ultimately have little effect if they are not accompanied by earnest attention to the continuous fluctuations in the entire internal system. So, it is not enough to try to change a single, isolated helper or hidden observer, one punitive or aggressive part, a solitary inner child, one numb part, a part pretending "as if" she's functioning normally, or a single self-hating or guilt-ridden part. An effective treatment model must consider the entire inner ecology. The IFS model tracks the sequential changes within the internal family, helps relationships among parts incorporate change, anticipates which parts are likely to be adversely activated, and then directly and respectfully addresses the concerns of those parts.

A systemic approach views the internal world through a wide-angle lens—an ecological perspective. This in turn helps both therapist and client understand how parts have become mired within the system as a result of various constraints. These constraints are discussed throughout the book as we identify common problems that hamper internal systems. Typical examples of constraints occur when (1) the leader is not available or is discredited; (2) a part is frozen in time; (3) a part holds extreme beliefs or feelings; or (4) a part is burdened by a sense of shame, worthlessness, rage, or perfectionism. Using a systemic approach to the psyche also permits the therapist to find ways to enter the client's internal system safely, to respect the natural pace of change, and to anticipate and avoid harmful reactions to the changes. (The client's external world can be understood in the same way.) Finally, systems thinking facilitates an appreciation of the common patterns of protectiveness and fear seen in those who have suffered trauma.

The systemic premises that organize the internal system of an adult who suffered severe trauma as a child closely resemble those of a person who passed through a more normal, undisturbed development. The essence of a person, whether or not she has suffered abuse, is how the internal system's components organize themselves, how they fit together as a whole, and who governs the existing system. An abuse survivor's inner world (and often her outer world) is typically more polarized, reactive, unbalanced, fragile, explosive, rigid, and lacking in leadership than the inner world of a non-abused person. Consider the chaotic response of Lorene's system after she stomped out of the therapist's office during a session:

Victor: *I'm never talking to that useless therapist again. He's negligent in forgetting to check on Andy. I waited half the session and he never asked about Andy—not once!*

Super-She: *Oh, and you didn't distract him much today, did you?*

Victor: *It was Nicholas who walked out this time, not me.*

Super-She: *What about when you accused Bonnie of having sexual feelings for that new guy she met?*

Victor: *But that's valid!*

Alexandra: *I don't suppose you ever felt sexual?*

Victor: *No, I don't suppose I did. Why don't you quit supporting Bonnie's whore tendencies. She'll be in bed with the next guy she sees.*

Alex: *So what?*

Victor: *I thought you promised to stay away from sex.*

Alex: *That's got nothing to do with you, Mr. Purity.*

Victor: *Why don't you stay out of this—let Bonnie stand up for herself.*

Alex: *She can't—you have too much influence over her.*

Super-She: *Why don't you worry about your own sexual feelings, Alex, instead of Bonnie's?*

Alex: *I don't have Victor punishing me every three minutes. He has no influence over me.*

Super-She: *Nicholas does.*

Alex: *Well, yeah, sometimes.*

Victor: *I hate to break this up girls, but the bottom line is, I don't want to talk about this stuff with Dick.*

Super-She: *What are you afraid will happen?*

Victor: *He'll be kind to me.*

Super-She: *So?*

Victor: *I'd rather be tough. I like Andy being angry and running back to Dad in the dark basement. That's better.*

Super-She: *Why don't you try being friendly to Dick?*

Victor: *No way!! I was just kidding when I told him I wanted love and safety and a new function in Lorene's life. I just made that up to give us something to talk about because I was so bored.*

The internal system of an abuse victim differs from the non-abused system with regard to the consistent absence of effective leadership, the extreme rules under which the parts function, and the absence of any consistent balance or harmony. Typically, the parts operate around outdated assumptions and beliefs derived from the childhood abuse, believing, for example, that it is still extremely dangerous to reveal secrets about the childhood experiences which were endured. Before encouraging a young part to expose secrets, then, the survivor and therapist must address the concerns of any protective part who believes he or she must prevent the perpetrator's threats from coming true.

In *You Don't Love Yourself*, there is a full systemic reaction of panic when one of the parts considers revealing an intimate, secret emotion to another person. Once the system is successful in stopping the part from blurting out secrets, the protectors return to their collective reclusiveness:

After that bad dream, how wonderful to be back amongst ourselves
again...
   It's so good to be together again, to merge, to melt...
   Everything is coming back to life, quivering... something intangible protected by silence is passing through the same substance in us, returning to
the same source... (pp. 130–131)

Ignoring the protective parts only increases the likelihood that they will
respond violently to the attempted invasion of the system. Like Jung's
concept of the shadow, when "repressed and isolated" it is "liable to burst
forth suddenly" (Jung, 1938/1940/1969, par. 131). Thus, failure to understand the internal ecology dooms most attempts at lasting, therapeutic
change and can even invite retaliatory behavior such as self-mutilation,
severe depression, binge eating, or substance abuse.

COMMUNICATION AND BOUNDARIES

How do therapists find their way within this invisible but volatile system? For guidance, Schwartz (1995) has identified four principles — balance, harmony, leadership, and development — that distinguish human systems from mechanical or biological systems. The principles are thoroughly
explored in *Internal Family Systems Therapy* (Schwartz, 1995). For our
present purposes, we wish to emphasize the difference between a non-
interactive system with only a sterile, mathematical balance between its
parts, and an integrated, harmonious system with permeable boundaries
and paths of communication between its component parts. Once the internal psyche is recognized as an *interactive* system, we can focus on the
problem of fluctuating boundaries and effective communication between
the various components of the system. Effective communication requires
that each member of a system be viewed as a separate entity who speaks
through a separate voice and can choose to join or not join the group's
present activities or thoughts at any given moment. In *You Don't Love
Yourself*, one part (#2) demonstrated his ability to feel his own boundaries,
to differentiate himself from other parts:

   [*Part #1*]: Silence! This is no time for joking. Let them go to work, those
   of us who are the most gifted...
   [*Part #2*]: In the first place, don't say "those" of us any more. Say: let him
   go to work... say "the one"... Yes. Me. I am only one. And not simply as one
   of our delegates whom we send when we have to present ourselves to the
   outside world... I am "one" inside myself. I am all of a piece. Yes. In my own
   eyes. Because I can see myself. I only have to stand aside a little... I look at
   myself: here I am. The sum of my qualities and defects. (p. 56)

Once each part becomes familiar with his or her own boundaries, feelings and thoughts can be communicated while the part successfully avoids
total isolation — or its opposite, blending. Consider the *systemic* reaction

when a friend invites the narrator of *You Don't Love Yourself* to spend a month's holiday alone with him. The narrator arrives at the vacation spot and realizes that her worrying, managerial-like parts have taken over, eager to please the friend in whatever way possible, by blending with her and relinquishing the other parts' sense of boundaries and identity:

> We all began to tremble... Our committees met with all possible speed, conferred... there isn't a moment to lose... we must get one of our delegates to... Ah, but that's just it, which delegate? Whom did she want to invite? Whom does she want to meet? What is she expecting, hoping for? (p. 70)

These parts felt they had to become more and more ingratiating toward the friend whom the narrator was visiting. "You begin to feel nothing, to think nothing other than what the people around you feel, think..." (p. 105).

Instead of isolation or blending, the IFS model encourages parts to connect and share their energies, thoughts, and feelings within the system. They may sometimes choose to form a single voice — but without losing the differentiation of each part. Zohar (1990) describes a harmonious relationship in quantum physics terms:

> Two people who are in the same state, for instance, will have a more harmonious intimate relationship than two people who are in different states, as the wave fronts of their personalities meet in a superposition, one on top of the other or one entangled with the other more or less harmoniously. . . . An analogy with musical harmonies (themselves patterns of sound waves) brings this out. If two musical notes played simultaneously are exactly the same, they can be said to be in the same state, and the result is a single, unified sound. (p. 137)

Once communication is established between parts who are confident of their individual boundaries, it becomes possible to share a common goal or vision. This may be a small goal, like when many parts want to show enthusiastic curiosity in a conversation with another person. In *You Don't Love Yourself*, the narrator's internal system chooses which part to present to the outside: "Out of our seething mass an 'I' steps forward, we propel him outside..." (p. 37). Or, the common vision may be larger, permitting each part to achieve its potential in such a way that the person could also achieve broader goals for the whole system. At one point in therapy, Lorene's rather intellectual part, Vincent, said that he longed to be able to "leave his brain turned on" all the time. Whether Lorene was jogging (at Dashiell's request), playing the flute (as Destiny), writing a thesis (as Super-She), or playing with her child (as Jenny), Vincent wanted to observe, wonder, and *think* about the activities. Prior to achieving balanced boundaries and communication in the system, his participation had not been possible. Like other parts, Vincent had been isolated and often condemned to acting blindly. In this state of oblivion, Vincent could not actively participate in many of the activities or thought processes of the system. The impermeable boundaries were necessary system-wide, because without them the extreme state of imbalance caused parts to constantly trigger extreme reactions in each other. For example, Dashiell's exercising made Alex afraid of sexual arousal; while Destiny played the flute, Super-She was screaming about how Destiny should have worked harder to audition for the Chicago Symphony Orchestra; while Super-She pounded out a thesis, Victor was taunting her with accusations about her stupidity; or while Jenny played with Lorene's nieces, Super-She insisted that letting Jenny out might trigger horrible memories of childhood.

With the achievement of more permeable boundaries and communication among parts in a balanced system, Vincent could remain mentally active and participate ("brain turned on") in any of Lorene's activities and thereby attain his personal goal of being able to ponder and think continuously. Sometimes, however, Vincent had to sacrifice his own goal temporarily for the sake of the system. Whatever "size" the common goal may be, it inevitably requires some sacrifice and compromise by each part, since the goals of each part are never identical to the goals of every other part. There will never be complete unity on individual issues, and some parts simply are not concerned with certain issues. In *You Don't Love Yourself*, the narrator's parts feel wounded, and managers attempt to marshal a unified response quickly:

> We must get the majority of us together, to examine...
> The thing is that we never all manage to get together at the same time... some of us are always thinking of other things, with "our heads in the clouds"...
> Or apathetic... Lazy... Dozing... To manage to wake them up... And there are others...
> But what's the use of trying to collect them? There are so many of all sorts... we have no time to lose... Words arriving from outside have wounded those of us who are usually the most sensitive... (pp. 89–90)

Lorene's part, Vincent, discovered that — for the first time — he was willing to sacrifice his singular point of view, because he was now in communication with, was aware of, shared connections and experiences with, and even *cared about* his companions in Lorene's internal system. Vincent was now willing to "turn off" his brain power if other parts respectfully asked him to, so that they could daydream in a hot tub, relax at a concert, or enjoy a trashy novel without analyzing its quality. Also, after Lorene's parts met one another directly, there was a greater willingness to sacrifice for each other because each part could see past the rigid images they had of one another to their common interests and qualities.

INTERNAL RELATIONSHIPS WITHIN A
QUANTUM SYSTEM

In Chapter 2 we discussed the existence of separate parts and focused on their individuality. In this chapter, we have been exploring the relational or connecting aspect of parts within the inner family's system. We can view the relational aspect through the lens of quantum physics principles. Jung worked with the physicist Wolfgang Pauli, learned of the invisible units of matter that can behave either as waves or particles, and used these premises as a basis for understanding the nature of human consciousness. Storr (1983) explains how "Jung came to believe that the physicist's investigation of matter and the psychologist's investigation of the depths of the psyche might be different ways of approaching the same underlying reality" (p. 25). Zohar (1990) offers a contemporary explanation of the wave/particle duality concept:

> The most revolutionary, and for our purposes the most important, statement that quantum physics makes about the nature of matter, and perhaps being itself, follows from its description of the wave/particle duality — the assertion that all being at the subatomic level can be described equally well either as solid particles, like so many minute billiard balls, or as waves, like undulations of the surface of the sea. Further, quantum physics goes on to tell us that neither description is really accurate on its own, that both the wavelike and the particlelike aspects of being must be considered when trying to understand the nature of things, and that it is the duality itself that is most basic. Quantum "stuff" is, essentially, *both* wavelike and particlelike, simultaneously. (p. 25)

The wave/particle duality reinforces IFS systemic understanding of parts' functioning in both individual and relational capacities (figure 4.3). In the wave/particle duality of physics, the individual members of a system carry the properties of both waves and particles (Zohar, 1990, p. 113). Using IFS principles, we sometimes need to identify, isolate, and work with a single part (figure 4.4). This becomes possible because "in their particle aspect [part-selves] have the capacity to be something in particular that can be pinned down, if only briefly and only somewhat" (Zohar, 1990, p. 113). By turning the spotlight on one part, it loses its relational "wave" quality and is seen in its individual "particle" state. "The act of paying attention focuses our mental energy, so through the mechanism of selective attention we can channel more energy into some particular aspect of the self, thus 'lighting it up' (giving it more coherence) while others recede into the background" (Zohar, 1990, pp. 116–17).

But the uniqueness of the IFS model also rests on the concept of each part's intrinsic connection to the internal *system* where a multitude of relationships coexist. The parts of a person's psyche must always be viewed within the context of the internal system as a whole — in quantum terms,

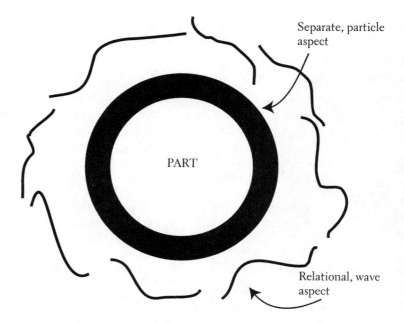

Figure 4.3. A superpersonality's wave/particle duality.

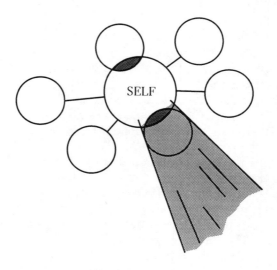

Figure 4.4. Focusing on a single part

as particles and waves simultaneously. (See figure 4.5.) We are looking at separate parts that are "so integrally linked that their bond mocks the reality of both space and time. They behave, instead, as multiple aspects of some larger whole, their 'individual' existences deriving both their definition and their meaning from that whole. . . . The oneness of the overall system is paramount" (Zohar, 1990, p. 34). To understand the personality sufficiently and to permit effective changes in a person's life, it is necessary to actively facilitate an ongoing inner dialogue between subpersonalities. Zohar (1990) explains the quantum view of this system: "What we recognize as our full-blown conscious life . . . is actually a complex, multilayered dialogue between the quantum aspect . . . and a whole symphony of interactions that cause patterns to develop" (p. 90). The IFS model, then, permits us to direct our spotlight to both a part's individual existence (particle aspect) and its relational context (wave aspect).

MOVEMENT AND RHYTHM WITHIN THE SYSTEM

The interweaving parts constantly reconfigure within the psyche's kaleidoscopic environment. This constant flux is both fascinating and essential to understanding systems thinking. The therapist and client learn to perceive and respect the rhythm and movement of the client's internal family. Zohar (1990) aptly describes the internal family as a "quantum self" that is "from moment to moment . . . a shifty thing with fuzzy and fluctuating boundaries" (p. 117). This quantum self is a "more fluid self, changing and

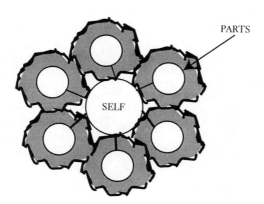

Figure 4.5. Parts exist in relationships with each other through overlapping wave functions.

evolving at every moment, now separating into subselves, now reuniting into a larger self" (p. 124). She explains further:

> [The] "I" might contain within itself several subselves, several smaller regions of quantum identity. We could picture the self as a system of emerging *whirlpools* [italics added], each discrete and individual at its center but overlapped and merged with others at the periphery. The great American psychologist William James developed in the last century such an idea of the self as a "seething cauldron . . . where everything is fizzling and bobbing about in a state of bewildering activity." Yet in all this "fizzling and bobbing about" there is always a center, the emergent reality of the "I" that conjoins the indeterminate characteristics of the subselves. (p. 114)

Our view of the internal family as a system of overlapping whirlpools is shown in figure 4.6.

We believe, then, that focusing on the rhythm and movement of the personality, a single part cannot be excised from the system in which it exists. One part's relationship, or absence of relationship, with another part necessarily affects how that part lives. We find the language of physics helps us envision this inner world:

> Because electrons are both waves and particles (both at the same time), their wave aspects will interfere with each other; they will overlap and merge, drawing the electrons into an existential relationship where their actual inner qualities . . . become indistinguishable from the relationship among them. All are affected by the relationship [and] they cease to be separate things and become parts-of-a-whole. . . . Indeed, it is no longer meaningful to talk of the constituent electrons' individual properties, as

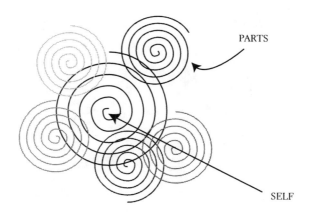

Figure 4.6. Whirlpools show each part's individuality
and movement among their relationships.

these continually . . . change to meet the requirements of the whole. This kind of *internal* relationship exists only in quantum systems, and has been called relationship holism. (Zohar, 1990, p. 99)

The IFS model focuses on these continual relationship changes among the parts' differing personalities. Figure 4.7 shows parts as they continually move within the system as parts-of-a-whole while maintaining their individual personalities.

One of the fluctuating patterns of movement within the system is what we call "blending," which we will be discussing throughout the book. Blending occurs when the person is overwhelmed by one part's emotions so that the wave aspects of a single part eclipse the Self and other parts. "We may even at times be 'taken over' by one of our subselves—as for instance when an angry person can think of *nothing* good about the person he loves during a row, or a depressed person can think of *no* reason to be happy when suffering his affliction" (Zohar, 1990, pp. 116–17). Figure 4.8 depicts how the system reacts to an angry part "taking over" the person. The significant movement within the system extends beyond the angry part taking over the person's awareness; it is also seen in the reactions of other parts as they move away from, or toward, the angry part. The Self in

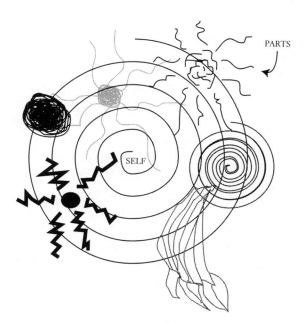

Figure 4.7. Movement of unique personalities within the system.

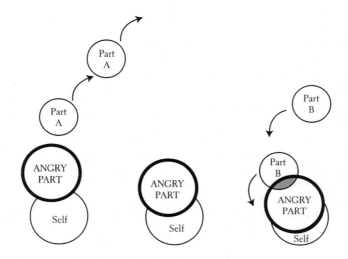

Figure 4.8. One part takes over, blocking the person's awareness.
- Part A reacts negatively to the anger, quickly moving away from it.
- Part B experiences anger as a magnet, and moves to join it.

figure 4.8 has become inaccessible due to the manner in which the inner mosaic has shifted.

We explore many of these types of continual internal movement in the following chapters. For now, we wish only to introduce the reader to our view of consciousness as a *moving mosaic*.

A SELF-REGULATING SYSTEM
AUTOMATICALLY STRIVES
TOWARD HARMONY

The movements of the shifting parts are not arbitrary or random; a balanced internal system automatically adjusts as it seeks out harmony. An imbalanced system will heal itself if the burdens constraining it are released. Jung (1955/1968) found that the internal system's *"attempt at self-healing* on the part of Nature . . . does not spring from conscious reflection but [instead] from an instinctive impulse" (par. 714). The "self-regulating psychic system" attempts to "restore the balance" (Jung, 1935/1976, par. 389), and can be compared to the body's internal regulatory systems (Jung, 1934/1966):

The psyche is a self-regulating system that maintains its equilibrium just as the body does. Every process that goes too far immediately and inevitably calls forth compensations, and without these there would be neither a normal metabolism nor a normal psyche. In this sense we can take the theory of compensation as a basic law of psychic behaviour. Too little on one side results in too much on the other. (par. 330)

We believe that movement within the internal system is purposive, as all parts seek to restore balance. Our innate drive for health, once freed from the beliefs or burdens which constrain it, steers internal fluctuations toward more tranquil waters.

DESTRUCTIVE POLARIZATIONS AND COOPERATIVE OPPOSITES

Jung's (1917/1926/1936/1943/1966) theory of internal self-regulation recognized the existence of opposites within the system. "There is no balance, no system of self-regulation, without opposition. The psyche is just such a self-regulating system" (par. 92). When systems split into opposite positions or behaviors, the diversity can be positive or negative. While *opposites* are valued for the diversity and richness they bring to a system, IFS uses the term "polarizations" to describe discordant and often destructive positions — what Jung might have described as uncoordinated, paralyzing positions. Jung wrote: "The reconciliation of these opposites is a major problem. . . . Thus, the 'adversary,' is none other than 'the other in me'" (Jung, 1938/1940/1969, par. 133).

Many mental health theorists have noted the prevalence of opposites in the psyche. Redfearn (1985) writes: "The image of opposing elements meeting, with the liberation or absorption of immense quantities of energy, good or bad, is so all-pervasive that it is hardly possible to exaggerate its psychological importance" (pp. 34–35). Johnson (1986) writes: "The psyche spontaneously divides itself into pairs of opposites" (p. 46). Beahrs (1982) agrees: "Even a seemingly rigid and limited ego state can reveal within itself the paradoxical elements and polar opposites we know we must look for in whole organisms" (p. 164). Beahrs also writes that "each polar opposite needs the other, is attracted to it and is in some sense inseparable from it" (p. 164). Stone and Winkleman (1985) warn that if we let the more powerful voice take over and "identify with it because it feels so good, the opposite energy will not be far behind" (p. 161).

It is the need to resolve *destructive* or *paralyzing* polarities that IFS principles emphasize. When events precipitate a takeover by one part (or an alliance of parts), the entire system becomes polarized; parts become extreme, which only confirms other parts' assumptions about those errant parts, thus perpetuating the polarization. Schwartz (1992) describes the IFS concept of polarization:

> Members of the system shift from their valuable, harmonious state and take extreme and opposite positions relative to one another. When two members of a system are polarized, they become rigidly locked into roles that are often a far cry from their natural desires, because they fear that if they back down from these extreme positions, the counterpart will gain the upper hand. Each one often believes that his or her extreme behavior is the only way to protect the system from the extremes of the other and will escalate these extremes in response to any perceived escalation on the other side. As a result, the behavior of each polarized member is destructive to the health of the system, even though each member's intention is protective. Thus, highly polarized systems are delicate, with any change likely to trigger escalations. Consequently, they are fearful of and resistant to change. (pp. 13–14)

Circumstances such as child abuse force some parts into extreme and destructive roles; this almost always motivates other parts to take the opposite extreme roles. Opposition degenerates into destructiveness when one or more parts take complete control, blocking out all other voices, or when all the "parts of an individual are sufficiently discordant and equally matched so as to paralyze the overall self's power for action" (Beahrs, 1982, p. 8). As Johnson (1986) describes it, when one attitude "seems exaggerated, it usually means that the unconscious is compensating for an equally off-balance, exaggerated position in the ego. . . . As the ego attitude becomes more moderate, the unconscious attitude also relaxes toward the center" (p. 73). He also notes:

> It takes courage to look directly at the fragmentation of our desires and urges. One side seems to argue yes while another side vehemently says no. One side of my psyche argues for relatedness, rootedness, and stability. Another side wants to go on heroic crusades and have great adventures in exotic places, travel to the other side of the world and live like a gypsy. Yet another personality wants to build an empire and consolidate my power systems. (p. 37)

Often polarized parts fear they will be eliminated or punished by their internal enemies. For example, Lorene's part, Victor, at times became so identified with his role as warrior and protector that he believed there was no other function he could perform. He also feared that other parts, like Alexandra, would punish him if he backed down, or that a part like Nicholas would take over and harm Lorene, perhaps by pushing her into promiscuous relationships. Polarizations are readily apparent in survivors of childhood abuse. Lorene often wrote about her inner turmoil:

I feel like my parts are playing a ping-pong game. Nicholas and Victor want me to be cold to my boyfriend and just turn off all feelings so I can't be hurt. Alex wants me to have sex so she can have fun. Victor says that I should be punished for even thinking of sex. Bonnie wants to play dress-up-for-a-date. Jenny feels sad and wants my boyfriend to hold me.

Herman (1992) highlights how trauma victims fluctuate between extremes, including: "uncontrolled expressions of rage and intolerance of aggression in any form"; paradoxical withdrawal from close relationships and desperate seeking out of intimacy; the contradictory identities of a debased self (malignant badness) and an exalted self (the self-sacrificing martyr); and other "frequent oscillations that are the hallmark of the traumatic syndromes" (pp. 56, 106, 140). Similarly, Courtois (1988) points to Lees' observation of "common bipolar patterns of affect, behavior, and cognition. Some survivors rigidly maintain one extreme, others the polar opposite, and some alternate between the two" (p. 135). Courtois lists examples of some of the simultaneously felt opposite positions that survivors carry (pp. 135–36):

Feeling bad or no good, "lower than the lowest"	vs.	Feeling superior to, better than anyone else
Feeling totally mistrustful of others	vs.	Feeling totally (naively) trusting of others with no ability to discriminate
Feeling powerless and victimized in life with difficulty saying "no," helpless and out of control	vs.	Feeling powerful with special or magical powers or behaving rigidly and in an overbearing and controlling way towards others
Behaving in an overly nice and pleasant fashion	vs.	Behaving overly unpleasant and "unnice"
Selflessly taking care of others, attention is other-directed	vs.	Selfishly not taking care of others, expecting to be taken care of
Behaving in an over-responsible manner, taking the blame even when it belongs to someone else	vs.	Irresponsible, blaming of others

Feelings of total despair and desperation	vs.	Denial of negative feelings (everything is fine, just right)
Extreme isolation and withdrawn	vs.	Hypersocial, inability to tolerate being alone
Abhorrence of physical touch or sexual activity	vs.	Compulsive sexuality and promiscuity
Feeling different from others, inhuman	vs.	Feeling and living in an overnormal, overconforming way
Compulsive/addictive behaviors	vs.	Excessive inhibition

Differences within the internal system are not "bad." The opposing inner forces can complement one another as "two facets of one stream of energy" (Johnson, 1986, p. 47). This only occurs, however, if the opposing forces are willing to acknowledge each other, communicate in a direct and respectful manner, and trust the Self to act as the leader in the internal system. With these provisos in mind, we agree that it is most enriching to "*embrace* the conflict, *embrace* the duality, bravely placing ourselves in the very midst of the warring voices and find our way *through* them to the unity that they ultimately express. . . . It is our lot, if we are honest, to live in duality and paradox. The dialogue of those paradoxical elements is the stuff of life" (p. 40). Beahrs (1982) explains this position further:

> Within the continuum of all that is, seen as polarity, each polar opposite needs the other, is attracted to it and is in some sense inseparable from it. . . . Within the constraints of language, this is perhaps the closest we can come to describing the organizing principle of existence. (p. 179)

The IFS model similarly teaches that inner differences are not to be extinguished. Opposing viewpoints enrich our lives. The key is to be aware of them, to facilitate respectful communication between the opposites, and to encourage parts to relinquish their long-held extreme positions. We work to avoid situations where the opposing forces refuse to speak to each other, rely on sneaky ploys to reach their goals, and attack parts who do not immediately agree with them.

CHAPTER 5

The Self as System Leader

*If we are going to conceive of ourselves as a collective
whole, we must have an organizing leader of this whole
to avoid chaos.*

—*John Beahrs, 1982*

THE FIRST MAJOR PRINCIPLE underlying the IFS model is the existence of a system of individual parts. The second major principle is the existence of a healthy, intact Self who acts as a binding force for the parts. This healthy system leader exists, no matter what level of trauma the person has sustained. Decades ago, Jung (1957/1964) spoke of the need for organization of the personality by some internal quality: "The natural state of the human psyche consists in a jostling together of its components and in their contradictory behavior — that is, in a certain degree of dissociation. . . . Such a condition cries out for order and synthesis. . . . The individual in his dissociated state needs a directing and ordering principle" (para. 540–541). More recently, Hilgard (1986) notes that for a long period of time, psychologists "evaded the problems of a planning and initiating self," and consequently adopted a view that no central control existed, instead substituting a "hierarchy of possible thoughts and actions determined by the competitive strengths of the activated subsystems," which would then "fight according to their strengths for control of the final common path leading to action" (p. 217). Hilgard found that a better interpretation envisioned a central control system. "[N]ow that planning and control functions are gaining recognition, the entire manner of central processes requires reexamination" (p. 217).

Scientists have also sought a central or unifying force in consciousness. Lancaster (1991) writes: "Given [our natural] multiplicity, it seems reasonable to assume further that there needs to be some form of integration of these parts — an overall self" (pp. 169–170). Zohar (1990) describes the quantum physicist's view of a "better integrated self that binds together the subselves more completely" (p. 114).

WHO SHOULD LEAD?

There is clearly a need for a leader. "All systems — families, organizations, nations — function best when leadership is clearly designated, respected, fair and capable. The internal family is no different" (Breunlin et al., 1992, p. 70). The need for a leader is less in dispute than the question of *who* should lead. Putnam (1989) notes that one of the initial steps in therapy is to "lay the groundwork for an internal decision-making process. Some sort of decision-making process has always been in effect, but usually one of several dominant alters [has] imposed their will on the system, with other alters seizing control at various times to impulsively act out forbidden wishes" (p. 159). Beahrs (1982) explores the dilemma of choosing a leader for our multiple selves:

> The most central unresolved issue which all of this poses ... is by what means one's sense of continuity of overall Selfhood proper becomes established, given a potentially infinite number of separate selves within. Looking upon an individual as like a symphony orchestra, how is the conductor set up and maintained in office? And in disturbed psychiatric patients where stable selfhood is lacking, what should be our priorities in determining who should wield the baton? (p. 183)

Beahrs (1982) pushes further, seeking to answer the "major question" raised by Hilgard: "Who is the I determining which role to play of various alternatives, choosing from the many competing at any given moment for priority?" (p. 65). Beahrs searches for the "central executive, that intrapsychic leader who organizes and presides over the family of Self comprising a single human individual" (pp. 73–74). Finding no clear answer on the question of who should be in control, "except to strive for whatever works best," Beahrs concludes that "the conductor is he who conducts best, considering the unique needs of the overall person" (p. 136). The problem with Beahrs' position is that it equates the leader of the system with whichever subpersonality is able to gain power. Beahrs (1982) states:

> If an overall executive or conductor is not clearly defined, different part-selves will vie with one another for the conductor's baton. There are no rules accepted across the board even by experienced therapists as to who should take the baton. The primary personality, "original" personality, most healthy secondary personality, and an [Internal Self Helper] have all been declared as candidates, no rule of procedure having withstood all the tests. . . . The therapist can only be a potent facilitator or internal diplomat, the decision necessarily having to be made by the collective of part-selves comprising the patient's whole personality. What is required is that there be some persistent

organizing force or central executive, however set up and maintained in office, and that he as well as his constituents know who is in charge and who is responsible for what. Only then can the individual function harmoniously like an orchestra, a cohesive whole comprised of parts that take joy in their own individuality, all doing what they do best. (p. 125)

The search for this "central executive," however, can be endless. In Lorene's system, there were any number of parts willing to take the conductor's baton. Each would announce candidacy in his or her own way:

Vincent: *I'm the best choice for leader—I'm wise, impartial, knowledgeable, and respected by all other parts.*
Super-She: *You're a passive lump on a log! Go back to your ivory tower. I, however, am energetic, super-competent, and a modern wonder—a true leader in every sense of the word.*
Nicholas: *I'm in the lead most of the time, anyhow, so I'll be chief leader around here. I have more guts than all of you put together.*
Alex: *I think my youth and vigor would serve us well. I could be a great leader.*
Vincent: *It's kind of you all to offer to help. I'll decide who the leader will be.*

Putnam (1989) refers to the "revolving-door crisis" that tends to occur "when no single alter personality is able to gain and maintain control over the patient's behavior" (p. 63). Redfearn (1985) also notes the internal competition: "Our feeling of 'I', as well as our behaviour, is being competed for and dominated by our various selves, one of which is in charge at one time, another at another" (p. 115). But Redfearn turns to Humbert's definition of the Self: "If you were to ask what the self signifies for me, I should reply that it is, above all, the inner voice which tells me frequently and precisely how I am to live" (p. 11). Unfortunately, there are many inner voices willing to dictate to us "frequently and precisely how [we are] to live." Listen to Lorene's cast of characters and their conflicting viewpoints on dating:

Andy: *Maybe I should ask someone like Victor or Nicholas to keep me safe.*
Alexandra: *It might be a good idea to have a man keep us safe.*
Super-She: *You want me to always have a man nearby, right?*
Alex: *Well, it's a pretty good idea, isn't it?*
Super-She: *It might not be a good idea to get involved with certain men.*
Vincent: *You have to consider many different factors. Anyhow, I like talking with that new guy you date. He awakens my mind.*
Bridgette: *And my soul! He explores the depths of values and spirituality within such a broad, rich context.*

Alex: Well, that's rather silly. I just like telling jokes with him.

Victor: Ha! You like the sex—admit it!

Alex: That's none of your business.

Victor: You and Bonnie are manipulative whores and I will put an end to it—or to you.

Alex: Do I look scared?

Super-She: Don't you two ever shut up? I have a lot of work to do today to make up for everything you guys have screwed up at my new job.

Victor: I will not permit sex to rule every relationship. You know what's happened in the past.

Vincent: Perhaps your half-truths are effective, but this time I think you should back off a bit, Victor. I'm keeping an eye on things.

Victor: Don't get me wrong. I don't care who she has sex with—look how I used it to scare Andy back into the basement. Even while she's sitting safely with Dick, I can convince Andy he's in Dad's basement! Ha! What an amazing feat! I'm incredibly powerful!

Vincent: You should be ashamed and disgusted with yourself. You've been hoping she'll pull away from Dick, too, right?

Victor: Well, that hasn't been so hard to accomplish—they're both so busy, too tired, too stupid, easy to fool.

Vincent: I'm ashamed to be in the same system as you. You frighten and sadden me. I'm going to sit with Andy so you won't bother him.

Victor: I don't care. Dick is an idiot. I know he'll do more "experiments" to let Bonnie examine her feelings. Then I'll show you she's a whore.

Vincent: Bonnie may surprise you and stand up for herself. Alex, Super-She, and Bridgette have all been working with her.

Victor: Then I'll burn her face off!

We believe that none of these parts should be the system's leader for any significant length of time, not just because these parts are extreme, but because a part differs considerably from what the IFS model calls the Self. Other theorists also reject the idea that the internal system can run on a "laissez-faire approach, involving competition and perhaps some bargaining," and they turn instead to the "possibility that there is some kind of 'governmental' regulation of all of this (for example, by the self)" (Samuels, 1989, p. 3). Stone and Winkelman (1985) refer to the ego as the "executive function of the psyche, or the choice maker. Someone has to run the operation and the ego does the job" (p. 21). Briere (1989b) also explores the issue:

> This dialogue [between warring components of the psyche] stimulates the development of an overbridging perspective [somewhat equivalent to Hilgard's "hidden observer"] that must orchestrate the component-to-component

interaction. As awareness grows to accommodate both ego states or split-off components, the defensive value of being or knowing only one side or the other is to some extent lost. (p. 91)

This overbridging perspective, which portrays a Self separate from the collective, suggests a position that is not inconsistent with the IFS definition of Self. But the IFS view of the Self goes beyond the abilities of a hidden observer. The Self is neither the strongest part of the moment nor a totality of the parts. For this reason, we should not hand over the reins to one part. Johnson (1986) warns: "If you do that, you will abdicate your rightful role and turn your entire consciousness over to only one part of yourself." This should not be done, "no matter how wise or 'right' [that part] seems to be. Only you can run your own life; you can't [successfully] turn that role over to anyone else" (pp. 190–191). But who in you should lead? Who exactly *is* this Self that IFS identifies as the internal leader of choice?

DEFINING THE SELF

The IFS model identifies an internal state of consciousness that acts both independently and through its relationships. Schwartz (1987) labeled this being who is both solitary and relational the *Self* because that is what his clients called it—my self, my true self, my core self. From its dual capacity of being both joined with and separate from the parts, the Self gains a unique meta or systemic perspective that endows it with an inherent capacity to lead effectively. The Self is experienced most vividly when it *stands alone*, differentiated from the parts. Schwartz (Nichols & Schwartz, 1991) describes his attempts at "guiding clients to separate from not just a few, but all the parts they could identify" (pp. 503–504). He invariably discovers that "when separated from their parts, everyone [has] a similar experience described variously as 'feeling calm,' 'lighthearted,' 'confident,' and 'in the present'" (pp. 503–504). Storr (1983) notes that Jung's concept of individuation is a spiritual experience that connotes the Self: "By paying attention to the voice within, the individual achieves a new synthesis between conscious and unconscious, a sense of calm acceptance and detachment, and a realization of the meaning of life" (p. 19). In his study of myths, Campbell (1988) discovers a state of being which IFS might attribute to the Self: "If you do follow your bliss, you put yourself on a kind of track that has been there all the while, waiting for you, and the life that you ought to be living is the one you are living. Wherever you are—if you are following your bliss, you are enjoying that refreshment, that life within you, all the time" (p. 120).

But we also experience the Self in its *relational* capacity as it interacts with parts in a decidedly different manner than parts interact with each other. Schwartz (Nichols & Schwartz, 1991) explains this relational concept further:

> In the IFS model ... the Self is not [merely] a passive, observing state of mind, but instead is [also] an active internal leader, who helps the system of parts continuously reorganize to relate more harmoniously. In this leadership role the Self listens to each part and what it really wants, nurtures or comforts some parts, helps change the role of others, and negotiates with polarized parts to resolve their differences. For example, the Self may comfort and soothe frightened or sad parts, calm rageful defenders, or get striving achiever parts to compromise with parts that demand more relaxation. In this sense, then the person's Self becomes a therapist to their internal family. (pp. 503–504)

Thus we have a Self that both stands alone, and connects with internal parts and with the external world. This "quantum" perspective of the psyche "gives us a view of the human self that is free and responsible, responsive to others and to its environment, essentially related and naturally committed, and at every moment creative" (Zohar, 1990, p. 237).

THE HIDDEN SELF IN
ABUSE SURVIVORS

The most frequently asked question by therapists and survivors alike is, "What if she doesn't *have* a Self?" They wonder if, destroyed by trauma, fractured by terror, the Self of an abuse victim can be annihilated or wounded beyond repair. The IFS model wholeheartedly rejects this possibility. Without exception, clients who have participated in therapy using the IFS approach have revealed a Self (though sometimes not without a prolonged struggle from protective parts). These clients include many who were severely abused as children and who could be diagnosed with borderline personality disorder, major depression, or multiple personality disorder. What some therapists might characterize as an absent or weak Self is actually a hidden or blended Self. In severely abused systems, it may be difficult to differentiate the Self, but it *is* present.

This portrayal of a highly competent Self within all of us may seem idealized and unrealistic. How is it possible that people who have been tortured and betrayed as young children could have developed or maintained such an internal leader? The answer lies in our capacity to protect the Self. In the face of severe trauma the Self tends to be hidden by protective parts.

> Typically the original [personality] is not active and is often described as having been 'put to sleep' or otherwise incapacitated at some much earlier

point because he or she was not able to cope with the trauma. The original usually does not surface until late in the course of therapy. (Putnam, 1989, p. 114)

All parts invest a great deal of energy in protecting or hiding the Self. "When any human system—a family, company, or country—suffers some kind of threatening or overwhelming trauma, the system organizes to protect its leadership. . . . In the face of danger, the tribe moves the Self to a place of safety and certain parts come forward to deal with the danger" (Schwartz, 1995, pp. 44–45). The system instinctively organizes so as to protect its leader (notwithstanding the fact that the Self may be doing very little effective leading all the time), sometimes by moving the sense of Self "out of body" in the face of perceived danger or by creating strong bodily sensations that signal danger. The Self may be forced into concealment even when it does not intend to acquiesce to the demands of its protectors ("Danger! Get down!"). The Self is shoved aside by the protective parts, like a president thrown aside by secret service agents who willingly put their bodies between the bullets and their leader.

THE INTERACTIVE SELF

Before talking more about the hidden Self in abuse survivors, we explore the Self in a person with a more balanced inner family where the Self functions in a leadership position. To help the reader identify the Self, we'll look at what the Self *feels*, what it *does* that distinguishes it from parts, and what role it plays within the system. We emphasize that the Self we describe in this section is differentiated, i.e., separate from the parts. A Self that has blended with, or been hidden by, extreme parts will not exhibit the qualities described here.

The Self as an Active, Unifying Force

Earlier we talked about the illusion of unity. The organizing function of the Self provides the cohesiveness necessary to create that vital sense of wholeness without which we would flounder. (It is this sense of coherence and connection that is absent in people who are labeled with "MPD.") The differentiated Self depolarizes and reconnects parts to one another, facilitating steady internal communication to ensure that the parts maintain healthy boundaries. Jung (1958/1964) described this mediating quality: "I have called the mediating or 'uniting' symbol which necessarily proceeds from a sufficiently great tension of opposites the 'Self'" (para. 779–80).

To understand the Self's role as a connecting or unifying force, remember that the Self both *stands alone* and exists as a *relational* being. The

Self may stand alone to monitor relationships and roles of the parts in a nonjudgmental and nonattached state. Or, the Self may foster relationships between it and the parts by interceding as a mediator, facilitating changes in those relationships. Zohar and Marshall (1994) describe this concept in terms of what they call quantum reality: the duality of waves (an indeterminate spread of possibilities) and particles (the individual, determinate aspect) create the relationship between parts and the Self. The Self exists separately, a substantial entity that is "a thing in itself that exists in its own right" (Zohar, 1990, p. 115). Zohar and Marshall (1994) introduce the concept of a central integrating force in the personality that is consistent with the IFS view of the Self:

> No mechanistic system consisting of separate, interacting parts . . . could give rise to the indivisible unity of our sense of self, but an emergent, holistic quantum substructure possibly could. That is, a structure that is greater than the sum of its parts, that has some identity over and beyond the identities of those parts, could account for how something like self could emerge and evolve over time. (p. 73)

The Self's dual capacity to function as both an isolated particle and a connected wave is contained in the metaphor of a symphony orchestra that several theorists have used to understand human behavior (Nichols & Schwartz, 1991, p. 504). While the conductor remains peerless, viewing the orchestra before him from his unique perspective of a raised platform, he also flows throughout the orchestra, communing with each section, unifying the group, and allowing the music to come alive. Beahrs (1982) describes this analogy:

> Like the overall Self, the orchestra is a complex whole with a personality of its own. Like any multicellular organism or social group, it is composed of many component parts or orchestra members, each with its own sense of identity and unique personality, but all of which function together in a coordinated cooperative endeavor to the advantage not only of the whole, but of all the parts. While the music is made entirely by the composite of parts, which transcends being a mere algebraic sum, it is *held together and organized* [italics added] by the leadership of an executive, the conductor. Although he makes none of the actual music, the conductor is in charge — at one level a fundamental paradox, at another simple commonsense knowledge available to all of us. (pp. 6–7)

The Self's fluidity and its relational capacity extend to things external to the individual. The Self is especially adept at connecting with people because of its confidence, its lack of fear, and its wisdom that within each person lies a similar Self. When the Self acts as internal leader, the individual experiences an extension of boundaries, a sense of transcendence of and connection to humanity. Thus, the Self encourages both *differentia-*

tion and *connection* among parts (and between the individual and other people). Csikszentmihalyi (1990) describes a similar process:

> Complexity is the result of two broad psychological processes: *differentiation* and *integration*. Differentiation implies a movement toward uniqueness, toward separating oneself from others. Integration refers to its opposite: a union with other people, with ideas and entities beyond the self. A complex self is one that succeeds in combining these opposite tendencies. . . .
>
> Complexity is often thought to have a negative meaning, synonymous with difficulty and confusion. That may be true, but only if we equate it with differentiation alone. Yet complexity also involves a second dimension—the integration of autonomous parts. A complex engine, for instance, not only has many separate components, each performing a different function, but also demonstrates a high sensitivity because each of the components is in touch with all the others. Without integration, a differentiated system would be a confusing mess. (p. 41)

Zohar and Marshall (1994) use the analogy of a company of free-form dancers (we would call them parts). Neither the Self nor the parts are "isolated atoms (particles) bouncing about in the void, nor is their dance an indivisible whole without individual parts (waves)" (p. 103). Instead, the dance creates a relationship: "The dancers *need the dance* to become fully *themselves*" (p. 108). Similarly, the Self needs the dance of interaction with its parts to become fully itself. The Self acts as a "conduit through which the emergent properties of the community get expressed" (p. 108) in a manner that creates "the most highly ordered and highly unified structure possible in nature. Its many 'parts' are so unified that they get inside each other (their wave fronts overlap). They share an identity, or become as one whole" (p. 74). The Self, then, embodies the "inseparable duality" (Zohar & Marshall, 1994) manifested in quantum physics (p. 201).

The Self *acts* when it unifies, connects, and brings order into the internal system. If the Self only watched, impassively observing the person's daily behavior and emotions, we need only search within for a nonjudgmental and passive space that other philosophies describe. Certainly the Self listens and observes. But a mere listener would simply retain the information gathered until someone requested it, and then regurgitate that information without feeling compelled to make recommendations or take action based on it. A true "hidden observer" acts only as a receptacle, not as an active leader. Lancaster (1991) describes the difference between the Self and a mere observer:

> What exactly is being observed and what does the observing? . . . It would appear that in order to observe the coming and going of 'I's, the individual begins to operate from a *qualitatively different region of the mind*. This shift within the individual is itself part of the desired self-change. In other words, the importance of self-observation in this scheme is not only to gain information about what may be observed, but also to *change the centre of gravity of*

consciousness [italics added]. Self-knowledge, beloved of the ancients, is not simply a question of one of the multiplicity of 'I's gaining greater understanding of its fellow actors. It is a state of being which, by comparison, is all-knowing; the view as given from the top of the mountain. (p. 99)

Beahrs' (1982) description of the function of the conductor/Self in the internal system as lending quiet strength to the person describes Self-leadership in a harmonious system:

> He sits back quietly, exerting little conscious effort, while group members pursue their tasks enthusiastically and autonomously. . . . The orchestra performs by itself, the strong conductor doing little beyond providing gentle guidance at occasional trouble spots or calling upon a certain orchestra member or section he wants active at a particular moment. (p. 70)

This "gentle guidance" is all that is required once a person's system is balanced and in harmony. For polarized or imbalanced systems, however, the Self needs to be more active, interacting with the parts, working with each of them in accordance with each part's special abilities, needs and desires: "Good leadership means all kinds of things, including nurturance, encouragement, self-sacrifice, wisdom, and compassion. When leaders exercise these qualities, there is little need for control or discipline. Fortunately, when differentiated, a person's Self already has these abilities" (Breunlin et al., 1992, p. 12). Being in a state of Self, then, does not mean passive relaxation. Connection to life through the leadership of the Self involves change and movement from both inside and outside. The Self naturally uses its entire range of energy, abilities, and concentration, and can choose to either act or be still.

Distinguishing the Self of an abuse survivor from her parts—especially her non-extreme parts—is challenging and fascinating. Examples are interspersed throughout our discussion below to aid readers in learning how to make this distinction. Each example begins with a comment the survivor might hear from an unidentified inner voice ("I really feel depressed"). The therapist or survivor might then ask for inner responses to the comment. Three typical responses are identified: a response from an *extreme part* ("I'm going to kill myself"); one from a part who is *not extreme** ("The depression will pass sooner or later"); and one from the *Self* ("I'm going to explore what triggered the depression, remind myself that I am separate from that depression, and then I'll work with the parts involved to help change it"). Commentary from an IFS perspective about the nature of the three responses is in brackets. Remember that initially a non-extreme part

---

*Sometimes even a *non-extreme* response does not sound particularly balanced or mature. The remarks often reflect either a part's young age (and are appropriate for that age) or a part's narrow, individualized role in the system.

and the Self may sound the same, their differences are revealed in the consistent patterns seen over time.

Meta-Perspective of the Self

Parts are tremendously helpful in the internal decision-making process, imparting valuable advice often based on well-reasoned, perceptive thinking. But ultimately, complex or highly-charged decisions land in the Self's lap. Unlike the parts, the Self can fairly assess all parts' advice, attitudes, and fears from a meta-perspective that provides a systemic or contextual appreciation of the internal system as well as the external environment. Only the Self can fully view the whole system and embrace all aspects of the internal family. When the "Self is differentiated and allowed to lead internally, people are not all-knowing, all-judging, or all-powerful, but they do have a sense of what is healthy and unhealthy—not for everyone—but for themselves" (Schwartz, 1993, p. 25).

Inner Voice: "Most men are dangerous and I refuse to have relationships with them."

Extreme Part: *Yes! That's been well proven by Dad's abuse of me and by other men I met as a teenager and adult. Men are an unpredictable risk.*

[This is a righteous, defensive remark that conceals the underlying fear and contains no insight into healthy alternatives.]

Non-Extreme Part: *No, that's not true. Only Dad and a few guys I've met are bad. There are nice men out there, too. We just don't always see the difference.*

[This view is broader though still limited because it ignores the underlying fears that must be addressed if the extreme part is to stop interfering on the path towards emotional health.]

Self: *It's true that men can rape, but I am an adult now. I can protect us in numerous ways. I am also capable of recognizing the difference between men who hurt us, and men who do not. And if we are hurt emotionally, I can help us all feel better and none of us will be exiled again.*

[From this broad perspective, the Self takes responsibility for future relationships or encounters. Recognizing that some parts still fear re-abuse or re-betrayal, the Self offers assurances that as an adult she can distinguish healthy relationships from bad ones and can deal differently with the consequences of any mistakes.]

Free of undue influence by any extreme part, the Self is capable of making fair, balanced decisions. The parts learn that the Self possesses a guaranteed, limitless integrity upon which they can rely. Some of this trust grows out of the fact that the Self always works voluntarily; if it is not blended with or hidden by parts, it cannot be "forced" to do anything. In making its decisions, the Self does not purport to know everything. It does, however, have potential access to all internal information; it merely needs to learn who and how to ask for that information, and needs to convince parts to release constraints on essential information.

Inner Voice: "We can choose to attack friends before they attack us."

Extreme Part: *Absolutely! I choose to take the offensive: hurt before being hurt; attack before being attacked; abandon before being abandoned.*

> *[This is an extreme position that indicates the part may still be living in the past, feeling like a child pitted against a powerful and sadistic adult.]*

Non-Extreme Part: *It's wise to keep a reservoir of energy set aside, so we'll be ready to defend ourselves against anything that happens to us. Wait and see what comes; no use blindly jumping into unknown situations.*

> *[This part doesn't fully believe the adult survivor now has the capacity to act and to make choices that will keep her safe and happy.]*

Self: *It's true that choices were once made for us; things were done to us. But this is no longer true. I am an adult now. We can exercise choices — for example, by saying where we want to live, who we want to live with, when or what to eat, when to sleep. It's also true that preparing for bad things makes us feel safer, but we miss too much if we live that way constantly. We lose many wonderful things if we are always preparing for the possibility of future pain and never participating in the present. Also, if bad things happened now, I would take care of the consequences, whereas I could not do that before.*

> *[In making fair, healthy choices the Self is able to explore alternatives, look beyond the immediate moment, and easily distinguish past from present.]*

The Self's wisdom rests upon a keen sense of fairness and justice. Parts have wisdom, too; but the Self has a unique perspective from which it can accurately evaluate whether or not a part's opinion is wise in terms of the good of the whole. A part often demands or suggests something — even something healthy — with a strong tone of righteousness. ("You absolutely must . . . stop dating Tom . . . make more money . . . lose weight . . . quit your job.") In contrast, the Self rarely acts in an adversarial manner in relation to parts. Although a part might present valid "evidence" to support his or her opinion, the presentation is often offered by an advocate of that position. In contrast, the Self presents suggestions, decisions, or questions only after considering *both* sides. The Self is incapable of ignoring a part as long as the part presents his arguments in a direct and respectful manner.

Inner Voice: "Should we quit therapy?"
Extreme Part: *Yes, it's too expensive and too upsetting!*

[*This is a stilted response suggesting an underlying, emotion-laden reason for wanting to avoid therapy.*]

Non-Extreme Part: *No. We've changed a lot, so the therapy seems useful.*

[*Although more reasonable, this response still lacks any exploration of the disadvantages of continuing in therapy, of alternatives and the future, which all must be addressed if the more extreme part is not to be ignored, and the decision to remain in therapy is to have full support from as many parts as possible.*]

Self: *It's true that therapy uses up financial, emotional, and time resources. But the changes have been worthwhile, and we want to live in harmony, so despite the disruption, we'll stay. Therapy has good points and bad points, all of which we can consider and talk to the therapist about. Therapy can be whatever we want to make it.*

[*The Self addresses both sides, looks to the future, and shows a willingness to take responsibility for whatever happens in the future.*]

Inner Voice: "Should we stop self-mutilating?"
Extreme Part: *No. It makes me feel calmer and more in control.*

[*This response reflects a narrow focus on the need to stop pain immediately.*]

Non-Extreme Part: *Yes. It's hard to explain to people who see the cuts.*

[*While this response fosters a positive result, the focus is still on the immediate present and does not include a perspective on how self-mutilation affects the internal system.*]

Self: *It's true that cutting acts as a powerful release, but it also creates a massive cover-up for feelings that cannot be freed unless they are experienced or addressed directly—and it scares many parts.*

[*Here the goal is to find an alternative and resolve underlying problems. Focus is long-term and includes awareness of all the parts. In addition, there is a willingness to experience the present discomfort of intense emotions in service of the vision of more balanced emotions in the future.*]

Inner Voice: "I direct your conduct and guide your actions."
Extreme Part: *No! Trust no one's direction.*

[This limited, emphatic perspective prevents even a modicum of trust in any relationship.]

Non-Extreme Part: *Yes. I am the guide you seek. I'll show you how to live.*

[This response conveys a wish to sit back and impart wisdom without actually listening to or cooperating with other parts in the system.]

Self: *It's true that some parts are very wise—but I am the one who ultimately makes final decisions, although those decisions will be made with as much input from you as possible.*

[The Self's response shows an ability and willingness to listen to all parts, encourage their participation so that each lends a unique value to the system, and still assert authority when necessary.]

Although the Self has a unique meta-perspective, not all of the hundreds of decisions we make daily need be made by the Self. As Beahrs (1982) notes: "While the conscious mind or executive can control at the most only two or three simultaneous activities, the unconscious collective can take part in a potentially infinite number" (p. 64). Hilgard (1986) explains that having a central control "does not mean that all behavior and experience has to be referred" to that place (p. 223). The Self's natural leadership role does not preclude a part from taking on such responsibilities temporarily. There are some situations for which the abilities of certain parts make them the best temporary leader. "At other times it is fun or thrilling to let some parts take over. The point is that when Self-leadership is restored, parts can still take over, but not for the same protective or polarized reasons and with the permission of the Self. They will also withdraw from leadership when the Self requests it" (Schwartz, 1995, p. 58). A harmonious internal system requires little minute-by-minute oversight by the Self. Each part operates in a role he or she desires and has the ability to perform. Also, each part remains connected to the larger system by a shared vision and sense of belonging.

THE SELF'S VALUES AND
GUIDING PRINCIPLES

The Self does not merely parrot rules such as, "honesty is good." It explains to each part the underlying purpose of the rule and how it relates to the vision shared by the Self and the parts. It also defines guiding principles for the system. In this way, the Self reminds parts of the possibility of making moral choices in the present. The Self does not pretend to be the source of all answers to questions of morality. Rather, the Self explores questions and problems of morality and seeks answers with the help of the parts. It also poses moral questions when parts are extreme and brings them back in touch with their own morality.

Inner Voice: "We should not steal or lie."
Extreme Part: *Why not? The world owes me.*

> [*This response reveals a part bearing heavy burdens of pain and betrayal with no insight into who delivered the blows (emotional or physical). It lacks an understanding about what the part wants from the world and how that would change things.*]

Non-Extreme Part: *True. People usually end up finding out and getting mad. It's better to be good.*

> [*This response produces a better result, perhaps, but the underlying problem is the same. The part focuses on the immediate moment—and ignores the survival aspects of the person's past need to steal, lie or otherwise "act out," or the person's hope of avoiding such behavior in the future.*]

Self: *It's true that we've suffered some horrid experiences, but the kind of compensation gained from stealing or lying isn't going to make us feel better for very long, is it? What do you really want?*

> [*Here the Self addresses the real problem and explores with parts whether a given remedy will help either now or in the future, which prepares them to seek an alternative.*]

The Self is Trustworthy

A principal function of the Self, like any unifying leader, is to earn the respect and trust of the parts. The Self does not automatically receive their trust. However, the Self is inherently worthy of the trust because of its deep-seated integrity. "Integrity is the capacity to affirm the value of life in the face of death, to be reconciled with the finite limits of one's own life and the tragic limitations of the human condition, and to accept these realities without despair. Integrity is the foundation upon which trust in relationships is originally formed, and upon which shattered trust may be restored" (Herman, 1992, p. 154). Trust grows because the Self consistently remains sincere, truthful, scrupulous. The Self will not lie or be sneaky or evasive. It is usually easy to distinguish this quality from a compliant part who is afraid that if she isn't good, someone might get mad and hurt her.

Inner Voice: "You can trust me. I'm honest, scrupulous, caring."
Extreme Part: No way. It's better to trust no one.

[*This emphatic response ignores any emotions that accompany this inflexible stance. This type of part usually has difficulty expressing what he thinks might happen if he did trust someone.*]

Non-Extreme Part: I'm not sure about you — but I can certainly be trusted. I've never done anything to hurt anyone.

[*Although this response is more emotionally honest, it still does not address the underlying problems that created deep mistrust in others.*]

Self: It's true that some people (and parts) have not been trustworthy. But if we trust no one, we cannot connect with anything in life. We'll remain isolated and growth will not be possible. Trusting me for a few minutes at first, then for a longer period, will help you attain your goals. Only good will result from this trust, but I know I have to earn it.

[*This response acknowledges painful past realities, while not succumbing to them by closing off future possibilities. It also acknowledges that trust is a process, an empirical experience, which parts must experience for themselves.*]

Unless they learn to trust the Self, parts will blend with or hide the Self, overwhelming it and obscuring its abilities. The Self must keep practicing its skills, gain the trust of the parts, and maintain that trust. This is not an easy task, although it is aided by the wave aspect of the Self mentioned earlier. This wave quality permits the Self to feel the fluctuating emotions and rhythms of the internal system. It also explains why parts are ultimately willing to trust the Self: Its communion with the parts, its lack of bias, its empathy, and its broad perspective combine to create the most trustworthy element within the psyche.

Distribution of Internal Resources

The Self ensures that resources are fairly distributed to the parts. The distribution need not be equal; instead, it is determined by each part's individual needs:

> I am not suggesting that each member should at all times have equal influence, resources, or responsibilities, or that boundaries around subsystems should never be rigid or diffuse. People have different roles within a system. Ideally, a person's role will be determined by his or her age, ability, vision, temperament, and desire. People also have different needs, according to their roles and levels of development. (Schwartz, 1995, p. 141)

Some parts need more nurturance and comforting, especially the younger ones; some need more time, perhaps ten hours for a work-related project while only two hours goes towards relaxation; some need increased tolerance, perhaps a malevolent-acting part who has tried much harder than usual to give up substance abuse or self-mutilation. The internal family system resembles an external family: The college-age child might receive most of the family's financial resources, the pre-schooler receives the most time and attention from the parents, and the 16-year-old benefits from more tolerance and flexibility as the parents try to permit him to grow without losing all sense of discipline and cohesion within the family. It is not necessarily the Self that gives the actual attention, time, and other resources; parts may provide these services, also. The Self, however, oversees the distribution of the resources and resolves related disputes.

Inner Voice: "You should set aside more time to cry, to remember the past."

Extreme Part: *No! I refuse to ever cry. It's too draining, a waste of time.*

[*This is a typical response from parts afraid to experience long-buried emotions.*]

Non-Extreme Part: *Yes, immersing myself in the sadness of my past is cleansing and healing.*

[*An often-heard response from a part who believes that healing (or being in therapy) means being completely immersed in depression, pain, and suffering. This part will clearly be at odds with the more extreme part.*]

Self: *Ignoring the past won't help, and complete immersion in it will scare too many of you. We need to balance the two.*

[*The balanced perspective is obvious; it more evenly allocates inner resources and serves as a guide to parts who think nothing exists beyond either uncontrollable, overwhelming emotion or a cold, cerebral life.*]

The Self as Mediator and Disciplinarian

What does this internal leader do when parts refuse to cooperate? The Self typically uses its power to control or discipline parts sparingly and with caution. The Self can be firm without being punitive or righteous. While discipline may be necessary until the extremeness of parts has abated, later it is rarely needed. Once parts feel accepted and are in a role they prefer, they cooperate. The Self is not burdened with shame and guilt, so it is neither accusatory nor critical; nor does it slip into blind acceptance. The differentiated Self is "more inclined toward cooperation and openness; less toward moralizing or coercion" (Schwartz, 1993, p. 25).

In facilitating internal cooperation, the Self usually mediates the most difficult negotiations. (Day-to-day negotiations may be delegated to various parts, who often exhibit special skills in this area.) Also, the Self is incapable of misusing power or imposing tyranny on the system—in fact, quite the contrary. The parts hold the power-moves, not the Self. The Self must gain the respect and trust of the parts instead of trying to outmaneuver the parts. The Self's power lies in its ability to lead effectively, not in its ability to dominate or coerce parts.

Inner Voice: "You two parts must stop fighting with each other."
Extreme Part: *Not a chance! He has to be stopped.*

> *[This part reaches for the most expedient solution and exhibits no sense of understanding that alternatives exist.]*

Non-Extreme Part: *Maybe they just need to fight it out and see who wins.*

> *[This is a less destructive stance; nonetheless, this perspective offers little hope for resolving the internal war for any significant length of time.]*

Self: *It's true that you two are far apart in the positions you take. You can disagree, but you must each present your side to me as directly as you can. I want you two to express your differences, while I make sure that both of you remain respectful to me and to each other.*

> *[The Self boldly steps into the middle of the conflict and plays an active role in bringing about both short-term and long-term resolutions of the ongoing dispute.]*

The Nurturing Self

The Self has no favorites or part-time commitments; it nurtures all parts equally. (Parts nurture, also, but usually they nurture parts they are responsible for, or parts they like.) The Self does more than comfort individual parts; it can create a *sustaining environment* that fosters growth.

Inner Voice: "I am willing to hear your memories, know in detail everything you experienced."
Extreme Part: *No way! It's not safe to tell. I'll be rejected again.*

> *[The extremeness of this position is obvious. The part is trapped by its own response, which precludes all alternatives.]*

Non-Extreme Part: *Yes, I'll listen and comfort you. You can tell me anything.*

> *[Although a more nurturing, caring response, this perspective still lacks a sense of direction.]*

Self: *It's true that not telling may feel safer. But if I listen, I can help release you from this burden you've carried so long. Then you can go forward, exploring new interests and activities.*

[The Self expresses caring as well as the ability to sense the direction in which the exposure of painful memories will take the person.]

Inner Voice: "I am furious, cold with anger at Dad's abandonment of me."
Extreme Part: *Yes, he betrayed me! He deserves my hatred and wrath.*

[A common stance for protective parts, this position offers little opening for confronting the underlying fear and pain.]

Non-Extreme Part: *No, I'm not angry. I never really get angry at anyone.*

[Certainly a more pleasant attitude to work with, but this stance still fails to address the underlying problems and the anger which lurks below the surface.]

Self: *It's true that we sometimes feel uncontrollable rage at those who abandoned us in the past. But now that I am an adult, I can help us make choices about our relationships — choices about how to start them, how to maintain them, or how to end them.*

[Here the Self offers a broader perspective, evidenced by acceptance of both the rage and the underlying pain from abandonment. It looks to both the present and the future — within the context of what has occurred in the past.]

Inner Voice: "We experienced a horrible, evil thing."
Extreme Part: *True, so nothing can be done to make this a happy life.*

[A unilateral position anchored in the past, this position contains no possibilities or alternatives.]

Non-Extreme Part: *True, but it wasn't that bad, and it isn't happening now.*

[A more congenial attitude, but this position uses denial and a limiting focus on the immediate moment to minimize what actually did occur.]

Self: *It's true that the incest was horrible, but life consists of more than the incest, more than that time period.*

[The Self's view encompasses the past, present and future, thereby providing a larger life context in which the abuse is seen as just one segment and nurturing can now occur.]

In looking for a person's Self, remember that the Self *feels*. The differentiated Self experiences emotions such as curiosity, courage, compassion, joy, and peacefulness, but it does not experience extreme or troubled emotions. If the person feels rage, despair, or a numb detachment, that emotion comes from a part. The Self is able to nurture because it carries an intense sense of connection to both the inner parts and external people. It reaches out with curiosity and compassion to all life around it. The emotions surging through the differentiated Self are always life-enhancing. The feelings, though, have a unique rhythm that the person learns to listen for and identify. It is always a part and never the Self who creates crashing waves of thrill and ecstasy—or of despair and terror. (Similarly, parts who willingly work to relinquish extreme beliefs and conduct do not calmly disappear into the psyche; they still exist and want to remain actively involved in the person's life.)

Inner Voice: "The emotional roller coaster I live on is exhausting, draining."

Extreme Part: *True. I can't function at home or at work.*

> *[This response focuses on the immediate present and does not look at underlying problems or explore alternatives.]*

Non-Extreme Part: *It's not too bad. Therapy is helping us learn to live with these extreme vacillations in emotions.*

> *[Though more reasonable, this response still does not incorporate an awareness of the real problem.]*

Self: *The roller coaster will slow down as we finish some of our work in therapy. In the meantime, I can pace therapy so that it doesn't completely deplete us of energy. We can do restorative things, too, like listening to wonderful music and reading enjoyable books.*

> *[Here the Self takes responsibility for the future and explores alternatives to sustain the parts, as all move forward.]*

The Self Helps Uncover Preferred Roles for Parts

One of the most beneficial aspects of the Self's leadership is seen in its role of guiding all parts within the system into non-extreme roles they prefer. The Self, more than any single part, can be completely trusted to help parts explore new roles or activities they will enjoy. Because the Self is incapable of tricking, endangering, or competing with parts, its perspective serves the parts well in finding these preferred roles. Thus, the Self works to provide a safe context where opposing parts can stop activating each other and focus on the question of their own needs and hopes.

Inner Voice: "Victor cut up my arm again last night, but he deserves another chance."

Extreme Part: *No! He's too destructive and angry. Lock him up somewhere.*

[*This part fails to see, or is unwilling to expose, underlying fears about Victor's destructiveness. The position necessarily blocks any movement.*]

Non-Extreme Part: *Yes. He has to stay, so we might as well find something useful for him to do.*

[*Though a kinder response, this position fails to explore alternatives for resolving Victor's destructiveness. Agreement to "keep" Victor is a product of circumstances rather than active caring.*]

Self: *It's true that Victor has hurt many parts and other people, also. But I've decided to have Victor stay with Dashiell for a while. He won't have much contact with other parts there, and I can work with him to find out what he needs. I can also ask him to tone down his responses for a while.*

[*Here again the Self takes responsibility for the future, and demonstrates a comprehensive understanding of Victor's need to be destructive, the need to change that behavior, and his value to the system.*]

Inner Voice: "Nicholas needs a new role."

Extreme Part: No—just get rid of destructive parts like Nicholas!

[*This part focuses on an expedient solution to the problem. Yet the proposed solution would actually frighten this extreme part more, because the part would wonder, "If it's possible to get rid of one extreme part, why not another?"*]

Non-Extreme Part: *Well, Nicholas could be in charge of watching for danger from men.*

[*Although a better solution, this position assumes that danger permeates daily life, that the person somehow invites danger, or that the watchman role is the only one for which Nicholas is suited.*]

Self: *It's true that Nicholas can be very disruptive and destructive, but his annihilation or banishment is neither possible nor desirable. Instead, let's consider his skills and attributes, talk to him about his interests, and discover his preferred role.*

[*The Self's solution acknowledges the reality of Nicholas' behavior, but takes responsibility for working on realistic alternatives that will serve both Nicholas and the internal family.*]

The IFS model assumes, then, that a natural, healthy leader exists within each person. The model facilitates therapists' and clients' abilities to confront the many difficulties faced in locating this internal leader. Two of the most serious difficulties—blending with or hiding the Self—are discussed in the next two sections.

THE SELF BLENDING WITH PARTS

The concept of blending is one of the most exciting and significant patterns revealed by the IFS model. Blending describes a condition in which the Self over-identifies or over-empathizes with a part. It is the opposite of differentiation and healthy boundary-making. There is a leakage of feelings, a blurring or merging of boundaries between parts and the Self. Jung (1939/1968) discussed this ability of unconscious complexes—what IFS calls parts—to take control of the person: The unconscious does not "follow meekly in the footsteps of the conscious." Instead, "consciousness succumbs all too easily to unconscious influences" (para. 503–504).

Childers (1988) describes "over-identified" parts or subpersonalities as having tremendous energy. "These parts on occasions may take over the individual's personality and determine the ongoing process of behavior and choice that should properly be the domain of a healthy ego" (p. 19). Zalaquett (1989) identifies a similar process: "In general, when confronted with a problem, the person tends to identify him- or herself with only a part of his or her feelings, desires, thoughts or behaviors" (p. 331). Redfearn (1985) writes: "A 'sub-personality' or 'part-self' may carry the feeling of 'myself' at times, or it may possess the individual behaviourally and be acted out relatively unawares. . . . Each sub-personality is potentially able to take possession of the feeling of 'I', of behaviour, or of both" (p. 16). He describes this process further:

> Various sub-personalities and complexes comprising his total personality are successively experienced by him as the whole thing—the whole truth, the whole of himself, the will of God, ultimate good etc. In other words, parts of the total personality take over the feeling of "myself" and seem like the whole of the self or even of the cosmos. . . . It is as if different actors successively occupy the whole stage, each thinking he is the whole show. (p. 12)

Stone and Winkelman (1985) also note a blending process: "Very early in this work it becomes clear that the ego has succumbed to a combination of different subpersonalities that have taken over its executive function" (pp. 21–22). Beahrs (1982) describes the situation "in which the conductor either abdicates or is over-powered to the extent that a variety of destructive or mad behaviors occur over which the patient's conscious self feels he has no control" (p. 20).

Particularly in victims of abuse, the Self will easily over-empathize and "blend" with a part, leaving the person feeling as if she is nothing more than that part. The clinician can be certain that blending has occurred if the client is aware of nothing but feelings of isolation, revenge, bitterness, fear, or other intense emotions. For example, if the Self blends with a young, frightened part, the whole person feels frightened. In this early journal entry made before her father died, Lorene blends with, or feels like she actually becomes, Jennifer:

Lorene's Self *[blending with 4-year-old part Jennifer]: Even though I was grown up, when I sat at Thanksgiving with my Dad last year, everything inside of me felt like a raw sadness. I felt completely alone, frightened, abandoned. I was consumed by feelings of terror, as if I were still inside a fragile four-year-old's body. I was afraid I'd wet my pants, or I'd cry, or make him mad. I couldn't find any adult-like, confident feelings inside of me.*

Blending caused Lorene's Self to merge with Jennifer until she became completely absorbed by and attached to Jennifer's emotions and thoughts. Lacking any boundaries between the Self and the part Jennifer, Lorene no longer had the experience of a Self who could "remain outside and observe what is going on. Instead of noting that a feeling, for instance of depression, is passing through us, we '*become* depressed.' 'I *am* depressed'" (M. Watkins, 1976, p. 16). Lorene found that with practice, it became easier to recognize when she was either blending with, or hiding behind, her parts:

Lorene's Self: *I don't worry about killing myself except when I blend with Destiny. I can stay separate from Nicholas now, but I can't do it with Destiny. I feel overwhelmed by her utter despair. She craves death as an end to her pain.*

Later Lorene began to understand more about the murky confusion between her parts and her Self:

Lorene's Self: *When I cannot rid myself of an overwhelming sense of sadness or anger or even zestful fervor, I know I am too close to the part who feels that emotion or energy. In effect, the part and I have blended, become one. I cannot differentiate. I cannot make judgments about what the part urges me to do. Should I skip the party because I'm so depressed? I don't know; I am paralyzed by the depression. Should I go with the fervor to begin a huge project that will require late nights and weekends at work, despite my family's objections? I cannot judge.*

Frequently a client will insist that she is thinking clearly and independently as her Self when, in fact, she has blended with a part who acts in a reasoned, logical manner. Lorene provides this example:

Lorene's Self [blended with Vincent]: I've thought this through very care-
fully, as my Self. I have to conclude that I feel totally unworthy of
anyone's help. I simply deserve nothing. Perhaps only death would
make my head stop hurting and spinning and exploding. I have strug-
gled, I have searched for answers, and I find nothing but blackness. It
overpowers my senses, my thoughts, and I quit. I repeat the process,
again to no avail. I quit again. It seems like therapy only exposes the
futility of my efforts.

Whenever a negative message such as this one is delivered, it always means
blending has occurred between the Self and a part. The Self is *incapable*
of agreeing with an extreme part unless it has actually blended with that
part's fear or anger. Blending is also the problem when the Self adopts the
extreme part's thoughts, feelings, or advice, making comments such as:
"The parts must be right because they all seem so sure"; or "They've
exhausted me"; or "They're obviously right since they *feel* so strongly, and
I don't have intense emotions like that."

When the Self over-identifies or blends with a single part, the system
experiences chaos and danger. The danger in blending lies in the Self's
inability to maintain a leadership position and an extreme part's taking
control of the system. The Self can learn to stop the blending process. It
should be encouraged not to rigidly identify with any one part. Instead,
the Self must learn to separate itself enough to permit it to experience its
natural identification with the internal movement of the *whole* system.
The Self can be close to a part and witness his or her story, without
eliminating all boundaries and without being overwhelmed by the part's
intense emotions. Lorene's Self often fought against blending with her
extreme parts, but the struggle was particularly difficult at the beginning
of therapy:

I try to work with Nicholas between sessions. I used to drown in his raw
sadness and rage—his feelings consumed me. Now I'm forced to keep him
at arm's length or I'll slip back into that sea of despair he drags around with
him. I hold Nicholas away, because I want to prove to other parts that I
can, in fact, continue to function in the outside world while we work with
Nicholas. But I have to stay far enough away to ensure that Nicholas won't
suffocate me (blend with me), yet get close enough to be able to listen to
Nicholas and maybe even comfort him without other parts pulling me
away from his intensity.

While the Self can control the blending process without the help of the
parts, it is much easier if the parts cooperate and join the effort to stop
blending. It is extremely difficult to convince parts not to blend, especially

hurt, younger parts. The Self of an abuse survivor is particularly suscepti-
ble to becoming frequently overwhelmed with a young part's pain or despair. Often these younger parts experience life as if they remain in the
original abusive situation. They will seize any opportunity to blend with
the Self or take over, often in a misdirected attempt to feel less alone and
to relieve their pain. For the Self to function as a compassionate and
effective leader, the parts must learn not totally engulf it. The parts must
learn to control the release of their feelings. In this journal entry, Lorene's
Self recognizes how she blends with young parts who are scared of Nicholas:

*Nicholas, I can ignore all your fighting and screaming and cries of danger.
I can ignore your threats and accusations. But sooner or later I become
overwhelmed by the fear of other, younger parts. I merge with them,
wondering if maybe the memories we face are too unbearable and will
destroy us.*

In contrast, Lorene's differentiated Self (not blended with any parts),
could compassionately view the situation of Jennifer while remaining separate.

*When Jennifer feels terrorized and raw, like her skin has been peeled off, I
remind her over and over that I have a body, and I have skin, and she is
inside of me. I don't blend with her. I stay separate, reminding her that I
am real—my physical existence is proof of that. And the childhood molestation she is feeling right now—no matter what triggered it—is not really
happening.*

Lorene frequently experienced the blending of her Self with her parts
and learned to fight successfully to keep her Self differentiated:

Vincent: *I think it would be best to admit Nicholas to a psychiatric hospital.*
Self: *I can do that (in my imagination). Do you think Nicholas will be
calmer there and stop pulling me away from the issues we're working
on in therapy?*
Vincent: *Well, I don't mean to be too stubborn, but Nicholas simply
might not be able to live up to Dick's standards.*
Alex: *That isn't your decision to make. You're wrong to take over and
make this hospital decision yourself. I don't want to run and hide.*
Self: *Don't blame Vincent. It's my decision. I thought the hospitalization*

was best. I just didn't think to ask you about it, Alex. I forgot it would affect you, too.

Nicholas: *I want to go to the hospital now.*

Self: *Why?*

Nicholas: *It's a place where they'll let me curl up and cry and cry and stop trying to pretend I'm tough and normal.*

Self: *It's okay for now, but sooner or later you'll have to face the same questions about your sadness, your sexuality.*

Nicholas: *I'm sorry I threw my shoe at Dick.*

Self: *What happened?*

Nicholas: *He seemed kind of spaced out. It seemed like he was leaving me alone.*

Self: *What did you want him to do?*

Nicholas: *Reassure me that my sadness doesn't disappoint and irritate him.*

Vincent: *Let's talk about the hospital.*

Alex: *No! Let Dick decide — you stay out of it.*

Nicholas: *But I can't stand the sexual feelings I have.*

Alex: *Hospitals don't erase sexual arousal.*

Nicholas: *They should. They could make everything around me neutral.*

Vincent: *Why not ask Dick for help?*

Nicholas: *I don't deserve to. I don't have the right to ask him for anything.*

Self: *Nicholas, unlike a few weeks ago, I now believe completely in your wise suggestion to talk with Dick about the "secret world" I often live in. But you have to be direct and honest. Stop slipping into the coldness or anger to misdirect me. I'll agree to talk with Dick about hospitalizing you. I understand that Dick should've said he was spacing out for whatever reasons, and I should have stepped in and told him I was having a problem.*

Vincent: *So you were both irresponsible.*

Self: *Yes.*

Blending in and of itself is not unhealthy. The overlapping of parts and the Self is common within the ever-fluctuating system. Zohar (1990) writes from a physicist's viewpoint: "The selves within selves of the quantum person undulate and overlap, sometimes more, sometimes less (each is a quantum wave function), and their region of overlap at any one moment accounts for the sense of 'I' at the moment" (p. 114). Indeed, it is extremely important for many parts to experience this overlap, to have their feelings temporarily and partially shared by the Self or by other parts. But the overlap or sharing need not degenerate into an unhealthy blending. When body surfing in the ocean, it is crucial to keep one's head up out of the waves. The minute your head goes under, you are thrown down, hitting the sand. Likewise, the Self can experience a part's "wave" without becoming totally overwhelmed if it keeps at least its "head" up out of the "water" (Schwartz, 1995, pp. 97–98).

THE SURVIVOR'S HIDDEN SELF
(REVISITED)

Earlier in this chapter we talked about the Self being hidden by protective parts. We expand on that here and distinguish the *hidden* Self from the *blended* Self discussed in the previous section. The IFS model describes the astounding process of an entire internal system of parts scurrying around, whisking the Self off to a hidden, "safer" world whenever those parts perceive danger. The survivor's Self may be separated from the sensations of the body, hidden away while all parts are organized to protect the Self at all costs. Wrapping the hidden Self in a protective gauze of nothingness differs considerably from blending, where the non-protective purpose is to submerge the Self in the part's intense emotions. The parts might treat the hidden Self as a rather weak yet venerable entity, an aging grandparent who doesn't always hear too well or see too well, blind to incoming danger.

Few internal processes cause as much turmoil. The rigid separation of the abuse survivor's parts, with the Self safely hidden, presents an extremely difficult aspect of therapy. The experience of the Self being "out of body" leaves the system feeling like it has no boundaries, is not grounded in reality, or is trapped in a void. Consequently, when the Self is kept from the leadership position for extended periods of time, chaos infiltrates the system, and paralyzing and destructive polarizations between the parts become rampant.

It might seem that the Self would remain elevated, filled with undaunted courage in the face of all sorts of extreme behavior and thoughts from parts. Why isn't the Self strong enough to demand trust and override the advice and conduct of parts? Isn't the Self purer and stronger than the parts? The Self, like any other leader, cannot just make loud proclamations to unhearing, skeptical, or even riotous troops. The Self's words mean little to sneering, suspicious, or angry parts. Instead, the Self has to *work* with these parts, gain their trust, and prove it is qualified to lead. Thus, when the Self is not leading, it has not surrendered or abdicated so much as *it has not been heard or trusted.*

The extreme parts might stage a revolution or uprising, attempting to overthrow the Self. The Self can be ousted for the same reasons as any dethroned leader. As a leader, the Self may be confronted daily with rebellious, unhappy parts, or worse—with vicious, suicidal, or anarchic parts. The survivor's Self does not abdicate its leadership position voluntarily, or choose to relinquish its duties by permitting parts to become extreme. Rather, it faces confrontations, resistance, insubordination, and outright defiance on a regular basis.

Also, in abuse survivors just entering therapy, the Self initially *lacks staying power*. The protective parts of a survivor learned very early that by demanding to take over they could push the Self aside. Unlike blending, where the Self has some voice or power in the decision to merge with a needy part, the Self who is to be put in hiding has no vote. The extreme protective parts are working in overdrive and have more vigor and durability than the Self; they do not need the Self's agreement to be hidden. Other parts don't interfere and are rightfully impressed by the protectors' power to ensure survival for the child throughout the years of abuse. However, all parts now need to learn that the same coping strategies are no longer helpful. For example, Lorene's part, Alexandra, continually whisked her Self into hiding whenever Alex perceived danger.

Alex: *If a man says to take off your clothes, you must obey him. Then, quickly escape from any physical awareness of him. That external place does not exist anymore. It is gone. It is now only a world for other people. Be very quiet. I will hide you. I will take you quickly back to my other-world.*

The Self can be pushed aside by the sheer intensity of the parts' warnings of danger. Parts functioning as managers, like Lorene's Super-She or Vincent, often remain in control of the system after the Self is concealed.

> [Some] people become dominated by their protectors and often report feeling no sense of self. They are often seen by therapists as having little or no ego strength. It is sometimes difficult but always important with such a client to remember that the Self is still there, although it is not allowed to use its resources, which are obscured by protective parts. (p. 46)

The problem is that after a person's parts have had to protect the Self in this way, they lose trust in its ability to lead and increasingly believe that they *have* to take over—even if they dread the added responsibility and would rather do other things. One major goal of therapy becomes helping the client differentiate the Self to the point that the parts can begin to trust it again. For many clients this happens rapidly, and things improve quickly. For others, however, the parts are reluctant to trust the Self, and it is a struggle to convince them to release the Self from its hiding place.

Because the protective parts strive to keep the Self hidden, the Self may be so unavailable at the beginning of therapy that the therapist's Self must act as leader for the client's internal system until the parts trust the survivor's Self. If the Self is not functioning effectively, it is being constrained by extreme parts who are afraid. The Self possesses the necessary qualities for effective leadership; the therapist and client need only work with the extreme parts who constrain its leadership. The therapist and survivor must be patient as they work through the layers of defensive strategies, confront loyal parts guarding what they perceive to be the Self's vulnerabilities, and re-educate parts who long ago lost trust in the Self's judgment. Once Lorene's parts permitted the Self to come out of hiding (after first learning to trust the therapist's Self), Lorene became adept at differentiating her Self and maintaining a leadership position as she worked with her parts:

Self *[attempting to calm a frightened Jenny, the four-year-old part]: Focus on your healthy life-forces, not your pain. I will support you.*

Alex *[16-year-old part]: This is absurd.*

Self: *You don't believe that.*

Alex: *I can kill all of you!*

Self: *Why are you so angry? So destructive? So secretly destructive? Are you protecting something?*

Alex: *I'm not even sure sometimes. I'm on automatic pilot.*

Self: *Do you want to give up that role? I think it's possible to do that.*

Alex: *It's very draining. I don't know how to give it up. I'm afraid of what I'll find behind the anger. Maybe I don't exist beyond the anger itself.*

Self: *What makes you stay angry all the time?*

Alex: *Jenny was betrayed by so many people we trusted. The betrayal never goes away.*

Self: *But you magnify the betrayal with such intensity that your anger suffocates all of us. There might be alternatives.*

Alex: *I don't deserve a healthy, real life.*

Self: *Then we'll all die. You'll pull us down.*

Alex: *So what? I don't care. I can kill all of you.*

Self: *Is this some sort of super power that I should be impressed by?*

Alex: *Yes, absolutely. I can kill you.*

Self: *That would just guarantee your own demise.*

Alex: *Maybe that's the point.*

Self: *I doubt it. I think you're just plain scared — scared of hurting so much with no control over the source of the pain.*

Alex: *I feel like someone's always punching my face, slicing up my stomach, sawing off my legs. If only I could stop hurting, then I could give up the angry armor.*

Self: *Tell me why you're so angry.*

Alex: *I've had enough of Dick's idiotic healing and health and wisdom. I can frighten you, I can do it. I can make all this "healthy" change and exploration stop. I can scare you so easily with images of blood and pain — you won't have a chance. You'll be too damned frightened to work on any issues. You should never think I can't scare you.*

Self: *Alex, I know that sometimes I blend with parts who are scared of you, and then I feel scared, too. But even if I run away temporarily, I'm never gone for long. I always come out from under your spell sooner or later. Plus, Dick will support me — and he's used to helping frightened parts like you.*

Alex: *We'll see. Look at the nightmare world I'm building for you.*

Self: *The images you flash do scare me, even right now, but I'm still separate from your "nightmare world." I remember that I exist separate from that place. You know, when I stop being so passive, you stop scaring me so much. I can release myself from your noisy, blinding anger and can make my own choices about how to live every day.*

Alex: *You're so stupid! There's no way you can make things okay. They'll crash downhill again and again, until you're dead.*

Self: *I don't want to talk to you anymore. Let me know when you can talk about what frightens you or how I can help. Otherwise, stay away from the other parts, especially Jenny. Maybe we do things in a slow, awkward way without your youth and energy and power — but at least we're not doing them your way.*

The brutal effects of severe child abuse, therefore, often result in the parts' obscuring the Self. Yet this devastating effect is not a mortal wound; it does not mean the Self has been permanently crippled or somehow irreparably damaged. It is relieving for a survivor to learn that her Self is buried or hidden — not destroyed. The therapist and survivor seek not to repair or restructure the ego, but instead to release the Self from its cocoon. As M. Watkins (1986) observes, working with the psyche of any individual "does not have to do with the enlargement of the ego or with the building of ego strength in all its aspects. It does, however, have to do with an increased ability to allow other voices to speak (which relativizes the ego) and with the increased ability of an observing ego which can be attentive to these imaginal dialogues" (p. 125).

Ellenson (1989) wisely concludes that clinicians have "overapplied" the notion that "childhood sexual abuse result[s] in persistent structural damage to the ego or self." She notes the possibility that "such formulations have arisen from observations of apparent ego fragmentation," but these fragmentations, she contends, are actually "sophisticated defenses of survivors." Thus the "ego structure is not so much damaged as it is actively organized by the survivor to cope with cataclysmic rage" (p. 592). The IFS model partially rests upon the abuse-oriented principle described by Ellenson (1989):

> In general, mainstream theories largely suggest that the consequences of notable childhood trauma are structural or organizational deficits in the ego or self, due to arrested development, maldevelopment, or the outright

shattering of existing structure. Although this statement oversimplifies matters somewhat, from this point of view, severe symptoms are thought to result from the inability of a poorly organized ego or self to cope with drives and affects. To begin with, such formulations are not altogether consistent with the rather sophisticated defenses and intricate defensive maneuvers discussed above. (p. 593)

Initially, Lorene had an extremely difficult time convincing parts to let her Self emerge into a position of leadership. Lorene's 16-year-old part, Alexandra, would often leap in to protect another part from any perceived danger—like the danger Alex sensed when Lorene was about to start a new job. Lorene's Self struggled and practiced, finally confident in her ability to remain differentiated from the frightened Alex. In this example, Lorene's Self was successful in not letting Alex's extreme feelings interfere with Lorene's decision to function well in the new job:

Alexandra: All I see are horrible images of terror.
Self: That is a predictable reaction to the new job I'm going to start. It's just your old reactions to any kind of change, which you always perceive as danger. But I am still here. You will all calm down when you realize I am here. Then I will decide what is dangerous, and how to handle the danger, if any in fact exists.
Alex: Dick didn't help. He didn't make the terror go away.
Self: You're not giving him much of a chance, as usual.
Alex: I know, I just think about blood and pain. I'm not going to therapy anymore.
Self: That's my decision. I choose to go there.
Alex: Everything is crazy. You are crazy.
Jennifer [four-year old part]: When Alex is scared, I'm scared. I'm alone in the basement and Dad will come to hurt me. Is he coming? Now?
Alex: He might be. I don't know what's real anymore. Danger is everywhere.
Self: Okay. Everything inside of me is starting to feel frightened. I'll concentrate on simply staying separate and not listening to all these frightened voices for now. But I promise you I will listen later. Know that you can wait that long. We'll talk about it in the next therapy session, where I can get some help.

We have seen, then, that the Self seeks what is best for the person and for the parts, keeping in mind a shared vision of the future. Seeing our potentialities, continuously adjusting to the normal rhythm and flux of life, the Self both glides toward the future and fully experiences the present. One of the Self's unique qualities is that, despite the leadership challenges, it always remains stable, predictable, purposeful, with unfaltering intent and goals. No part (even a non-extreme part) consistently exhibits this type of stability. In fact, the Self cannot be selfish; it cannot be concerned with only its own desires or pleasures, for unlike the parts, the Self cannot separate its needs from those of the system as a whole. When differentiated, the Self consistently displays courage, compassion, and curiosity as it leads this internal system of subpersonalities. It emanates a sense of wholeness, integrity, and oneness. The Self alone always maintains a feeling of being intact and autonomous. It is sure of its boundaries. The Self understands its value and respects itself. Thus, the IFS model assumes that a natural, healthy leader exists within each person and guides the therapist, who may confront difficulties in locating and differentiating this internal leader.

The error of believing that trauma has destroyed the Self, if the abuser is successful enough and the damage severe enough, results in severe consequences. The survivor and the therapist will not try to locate and use the Self as a vital resource; instead, the client may become highly dependent on the therapist. The clinical experience underlying the IFS model consistently reveals that all individuals have a Self-reference. The Self may be buried under layers of defensive protection, it may be "out of the body," it may have to be repeatedly and painstakingly differentiated, perhaps at first only for a few minutes at a time—but it *is* present, a well-hidden resource, buried under layers woven together by creatively protective parts. The Self is present, naturally competent, a "born" leader, and a valuable asset to the entire internal system. What many severely abused people have lost is not the Self, but trust in the Self.

CHAPTER 6

Three Groups of Parts

Don't force them into a mold. Let them be who they are.
— *Robert A. Johnson, 1986*

THE IFS MODEL RECOGNIZES that each part of an adult survivor experienced the childhood abuse in a unique way. Each part learned or was forced into a particular role to ensure that the child would survive in the abuse environment. We find it useful to organize these roles into three groups—exiles, firefighters, and managers. The three categories of parts are apparent in all people, but the roles become more extreme in abuse survivors.

The first type of role is usually taken by the younger parts, whom we call "exiles" (often referred to by people as their "inner children"); in a survivor the child-like parts are intensely needy and frightened. The second set of roles taken on by parts, called firefighters, is a more assertive and highly energetic presence; in a survivor they may take on characteristics of the perpetrator or act out in unprincipled, impulsive, and destructive ways (substance abuse, promiscuity, self-mutilation). And finally there are the more rational-sounding, detached managers, sometimes referred to as the "hidden observers"; in a survivor these parts can be cold, numb, aloof, dedicated to concealing pain or fear so as to appear normal. Sometimes, like Putnam's (1989) "host," one of these parts might not be a single part but an alliance—"a social facade created by a more or less cooperative effort of several alters agreeing to pass as one" (p. 107).

All people experience conflicts between parts because they have such differing goals and behaviors. Some try to push the person to achieve or produce (managers), other parts want to play and laugh (the young exiles), and still other parts want to jump into every situation both feet first (firefighters). The conflicts experienced by survivors, however, is more intense because all three groups of parts are extreme. As adults, then, survivors face the complex task of discerning how one group of extreme parts opposes or interacts with the goals or beliefs held by the other two groups of extreme parts.

Before going on to discuss the behavior of the three groups when they are extreme, we pause to qualify our act of affixing labels to parts. A label may undermine therapeutic goals by causing the survivor and the therapist to define the part's essence by the extreme role it is stuck in and to ignore the part's other qualities and the new functions it could serve. For example, although Lorene might label Super-She the "achiever," Alexandra the "sexual part," Jennifer the "inner child," Nicholas the "rageful part," and Vincent the "hidden observer," each part carries a full range of emotions. Assigning a label derived from a part's extreme state resembles the practice of labeling a client as the dominating, aggressive husband, or the passive, dependent wife. This practice reduces the person to one characteristic, ignoring the fact that each person (or part) experiences a broad spectrum of feelings and beliefs as well as an idiosyncratic style and personality. Schwartz (Breunlin et al., 1992) writes:

> [Therapists may] try, admirably, to avoid traditional diagnostic categorizing. But since they lack a language that conveys their optimistic and systemic philosophy on the individual level, such discussions can easily become pessimistic: "Johnny is a needy, dependent child who is trying to protect his parents' marriage. His mother is enmeshed with him and afraid to let him grow up. His father is overly rational and afraid to deal with his wife's feelings." Depictions like this are presented in case conferences across the country and portray family members unidimensionally, with the focus on the aspects of their personalities that are thought to be causing the problem. (p. 62)

A monolithic label tries to encapsulate a person's character, but necessarily misrepresents the total person because it only focuses on a person's most extreme feelings or behavior as the essence of the person. Furthermore, labeling parts also increases the danger that the therapist will underrespond to each part's needs when those needs deviate from the narrow expectations contained within the label. "If a therapist sees [a part] as just a mental state, the therapist will be less interested in helping the part discover the best role for itself, based on its feelings, talents, and desires" (Schwartz, 1995, p. 131).

We might too quickly identify Lorene's part, Nicholas, as the "persecutor" or "malevolent" firefighter because he would often lash out at anyone, seemingly without remorse. Granted, he would scream at Lorene's friends and family, self-mutilate because some part told a secret in therapy, and seek out abusive sexual relationships. Yet once past the facade of extreme toughness of Nicholas' demeanor, it was clear that he was also very frightened. He remembered the childhood abuse in a different way, for example, than Jennifer, who recalled the need for her father's attention and love while accepting the molestation as a scared child would experience it. Nicholas was guilt-ridden, because he felt he should have been able to protect Jennifer at the time of the abuse, yet he found himself helpless. He concluded that if he now acted more like the powerful abuser, he might gain some control over the external environment and lessen Jennifer's terror. But Nicholas also felt fear, embarrassment, shame, and the need to be accepted by the abuser. Thus, to merely label Nicholas as a malevolent, perpetrator-like part would discount any other feelings (like sadness and loneliness) and motives (comforting Jennifer) underlying his actions.

Similarly, simply labeling a part a "protector," because at one time it successfully built protective walls of dissociation to remain isolated and safe, would overlook the fact that *each* of Lorene's multidimensional parts has ways of protecting itself. Jenny, whom some would label an "inner child," senses danger everywhere and is able to protect herself by leaving her body, curling into a ball, or pretending not to exist at all. But Alexandra, the promiscuous teen, also senses danger all around her, leaves her body, and loses touch with the realities around her. Vincent, easily labeled the "Inner Self Helper," can avoid any troubling emotion by looking the other way and minimizing or intellectualizing whatever Lorene encounters. Nicholas, the "demon," can turn on his self-hate "tapes" and send all parts running. They *all* have protective abilities and functions. Schwartz (1988) cautions, then, that the "danger in describing these [common roles of parts] is that therapists will impose on the client theoretical preconceptions about the partial selves rather than listening closely to and trusting the client's own description of his or her inner world" (p. 23).

Keeping in mind this caveat, we find that in using a systems approach, it is helpful to map out the internal family in a way that provides guidelines for perceiving and understanding the relationships between groups of parts. The IFS model's tripartite organization separates these three functions or roles of parts into managers, firefighters, and exiles, hopefully avoiding the limitations of labeling by addressing *function* rather than *essence*. A part can be seen as serving identifiable functions, but the part's nature or essence is not subsumed by the function. Its essence cannot be predicted by its role, because each part is a unique individual that eludes preconceived schema.

MANAGERS

Parts who perform managerial roles permit individuals to function on a daily basis. A managerial part goes to work, eats nutritious meals, drives the children to school on time, gets a haircut, and attends church committee meetings. Some parts acting in a managerial function appear very effi-

cient, competent, smart, and in control. Many people are quite comfortable with their managers. Managerial parts can be very likable, quick, and
funny. "We all like our achieving subselves the best; it is they who are
largely responsible for whatever worldly success we have — the praise, pro-
motions, Phi Beta Kappa keys, new cars and country-club memberships,
those perks that reassure us that we are acceptable in the eyes of our fellow
creatures" (Schwartz, 1992, p. 36). The problem for abuse survivors arises
when the managers become extreme and dominating, trying desperately to
maintain a facade of normalcy. Sargent (1989) voices the viewpoint of a survivor's managerial part: "I believed that if anyone saw beneath my 'perfect
exterior' I'd be abandoned because I was disgusting" (p. 184).

The parts of Lorene who most frequently fill a managerial function are
Super-She, Vincent, and Dashiell. By the time she was an adult, Lorene
(and her parts) had learned to rely on these managers to keep her life
going each day. They ensured that she performed well at work, bathed,
visited with friends, attended school plays, played tennis, and paid the
mortgage. Initially Lorene's managers made it clear to the therapist that
they would do almost anything to keep Lorene's life as normal *looking* as
possible. They believed that if everything appeared to be "business as
usual," perhaps no one would notice Lorene. Efforts by managerial parts
to look normal are usually triggered by the survivor's perceived need to
conceal an immense well of raw vulnerability and shame. Managers believe
the only possible way the survivor can get through the day is to block all
conscious awareness of horrible memories. (To their credit, this is often
quite accurate, if the person does not have the benefit of the able leadership of a differentiated Self.) Managers like Lorene's create what Briere
(1989a) calls "conditional reality," in which reality is defined by the perceived current conditions, not by any point of self-reference:

> Survivors work so hard to look normal and be okay. They may get college
> degrees; they may be very "with it"; they're wearing good clothes; [and are]
> intelligent and witty. . . . There are parts of them that are damaged, but they
> can hide it and make it look okay, but they're not really okay. A number of
> people have talked about this quality of more functional sexual abuse survi-
> vors: The ability to look like you're really in good shape, when you're not.

An excellent way to protect vulnerability within the system is simply to
not let anyone near the survivor. Intimacy cannot be tolerated. Managers
typically avoid unnecessary encounters with people, since interacting
would inject innumerable variables into the fragile facade of normalcy.
Lorene's managers explain that it is better to avoid a close relationship
because of what it might activate: A man's flirtatious comment, for example, might trigger Alexandra's desire for physical intimacy, Nicholas' desire
to punish any sexual arousal, or Jenny's fear of re-abuse. A friend's angry

outburst might activate Victor's fury at any perceived wrong or Destiny's certainty that she deserves to be punished. Because of these potential triggers, parts often cannot tolerate more than dinner with friends; an entire weekend would be an unbearable strain.

Managers, then, are those parts who help survivors develop "patterns of relating to others that are not conducive to intimacy. . . . Establishing multiple superficial relationships helps survivors avoid intimate contact. We call this 'busyness,' as the individual has established a pattern of interacting that keeps him or her busy with many tasks (membership in social organizations, parenting, multiple jobs) and gives the illusion that he or she is connected not to tasks, but to people" (Sgroi & Bunk, 1988, pp. 184–85). Managers can also appear to be "cold, distant, and authoritarian. Their aloofness discourages any familiarity that could disclose the existence of other personalities" (Putnam, 1989, p. 112). Managers might describe themselves as "those of us who make us most resemble what we ought to feel we are" (Sarraute, 1990, p. 25).

Ironically, managers sometimes accomplish the "don't notice me" goal by performing outstanding achievements and maintaining a successful (and noticeable) career. However, managers never remain in the limelight, quickly murmuring, "Oh, it was nothing at all." Their purpose is only to maintain a high enough achievement level so that people will not look any deeper into the person, for they surely will see the evil rage, the buried secrets, the tainted soul, the very inadequacy of her humanness. Lorene's performance at work, for example, must be of high enough quality that she is left alone—but not so outstanding that others will insert themselves further into her life in any way. She has learned that it's even better to make a few mistakes so that co-workers and superiors won't always count on her.

Different types of managers may clash. For example, there is one type of manager who forever finds fault in the person, grooming her to be perfect in order to forestall attack. Another kind of manager prefers to repeat numbly, "Everything's fine." When one of the striving managers comments on a few minor imperfections, the "everything's fine" manager jumps in: "Oh come on, I don't notice [any imperfections] . . . [I]f there are any, a protective varnish flows out of my gaze and covers them up" (Sarraute, 1990, p. 60).

But generally, all managers find it useful to please other people. A manager ensures "our acceptance by others. It decides how emotional we can be. It makes sure we do not act foolishly or in ways in which we might embarrass ourselves" (Stone & Winkleman, 1985, p. 15). However, managers often overshoot their mark, offering "obsequiously placating behavior toward other individuals which almost always meets a response of disgust, avoidance, or anger. It might involve turning the other cheek in a manner that does not paralyze another individual with love, but is more likely to invite a retaliatory blow for something that another part-self has just done" (Beahrs, 1982, p. 109).

Other parts often deride and ridicule the managers, manipulating and frightening them further into emotional paralysis. The managers make the rageful parts feel smothered, buried in superficial goodness and appropriate behavior. These rageful parts may attack the frequently exhausted managers at will, creating emotional chaos. Lorene can have a wonderful day performing at work and then go home, close all the blinds, refuse to answer the telephone, and self-mutilate. After expending tremendous energy while in public during the workday, the managers retreat and let others take over in the dark, secret world at home.

Despite the underlying antagonism or polarity between managers and other parts, however, the other parts also trust and rely on the managers, further burdening them. Like Stone and Winkelman's (1985) protector/controller, a manager may establish "a set of rules that it feels will ensure our safety" (p. 15). A manager may also serve to protect the body from perceived external dangers or to balance and counteract some of the self-destructive behavior in the survivor, even to the point of ensuring that the person gets help if a suicide attempt is made (Putnam, 1989). "The more competent [the managers] become, the more the system relies on them, and the more they become overwhelmed with their responsibilities and power. They come to believe that they alone are responsible for any success and safety the person has experienced, and increasingly they lose trust in the leadership of the Self" (Schwartz, 1995, p. 50).

Managers are often exhausted because of the energy needed to maintain barriers against all strong emotions. They can never eliminate their pain, so instead they "merely abandon it. Temporarily, at least, clients reduce their level of anguish, but they also experience little joy or intimacy. In effect, they live under siege by the fear of awakening those exiled feelings and being drowned in them" (Schwartz, 1992, p. 36).

The effect of the managers' well-meaning attempts to "create some sense of safety and to control their pervasive fear" is to impose an excessive restriction of the survivor's life (Herman, 1992, p. 46). Thus, a manager is often "afraid of psychological work—it does not necessarily seek expansion and growth. It tends to be conservative in outlook and distrustful of new ideas" (Stone & Winkelman, 1985, p. 91). Managers monitor and constrain all emotion-triggering activities that connect the survivor to everyday life. Indeed, "this narrowing applies to every aspect of life—to relationships, activities, thoughts, memories, emotions, and even sensations" and ultimately, the ability to take initiative and make choices must be relearned (Herman, 1992, pp. 87, 90). Unfortunately, under this constrained way of life, some managers can become completely passive, believing that "any action has potentially dire consequences" (Herman, 1992, p. 91). While they possess a tremendous amount of know-how, they have little power for non-protective action. The greatest gift the survivor can give her managers is to help them shed their passivity and learn to take action, for example, by stepping forward and giving advice without waiting to be asked, by crying, by complaining, by exploring. In many ways, they have sacrificed the opportunity to express and experience their own desires and emotions, their own sense of abandonment and despair, and their own interests and talents in order to hide and protect the vulnerable exiled parts, who continue to experience intense emotions. Like a mother who pushes aside her pain after the death of a spouse in order to attend to a child who cries incessantly for her father, the managers' protective behavior ensures that these "disowned selves remain disowned" (Stone & Winkelman, 1985, p. 91). Schwartz (1992) describes the managers of one abuse survivor:

> The managers/protectors thought that since the damage had already been done, all they could do was isolate Marcia's hurt little-girl selves so that they would not overwhelm Marcia and make her vulnerable to being hurt again. They strove to control Marcia's relationships and make her tough, successful and self-possessed so that she would never be vulnerable to hurt and rejection again. (p. 35)

The most common error made in working with managers in therapy is to assume that they can be nothing more than passive gatherers of data. For example, Putnam (1989) describes ISHs as "physically passive and relatively emotionless personalities, who provide information and insights into the inner workings of the system" (p. 110). But being emotionally paralyzed does not necessarily mean passivity reigns. Viewing managers as being passive ignores the fact that they can be cunningly manipulative in their very active pulling of the ropes behind the scenes. Like Putnam's (1989) description of ISHs, a manager "almost never plays all of his cards at once. The therapist must learn and understand that for the most part the ISH can do more and exert more influence than the therapist realizes" (p. 203).

The passivity label also ignores the fact that managers often contain a well of forceful emotions that they are rarely allowed to express. In addition to being overly cautious about change, managers are generally opposed to anything which requires direct contact with emotions. Managers are so busy providing information and insights that they do not allow themselves to focus on their emotions. In viewing a survivor's passivity or helplessness, therapists who look beyond the apathy discover that "a much livelier and more complex inner struggle is usually taking place" (Herman, 1992, p. 91). It takes a tremendous amount of reassurance before a manager will voluntarily recognize or voice his emotions. Lorene records:

Self: Vincent was very sad and scared. He cried—Vincent did! So the
long hours working with him yesterday seems worthwhile because he—
finally—could reach his own feelings.

A managerial part might spend hours discussing intellectual concepts
with the therapist, while hoping desperately to be encouraged to explore
their paralyzed but still painful resevoir of emotional undercurrents. Lorene notes:

Self: Although Vincent encouraged theoretical and conceptual discussions with Dick today, he was disappointed that Dick didn't insist they
focus on Vincent's feelings.

Thus, sometimes managerial parts protect their own vulnerability, even
as they protect exiled parts, but at the same time they yearn for disclosure.
Uncovering the rational-sounding protectiveness of a manager often reveals a deep fear of abandonment or physical harm:

Vincent: Halfway through the session today, I thought Dick seemed to
say I should leave when he mentioned he'd been very busy lately. I was
very quiet and picked up my coat and keys and then just walked out
quickly. Don't make him mad. I couldn't bear to lose him. He'll be
disgusted if we show him the terror and raw sadness we feel. Just be
quiet and politely leave. It's better not to upset him. Just comply with
whatever you guess he might want. Guess and obey so he'll still like us.

Many clinicians and clients alike make the mistake of believing that
managers are superficial. M. Watkins (1986) describes a "manager-
organizer" part as a "dictatorial woman, immersed in a mania of doing, of
endless details. She is tense and somewhat shallow, working like an autom-
aton without a deep sense of meaningful priorities or heartfelt commitments" (p. 160). Despite their presentation, managers are not shallow.
They have great depth and passion for life. However, managers often have
diverted an inordinate amount of psychic energy to ensure the repression
of parts who carry the abusive memories and related affect. Managers are
seldom permitted to explore, develop, or voice their "heartfelt commitments." Indeed, managers should be encouraged to express their concerns,
fears, and desires. Once released from their role as guardians of normalcy,
the managerial parts lend much joy and energy to the system. Relieved of
their fear and the inflexibility it creates, managers often prove to be loving
caretakers and are thoroughly enjoyable, interesting parts.
Managers use a variety of techniques to protect the system:

1. *Distracting.* The survivor may appear very intellectual and functional. "No problems here!" A manager might find that it is especially important to distract from (or compensate for) the survivor's inner shame, fear, sadness or despair. This is especially true for survivors who are highly functional in their lives. Low-functioning survivors tend to be more dominated by firefighters who block the managers from functioning very well and restrict the managers to the job of keeping the person totally withdrawn from life.

2. *Numbing.* This behavior results in the survivor's feeling very little emotion. Her focus may turn to career success, wealth, or power. It drains a tremendous amount of energy from the managers to maintain the numbness. Managers numb by rationalizing ("Dad couldn't help himself"), minimizing ("This type of thing happens all the time—it's no big deal"), inappropriately making important issues into jokes ("No one will know what I'm feeling if I entertain them with wry remarks"), spacing out ("I knew Dad was talking to me on the phone yesterday, but I kept staring out the window and forgetting who I was talking to"), denying ("I've pretty much resolved any abuse-related problems"), forgetting ("I know my sister says she *saw* Dad molesting me, but I honestly can't remember"), and blatantly ignoring obvious problems ("I don't have time to think about why I cut my arms"). Unlike their distracting behaviors, the managers' numbing tends to produce an almost autistic response to certain emotional triggers. Given the chance, however, these stifled managerial parts eagerly display the extreme emotions they carry.

3. *Pleasing others.* Keeping the survivor's behavior perfect helps to please everyone and prevents abandonment. It's difficult to dislike or harm someone who helps you paint your house, lends you anything you need, watches your kids, and shows up with dinner whenever you aren't feeling well.

4. *Reinforcing her victimhood.* Managers may find it beneficial to make the person ill frequently or facilitate injuries. This ensures that other people will take care of her. It's difficult to blame someone for having a serious illness, for being beaten by an ex-husband, for being raped as she returns from work late at night, or for falling down icy stairs and breaking her leg. If family or friends get tired of the constant revictimization, there are a host of physicians, hospitals, physical therapists, chiropractors, and pharmacists who can take over.

5. *Avoiding risks.* A manager might erode the survivor's confidence or sabotage performance in order to drain off any remaining courage to take risks or pursue personal goals. For example, eroding confidence results if the survivor applies for jobs for which she is

not qualified or tries to date someone who is clearly unavailable. Either the job is too difficult, the salary too low, the church too conservative, the potential girl friend too stupid, or the neighbor too nosy. A manager also might accentuate any flaws in the object of desire in order to dissuade other parts' attempts to obtain it. Survivors often live in social isolation in order to avoid situations that might arouse anger, sexuality, or fear. It is a difficult task to balance the goal of looking normal and the goal of remaining as socially isolated as possible. While certain social relationships are necessary in order to appear normal, they must never develop into intimacy. This type of manager flashes worst-case scenarios in front of the person who contemplates taking any interpersonal risk. A manager calmly advises the survivor: It's better not to go to the neighbor's for dinner because your headache might make them think you're stupid. Or, you really shouldn't date that woman for the third week in a row, because she'll end up hurting you somewhere down the line. Or, don't waste too much energy trying to get that new job since there are many applicants more qualified than you, and you'll just end up feeling disappointed and crushed. Life becomes a "series of half-hearted attempts and failures, which provide protection from [exposure to] responsibility or disappointment" (Schwartz, 1994, p. 49).

6. *Caretaking.* Women especially are socialized to rely on a caretaker part who goes beyond merely pleasing others. This part encourages her to sacrifice her own needs and take care of others, sending inner messages like these: How dare she take a night class to help her get a promotion when her husband needs companionship and attention in the evenings after his long, hard day at work? How could she possibly even think about going out to dinner and a movie when her mother is confined to bed and could use some company?

7. *Denying.* The survivor distorts perceptions in order to keep himself from seeing and responding to risky feedback. For example, a manager will maintain that nothing is wrong with him and he doesn't need help from anyone, even in the face of information from a succession of therapists and a multitude of books that self-mutilation, promiscuity, and cocaine abuse are serious problems. After all, if something were wrong, he wouldn't be a vicepresident at the bank or a wonderful marriage and two delightful children, right?

8. *Controlling the internal world.* One final technique a manager might use to protect the system is to constantly monitor and control all other parts. It resembles a parent who controls every minute of the day for his children—when they play, who they

play with, what games or activities they can play, what to eat, what to wear, and what to say or feel at any given moment. A manager notes when the exiles are more scared than usual and moves to hide or banish their fears; stops the firefighters when they plan to burn the survivor's face, because other people would notice; or tries to instruct firefighters when they can surface and when they must stay hidden. This behavior often chills all spontaneity in other parts, who may grow more watchful and agitated under the managers' smothering manipulations.

Each of these techniques has a hundred variations, all of which are aimed toward protecting the survivor from pain, disappointment, humiliation, or some other perceived danger.

FIREFIGHTERS

Firefighter parts can appear ferocious, extremely destructive, filled with nothing but evil intentions. They listen for alarms announcing incoming danger and then jump to put out the fire. The survivor must learn that, like all of his parts, the firefighter needs and wants the help of the survivor's Self to change. The poet Ranier Maria Rilke described this need: "Perhaps everything terrible in its deepest being is something helpless that wants help from us." Firefighters who act like tyrants or bullies are often concealing fear like a scared child. The firefighters' destructiveness comes from a position of helplessness. Still, it is often the only power the abuse victim believes he has, and thus, must not be tampered with lightly.

While managers are usually reluctant to *act*, firefighters do not hesitate. Nicholas sadly confesses:

Nicholas: *I hate it when Dick gives me hope that I can leave my crazy world and be loved someplace safe. That hope makes it so hard for me to stay cold and to act. And I need to* act *if I'm going to survive each hour.*

This difference is reflected in the tactics used during therapy sessions where both managers and firefighters want to avoid exposing vulnerability. Managers superficially comply with the therapist by letting the therapist think the survivor is being insightful and trusting; firefighters use blatant, tyrannical efforts to disrupt the therapy relationship. For example, if Super-She proves to be inadequate in controlling access to sadness, a firefighter will have to step in to help ensure that Lorene does not shed a tear in front of the therapist. The therapist will even see very different physical responses: The cooperative, apparently docile manager part sits quietly during a session, barely moving a muscle; the firefighter, sensing an onslaught of tears, might simply stand up and march out of the therapy session. When an angry manager coldly recites evidence of the therapist's negligence and incompetence, a firefighter hurls accusations at the therapist. Nicholas was one of Lorene's best firefighters:

Nicholas: *I forbid you to go to therapy! Don't go to that place. Don't sit in that chair. Don't go. Do something else. You'll die in there. Don't look at his face. Don't talk. Don't listen to his voice. You absolutely will die there. Stay home. Do something else. Like hammer your arm.*

Firefighters have been called malevolent, rageful, disowned, persecutors, tyrants, avengers, and demons — or impulsive, reactive, and addicted. Most of these labels, even when earned, are unfair, because in an unbalanced internal system firefighter parts have little control over their own actions. They can agree not to do something, but when the alarm sounds again, the behavior automatically returns. If they stop one behavior, they soon find an equally destructive and distracting substitute. Firefighters instantaneously serve protective functions in much the same way that our bodies automatically regulate body temperature, send rushes of adrenalin to counter immediate threats, and signal when water or food is necessary. There is little or no exercise of judgment — just action. Managers perform tasks of cognitive deliberation; firefighters go out into the trenches and gather information, allow life to touch them directly, and return with data that the managers will digest and analyze.

Firefighters long ago learned to focus on keeping the child-victim as safe as circumstances permit by ensuring her emotional and physical survival by quickly responding to emergencies. For example, when a child awakens to hear her father entering her bed, it is often the firefighter who steps in to block the child's conscious awareness of the sexual act that follows. Or, when a child's abusive father arrives home drunk and angry, the child's firefighter part may offer oral sex in the hope that it will forestall a more painful or frightening sexual act.

At the time of the childhood abuse, this job of acting aggressively in an emergency was thrust upon the firefighters, and they continue to perform that function in the adult survivor's life, unaware that there are now other ways to ensure physical and emotional safety. They are often convinced that either the firefighter or the entire person will be annihilated if the firefighter walks off the job. The firefighters continue, then, ever-vigilant in watching for and leaping out to stifle perceived danger.

An initial problem therapists encounter is understanding the firefighters' definition or perception of danger. It might be signaled when the person: feels sexual arousal toward a spouse, a neighbor's child, or a stranger met at a party; decides to make any level of change, such as quitting a job or driving a different route to work; talks to the therapist about childhood incest or cries for the first time in front of the therapist;

loses weight or gives up alcohol; learns to trust and love another person; self-mutilates or masturbates to fantasies of the incest; talks to her father on the phone or sees a man who walks like her father; or simply smells beer, which triggers memories of the incestuous nights. While a particular firefighter's definition of danger cannot be assumed, usually firefighters readily lecture therapists on what is dangerous.

The next problem the therapist confronts is what happens when the perceived identified danger occurs. The part who identifies danger must either put out the fire herself or ring the bell for another part to put out the fire. The minute the alarm goes off, the firefighter charges ahead. The firefighter might choose to extinguish the danger by creating a different danger that feels more controlled, familiar, or safe. For example, self-mutilation might replace frightening masturbation, or an abusive encounter might be substituted for a loving, trusting one. If Lorene had an intimate, trusting conversation with a person she was growing close to, for example, her firefighter might create sexual arousal at an inappropriate time or flash memories of her participation in childhood sexual rituals to remind Lorene that she is damaged goods, evil and tainted, and undeserving of normal love or friendship.

The firefighter often chooses protective behavior that is expedient and unwise. We are all familiar with common, socially acceptable behavior that is self-destructive, such as overeating, drinking too much alcohol, or working for long periods under overly stressful conditions. From the point of view of an abuse survivor's firefighters, their conduct is no different. Other extreme examples of this type of reasoning, taken to its logical conclusion might be: "I can't handle news that I have cancer, so I'll skip my pap test or mammogram." "If I find out I'm pregnant, I'll have to decide whether to have an abortion—a decision I never wanted to face—so I'll just ignore the fact that I've missed my period twice." "Knowing my wife no longer loves me would be devastating, so if she tries to raise that issue, I'll quickly change the subject or think of an errand I have to run."

Other examples of firefighter-type active "protection" which is ultimately destructive include: "I need a drink every morning when I wake up or else I'll never be able to face the job I hate, and my family responsibilities will overwhelm me." "I must have chocolate treats everyday, so that I'll quit hearing those inner voices who are always whimpering that my spouse does not love me." "If I keep charging new things for our home (another gourmet cookbook, some beautiful plants to crowd into the sunroom, new bedspreads for everyone), it won't seem like we're having financial problems at all, since we'll own all these new things." Such firefighter logic will be encountered frequently in therapy.

A child abuse survivor's firefighters take this protection-by-destruction behavior to an even further extreme. It is the type of mentality sometimes employed during the Viet Nam war—destroy the village in order to save it from being taken by the enemy. Behavior like self-mutilation or substance abuse falls neatly into the firefighters' well-intentioned definition of what is necessary to ensure survival. Lorene's firefighters explain the paradoxical helping-by-hurting:

Nicholas: *Alexandra feels rejected and devastated, because Lorene's new boyfriend accused Lorene of being cold—he means frigid. Lorene can't handle this abandonment and shame, so I'll help. I know that if I cut her leg 15 or 20 times, I can match (and thereby negate!) the suffocating pain Alex feels.*

Another example by one of Lorene's firefighters:

Victor: *The memories Lorene is dealing with in therapy have made her unable to function at work. I have to do something to help, and fast! If I eat junk until she vomits, I will surely have given her something more immediate and concrete to think about.*

A firefighter could also make a seven-year-old child wet her bed or vomit so her father would find her repugnant and reject her as a sexual partner (at least for that night). Or, a firefighter might cause the young child abuse victim to seek out an incestuous incident in order to provide a feeling of control, to get the sex out of the way, or to pass the test that makes her deserving of her father's love. In the adult survivor, the firefighter might seek out strangers in bars and have sex with them, thinking that it cleanses the survivor's soul and gives the younger parts a chance to be loved by someone. So, protection as defined by a firefighter often differs from how a "reasonable" person might define protective behavior.

The Firefighters' "Power To Do Bad"

Survivors typically carry within them one or more parts who feel powerful in a negative sense—what Briere (1989b) calls the "power to do bad." The concept of "negative specialness" is a concept foreign to many people. The idea of being the best seductress or the best arsonist or the best self-mutilator does not occur to most people. Survivors, however, are intimately familiar with the concept. Briere (1989b) describes negative specialness:

Despite the self-hatred of many sexual abuse survivors, they may experience a paradoxical, almost magical sense of power—the ability to do harm.... This specialness, however, is usually confined to sexual or sexualized interactions and is often seen by the survivor as further confirmation of the "badness" in herself and in the object of her "power."... The facade of cynicism and streetwise arrogance may be quite important to the survivor, who needs to feel control over at least some portion of her or his interactions with others, if only those related to further exploitation. More deeply, this "power to do bad" is a projection of self-hatred that may increase over time as a self-fulfilling prophesy: "I do bad because I am bad, and I am bad because of what I do." (pp. 44–45)

One of Lorene's firefighters, Nicholas, is immensely impressed by (and terribly frightened of) the power he perceives himself as having. The power revolves around the ability to do bad things. He aptly describes the negative specialness that burdens survivors:

Nicholas: *I am the worst secret, the worst fear you can hide. I can shred you into pieces, can rape you, can overpower the weak, snivelling cry-baby parts you pamper so much. Watch how I cut up your arm. Most people can't pour boiling oil on their stomachs. My powers are amazing. I make you different from — stronger than — any other human being!*

Another of Lorene's firefighters, Victor (who likes to refer to himself as Victor-the-Victorious), proclaims his negative specialness — and the accompanying shame:

Victor: *I am the one who is most crazy. All the parts know me. I let you become both the punisher and the victim blended together. I make you both the rapist and the rape victim. I feel frightened and physically ripped apart when I think of the incest; yet I think of it over and over again, masturbating, changing the storyline with a hundred variables. I already have created ten thousand times more pain than I can bear.*

Most survivors have a part like Victor — usually an adolescent or young adult firefighter part, either female or male, who frequently acts tough in stressful situations, is disdainful of any offers of affection or support, and makes loud threats at the first sign of danger. The negative power of the firefighters frightens a survivor the most, yet she is drawn to its seeming magic. Many of the powers revolve around sexual behavior.

Alexandra *[16-year-old part]: I can make you die faster by pushing your therapist away quickly and isolating you. All I have to do is try to seduce him. Either he'll get scared and run, or he'll give in and have sex. Either way, you lose your therapist. I'm sick of this healing and inner wisdom garbage. I told you I can scare you with blood and pain and sex. Look at the nightmare world I'm building for you. Look at the power sex slides and movies I make up for you. That's who you are. No one can stand to be near you unless you let me screw them.*

Herman (1981) notes that some survivors even embrace "their identity as sinners with a kind of defiance and pride. As initiates into forbidden sexual knowledge, they felt themselves to possess almost magical powers, particularly the power to attract men. They seemed to believe that they had seduced their fathers and could therefore seduce any man" (p. 97). Herman (1981) describes one women's boasting about her sexual powers over lovers who beat, exploited, and deserted her: "The belief that she was possessed of a diabolical power which drove men mad and caused them to mistreat her was easier to bear than the humiliation of powerlessness." Thus survivors speak of "feeling that they had extraordinary powers over others, especially sexual powers over men, and destructive powers over both men and women" (p. 98).

Firefighters as Pure Life Energy

We are more likely to turn away from our firefighter parts than any others, ignoring the fact that these "powers slumbering in the psyche" usually prove to be "potentialities of the greatest dynamism, and it depends entirely on the preparedness and attitude of the conscious mind whether the irruption of these forces, and the images and ideas associated with them, will tend towards construction or catastrophe" (Jung, 1957/1964, par. 582). Firefighters' slumbering powers awaken with a roar, offering enormous energy that the person desperately needs; these valuable entities should not be hastily locked away with the label "demon" blazing on their foreheads. Beahrs (1982) writes:

> As I use the term, the demon is largely pure life energy. Initially suppressed and disowned out of fear, it then turns back against the self in rage. What we see as a persecutor is merely a normal child response to being the recipient of persecution, that rejection inherent in the original disowning or suppression. This reversal is the critical awareness for making friends with a demon, who may then become the patient's greatest asset. (pp. 126–127)

Beahrs concludes that the tyrant-like part "was really the same as the desperate, terrified child who finally had to be protected by whatever means" (p. 156). The ferocious firefighter reeks of fear. Beahrs asks: "Is the tyrant, like many real-life tyrants, really a scared child underneath? If so, why does he not own up to it at the outset and seek protection?" (p. 156) Lorene offers one answer:

Self: *Victor likes to tell me how evil he is, so that I'll think he's more powerful than I am. But I tell him that even if evil equals power, that kind of power serves only to conceal fear. He doesn't disagree—he seems embarrassed.*

In therapy, the firefighter Nicholas initially appeared to be a trouble-maker, constantly urging Lorene to fall further into a quagmire of self-mutilation, depression, and self-hatred. He often resisted any communication with the therapist, snapping angrily whenever he heard words like *trust* or *caring*. He continually sought to prove the therapist wrong or traitorous. But when viewed in the context of the role he perceived himself to fill—the role of realist ("don't expect Dad to make you feel safe or loved") that he had been forced into within Lorene's internal family—it became clear that he did not truly want the extreme outcomes he urged. What he wanted was to protect Lorene from any person—the therapist was a prime suspect—who planned to reveal Lorene's repulsive past and then abandon her when she let down her guard and agreed to trust the therapist and let him help her. With Nicholas, the therapist and Lorene drew boundaries: He would be allowed to express his accusations and mistrust only directly and with a minimum of rudeness, and he also needed to let the other parts participate in therapy.

Eventually, Nicholas recognized that the other parts were safe in therapy and did not need his protection. He even admitted that he wanted to give up the role of protector if he could believe that the younger, abused parts would be safe without him. In time, Nicholas discovered that, even after giving up the distracting and destructive behavior, the exiled parts were in no danger. Nicholas also realized that much of the danger Lorene experienced in adulthood had been created by his own destructive behavior. This insight motivated Nicholas to explore his own personality. He was surprised to find a mixture of rage and sadness, and he fought hard to maintain his tough exterior. Lorene reports:

Self: *Nicholas was close to tears and furious all day. Angry/sad seems to be his trademark. He uses food as a secret weapon—not just a shield to protect him—it's actually a weapon. Sometimes cutting or burning is a weapon, also. He acts like it's against another person—not against another part. His attitude of "I'll show him" is one of vengeance against the men who betrayed and hurt him, but my body happens to receive the punishment instead of the men. Why? Maybe other parts think it would be too dangerous to let Nicky lash out at a real man.*

Nicholas told Dick he was going to leave the dark place, whether Dick liked it or not. Nicholas likes to stir up trouble, no matter what the price. If he's told that our reaction to his leaving the dark place could be drastic, he says, "So what? Nothing is real anyhow; this is all pretend." Has he left the dark place? I have no idea. I keep asking him questions, but he rarely answers.

I can't understand why he tries to hide all his sadness. He remains mired in anger, his body tense and brittle—but he has tears in his eyes.

One of the firefighter's roles is to gather gifts for the survivor. Firefighters are not afraid to leap up and grab material things for the person— money, food, and any material belongings. This role either soothes the firefighter ("I work hard, I deserve this"), or the young, exiled parts ("They suffered a lot" or "This will keep them quiet").

> When activated, a firefighter will try to take control of the person so thoroughly that he or she feels nothing but an urgent compulsion to engage in a dissociative or self-soothing activity. These firefighters can make the person self-absorbed and demanding (narcissistic), driven insatiably to grab more material things . . . than anyone else. (Schwartz, 1995, p. 51)

Other parts often detest and fear the firefighters, who more often than not disrupt, frighten, and provoke. This fear is intensified greatly when a firefighter takes on the attributes of the original abuser. Yet the other parts only create more havoc when they reject the firefighter. This does not mean that firefighters don't create danger. They do. However, they often feel it is their duty to warn loudly, "DANGER!" because the other parts are merely denying, shaming, coercing, or acting fearful—behaviors that only increase vulnerability.

Beahrs (1982) notes that in working with a persecutor or demon part, often it is *other parts* who create resistance. The demon "is often all too eager to become a cooperative part, and it is the patient in his usual self role who becomes resistant" (p. 122). The other parts work hard to ignore the full extent of dissociation; they are terrified that a demon will divulge this previously buried knowledge. Managers fear that firefighters will carelessly expose an intense emotion like rage just to see what happens. The negative power usually displayed by firefighters "is often due to the fact that they are the keepers of pain and rage, which frees up the 'good' personalities to function" (Putnam, 1989, p. 162). Huge polarizations develop between managers and firefighters because their strategies differ so vastly:

> Both the firefighters and managers try to contain feelings and memories of the exiles. Unlike the managers, however, who strive to keep the internal system under control by being painstakingly correct and pleasing everyone, the firefighters take the person *out* of control and *displease* everyone. Consequently, the managers often hate and criticize the firefighters even though they rely on each other. (Schwartz, 1992, p. 36)

Clearly, managers and firefighters are often uncomfortable with or hostile towards each other. While managers rely on firefighters and call on them for help from time to time, later they attack the firefighters for making the survivor weak and disgusting. Managers tell the firefighters: "You can't count on us, as you well know... we're busy elsewhere, we have better things to do... it's up to you to defend us" (Sarraute, 1990, p. 92). But as the firefighters look for "an opportunity," the managers become timid: "No, no and no... we don't want anything to do with those retaliations, those regurgitations, that cold revenge... we can't stand them... we're the ones they humiliate, they degrade us all." The firefighters, in return, taunt the managers with: "Don't forget your fear of action... your laziness... whatever you do, don't move. Play the ostrich..." (p. 93).

We all must learn that firefighters have great value and are not to be disposed of or somehow exorcised from the personality. Beahrs (1982) writes: "This alarms me, as it not only plays into the original pathogenic category error but also is persecutory in itself. . . . I do not accept that any part-self is so bad in its basic being that it should be exterminated and doubt that such riddance is even possible, short of biological death" (p. 129).

Firefighters have enormous resilience and energy. Relieved from their rescuing duties, they are free to provide strength and passion to the person's life. The mischievous firefighter happily exhibits enormous curiosity about a myriad of subjects: "An inquisitive child who wants to see how it's made, who amuses himself by scratching off the varnish, who attacks it on all sides, dismantles, demolishes..." (Sarraute, 1990, p. 60). Often the therapist and client find the firefighters to be one of the survivor's greatest asset and their strongest ally in healing. For example, Beahrs (1982) asked a patient, "Why would you want to get rid of an important part of your own basic being?" This question caused the patient to

> do a double-take and enter into careful thought, while the demon senses a potential ally and relaxes some, allaying some of the anxiety in the primary patient as well. A beneficent circle may already be in the offing. If a patient angrily says "I hate myself!" I may unobtrusively ask how it feels to be hated by one's own self, generally eliciting a response from a secondary part of either sadness, bitterness or rage. In a classic demon, the reply is to disown its sadness and to take sadistic delight in describing his means of torturing his victim, in a way both terrifying and yet likely to arouse vicarious delight in most listeners. Here, as in a great flood, is the patient's life energy, formerly experienced as not-me. (p. 127)

Under all their noise, then, the ferocious firefighters are no different from other parts who bear the burdens of loneliness and pain.

EXILED CHILD-LIKE PARTS

The youngest parts are usually hidden away, buried with their memories and shame. They feel sadness and other intense emotions more directly than any other part. The intensity frightens other parts immensely, and thus the young ones are banished or "exiled." They are usually over-

protected, and often a source of great shame and concern for the managers
and firefighters. The exiles usually include the many inner children who
retain the most vivid memories of the abuse. Unlike the other parts, who
have to deal with the external world, the exiled children need not actively
cover up their memories. Because they are hidden, exiles can retain more
vivid memories. The other parts work hard to bury the exiles, preventing
any communication with the Self, purportedly for the Self's own good.

Stone and Winkelman (1985) write that the "exiled selves that represent
various aspects of the inner child are [a] . . . major group of selves that
are usually disowned" (p. 149). The exiled child "embodies the subject's
sensitivity and fear. Its feelings are easily hurt and it generally lives in fear
of abandonment. It is almost always frightened of a multitude of things
that the protector/controller and the heavyweights know nothing about"
(p. 149). It is the other parts who decide that the exiles must be sent away:
"We had banished for ever the one who committed the offense" (Sarraute,
1990, p. 33). The protective parts might justify the banishment in a number of ways. For example, Jennifer might be buried more deeply whenever
other parts believe she has done something evil—like trusting a friend,
feeling a desire for physical intimacy, being happy, missing the abuser's
attention, crying, or telling her story of the abuse. The other parts also fear
that the exiled part will lead them into danger while indiscriminately seeking a redeemer—often someone whose behavior resembles that of the
original abuser. Even the protector parts often have no idea *why* the survivor feels frightened—they only know enough to bury the fear. It is the
exiles who are permitted to hold the fear, while the other parts push away
their own fear by busying themselves with protective functions. Although
other parts might like the opportunity, it is only the exiles who are allowed
to feel the acute despair, abandonment, and betrayal.

The sense of vulnerability which permeates the internal system of an
abuse survivor cannot be overemphasized. Its impact on the system is
enormous. Every survivor is all too familiar with the internally murmured
accusations of being tainted, shameful, weak, bad, and grossly disfigured.
In *You Don't Love Yourself* (Sarraute, 1990) there is an extraordinary
passage that captures the pain carried by young, exiled parts. As the exiles
desperately reach out, other parts step in, push the exiles away, abandon
them—and still other parts just watch.

> Still those same emaciated arms being held out, those washed-out eyes
> from which tears are coursing, that trembling voice... "Take me with you..."
> At other times it's sobs, entreaties, a child's arms held out towards us...
> Or again...
> But what's the good of recalling everything that comes back to us at times
> and revises the same stabbing pain in us...
> Agonizing twinges like the ones that suddenly return in a certain point in
> our body...

We prod, we press... it hurts...

But not like we are hurt... not in the same way as we are hurt by all the apparitions of entreating arms and faces bathed in tears that come to us from all over the world.

It's something we ourselves have created...

We have manufactured it... And we have wounded ourselves with it... It's made a deep gash in us...

Splinters have entered us and become embedded, there's no way to extract them.

And yet, when it was still incomplete, we could have transformed it, we were going to do so, we were going to lean over and let those emaciated old arms raised up to us hug our shoulders, let the child's arms be clasped around our neck... let smiles and words radiate appeasement, tenderness...

But you intervened... You poured lead into those arms that were going to throw themselves around us... We could already feel how we were sagging under their embrace, we were staggering, were going to fall, remain prostrate, unable to get up...

And we allowed them to become what they remained for ever... those helpless arms stretched out towards us, those heartrending appeals...

We have turned them into that petrified thing. Immutable.

No fluctuations. Never anything nebulous, cloudy, nothing obscure, no shadow...

A hard object. Very distinct. Sharp.

Made of an unalloyed material, which bears a name everyone knows: "Abandon."

It entered into us and has become part of us... a point in us where at times an incurable pain returns... (pp. 157–159)

When a child expresses fear or pain, adults often react with impatience, denial, criticism, or distraction. The internal family is no different:

Managerial parts of the child soon learn to adopt these attitudes and constrain the Self from taking care of the younger tribe members. This makes many people quite vulnerable to polarization from trauma. They become inclined to try to forget about painful events as soon as possible, which means pushing the hurting parts out of awareness. In this way, insult is added to the injury for these child-parts. They are like children who are hurt and then are rejected and abandoned because they are hurt. They become the exiles, closeted away and enshrouded with burdens of unlovability, shame or guilt. (Schwartz, 1995, p. 47)

Because the other parts cannot focus on their own emotions, they might also (intentionally or not) *dump* their feelings into the exiles. Thus, managers may go so far as to transfer their burdens of extreme feelings to exiles so that the managers do not have to be reminded of their own fear or pain. Managers believe that the only way to continue their managerial activities (which permit the survivor to function from day to day) is to expel those emotions by transferring them to the silent exiles.

An important distinction between exiles and other parts involves the exiles' perpetual search for opportunities to break out of their prison and tell their stories. Like any abandoned child, they desperately want to be cared for and loved, so they search endlessly for a rescuer and redeemer. It is not that managers and firefighters do not ultimately hope to be rescued and loved. Exiles, however, *do nothing but* watch for chances to express (leak) their emotions and be cared for. Managers and firefighters are kept busy functioning in a hundred protective duties to keep the survivor from being exposed to danger, while exiles simply wait for a chance to be exposed to the world, often exerting tremendous unconscious influence.

While all parts can become "frozen" in time—believing that they still live in a time when danger and abuse surround them—this quality is most apparent in the exiles. A manager might pretend to be functioning in the present by going to work, driving a car, and cooking dinner, while holding anachronistic beliefs that danger is everywhere and the original abuser could arrive at any moment. In contrast, an exile does not even pretend to function in the present. She constantly senses her abuser's presence, feels her father's bed pressing against her back, and cries within a tiny body. An exile frozen in time lives as though she remains fixed in the abusive situation, with all its attendant emotions and physical sensations. Consequently, exiled parts continually drain energy from other parts who must work endlessly to keep the exiles hidden and secretive. Lorene describes her "seven-year-old" part:

She's a secret. The other parts let her talk directly to Dick, but they don't let her write in the journal. Vincent usually describes her feelings and thoughts. So much secret surrounding her. She can't even use her name, and can't talk to other parts. Although she thinks she has no power, her power actually lies in her secretiveness.

Careful, slow work with the protector (Vincent) gave Lorene some access to this young part:

I worked hard with Vincent for hours today. Finally he decided to let me talk to the seven-year-old. It was exhausting and eerie. She talks about the dark place. Very clear about worms in/on vagina; blood used to scare her; confusion between enema-induced pain and feeling physically alive. I tried to figure out what she was feeling, what Vincent was feeling, and what Vincent was trying to say. The only thing I figured out after hours of work with them is that it's definitely scary to all my parts.

At other times, direct contact with an exiled part is not permitted, but the protector part will give the therapist information:

Vincent talked to Dick for a long time, explaining concepts about seven-year-old type parts. For example: She is incredibly needy. Can't get enough love, food, punishment, possessions, diseases, redemption, etc. The other parts bring her presents, but they still see her as needy and so bring her more presents. I thought restrictions and setting limits would help her, but Dick disagreed. I want to discipline her so she'll learn she can't have everything—which part of me is saying that? (Super-She?) Her memories scare so many of my parts.

Some parts attack exiled parts, disgusted with their fragility, which the attacking parts believe weakens and endangers the entire system. Sadly, exiled parts may even welcome the familiar attack, a known danger that permits the part to feel redeemed or forgiven, since dues for her sins, whatever they may be, have been paid. The younger parts freely admit that they yearn for love, to be taken care of in some way, and to be heard. Unfortunately, these yearnings create great danger because the needy exiles will do most anything, including suffer additional abuse, in order to achieve their goals—and the protective parts know it. Often child victims are told by their abusers that the abusive situation is the only "loving" relationship of which they are worthy (Finkelhor & Browne, 1985). The adult survivor's parts still carry this belief, a burden of worthlessness.

Should these exiled parts who crave some long-deserved care look to the most maternal parts of the person or to the therapist? Anderson (1986) recommends that the therapist provide a "belated but genuine equivalent of parental love" and "provide the respect and concern that the patient lacked during childhood" (p. 69). In contrast, we agree with Putnam (1989) "that the reparenting process must occur from within. . . . The adult personalities must first acknowledge and then ultimately protect, care for, and raise the child alters" (p. 193). Beahrs (1982) also warns against the therapist reparenting child-selves (p. 138). Initially, however, clients who have suffered severe abuse need time and practice before they can perform internal parenting duties. In some clients, the Self is so unavailable at first that the therapist has to act as the Self to the younger parts—but only for a period of time. Slowly, the leadership is transferred to the client's Self, sometimes for a few moments, then for a full session, then for a period of time between sessions.

To believe otherwise would mean that survivors have suffered permanent damage and could never be strong enough to function independently as whole and happy people. The IFS model rejects such a position. "Especially insidious is the implication that the patient cannot serve these functions for himself—that lack of faith inherent in a 'defect' model" (Beahrs, 1982, p. 138). We agree that it would be "especially insidious" to imply that survivors will never be able to care for their younger parts. Once protective parts permit the Self to have access to needy, younger parts, the survivor's Self has the skills necessary to provide parental nurturing for all parts. Thus, under IFS principles, the therapist does not have to reparent the inner parts of the client. Every person has a Self, and once it is differenti-ated, it becomes clear to that person how to heal and bring the inner family into a state of harmony.

The process is far from linear, however. After working in therapy with Lorene's part Jenny, the young part began to feel quite strong, but other parts still maintained that she was too vulnerable to be exposed. They hid her protectively, whether or not she wanted the protection. They refused to let her "tell her story" for fear it would create total chaos, make the abuse recur, arouse parts who try to imitate the abuser, or even cause the protective parts to encounter their own long-buried emotions. The thera-pist and Lorene's Self encouraged Jenny to voice and demonstrate her newfound strength, knowing that the protector parts would gladly give up their previously inflexible stance once they trusted her strength. The poet Rilke eloquently describes the sadness many parts are frightened of, and the need to accept and honor that sadness as part of life:

> So you must not be frightened, if a sadness rises up before you larger than any you have ever seen, if a restiveness, like light and cloud shadows, passes over your hands and over all you do. You must think that something is happening with you, that life has not forgotten you, that it holds you in its hand; it will not let you fall.

Finally, when freed from their prison, the exiled parts pour tremendous life energy into the survivor. Indeed, it is this "maimed, speechless child that holds feelings, spontaneity, connectedness and creativity" (Matousek, 1991, p. 21).

PART II

Treatment Issues and Techniques

CHAPTER 7

Guidelines for Working with the Internal System

The unconscious is powerful: If we are going to approach it, respect and care are in order. With this attitude, we can derive the benefits of inner work while still protecting ourselves from the sometimes overwhelming power of the unconscious.

— *Robert A. Johnson, 1986*

B EFORE EXPLORING SOME of the more complex treatment issues, an overview of some of the guiding tenets used in IFS treatment may be helpful. Many of these rules are touched upon throughout the book; however, we believe those listed here are significant enough that they deserve separate emphasis.

SHOW RESPECT

It is vital that therapists approach each part of a survivor's internal system in a respectful manner. "Just as in international diplomacy, progress is more likely to result if the unique needs of all parts are given adequate attention and respect" (Beahrs, 1982, p. 9). Only then can the survivor discover what each part wants and believes. Ignoring, manipulating, or attacking parts invites retaliation. When protective parts are given respect and consideration, they become less protective, and the therapist encounters less resistance. The IFS model redefines resistance as the therapist's activation of protective parts by ignoring their concerns. Instead of searching for techniques to overpower or bypass resistance in clients, the therapist asks the client to listen to her protective parts and ask them respectfully—without derision and criticism—what they want or fear. The therapist may need to reassure those parts by respecting their fears and slowing the pace while they learn to better articulate their needs and trust the process.

BE DIRECT AND HONEST

One way of showing respect is to be direct, which is another way of saying "tell the truth" about what you're really feeling. Both the therapist's parts and the client's parts need to practice making direct, honest statements. For example, instead of stomping out in the middle of a session, Lorene could say: "Nicholas wants to leave now, because he's afraid Jenny will make me cry in front of you." This may be a difficult task for survivors, who carry layers of secrets known to some parts but not to others and who create new secrets for no reason, even keeping their most benign and mundane thoughts, activities, and feelings hidden from the world. Being direct and truthful may also be difficult for the therapist's parts who over-react to boundary issues with clients, or who want to appear "together" at all times.

In keeping with the rule of directness and honesty, both the therapist and the client should acknowledge interference from their parts. For example, a therapist should acknowledge if she puts a managerial part in charge (something the client will probably notice) because of a sleepless night due to sick children at home; and a client should acknowledge general crankiness caused by receiving a speeding ticket on the way to a therapy session. Lorene records:

Nicholas was so hurt that Dick seemed aloof last week. Today, instead of Nicholas attacking Dick and being rude, he just told Dick why he was upset. Dick explained that last week he'd been concerned about a problem at work that he needed to take care of. He apologized. It seems so simple! It even made Nicholas feel safe enough to cry—and he never cries in front of anyone.

AVOID CHANGING APPOINTMENTS

The therapist should be careful about changing appointments, since survivors' parts easily interpret any change as rejection. Give as much notice as possible and be honest about the reason for making the change (for example, a family emergency or a business trip). This consideration demonstrates that the therapist's commitment to the relationship remains, even though the regular Monday morning appointment has to be moved to Tuesday evening.

Similarly, the client should avoid changing appointments. Refusing to come to therapy may be the only power that managerial parts believe they have in the therapy relationship. Managers are often heard to complain that the therapist often controls where, when, and how in sessions. Those parts must learn to challenge the therapist more directly on power issues. Another part (usually an exile) may affect scheduled appointments by acting like a small child holding his breath until Mom pays attention; this part might seek attention by simply not showing up, in the hope that it will worry or irritate the therapist. It is a good idea to prohibit changing appointments and discuss the parts' appointment-related concerns at the next scheduled session. Any part's anger or distaste for the therapy process should be voiced directly to the therapist. (Also, appointments should be scheduled at times when the client will have time afterwards to decompress and work with parts who might be upset. It is a mistake to leave for a demanding job or other responsibilities immediately following an intense session.)

RECOGNIZE EXTREMENESS OF PARTS

An extreme part is often obsessed with a particular issue or theme. It has the narrowest perspective on what it real and on what is best for him or her. It becomes compulsive, repeatedly hammering on the theme with which it is obsessed (for example, guilt for having participated in an incestuous relationship or a desperate need to act normal in order to avoid being abandoned by people). With the therapist's non-judgmental help, parts can learn to understand that extremeness is destructive, because it keeps them from doing what they want to do.

Schwartz (1995) lists common factors that constrain a part from taking a healthy role, instead forcing the part into an extreme role in the system. Those factors include: The part needs to protect another part; the part is polarized with other parts; the part is frozen in the past; the external environment constrains the part; the part carries burdens; or something in the relationship between the therapist and client is activating extreme behavior in the part. Schwartz warns, however, that "one intervention is rarely enough by itself to release a part from its extreme role. The therapist often needs persistence and patience" (p. 111).

Most importantly, both the client's and the therapist's parts must learn that one part's extreme behavior does not reflect the true nature of that part's personality. Putnam (1989) warns: "The therapist should not make the error of believing that the patient has 'good' and 'bad' personalities and that the task of therapy is simply to promote the good and suppress the bad" (p. 162). Instead of criticizing and attacking the disruptive or offending part, the therapist's or the client's Self can negotiate with an extreme part to suspend its attacks or other extreme behavior temporarily. The part will often agree to give the client's Self an opportunity to handle a particular problem. For example, if the extreme part is convinced that the survivor will continue her promiscuous behavior, which frightens another part, the survivor might agree to not have sex for a certain period of time, until the part can be helped to feel less vulnerable. This agreement relieves all the parts, especially the manager called upon to numb the survivor or act reckless and impulsive (firefighter) in order to carry out the sex. If the therapist leads with his or her Self, it becomes possible to acknowledge the fears or pain under the part's extremeness. This Self-leadership helps extreme parts drop their tough facade and work with the therapist in a non-extreme state. Unfortunately, some parts need to prove their ability to take total control before they will discuss their true feelings; but once the power and status of the part are established, the therapeutic relationship with regard to that part can begin.

TALK WITH THE SELF

In the IFS model, it is the Self who coordinates the cooperative function among parts, the Self who helps each part define a preferred and valuable role, and the Self who ensures that mutual respect among parts continues. Speaking only to extreme parts can exhaust and confound a therapist. A helpful treatment principle is to talk with the client's Self for at least a few minutes during each session. This rule also helps calm the therapist's parts who keep muttering that therapy is futile with this client. In addition, a client "who is invested in a fantasy of rescue may resent having to do work and may want the therapist to do it" (Herman, 1992, p. 166). The habit of reasserting the client's Self as leader for at least a few minutes during each session helps counter tactics of parts seeking an all-powerful rescuer. With some clients (particularly those who suffered severe childhood abuse), this will not be possible for extended periods. But with each experience, however brief, of the Self in the lead, the survivor will typically strive harder to return to that centered place; in turn, the part who craves a rescue will feel less pressure and interfere less with the work in therapy.

USE A SYSTEMS PERSPECTIVE

In the IFS model, parts are worked with as if they belong to an internal family. Each part is treated as an individual entity, but all are members of an internal family. The therapist addresses each part's relationships with other parts. Negotiations among parts also reflect the use of structural family therapy techniques. The client learns to act as a therapist to his or her internal family. The client learns about appropriate boundary making. The self easily resolves huge polarizations among several parts simply by having those parts face each other without interference from other members of the internal family while the client's Self calmly leads the discussion.

COLLABORATE

Clinicians have found that attempting to implant insights and interpretations "doesn't work effectively with survivors of a traumatic invasion (e.g., incest). Instead, we employ a cooperative model in which individuals learn . . . to develop an alliance with their unconscious resources" (Gilligan & Kennedy, 1989, p. 10). The IFS model removes the therapist from the difficult position of having to construct and sell a new reality to the client. Instead, the therapist explores issues with the parts by asking questions, recognizing always that the client is the expert on how she experiences her subpersonalities and how they relate to each other. Instead of imposing interpretations, the therapist collaborates with the client, showing respect for her inner strengths and resources. If the therapist adheres to a framework that identifies defects and deficiencies in clients, then "the therapist will try to give clients what they lack, whether through reparenting, interpretations, information, reframes, directives, or drugs" (Schwartz, 1995, p. 89).

That is not to say that other types of additional support, such as medication, hospitalization, group therapy, or 12-step programs, are never needed; there are times when both the client and therapist decide such means will be helpful. But in conjunction with other aids, IFS therapy reassures survivors that they have the necessary internal resources to heal, instead of insisting that they need to become dependent on an authoritative relationship because the abuse made them somehow defective.

> In the reality of clinical practice, therapists will vacillate between these two positions. The collaborative therapist will sometimes give information, sympathy, or directives, and the authoritative therapist will sometimes encourage clients to use their own resources. The difference, then, is not so much in the therapist's behavior, but instead in his or her overall attitude toward clients and the messages that this attitude conveys. (Schwartz, 1995, p. 85)

We disagree with theories that focus on what the survivors *lack*. For example, Dusty Miller (1994) believes that a survivor (or any woman who hurts herself) should learn to develop within her a Protective Presence, which can be an internalization of the therapist. The internalization might be facilitated by the client's keeping a physical object to help her feel connected to the therapist or perhaps listening to "a tape of their therapist reading a comforting children's story" (p. 252). The Protective Presence can change over the years. It can be a spirit guide, close friend, a grandparent or sibling, or a composite of various positive aspects of people she has known (pp. 254–55). In the IFS model the internalization of a "healthy" person is necessary. Once clients differentiate their Self from their parts, they can do a great deal of work on their own, between sessions. People discover insights on their own, without receiving previous reframes or interpretations from the therapist. Using this facilitative approach, people learn quickly how to trust their own resources and, consequently, feel less dependent on therapists.

TIMING AND PACING

A therapist's intervention in the delicate ecology of the internal family must be well-timed.

> If certain parts, or relationships among parts, are addressed too early, other parts react protectively and may try to sabotage the change. If a therapist tries to elicit a vulnerable, child-like part of a client before having dealt with other parts that try to keep that one away from the client's Self or from other people, "resistance" will be encountered, and the client may be punished internally for allowing the intrusion. A family therapist who tries prematurely to get at a family secret or vulnerability encounters the same process. (Breunlin et al., 1992, p. 74).

It is important to check in with a client's parts periodically to see how they are experiencing the process of disclosure. Feinauer (1989) warns that to attempt to "force individuals to face trauma before they choose to do so is not effective and may be experienced by the victims as revictimization" (pp. 332–33). Swink and Leveille (1986) provide a trusting milieu:

> We have learned to trust each person's natural process without judgement. Clients who recover memories slowly are very tempted to seek hypnosis to get it all at once. This can be very dangerous if it overreaches the clients' natural pace and therapeutic process. . . . We prefer to let the natural process take its course with gentle prodding, and trust that all the material will emerge in its own time and within the client's control. (p. 132)

Gilligan and Kennedy (1989) also warn that using hypnosis with incest survivors may force the pace. Hypnosis involves "powerful reconnections with an 'inner self,'" which can only be effective when

> a person's rate and style of hypnotic processing is respected. Individuals who are frightened or absorbed in distracting inner processes will be unwilling or unable to participate in hypnotic experiences. Thus, therapists must actively encourage and coach incest survivors to remain sensitive to their unique styles of developing and experiencing trances, so that individual needs are respected. This will often mean slowing down, working with smaller "chunks" of time or material, expanding the trance to include more resources, and so forth. (p. 11)

Moreover, survivors are often disconnected from feelings that might warn them of extreme discomfort. Consequently, they may not realize that the pace is too fast. Cornell and Olio (1991) note: "They are unlikely to refuse a therapist's direction or may minimize the impact of overstimulating and intrusive interventions. Thus the therapist's responsibility for monitoring the intensity of treatment is crucial" (p. 67). For example, a survivor may act calm and open during a session in which traumatic memories are explored, but then go home and self-mutilate. This signals to the therapist that, while the parts worked with during the session were comfortable with the exploration, there are other parts of the survivor who feel the session was too intense, overwhelming, or dangerous.

Sgroi (1989) aptly describes the recovery process as "flowing from one stage to another in a spiral fashion" (pp. 121–22). Thus a client might express dismay at what appears to be a step backwards, saying, "I've been here before! I thought I was finished with this" (p. 121). The therapist may feel that the client is repeating steps in therapy; often it is because the same issue is being addressed with a different part (see chapter 19). The key, then, is to respect the fact that each internal system has a different pace of change, and that efforts to accelerate the pace will often have the opposite effect.

USING A VARIETY OF TECHNIQUES

Because IFS is a collection of principles, a variety of techniques can be used. IFS techniques are described in greater detail in *Internal Family Systems Therapy* (Schwartz, 1995). It is not necessary to use all IFS principles and techniques; instead, the therapist should use techniques that feel comfortable. Many techniques from other models can be grafted onto the IFS model.

TIME IN TREATMENT

The IFS model typically works rapidly to produce effective changes with non-abused clients. This has not been true with child abuse survivors. The therapy takes longer, although perhaps it is shorter than more traditional methods of therapy because of its user-friendly language and empowering principles. This extended timetable may activate various parts of the therapist: a "striver" part who needs quick proof of his capabilities and, when it is not forthcoming, demands that the client be immediately referred to a more qualified therapist; an "evaluator" part who experiences the therapy as failing and suggests an alternative career; or a "passive pessimist" part who is convinced that therapy will never be successful and suggests hospitalization for the client. Therapists must be aware of the activation of their own parts. From the position of the Self, the therapist should reassure those worried parts that therapy with the abused client is moving along at an appropriate pace and ask those parts not to interfere, especially during a session.

Most therapists are wisely reluctant to set an idealistic timetable for working with survivors. Putnam (1989) estimates that treatment of multiple personality disorder requires an average of three to five years of meeting two or three times a week for 90-minute sessions. In addition, special sessions will be a crucial factor in successful treatment. Herman (1992) notes that the initial stage of therapy, when the survivor's sense of safety is being established, may take months to years if the abuse was severe and chronic; the length of time expands "in proportion to the severity, duration, and early onset of abuse" (p. 160). In regard to the stage of recovery identified by Herman (1992) as remembrance and mourning, she warns that there is "no fixed answer to the question [of how long the process will last], only the assurance that the process cannot be bypassed or hurried. It will almost surely take longer than the patient wishes, but it will not go on forever" (p. 195).

WARNINGS

It is impossible to present all the considerations and guidelines for doing this work in one book. Perhaps the most salient principle is that therapists are dealing with a client's entire internal ecology, in which no single part can be changed without affecting every other part and the client's external life as well. Using the IFS model with clients can be so fascinating and powerful that a therapist may be tempted to ignore or underestimate the impact on parts who are less visible, or on the person's external context. It is dangerous to neglect some parts out of fascination with others.

While this book focuses on the abused internal system, it is recommended that the techniques described first be applied only to less internally extreme or polarized parts, until the therapist has more experience in dealing with this inner world. Therapists must use the model very cautiously until they become sufficiently familiar with the underlying principles and techniques, which are also outlined in *Internal Family System Therapy* (Schwartz, 1995). This is not meant to discourage survivors or their therapists from doing inner work, but only to remind them that the forces hidden within each of us are immense and powerful.

ULTIMATE GOAL: FUSION
OR COEXISTENCE?

Therapy using the IFS treatment model never seeks to unify or merge all parts. Instead, it aims at increasing differentiation of the self and internal harmony. No parts need to be inserted (e.g., the image of a good parent), no parts need to be removed (e.g., a malevolent abuser-like sub-personality), and no parts need to merge (although some "parts" may turn out to be subparts of others and want to return to the original). IFS is a "polycentric" psychology. Beahrs (1989) explains the term:

> A gradual assimilation of other portions of psyche by the ego is not the goal. In a polycentric psychology, once attuned to and respectful of the multiplicity of the Self, one would attempt to restore some autonomy to the colonies. One function of personifying is to save the diversity and autonomy of the psyche from dominion by any single power. (p. 119)

Beahrs discusses the active proponents of fusion, and rejects the notion, concluding that "the data of hypnosis show that co-consciousness is the rule rather than the exception" (p. 134). Thus it makes little sense to label a client with a diagnosis simply because he acknowledges his parts: "How can we . . . consider a multiple unhealthy if his part-selves communicate and cooperate with each other under the benign leadership of an executive, like the conductor of the orchestra?" (p. 134). Beahrs (1989) also points out that fused individuals do not stay fused due to the natural condition of multiplicity:

> Since a true alter-personality experiences himself as a separate self, he will fight that dissolution with the full force of the self-preservation instinct common to all life. . . . No part-self actually dies; rather it remains as a latent ego state, a normal part of the personality which may even have its own subjective experience but does not ever "come out" for public view. Watkins' discovery in healthy individuals of potentially infinite latent ego states or hidden observers, which may even have their own unique subjective experiences, raises philosophical issues about the nature of cohesive Self and selves, and their relationship to the universe at large, which are mind-boggling and only beginning to be explored. (p. 134)

In contrast, Putnam (1989) struggles with the possibility of fusing all sub-personalities:

> I do not know what fusion is or is about. At times I find myself quite skeptical of the process and wonder whether we have bought into a magical expectation about treatment outcome. . . . Yet I have seen some patients undergo a transformation over the course of treatment, so that the alter personalities lose their separateness and appear to be absorbed into a more integrated sense of self. (pp. 308–309)

Putnam acknowledges that "most 'fusions' probably never occurred in the first place. . . . [There] seems to be a temporary merging of alter personalities that fails to hold, and the alters reappear as separate entities," while at other times, patients deliberately "undo their fusion" (p. 313).

From the IFS perspective, the failure of fusion is due to the fact that fusion is an unnatural state. Putnam (1989) concedes that many people "experience significant difficulties following a final integration." Moreover, attempts at fusion can be dangerous, in that failure may trigger internal chaos. Putnam (1989) notes that some alters "evince profound disappointment" after a failed fusion and that "crises and suicidal behavior can be precipitated by renewed or new evidence of dividedness." Other alters may be "triumphant and gloating, viewing the failure of the fusion as a sign of their power and a victory in their struggle for control of the patient and the therapy" (p. 314).

A purported fusion robs parts of the opportunity to express their internal conflicts, contradictory experiences, hopes, and opinions. When a person is permitted to acknowledge a healthy state of multiplicity, he is "usually able to maintain sets of contradictory feelings toward the abuser(s) side by side. This is not as easily done in the fused state, which forces the patient to face and resolve these very different perceptions" (Putnam, 1989, p. 318). IFS permits survivors to "face and resolve" internal conflicts *without* destroying the boundaries around each part by an attempted meltdown. Dusty Miller (1994) describes the emptiness survivors (whom she refers to as "Trauma Reenactment Syndrome" or TRS women) feel when they extinguish boundaries surrounding each of their various parts:

> The process of identifying the three parts of the [Triadic] self and then banishing them by stopping the symptoms creates a deep loneliness for most TRS women. This is why it is so important for them to do this work in therapy rather than alone. The TRS woman can learn to identify the Triadic Self, and she can find ways to give up these familiar figures from childhood as she gives up her self- harmful behaviors or symptoms, but the next step is enduring the emptiness. (p. 250)

Putnam (1989) similarly finds that fused patients may "grieve for the loss of the alters" and recommends that the therapist "facilitate mourning for the divided state [which] contain[s] elements of fairytale beauty, perfection, and peace that must be surrendered with fusion. These losses should be identified and mourned also" (pp. 319–20). The IFS model does not support guiding survivors into such an unnecessary and cruel emptiness.

The idea of fusion rests upon the premise that we are unitary in nature and become multiple through trauma. In contrast, the IFS model is founded on the assumptions that multiplicity is natural and fusion is an unnatural state. Instead of fusion, IFS promotes *integration*. Watkins and Watkins (1988) distinguish between the two: "We realize that many of our colleagues do not conceptualize such a difference between integration as we define it (a working together of sub-ego states under an overall unifying jurisdiction, as in the United States of America), and fusion, which we define as the elimination of the boundaries and fusing of their contents, so they no longer function as entities" (p. 68). The goal of the IFS model is similar to that described by Johnson (1986): "Pull the different parts of you together that have been fragmented or in conflict; it wakens you powerfully to the voices inside you; and it brings about peace and cooperation between the warring ego and the unconscious" (p. 141). This kind of balanced and harmonious integration is best achieved by differentiating a Self who can lead the internal system.

ARE PARTS REAL?

Clinicians introducing the IFS model to clients have often shared the experience reported by Johnson (1986): "Whenever I start a patient on Active Imagination,* I get a series of questions: 'How do I know that I'm not just making all this stuff up?' 'How can I talk with someone who is only a figment of my imagination?'" (p. 150). Johnson explains that "imagination is a *transformer* that converts invisible material into images the conscious mind can perceive" (p. 22). Clients asked to speak with an inner voice or a part might initially retort, "You think I'm like Sybil?" or, "Sounds like New Age garbage for aging hippies." One of the most frequently asked questions asked by therapists and clients alike is whether inner parts are in fact *real*. Some therapists and clients using the IFS model answer with an unequivocal yes. The IFS model does not demand that the client *imagine* anything. But clients consistently report that when guided by an IFS therapist, they focus inward and discover an already existing inner world.

Some clients and therapists using IFS principles prefer to think of parts as metaphors rather than as internal people. In an ontological sense, clinicians need not believe that parts are real before they can make use of the model. However, we believe that clinicians will inevitably discover that parts describe themselves as people, in which case the most respectful response is to acknowledge that belief. Each part "is an *actually experiencing being* which we can contact and communicate with and with which we *must* communicate respectfully if we are to effectively fulfill our responsibilities as psychotherapists" (Beahrs, 1982, p. 13).

During the course of therapy, parts may accuse the therapist of concocting images. One of Lorene's parts (Vincent) is very cerebral and cautious about change, and vigilantly protective of young parts whom he believes are too quick to trust. In therapy, he particularly denounced Lorene and Dick for what he saw as their contrived manipulations of young parts:

Vincent: *I can't believe the stupidity of Lorene and Dick! They actually think these meaningless imaginings are worth something. Today they*

---

*Developed from the Jungian theory of Active Imagination.

pretended to move little Andy out of the dark basement where Dad always hurt him the worst. They pretended to move him from the past to the present despite the scientific fact that "time travel" is totally unverified, never tested objectively, and completely unproven. All they're basically doing is telling Andy that if he would just make the effort to envision a better world, he would magically find himself in a better world. What total idiocy to believe that these little imaginings have any significance. It changes nothing! There is no escape — at least not through Dick's absurd games. I find this to be an incredibly incompetent method of practicing therapy.

This is a typical (though particularly caustic) accusation. Remarkably, though, clients *rarely accuse the therapist of inventing the parts themselves.* When a therapist asks to speak with a vulnerable part, it is not uncommon for protective parts to conceal the younger part by insisting, "Oh, she's not in here anymore," or "She died last week after you abandoned her." But the protective parts do not suggest that the younger parts *never existed.*

Does any of this prove that parts are real? There are those who will maintain that the IFS therapist is subtly pushing clients into fabricating parts. They want objective proof of the existence of parts. It's true that parts don't have bodies we can see. They are not corporeal, three-dimensional, tangible, or discernible in a way that can be measured by a yardstick and scale. They have no fingerprints and no DNA. Parts cannot be photographed, and no one will recognize one of your parts when they pass it on the street. (Lorene has never had a friend say, "Hey, I saw you at the party last week. Definitely looked like Alex and Nicky were having a wild time.")

Certainly the behavior and beliefs of parts have a real effect on the person's life. Lorene had several parts who used to cling to the belief that she was bad or somehow tainted. This kept her from making friends ("no one could like me"), and from asking for a raise ("I don't deserve it"). If her boyfriend slapped her, she accepted the punishment — even sought it — as being deserved, and a known, almost comfortable danger. The beliefs held by each part affected Lorene's life more profoundly than any external event in her adult life.

Is Super-She a real, experiencing being? Her existence as an entity with whom we can identify and communicate helps explain how a victim of severe abuse like Lorene is able to function at high levels at work, and then go home to self-mutilate. Super-She provides Lorene with a real resource of organizational and managerial talents which have real, tangible results evidenced by her high production at work.

Is Nicholas, the teenage warrior, real? He is a real, experiencing being in the sense that Lorene can contact him and communicate with him.

Nicholas has a tremendous effect on Lorene's daily life. He provides confidence and energy in some stressful situations and attacks anyone he perceives as a threat. Certainly the cuts and burns he has peppered Lorene's body with over the years are real.

Most theorists who have struggled with this question and worked directly with subpersonalities are willing to conclude that parts are real. For example, Beahrs (1982) opines that "whenever we are talking about a component of the psyche, this part is not just an abstract 'mechanism' used to help us organize our thoughts" (p. 13). He does not believe that therapists using a multiplicity framework concoct their clients' parts. He cites hypnotic work in which there is a "spontaneous emergence of alter-personalities in normal subjects" and he asks, "Is it no more likely that the alter-personality was already there? Unless we believe in creation from nothing, the alter-personality . . . must have been present in at least latent form even in . . . normal subjects" (p. 112). Watkins and Watkins (1979) point to "the frequency with which these [ego-states] emerge in ways which are totally unexpected by the investigators or therapists, or in ways contradictory to requests made, [which suggests] that they are not mere artifacts created by experimenter demand characteristics" (p. 17).

Johnson (1986) argues that no one "makes up" anything in the imagination. "Imagination, properly understood, is a channel through which this material flows to the conscious mind" (p. 22). Johnson explains further the connection between images and symbols:

> The images with whom we interact are symbols, and we encounter them on a symbolic plane of existence. But a magical principle is at work: When we experience the images, *we also directly experience the inner parts of ourselves that are clothed in the images.* This is the power of symbolic experience in the human psyche when it is entered into consciously: Its intensity and its effect on us is often as concrete as a physical experience would be. Its power to realign our attitudes, teach us and change us at deep levels, is much greater than that of external events that we may pass through without noticing. (p. 25)

Clothing the invisible material in images permits the therapist and client to share a powerful language and provides a way through which the client can consciously interact with her internal processes. M. Watkins (1986) also offers an insightful discussion of the problem. She believes that "imaginal dialogues do not merely reflect or distort reality, but create reality" (p. 48). She states, "The Child [part] is not just 'in' an imagination, she has an imagination" (p. 162). Watkins notes further that in the "Romantic view, the imagination is not merely a replica of pre-existing external reality. It has its own 'internal source of motion'; it does not merely represent scenes but creates them" (p. 59). She concludes: "Instead of the real and the imaginal being opposed as the imaginal distorts, condenses, rearranges and negates the real, it is thought that through the imaginal the truer nature of the real is manifested" (p. 75).

Similarly, under IFS principles, parts are more than imaginary friends. They are seen as being inherent and vital to the human condition. Moreover, serious problems result when therapists ignore the reality of parts. First, underestimating parts forces them into one-dimensional molds. Therapists believe that if, for example, they can help a client just get rid of the anger, the client will be healed. But an angry part is not so easily assuaged. That part is like a "teenager and [is] not just a mental state, [and thus] it does not just need to be calmed out of its angry condition. In all likelihood it will also need to be talked to about its hurt or about the way the world works. It will need to see that the Self and other parts care for and appreciate it. It will need what a lonely or hostile adolescent needs to feel a sense of belonging and security" (Schwartz, 1995, pp. 228–29). Second, believing parts are not real means the therapist will fail to focus on "helping the part discover the best role for itself, based on its feelings, talents and desires." Schwartz (1995) concludes:

> Thus, if the therapist views parts simply as mental states or as introjected images, he or she will relate to them differently than the therapist who sees them as people. . . . The important thing is that when relating to [parts], their personhood is respected. (p. 229)

CHAPTER 8

Eliciting Parts

Try to give expression to all of these different parts of you. You cannot learn how to strengthen or reduce them without first giving each of them a voice and perhaps even a name.

— *J. Patrick Gannon, 1989*

THE IFS THERAPIST HELPS to acquaint the survivor with his or her unknown parts. The survivor may only have seen these parts when they were out of control; the therapist can help introduce them in a controlled environment. The initial identification of a part decreases its power to overwhelm or intimidate the client ("Only one part of me is filled with terror"). Moreover, clients discover that they consist of much more than their extreme parts; they also possess healthy internal resources that can help the extreme parts change.

The techniques used for accessing parts are not as important as the underlying principles. As mentioned earlier, techniques other than those listed here can be used. For example, in working with subpersonalities, Feinberg-Moss and Oatley (1990) note that techniques may include "emotional catharsis, Gestalt dialogue with subpersonalities, art and movement exercises, role playing and discussion with the therapist" (p. 119). Bogart's (1994) work with personas (a term he prefers to subpersonalities) might involve Fritz Perls' hot seat technique, Virginia Satir's family therapy techniques, psychodrama, or "journeying" while in a self-induced trance state. Zalaquett (1989) lists a variety of techniques for working with multiplicity, including verbal, position techniques such as empty chair, imagery, psychodrama, hypnosis, and arts (pp. 338–39). It is crucial that both therapist and client feel comfortable with whatever techniques are chosen. In general, however, therapists find that most abuse survivors have little difficulty eliciting a part, perhaps because their parts have long been so polarized and separated that they stand out in bold relief.

FINDING PARTS

An IFS therapist begins by introducing the language of multiplicity: "It sounds like a part of you wants this, but another part is frightened." Most people are immediately comfortable and familiar with this language. Survivors especially feel relief at knowing that having intensely opposing yet simultaneous feelings or thoughts does not make them crazy. The IFS therapist also introduces some of the basic ideas of the IFS model, explaining the concepts of a part and a Self, for example. Next the client is asked to identify a part who relates to a current problem. The client focuses on the part, however he or she experiences it. The client need not "see" an inner person; it might be a thought pattern or inner voice or feeling state. For example, the client might focus on one feeling or thought and ask, Where does this feeling come from? Who inside of me feels this way? What do you look like right now? Usually an image will eventually come into the client's mind. M. Watkins (1986) illustrates with an example of personifying depression:

> We need to know what the imaginal sense of the depression is and who, which character(s), suffer it.... Does the depressed part of one express itself as an abandoned child, an aging man, a struggling single mother taking care of everyone? Even when the person identifies at first with the depression ("It is just me who is depressed"), he can often give hints to the images beneath: "I feel so old"; "I feel like I never want to leave my bed, like an invalid." (p. 153)

Johnson (1986) offers another description of this initial step: "Any quality within you can be . . . persuaded to clothe itself in an image so that you can interact with it. . . . If you vaguely feel a mood controlling you, you can do the same. It is the image that gives one a starting point" (p. 147). (Remember that "seeing" a part is not necessary in the sense that a clear visual image appears in the person's mind. Many people simply sense the presence of parts and interact with them on that basis.)

Yet another accessing method is to simply wait to see who will show up. Johnson (1986) provides a helpful metaphor when approaching the initial problem of eliciting a part: "An inner problem that looks so difficult that one doesn't know where to start is an example of an inner Jericho. It is like a walled city within the unconscious. . . . Identify to yourself as best you can what the conflict is. . . . Invite the people out of the city and find out who they are and why they are opposing you" (pp. 204–205). For example, a client may find that depression is her "inner Jericho." Johnson explains how to meet the depression:

> How do you approach it? . . . Go into your imagination, and look for the figure, the image, that will represent your depression. Now begin your march around the walls of Jericho. Talk to your depression. March around

your depression, and view it from every side. Talk to the figures. . . . What do they know about it? Perhaps one of them will admit to being the one, inside you, who is depressed and can tell you in some detail what he or she is depressed about (p. 205)*

Feinberg-Moss and Oatley (1990) describe a technique used in psychosynthesis to access subpersonalities: "This guided fantasy started off in a sunny meadow. The client was asked to imagine reaching a cottage, and to invite four or five people out, one at a time, greeting each as she or he emerged, and exchanging whatever words occurred. In discussion after the daydream, these people were explained as possible aspects of the client's own personality" (p. 119).

In the "room technique"† that Schwartz (Breunlin et al., 1992) uses, a client focuses on one part exclusively: "As [the client] isolates the part, the therapist asks him if he can see what it looks like. Once he gets an image of it, he is asked to put the part in a room by itself. He is then outside the room, looking at the part through a window" (p. 80). Schwartz adds a second step which is vital, regardless of which technique has been used to initially elicit the part. In some manner, the client must be sure that it is his Self—not another part—in the room dialoguing with the part:

> The therapist asks the client how he feels toward the part in the room and whether he feels anything extreme toward it (anger, envy, extreme sadness, fear, hopelessness). If so, he is asked to find a part that is outside the room with him and is influencing him to feel extremely toward the original part. He then moves this second part into another room, so that it does not interfere with the Self's ability to see clearly and work with the original part. (pp. 80–81)

Thus, after the client has begun a dialogue with a part, it is important to be aware of other voices or feelings that may compete with the part being addressed. If the client feels more than curiosity and empathy (for example, irritation, impatience, anger or fear), then another part is interfering. The therapist directs the client to find the part who is generating those negative feelings and ask the part to briefly separate from the client's Self—to step away emotionally, so that the part's influence is not so intensely felt. Only when the client feels alone outside the room experienc-

---

*Survivors must be especially cautious with parts who feel "walled off," since these may be young parts who hold secrets and have been concealed by protector parts.

†The room is used only to provide some initial separation between the parts and Self, and to help other parts feel less worried about the target part taking over. Very often, with less polarized clients, this is not necessary. Also, some parts react severely to being put into a room (perhaps the survivor was abusively confined as a child). It is helpful, though, to use some image which depicts a sense of separation or boundary.

ing feelings like curiosity or compassion, should a dialogue with the part in the room be attempted.

Before initially eliciting the part of a survivor of severe abuse, therapists should be forewarned that the survivor might envision a child-part who appears covered with blood or feces, is frail and sickly, or is pathetically vulnerable in some way. Schwartz (1992) describes the initial contact with an exiled part of the abuse survivor he calls Marcia: "I asked her to focus on the part of herself that felt so scared and jumpy. She concentrated on these feelings for a moment and said she could see a five-year-old girl whose body was covered with open, bleeding wounds" (p. 34). Therapists must reassure the survivor's parts—and their own parts—who become frightened during an encounter with a severely wounded part. The highest priority at that point is providing a sense of safety. Therapists are most successful when they make consistent, caring statements to assure the survivor that protection and safety will remain primary concerns.

OPENING LINES OF COMMUNICATION

After meeting several parts, the client chooses to work with one or more, and begins to open lines of internal communication. Beahrs (1982) notes that "the essence of psychotherapy within the multiplicity model is communicating with and enhancing communication among all parts of an individual" (p. 120). Many clients discover that they have *never* permitted some of their parts to voice questions or share feelings. Some parts have been buried under the rubble; it's a tremendous relief to free these voices in a controlled, safe environment and find out what they have to say. Johnson (1986) provides a perceptive example of the first struggling communications between his "ego" or "conscious mind" and a newly discovered part he calls Japanese Artist.

Ego: What is happening here? I've been taken over by an unknown force. I can't sleep for the barrage of hues before my eyes. What are you doing? What do you want? Who are you?

Japanese Artist: (Sounds like a feminine voice in my imagination.) The colors are so lovely. See the interplay. See how they evoke different aspects of nature. These, in particular, go so well with the wood tones of the bookshelves—

Ego: Excuse me. Yes, it is indeed lovely, but I am very weary and I have other considerations in life to worry about. I have other things to balance with this effort. You have taken over.

(At this point I began to realize that the feminine voice inside me was not so much obsessed as thrilled at the colors.)

Japanese Artist: I have a clear idea of what wants to be created here. I am trying to find the right tools. We must find the right fabric and paint and design to make it happen, to make it physical.

Ego: That is fine. But must you do it all night???

Japanese Artist: Oh. Yes. I see what you mean.

(*The figure grows clearer to me. This is a Japanese figure. At first it looked like a masculine figure, but now I see that it is neither masculine nor feminine, but androgynous. I feel that this is an artist, dressed in orange Zen Buddhist robes. The being stays silent, as though wounded. I am suddenly "tracking" on this being's personality, and I "know" that it has sensitivity, a vision derived from a meticulous appreciation of physical nature. I feel that I don't want to lose this being. I feel my irritation and frustration evaporating. I am getting very interested in this creature.*)

Ego: Please don't retreat. I am not angry. We can come to an agreement so that we both can thrive. Why are you pushing me so hard?

Japanese Artist: I am afraid.

Ego: Afraid of what?

Japanese Artist: I am afraid that I will be locked up again.

Ego: Locked up?

Japanese Artist: There are rarely any opportunities for me to express myself. It seems I must work very fast and intensely while the door is open to me. Soon it will be over, and I will be locked up again.

Ego: I begin to see what you mean. In my life there have been very few outlets provided for you, so few that I hardly knew you existed. The culture I live in doesn't provide any place for you. And I have not stood separately from my culture in this matter to provide for you.

Japanese Artist: That is true. I feel that I've been starving. This may be my only opportunity.

Ego: It doesn't have to be. If I provided other vehicles for you, other ways to express yourself, would you feel less desperate? Could you decrease your intensity?

Japanese Artist: Yes . . .

(*There is a long pause. Then the being speaks very gently.*)

Japanese Artist: Do you—are you aware of what that implies?

Ego: (*I feel apprehensive. I am about to commit myself to something that perhaps I can't back out of.*) I think so. I know it hasn't been easy for me to give permission to purely creative efforts in the physical and sensation world. I have always let practicality get in the way. I always feel the pressure of my work, my responsibilities.

Japanese Artist: I have tried to express myself through you, but for the most part those "practical" matters always win out. The pure joy of creating, living in the physical side of life, is whole unto itself—without expectation of outcome or so-called practical benefits.

Ego: This is true. And, given my conditioning, my dominant attitudes, I

*know you had to make me uncomfortable to get my attention. I see that
I will have to stand independent of the values of productivity that
surround me and dominate me. I must deal with the negative masculine
production mentality that carries these ideas and crowds out everything
else. He uses my fear of failure, my performance anxieties. And I must
confront my desire to produce, to be a success in my work, that gets out
of hand. I must sort through the values connected with art, artistic
expression in the physical world, and I must make a place for you. More
directly, I have to provide some immediate vehicles for you. What do
you suggest?*

Japanese Artist: *Something like ceramics, watercolors. Plant flowers. Arrange flowers. Or you can do something less formal. I just want us to
work and play with form and color and aspects of the physical world.*

Ego: *Fine. I will need your help also. I need your awareness of the value
of the sensation world to strengthen me against the prejudice that has
ruled me.*

Japanese Artist: *You only need to still yourself and call to me, and I will
respond. I will come back to you. (pp. 144–146)*

In this conversation with the part he called Japanese Artist, initially
another part interfered: "I have other considerations in life to worry
about." "[M]ust you do it all night???" Then Johnson's Self moved in closer,
without the interfering part. "I see that I will have to stand independent of
the [parts that value] productivity that surround and dominate me." "I am
getting interested in this creature." "I must make a place for you." Johnson
then easily discovered why the Japanese Artist part of him behaved the
way it did, what it wanted to add to Johnson's life, how to negotiate with
it, and how to reconnect with it later. As he did so, however, he began to
over-identify with the Japanese Artist and started to see his striving managers through the Artist's eyes — as all bad (negative masculine production
mentality). This illustrates how easily the Self gets pulled between one
side and another in a polarization.

Typically, either the IFS therapist has the client ask the part questions
and report the answers to the therapist, or the therapist directly questions
the part. These two basic ways of entering the internal system are *direct
access*, in which the therapist talks directly to a part or uses open-chair
technique to have parts talk to each other or the client's Self, and *in-sight*,
in which the client looks inside and describes the parts and their conversations to the therapist (Schwartz, 1995).

When using in-sight and working through the client's Self, the therapist
can ask the client how he feels toward a certain part (to ensure that other
parts are not interfering), why he thinks it behaves a certain way, how
often he hears from it, how much influence it has over him, and how he
would like the relationship to change. When the therapist talks directly

with the client's parts, the questions should ensure a *differentiated answer;* that is, the part has to speak about itself as *separate* from the client. This is accomplished by asking questions that focus on the relationship between the Self and the part. Note how this early conversation with the extreme part, Nicholas, permitted Nicholas to see himself as separate from Lorene:

Therapist: What is it that you say or do to Lorene?
Nicholas: I tell her, "You're evil, I will kill you tonight."
Therapist: What do you make Lorene think?
Nicholas: That she is bad and worthless, and that everything is hopeless.
Therapist: How do you feel towards Lorene?
Nicholas: I hate her!
Therapist: How do you think she feels towards you?
Nicholas: She'd like to get rid of me.
Therapist: Why do you tell her you'll kill her and that she's evil?
Nicholas: To keep her away from other people.

As the series of questions continues, the therapist slowly focuses Nicholas on the possibility that a non-extreme role might be available for him. This entails finding out what he is really afraid of and what he would prefer to do if his fears were eased. Note, too, how the therapist does not react to the part's extreme answers, but steadily pushes ahead with direct, non-confrontational questions.

Therapist: What is it that you really want for Lorene?
Nicholas: To die.
Therapist: Why?
Nicholas: Then I would be free.
Therapist: Free from what?
Nicholas: From guarding her so she'll stay away from other people.
Therapist: What are you afraid—
Nicholas: I'm never afraid!
Therapist: What are you afraid would happen if you stopped telling Lorene you'll kill her if she gets close to other people?
Nicholas: She'll let Alex and Destiny loose, and they'll have sex with everyone they can get their hands on.
Therapist: If Lorene could keep that from happening—
Nicholas: She can't.
Therapist: Yes, but if she could, would you be glad?
Nicholas: Of course.
Therapist: If you were relieved of your job of keeping Lorene distant from other people, what would you want to do instead?
Nicholas: I cannot do what you are asking. This is my job.
Therapist: I know, but if you could have a chance to do something else—?

Nicholas: More physical things outside with Dashiell, like running and biking.

Through this straightforward line of questioning, Nicholas was able (however briefly) to step away from his extreme role in which he threatens suicide if Lorene gets close to another person. The therapist did not demand that Nicholas stop his suicidal threats or reprimand him for sounding cold or cruel. The encounter remained non-judgmental on the therapist's part. The therapist kept his Self in the lead; he did not respond to Nicholas with his scared part ("Oh, please don't kill Lorene"), or his judgmental part ("That would be a crazy thing to do"), or his controlling part ("If you continue to make such threats, I will have to hospitalize you"), or his aloof part ("I see. Hmmm . . . ").

Eventually, the survivor is asked to use his or her Self to lead an internal discussion without the therapist's direct participation. At the early point, however, communication continues to pass through the therapist. For example, the therapist asked Lorene's Self if she would agree to a three-month moratorium on any sexual relations. The therapist returned to Nicholas and asked if that would be acceptable for a trial period. Through this process, Nicholas learned to trust the therapist's Self — and ultimately Lorene's Self. The Self began functioning as an internal leader. Here is an example of Lorene's Self asking questions of Nicholas:

Nicholas: If I can't fit in with Lorene's sister and mother, then I belong no place.
Self: The only place you need to belong, or fit, is here in this system. Once you feel safe here, you'll create your own safety wherever you are.
Nicholas: I am nothing. I have no worth without the family. I am only layers of pain.
Self: What would stop the pain?
Nicholas: If Lorene's Dad could love me, despite my past misdeeds and present faults.
Self: He is dead. What do you want for yourself now?
Nicholas: Some strength — a strong base. But I'll never have that.
Self: So you want to die?
Nicholas: Yes.
Self: What makes you stay alive?
Nicholas: I don't really know. It's so tenuous most days.

At the risk of overwhelming readers with the complex beauty of inner systems, we make one further comment about the above interchange. Each part has his or her own Self, which lies within a complete *sub*system. In other words, Nicholas has subparts and a Self. A part's Self differs from the client's overall Self in that it has a meta-perspective only of its own subsystem—not of the client's entire internal system. In the first conversation quoted above, the therapist encouraged Nicholas to be his Self, which would require Nicholas to be direct and honest. Instead of accepting a response like "I'll kill Lorene" or "I hate Lorene," the therapist probed for a more specific, honest answer to what Nicholas was afraid of and what he wanted Lorene to do. The therapist could even have asked Nicholas to separate from his extreme subparts and speak as his Self for a minute. Consider this example as one of Lorene's parts, Andy, refers to the Self in his *subsystem*:

Andy: I saw Dick today. It felt awful. I wish he didn't know my name, so he couldn't call me out. I told Dick I was so ashamed of myself, the things I participated in. I felt full of crying, but no tears came. Dick said he wants me to be able to cry! What a strange thing to say. I wonder what he meant. Who would want to cry? I told Dick I've never, ever felt safe. Dick was very stubborn today. He persistently made me keep returning to my Self. Whenever I left, saying I shouldn't bother him, or trying not to cry, or telling him I have no feelings at all—he'd remind me to come back, to trust him, to focus on his voice, to look at his eyes, to remember where I was. He asked me hard questions (do I trust him?) and I tried to be honest except when my Self would leave and subparts would take over. Then Dick would stubbornly bring me back again. I think it'll be easier next time.

Again, we don't wish to confuse readers with parts, subparts, Selves of parts, the Self of the person, and so on. We point it out only because it is sometimes helpful to work within one particular subsystem in the same way that the person's internal system is approached—by encouraging the parts (or subparts) to trust and follow the lead of the person's Self (or part's Self).

The therapist might also question one part about how the client's behavior would be different if the part did not take over. For example, without having to promise *not* to interfere, Nicholas (as his Self) might acknowledge that instead of sitting at home contemplating suicide, Lorene might be out bike riding if she were free of Nicholas' interference. Nicholas might further acknowledge, as his Self, that he would *prefer* the biking.

A series of questions seeks to identify factors that lock a part into its extreme role, what the part needs in order to leave that role, and what kind of role the part would prefer. The typical questions that an IFS therapist asks (see Schwartz, 1995, pp. 117–18) a client's part include:

- What is it that you [the part] say or do to Lorene [the client]?
- What do you try to make Lorene do or feel?
- Do you like Lorene?

- Do you think Lorene pays attention to you and treats you well?
- Why do you make Lorene feel frightened? Angry? Depressed?
- What is it that you really want for Lorene?
- What are you afraid would happen if you stopped acting extreme?
- If Lorene and I could keep other parts from doing what you fear, would you feel free to do something else that you would prefer?
- Could I help get you into a new role in which you could do things you prefer, instead of protecting Lorene from the dangers you perceive?

At the conclusion of a discussion with a client's part, the therapist might ask if the part wants to say anything to the client's Self or to the therapist. Also, she asks if other parts had extreme reactions. Finally, the therapist returns to talking to the client's Self and asks how the conversation was experienced. The client's Self may report reactions of other parts or note a tendency to blend with either the part or the part's internal adversaries.

The client can be asked to focus between sessions on a certain part and monitor when, where, and by whom it is activated, how the activated part affects her, and how well she can calm the part or get the part to separate from her Self. The client may also want to write in a journal about the kind of personality she thinks the part has, what the part's characteristics, interests, and opinions are, and how other parts feel about this part.

Putnam (1989) encourages the therapist to ask each personality which gender he or she is, how old he or she feels, what age the patient or the body was when the part first came out, and the part's function or role. (Age ranges can be significant because "personality systems composed largely of child and adolescent personalities seem to have different dynamics than do systems with more adult personalities" [p. 143].) After these initial introductions, the client and therapist go on to discover where each part lies within the system; the size, composition, and structure of the internal system; and the system's dynamics. This initial mapping is revised over time, as more parts emerge.

DIRECT ACCESS OR IN-SIGHT?

Putnam (1989) notes that, while some therapists believe they should refrain from working "directly with the alter personalities, in my experience this is not possible" (p. 141). IFS agrees that it is not possible to avoid direct work with parts of a survivor. Moreover, researchers have found no evidence that increased dissociation or impermeability of boundaries results from working directly with parts (Napier, 1993). What usually causes those problems is working with certain parts prematurely or ignoring basic IFS systemic concepts, particularly those dealing with the existence of a healthy Self. The question that remains, however, is what method of working with parts is most effective and safe.

IFS therapists find that with many survivors, the best method is direct access in which the therapist, using his or her Self, works directly with parts of the survivor. This is beneficial, at least initially, for a number of reasons. First, many people (particularly survivors of severe abuse) have parts who need to experience the therapist directly. Direct contact reassures the managerial parts that the therapist is competent, reassures the firefighter parts that the therapist is not out to usurp their powers, and reassures the child-like exiles that the therapist is caring. In some cases this reassurance can only be evoked when a part talks to the therapist directly. For example, an adult client may be quite uncomfortable asking questions like, "Do you like me?" or "Will you hurt me?" but very willing to allow a part to do so.

Second, abuse victims inevitably have parts who stopped trusting the survivor's Self long ago. Scared and extreme parts need access to someone's Self. During the time it takes to rebuild this trust, an IFS therapist uses direct access exclusively with some survivors so that the therapist's Self can act as the system's leader (Schwartz, 1995):

> Sometimes a client has been hurt or scared so badly in the past that the parts have very little trust in the Self. With such a client—for example a survivor of severe and chronic incest—the therapist may have to be the Self for the client's system at first. That is, when it becomes clear that a client's parts will not cooperate with the Self, I have learned that continuing to expect and insist that the Self take the lead frustrates all members of the system. I have found that if I talk directly to each part and help resolve polarizations among them ... then I can also gradually help the parts appreciate the leadership potential of the Self.
>
> Thus, I begin as the Self for the system and spend much of each session talking directly to one part or another, or having two parts talk to each other. (p. 124)

Using the therapist's Self as leader of the survivor's internal system may appear similar to techniques described in the MPD literature. In fact, Putnam (1989) warns that in treating MPD patients, the "therapist should not become a fixed part of the internal communication process, or the patient will be unable to maintain an internal dialogue in the therapist's absence" (p. 154). Perhaps the warning arises because much of the MPD literature has no comparable concept of the Self to whom leadership duties can be transferred in time. In the IFS model, as the parts begin to trust the therapist's Self, the therapist suggests—quietly, but firmly and repeatedly—that the client's parts can trust the client's Self. Increasingly, then, the therapist shifts responsibility to the client's Self, which is especially useful for work done between sessions.

As a client becomes accustomed to this form of communication between a Self (the therapist's, at first) and a part, the therapist can take a less directive stance, asking open questions such as, "How do you respond to what the part just said?" or "What needs to happen now?" In this way, the therapist tests whether the client's Self is ready to take over in a central position. If the therapist asks, "How do you feel about what Nicholas said?" and Lorene responds, "Get rid of that maniac!"—that isn't her Self. A response from her Self would sound something like, "I really don't want to get rid of Nicholas; those feelings come from other parts of me who are frightened by him."

A third advantage to direct access is that it offers the therapist and the client a unique and dramatic view of the inner parts and how they relate to each other. The therapist is often amazed to watch the client's shifts in tone of voice, posture, and movement, as different parts emerge. This physical concretization of the personality of each part is especially helpful to survivors in learning not to blend with the parts and how to recognize when one part has taken over the system. For example, Lorene recognizes that biting her nails means Destiny is present; sitting so still that she's hardly breathing means Vincent is there; and pacing around or slamming things down means Nicholas is front and center.

A fourth advantage of direct access is the ease with which it permits parts to speak and feel in a full-bodied way. They have waited a long, long time to receive permission to talk, yell, cry, explain what happened to them, describe how they've managed to survive, and utter their hopes. It may be particularly important for survivors who have dissociated many of their feelings and memories to have the therapist talk directly to the parts. Often, the client says things she didn't know she thought or remembered, which gives the part a chance to more fully express itself: "As the therapist interviews a part, the part itself is frequently surprised to learn what it feels or thinks. Parts often value these opportunities for *sanctioned external expression* [italics added] and feel better understood by and connected to the listener" (Schwartz, 1995, p. 125). The sanctioned external expression often breathes life back into a part who has suffered dreadfully in its isolation. Simply listening to the part garners for the therapist an enormous amount of trust and commitment to the collaborative effort.

There are also disadvantages to direct access. It is necessarily less efficient than in-sight, since it takes a great deal more time to speak individually with each part and later switch to other parts for their reactions and more work. For survivors with very extreme parts who may have been hidden for years, it can also be dangerous to use direct access initially. Some of these hidden parts are not ready to speak—or the protector parts are not ready to give the hidden ones free access. For example, Schwartz (1992) wrote about Marcia's initial encounter with her five-year-old, bleeding, frail part. By failing to deal with the managers and firefighters before moving in too closely to this part, Schwartz lost all contact with the five-year-old simply by suggesting that Marcia envision bandaging the wounds:

> I asked her to imagine approaching that little girl to carefully wash and dress her wounds. In response to that directive, Marcia immediately closed herself off from me. She looked at me stonily and insisted she could no longer see anything, and had no more thoughts about it. For the remainder of the session, she remained detached, polite, and totally inaccessible. (p. 34)

Schwartz found that he could not access Marcia's five-year-old bleeding part until he dealt with the managers and firefighters who protected her. It is an IFS truism that when you access one part, others are not far behind. Beahrs (1982) reminds the therapist to always be aware that "there are multiple consciousnesses listening in on what we are saying, whether we are directing our words to them or not; how these are reacting can often be presumed by observation of nonverbal responses to our communication. Spontaneous body movements which are incongruent with the patient's words are communication from a patient at a different level" (p. 123).

The exiled young part of Marcia was banished for a reason. To suddenly release her, ignoring other parts, invites extreme reactions within the system. If the survivor insists on working with an exile or firefighter, the therapist should find the parts who are afraid and work with them first. Otherwise, the contact may trigger alcohol binges, self-mutilation, and other dangerous behavior. As detailed in later chapters, the key therapeutic responses are *protection* and *validation*: helping the protector parts understand that the survivor will be kept safe, and that the protector parts will be taken seriously.

When the therapist indicates that it is time to end the session, the part contacted during the hour may refuse to relinquish control to let the Self return. While this reaction may startle or frighten therapist and client, it is not typically dangerous. If possible, the therapist can ask the part why it wants to remain in control. But if the part remains obstinate, it is better to avoid attempts to coerce the part into relinquishing control. The client can then leave with that part in charge. The obstinate part, however, may simply be terrified to *leave* the therapist, fearing that the session was make-believe, that the abuser is lurking outside the therapist's office, or that the pain and sadness experienced during the session will become all-engulfing. If the therapist senses this intense underlying fear (even if the part *sounds* demanding, cold, and quite strong), the therapist should briefly reassure the part that the client's Self will be available to help and the therapist will still be there next week (or whatever guidelines they have developed for helping the client feel safe between sessions). Often this fear can be anticipated and the reassurance given as a matter of course.

CHAPTER 9

Differentiating the Self

By withdrawing the feeling of "I" from these "people" inside us . . . we begin to change. . . . Self-observation is the knife that begins to separate, to remove, what you take as you from what is real.

—Brian Lancaster, 1991

THE IFS THERAPIST TRIES to differentiate the client's Self as quickly as possible, because the Self ultimately acts as the therapist to the internal family by mediating between polarized antagonists and by restructuring relationships among all the parts. As described in the previous chapter, in the room technique used by Schwartz, after the client has placed a part in a room while her Self remains outside the room, the therapist asks the client how she feels toward the part in the room. If she feels anything extreme toward it (anger, envy, intense sadness, fear, hopelessness), she is asked to find the part who is outside the room with her and who is influencing her to have extreme feelings toward the original part. She asks this second part to separate from her and to move into another room so that it does not interfere with the Self's ability to see clearly and work with the original part. The client may have to separate her Self from several parts before the Self can speak to one part uncontaminated by leakage from other parts.

The room technique derives from the boundary violation principles. When two internal family members (perhaps a firefighter and a manager) encounter difficulties in their interaction, it is due to the interference of a third family member (perhaps another managerial part), who interrupts by making snide comments or taking sides so as to violate the boundary surrounding the original two parts. The technique of boundary-making was developed by structural family therapists (Schwartz, 1995). It involves simply asking the interfering person to not interfere, to respect the boundary around the dyad.

When the Self is standing outside the imagined room, preparing to talk to a part who is in the room, sometimes an interfering part refuses to leave the Self's side. The client must then work with that part before turning to the original part waiting in the room. The interfering part's refusal to leave may indicate that it has important information, perhaps warning the client and therapist that their planned intervention would be dangerous. In that case, the interfering part must be direct and respectful if the therapist and client are expected to hear the warning. Lorene frequently fought to keep her Self in a position of leadership, even as parts attempted to overcome her with powerful feelings:

Self: *I know parts of me are frightened because more memories are surfacing. Who is so scared?*

Alex: *Well, it's not a bad idea to skip this abuse memory garbage. Why don't you guys get off my back? I really hate that therapist you have.*

Self: *You hate him, but you don't hate Dad, who molested me?*

Alex: *No. Dad needed me and loved me.*

Self: *Alex, why are you fighting the memories other parts are revealing?*

Alex: *If you talk about it in therapy, Dick will be repulsed. Or worse, he might be kind and friendly. I only want someone to be nice if they're also going to hurt me.*

Self: *I know it's hard, Alex, but at least you're being direct and open. It's very unlike you to not calculate everything before even speaking. I'll help you while we're working with new memories. No matter how frightened you get, I will be here, unchanged.*

In this example, the interfering part (Alex) was able to be direct because of the respect shown by Lorene's Self. This respect greatly facilitates the Self's success in convincing parts to trust in its leadership.

In seeking the Self, the goal is to help the client find the place within from which she can reach out and connect with all the parts and listen to their fears and hopes, instead of a place chosen by only the dominant parts. One of the most empowering discoveries of the IFS model is that, once differentiated in this way, the Self is able to change its relationship with the parts and help them change relative to each other. The feeling of compassion or curiosity that the Self feels toward parts seems to be universal. Thus, if the Self is trying to work with a part, but feels strong emotions and thoughts thrust at her, other parts are interfering and the Self has not been successfully differentiated. Schwartz (1995) explains: "The key indication of differentiation is the person's response to the question 'How do you feel toward the part?' If the client's Self is separate from the influence of interfering parts, the answer will reflect qualities of the Self, both in content and tone of voice" (p. 116). Lancaster (1991) describes a similar technique, where the core essence of a person is separated from the "various aspects":

> Consider the nature of your "self." As you attempt to specify its nature, you will, no doubt, bring various aspects to mind. The exercise is one of detaching from each of these aspects in turn. What remains as you strip them away? Is there some core you can experience beyond the various aspects you have specified? . . . It is possible to strip away all the aspects (and more) mentioned above. Eventually you will be left with the feeling of "I." Not this or that aspect, just a feeling which cannot be put into words. And then . . . awareness. Simple Being. (p. 82)

Gilligan and Kennedy (1989) explain a similar concept derived from their work using hypnosis with incest survivors: "Trance is learned as an opportunity to set aside nagging 'internal chatter' and achieve a state of 'psychophysical centering' involving a somatic and psychological sense of well-being. We emphasize repeatedly that individuals can return to this state of inner security to access a sense of safety and self-protection" (p. 10). M. Watkins (1986) describes a narrator who has some similarities to the IFS concept of Self: "The narrator's position is like the one I described for the therapist. He or she has less of an investment in any particular character over another, and is more interested in the unfolding of the drama between the characters. The narrator is an observing presence who can reflect on and mediate between the other characters" (p. 154).

Similarly, the IFS model uncovers a Self who reflects and mediates, who sits in the place where people experience strong connections to each other and to the world. Schwartz (1995) writes:

> I consistently found that if I asked a client to separate from extreme and polarized parts in this way, most of them could shift quickly into a compassionate or curious state of mind. In that state, they often knew just what to do to help their parts. It seemed that at the core, everyone contained a state of mind that was well suited to leadership. It was through this boundary-making, differentiating process that I encountered what people called their "true self" or "core Self." This Self felt different to them from their parts. I later discovered that some other approaches described a state of mind like this Self. Generally, however, these approaches saw it as a passive, nonjudgmental observer or witness, in the tradition of Eastern religions, rather than as an active, compassionate leader. (p. 37)

Lorene described her first experience of her Self, with no parts interfering, with joy and amazement:

Self: *I found it!! I have a living core of strength within me—it's incredible! It radiates through me. I knew I had the colors of life radiating through some parts of me, but I did not know—I really didn't know there was a source for the colors of life—and the source is in me! I am not dead. Is* *this the big secret my parts have been protecting? Hiding my own life energy in a dark, still place, so it would not be consumed by the destruction of my childhood?*

Therapists sometimes fail to recognize the interference of parts who are preventing the Self from leading. Some of the common causes of interference are: the client's sudden loss of the image of a part, sudden distraction from the work during a session, or impatience with the therapist (Schwartz, 1995, p. 117). Unrecognized interference is signalled, for example, by the client's insistence that a part is correct in its extreme position. The therapist then must ask the client to identify the part who is creating the interference and find out the part's reasons. The therapist can also look within to determine if the interference is coming from the therapist's own parts (see chapter 19).

PARTS LEARNING TO TRUST THE SELF

When differentiating the Self, the therapist and client must work with extreme parts who fight the differentiation. It is essential to the healing process that the client's parts gradually learn to trust the Self. Particularly with a survivor of severe childhood abuse, the parts have not trusted the Self for a very long time. Lorene's much-needed Self was often hidden behind over-protective parts who insisted that the Self needed to be kept from the vulnerable position of leader. These parts saw danger everywhere, experienced many people as being unpredictably threatening, and were convinced that the pathway through daily life was a treacherous one. In the following example, Lorene's Self initially deals effectively with an extreme part (Nicholas), but then begins to retreat:

Nicholas: *Stop pretending that everything will be okay. Just take your tranquillizer again and let me hide in it. My brain is going to split wide open and all the crazy devils will spill out.*

Self: *Nicky, I need to gain some balance. I can't go on flipping in and out of extreme states every few hours. I have to carefully limit any external stimuli so you won't go completely crazy. Please let me finish this work in therapy.*

Nicholas: *Why can't you just ignore me?*

Self: *Sometimes I wish I could. You've exhausted me. Try to rest.*

Nicholas: *Impossible! The pain inside of me is so intense. I have to make it stop. I have to!*

Self: *I know, but you're smothering me. If I can't breathe, I can't help you.*

Despite the good intentions of parts who guard the Self, they must learn to step back and let the Self lead. The survivor pays too high a price when a part leads for very long. To help parts learn to trust the Self as a leader, the Self needs to become familiar with its own qualities. The thera-pist and client can create a context in which the Self can be accessed quickly and feel its ability to pilot the internal system, know that it can persevere longer than any part, re-establish harmony after a part has taken over, and re-explore its abilities whenever a part does take over the system.

For example, Nicholas protected Lorene's Self by keeping it separate from the young, exiled Jenny. Nicholas wanted to ensure that the Self did not blend with Jenny. He often displayed a tough, macho image and threatened to harm Lorene if she permitted Jenny to directly express her fears or her memories of the abuse. Over time, Lorene's Self learned to prevail in a conflict such as this:

Nicholas: *I'll cut up your arms and stomach if you keep asking Jenny to talk about her sadness in therapy. I'll go find a man to rape you. I'll cause chaos everywhere.*

Self: *Your dramatic statements scare parts of me, but even if you succeed in doing one of these things, I'll keep going, Nicholas. I'll be slow and careful with Jenny and not scare her, and I'll keep going.*

Nicholas: *I'll kill you!*

Self: *Nicholas, you can cut my body, burn my body, show me horrible images, and isolate me from my friends and family. Sometimes I can't deal with you directly, because you can out-smart me, out-argue me, out-maneuver me. So I fight back by doing things that are good for me to show other parts that I do exist and can act. I stand up for myself at work, take vitamins and exercise, go on new job interviews, buy healthy food. I know there are some things I can't do as well without you, but I'm going to keep moving steadily and slowly in the direction that I keep in my sights.*

With practice, the Self learns to face the most frightening tactics used by parts and continue on with certainty and trust in its own existence and goals. The parts, in turn, begin trusting the Self and respecting its ability to lead. The Self must earn this respect by steadfastly trying to remain in a leadership role. Although the Self can delegate functions, the parts will soon look to the Self for ultimate leadership. Initially, this arrangement might sound impossible to many survivors, but it is achieved through repeated practice in locating the Self.

If left to the discretion of the parts, the job of protecting and hiding the Self until no danger exists would be endless. These parts cling to their roles as bodyguards and protectors, acting like a mother who still walks her 12-year-old child to school, holding his hand crossing streets. It is helpful if the Self can convince key parts that it no longer needs that level of protec-tion. Parts are quite aware that the Self is not a part, but a different entity altogether. They know the Self *should* be the leader. They aren't sure, however, that the Self can be trusted alone at the helm just yet without their protection. As the parts observe the Self effectively handling stressful situations such as a new job, a welcome divorce, a fight with a friend, or the therapist's vacation, they learn to trust the Self. Parts express great relief when they relinquish the role of Self-protector, which in turn releases the Self's ability to communicate respect and caring to each part. Despite their loyalty to the Self, the parts can feel very little caring or love from the Self as long as they over-protect it.

In IFS therapy, the client learns to differentiate the Self and intervene in negative power displays in several ways. For example, the Self learns to stand firm and refuse to accede to a part's ideas or plans to self-mutilate or to inappropriately sexualize a relationship, without condemning the part. Lorene records her Self's reflections:

Alexandra had a tantrum today, demanding that I admit that Dick was only pretending to help, that he thrived on adoration and was trying to force Alex into revering him, that he just calls it "trust," and that the work he's done with me so far is no big deal. Alex said that she refuses to act like she needs him or trusts him, and that she could get along fine without therapy.

I asked Alex why she's so defensive about needing Dick. She says Jenny's blatant and undisguised requests for his support ("I wish you could help me," or "I wish you weren't going away") are embarrassing. I gently told Alex to leave Jenny alone. That's between Jen and Dick, and Alex needn't worry about it. Alex didn't answer, but she's been quiet and calm. Nicholas started laughing at Alex's failure to convince me that Dick is a fraud, but I told him to back off.

BLENDING

As noted earlier, problems arise when extreme feelings and thoughts blend with the Self for extreme purposes. For example, when the managers or firefighters fear that the Self will permit the young exiled parts to reveal secrets, they (managers or firefighters) might take control of the system by blending with the Self. Ironically, sometimes what the managers and firefighters *fear* is blending—but they fear the blending of the Self with *exiles* (instead of with protector parts). They fear that the exile's disclosure of secrets will release that part's intense emotions, which will overwhelm the Self and cause the exile and the Self to blend, such that the survivor becomes mired in pain and despair.

There are several reasons why managers and firefighters might be so afraid of a young exiled part blending with the Self (Schwartz, 1995, p. 100). The blending might overwhelm the Self with the young part's fear to the point that the entire system feels horribly vulnerable. The Self suddenly feels just as scared, sad, or young as the vulnerable part. The Self can no longer offer comfort or reassurance to any of the parts. In addition, the protectors fear that the exiles (unrestrained due to the Self's blending) may put the survivor in danger by rushing into relationships and getting abused or rejected. Also, the release of the exiles often triggers chaotic destruction by the firefighters, perhaps releasing their rage, threatening to hurt the survivor or other people. Moreover, the Self's blending with exiles may cause a manager or firefighter to leap in and shut down the system in order to punish the survivor, or distance her from the therapist. Firefighters may also explode with impulsive behaviors.

Why do the exiles insist on trying to blend with the Self? They may blend in order to rid themselves of the feelings that bind them, or to let the Self know what they have suffered. Or, they are looking for an external person to care for or redeem them. Finally, they may fear being exiled again by managers as soon as they give up the control they gained through the blending process. It is important to teach the young parts that their need to blend is understandable, but that they are upsetting the entire system and undermining the Self's ability to provide them with a caring, safe environment. If the child-like parts can refrain from blending, the Self can help them, and the managers won't be so fearful of them. While these hurt parts might have trouble believing that the Self can help them, often they can be convinced to at least give it a try. Schwartz (1995) describes the process further:

> The therapist asks the client's Self first to ask the managers not to interfere, and then to approach a child-like part but stop where the Self begins to feel overwhelmed by the part's feelings. Sometimes the child part is cooperating to such an extent that the Self can get very close and even hold the part immediately. More often, the Self has to stop several times and remind the part not to overwhelm it before they can become close. Sometimes this takes more than one session.
>
> Throughout this process, the managers should be consulted as to how they think things are going. They also should be encouraged to let the therapist or the client's Self know if they become highly concerned. If managers are shown this kind of respect, they can become cooperative consultants who give advice and monitor the pace. Thus, the IFS model views what has been traditionally called "resistance" as the managerial parts' often valid fears about people entering their delicate system. They do not resist, and can help, if they are respected and are convinced that the therapist knows how to work safely. (pp. 100–101)

Initially, the survivor's Self might assert its leadership for a while — but then, inevitably, it blends again. The survivor feels as if the Self has collapsed with fatigue, when extreme parts, with their seemingly limitless energy, take over. Lorene often found that she could differentiate her Self, begin to lead with it, but would then falter and finally blend with a part, giving in to its intense emotions:

Tonight I checked in with my parts. Destiny is terrified and hiding. Nicholas hates Destiny—her name, her feelings, her crying, the problems she causes when she remembers things about the past. Vincent seems hard, inflexible, determined not to go ahead with plans to work with Destiny's memories. Feeling very hurt and alone.

Jennifer is nervous, hanging around Alex. Alex is voting with Nicholas to stop taking my medication and see what happens, just to make the present changes somehow—even if it changes for the worse. Super-She and Dashiell don't seem too involved, perhaps because of Vincent's firm stance. Me? I'm tired. I remember to comfort Destiny, reassure her that I am going ahead with her "memory confrontation." I tell Destiny I'll take care of her, that I am separate from her. It helps to remind her that the terror is hers—not mine. That helps calm her more than anything. But Vincent's holding back makes me drag my feet. I feel like I don't really want to listen to Destiny. I don't want to know why she's sad, what she remembers.

It's very hard for me to shut out Nicholas' hatred speeches and Vincent's stubborn refusal to change things. This in turn gives Alex more room to manipulate everyone, including me—her manipulations seem tame, and preferable to Nicholas' and Vincent's cold demands. The truth is that I'm all alone in a terrifying place. What I've always told the parts—that I'll be there for them, my strength as the "Self" is sufficient—has proved to mean nothing.

It is not an easy task to convince parts to stop blending with the Self. This process of struggling to locate and maintain Self leadership takes patience, courage, and practice, especially for survivors who have such highly protective systems. The therapist's unwavering belief that the client does indeed have a Self often provides the safety net for those painful struggles. A part's insistent blending with the Self constrains the part from exploring its valuable place in the system, from interacting freely with other parts, and from receiving any consistent type of care or support from the Self. (This type of blending occurs when desperate parts carry extreme burdens—it is not the type of appropriate sharing that occurs when the Self controls the timing and extent of blending.)

If the Self respectfully asks a part to stop "leaking" its feelings, but the part does not comply, the Self may be forced to keep some distance from the part until it agrees not to overwhelm the Self with its emotions. Johnson (1986) describes this problem: "If an attitude comes roaring out of your unconscious that will destroy your practical existence, hurt your relationship with your family, cause trouble for you at your job, or get you into power struggles with everyone, then you have both the duty and the right to answer back, to present the ethical alternative" (p. 193). With practice, Lorene learned to remain separate from her parts and maintain her Self leadership, even in the face of extreme terror by parts:

Nicky is physically going crazy. Internal organs pulsating, trying to get out of body. I'm terrified—no!—he's terrified. Pure physical terror. Hours of terror. He slept for a while, but on and on the cycle continues. I wake again, hold my hands on my chest, helping Nicky breathe. Vincent helps. It's better for a few minutes. Nicky still crying sometimes. I keep reassuring him that I'll take care of him. Nicky talks about something awful. What? Even Vincent cries.

I think that I've taken away all Nicky's false strength and I can't figure out how to help him find a more natural, real strength. Nicky feels sick all the time, shaking, teeth chattering, then hot and sweating, my pulse beating way too fast so I think he'll explode. Sometimes I have Nicky search himself for signs of strength, but he's very exhausted. I don't know if he can survive this physically. I need help working with Nicky. If he wants to try and work, I want to give him the chance. But I have to think of something to do to help him. I'll let him talk to Dick and then we can think through the alternatives.

Particularly in abused systems, it is necessary to intercede repeatedly in the lightning-quick blending in order to help the Self return to its natural position of leadership. Don't assume that the process is complete once the Self is differentiated. On the contrary, differentiation will have to be done again—a few minutes or a few weeks later. Therapists can teach clients how to differentiate the Self alone, at first for short periods of time, and later for longer periods, as they learn to master this vital skill of reassuring parts that it is safe to separate. One of the most important recent discoveries in the IFS model is that a part can control the release of its emotions in a way that allows the Self to get close without being overwhelmed by (blending with) the part's emotions. The part must first believe it is in his best interest to contain his feelings within his own boundaries. This is not easy because blending often feels good. It is similar to people who are angry or depressed wanting more than sympathy from friends—they want the friends to share to the point that they also are angry or depressed. (Hence the saying, "misery loves company.") This type of leaking of one's emotions over to another person might serve to release or dissipate the emotion, or prove the person justified in feeling the particular emotion in the first place.

In order to convince parts to stop blending, the person can teach the parts that blending will ultimately do nothing to solve the underlying problem. Blending rarely changes whatever originally triggered the intense emotional reaction from the parts. The person can also explain that, while blending does make parts feel they have a kindred spirit, that they are not so alone, it ultimately leaves them even more isolated. Blending is a way to disown or give away the emotion, a way to get attention or help, a demand ("Fix me now!"), and a way to make the part into a non-entity (by erasing their boundaries they become nothing). Whatever the reason why parts blend, there is a common denominator: They are all attempts to go beyond the part's own boundaries. It is an intimate connection of sorts, but very twisted and ultimately not comforting for long. But they do not try to cross the boundaries by *connecting*; instead, they become "shape-shifters," trying to melt and change their own basic form.

CHAPTER 10

Depolarizing

[A survivor's parts] are scared of each other and con-
vinced that they must annihilate the other in order to
survive. The paradox is that they cannot live without
each other. If some communication can be established
... then they can work out a compromise so that they
can work together rather than against each other.

—*Kathy K. Swink & Antoinette E. Leveille, 1986*

WHEN ONE PART STEADFASTLY refuses to move from an extreme position, the survivor will usually find an opposing part in an equally
extreme position. The two parts (or groups of parts) noisily combat each
other. Each proves to be a formidable opponent. When one antagonizes
the other, the opponent returns fire from an equally uncompromising
position. The unseen polarization frustrates the therapist, who patiently
works with one part only to find that the opponent has become activated.
The central truism of polarization theory is that one part cannot change in
isolation if the change is to endure.

Because the polarization of the parts drains valuable inner resources,
the client teams with the therapist and works to return these parts to a
non-extreme state that immediately calms both of the warring parts. In the
following example of a longstanding polarization, a manager wants Lorene
to start a new job where she will earn more money and have more interesting duties, but a firefighter sees this as a dangerous move where young
exiled parts will be exposed to strangers. The manager (Vincent) and the
firefighter (Alex) argue:

Alex: *You can't have control of anything. I'll cut your face off and make*
you so sick you'll die. I'll stop you and stop you and stop you. I won't go

to the new job. NO!! I declare war. And I'll win. Now you are The Enemy.

Vincent: Alex, I want to do this. Let me make my own choices.

Alex: I hate what you're doing. Enemy!

Vincent: Is there no way to do this? I've tried everything. I try to work with other parts, but I keep running into you.

Alex: You cannot go there. It is not safe. Stop pretending—you'll never be normal.

Vincent: Why are you doing this? Lorene might not survive another internal siege.

Alex: I will do anything to stop you.

Vincent: Does Andy seem better to you?

Alex: HE SHOULD NOT BE BETTER!

Vincent: Does this work with Dick and Andy scare you?

Alex: I DON'T EVEN ACKNOWLEDGE DICK OR WHAT YOU DO THERE NOW. I WILL NEVER LET YOU START THAT JOB.

Vincent: Perhaps I'm not ready. Maybe I shouldn't go.

Alex: YOU'LL NEVER GO. I WILL KILL YOU FIRST!

Vincent: Can't you let Lorene keep you safe, and then I'll go?

Alex: NEVER! Don't forget for one minute that I'm in control. You cannot choose. You are too bad.

Vincent: Let me choose. My judgment is good. My choices are good. I had hoped the war was over.

Alex: The war is over when you give up.

Vincent: I want to have a body, like Andy and Nicholas.

Alex: NO NO NO BODY!

Vincent: Trust me.

Alex: What a worthless, stupid request.

As Alex and Vincent butt heads, their frustration and antagonism increase. They see no resolution and Lorene becomes paralyzed—should she start the new job or not? Indecision and emotional chaos reign. It is not unusual for clients to have parts who refuse to speak to each other. "By adulthood the host is often not on speaking terms with many of the alters and is terrified and tormented by the voices. [The therapist must] re-establish dialogue in the personality system" (Putnam, 1989, p. 153).

Before trying to disrupt a longstanding polarization, it is important to remember that extreme parts do not enjoy their extreme roles. They would rather engage in their preferred activities. Why do they leave preferred roles to take extreme positions? Usually out of fear. Parts may have remained functional in extreme roles for so long that they are afraid there is nothing else they can do. Some parts fear that they will be punished (by other parts) if they abdicate. If one part backs down, the parts opposing will take over and make the person extreme in the opposite direction.

IDENTIFYING THE POLARIZATION

The interaction between polarized parts resembles two people on a children's teeter-totter. If they refuse to recognize each other, the polarization cannot be resolved. For example, whenever Lorene's part Andy indicates that he wants to reveal a secret in therapy, he is effectively blocked by Super-She, who looks in the opposite direction loudly repeating, "Everything's Fine! Everything's Fine!" (See figure 10.1.) Thus, if a manager takes one extreme position (at one end of the teeter-totter), and another part opposes the manager, neither can safely step off. If one steps off, the other will crash to the ground.

In order to reorganize a clashing internal relationship it is necessary to have the parts communicate with each other (or with the person's Self) so that eventually each part can be brought closer to a middle position. If one part retreats a step, so will the other. If they cooperate, a balance can be maintained. If, however, one part wants to get off the teeter-totter, it cannot safely do so by itself. Whether the opposing parts blindly stare in opposite directions (figure 10.1), or face off in a bitter confrontation (figure 10.2), they cannot reach steadier ground unless they each move forward, inch-by-inch, towards the middle of the teeter-totter, where balance can be maintained and they can both climb down safely.

Often the two polarized parts can be identified by asking one part what would happen if it gave up its extreme position. To convey how parts cannot change in isolation and often become less extreme only when assured that their opposing part will also become less extreme, Schwartz (Breunlin et al., 1992) borrows a metaphor from Watzlawick, Weakland, and Fisch (1974), and reapplies it to internal family systems dynamics:

> If two sailors are leaning out on opposite sides of a boat and trying to keep it balanced, one of them is not going to move in unilaterally, because of the realistic fear that the boat will capsize. The sailors can move in only together

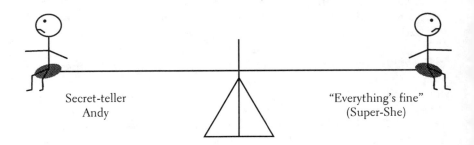

Figure 10.1. Polarized parts refuse to recognize each other's existence.

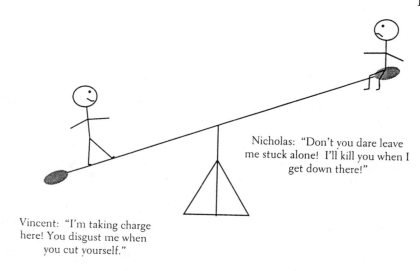

Nicholas: "Don't you dare leave me stuck alone! I'll kill you when I get down there!"

Vincent: "I'm taking charge here! You disgust me when you cut yourself."

Figure 10.2. Polarized parts vie for control.

and will not do so unless a trusted leader can ensure such coordination. Before the sailors move in—while they are both still leaning out in opposite directions (polarized)—they are stuck in their extreme positions. They cannot move freely around the boat and must counter each other's every move. Once they both move in, they are both free to do what they want to do on the boat, regardless of the other's behavior. This is the difference between rigidity of any polarized system (family, corporation), in which all parts occupy extreme, opposed positions, and the flexibility and freedom of a harmonious system, in which all parts have a much wider range of roles. (p. 82)

USING FAMILY THERAPY TECHNIQUES TO END INTERNAL WARS

Johnson (1986) describes an inner negotiation technique he calls horse-trading as a "blatant process of bargaining with the inner parts of oneself so that some agreements can be reached and life can proceed" (p. 200). Internal Family System theory develops this idea further, using family therapy techniques to work with the embittered internal adversaries. The goal is to clarify and strengthen the *boundaries* around each part and to improve the Self's leadership within the system:

Schwartz found that when he tried to get a client to interact with one part (we'll call it part A), frequently another part or parts that were polarized with A would interfere by making the client feel something extreme about part A—perhaps fear, anger, envy, or hopelessness. To counter this, Schwartz asked clients to find the interfering parts and get them to stop interfering, much as a family therapist gets interfering family members to respect a boundary around a family subsystem. Most clients could do this and when they did their perception of part A, which had been extreme, suddenly shifted to compassion for or curiosity about part A. (Nichols & Schwartz, 1991, p. 503)

Once an agreement to meet has been secured, the therapist and the client's Self can bring the warring parts together. The Self should set the tone with a prefacing remark such as, "I know you both have in common that you want something good for all of us; you just differ in what it is or how to get it." Or, "Your battles are unnecessary and self-defeating. I want you to talk about how you can help each other or at least get along differently" (Schwartz, 1995, p. 121). In this way, the Self acts as the internal family's therapist, while the therapist becomes an observing co-therapist who concentrates on ensuring that the client's Self remains differentiated.

At a depolarization meeting, the Self asks the parts how they would like their relationship to change. Frequently they express the wish for a dramatic reversal. For example, a critical manager who hated a child-exile might become a role model for the young part. Slowly, more parts are brought into these meetings to explore their previous relationships and alliances and to identify when and why they formed destructive coalitions or used each other as scapegoats. In this way, meeting individually with each part in polarized internal systems "gradually changes to dyadic therapy with two parts, which in turn becomes internal group or family therapy" (Schwartz, 1995, p. 121).

The initial meeting may be successful or it may result in no change at all. If no change occurs, it is often because the Self first needs to work with one or both parts *separately*. Each part must be encouraged to listen respectfully to the other part. Soon the parts learn to trust the process, and ultimately to trust the Self, so that it is no longer necessary for the two antagonists to be extreme in the presence of each other.

The Self plays a key role in depolarization. The more highly polarized the system, the more important it is to ask each part if it would be willing to talk to its antagonist in the presence of the Self. "The Self can reassure each that he or she can keep the other from becoming disrespectful or hurtful. . . . The Self can also tell each part what he or she has learned about the other's real nature, and can describe how much better things could be for each part if it could get along with the other" (Schwartz, 1995, p. 121).

POLARIZATIONS AND
TELLING SECRETS

One of the most extreme types of polarization occurs when exiled parts attempt to tell their story of the abusive place where they are stuck in time.

Jenny: Mom won't come. I call her and call her inside my head. Even when she comes home later, she won't love me. I'm all alone forever and ever and ever. Trapped in this body that I don't want to feel anymore.

Other parts inevitably react in strong ways to this vulnerability and desperate neediness. Consider Nicholas' crude response to Jenny's aloneness:

Nicholas: That's the most disgusting rot I've ever heard! Your groveling embarrasses all of us. Why don't you go hide your putrid fears, far away from the rest of us.

As the exiled child-parts remain emotionally isolated the past, they desperately seek opportunities to tell their stories. The client starts experiencing flashbacks, nightmares, and fleeting sensations of terror. Like abandoned children, the exiles search endlessly for a person who will care for, love, rescue, and redeem them. Unfortunately, other parts object, knowing that the child-like parts often will pay virtually any price for the smallest amount of love or redemption. (See figure 10.3.) Yet these exiles must be allowed to tell their "experiences and not be questioned, disbelieved, or denied. . . . The child inside is terrified, so [the client] must listen, allow the memories to come through, and encourage the child to believe that she is now safe" (Blake-White & Kline, 1985, pp. 397–98).

Before listening to the stories that each part has to tell, it is important to check with other parts who insist that silence be kept at all costs. Therapists and survivors learn that managers and firefighters legitimately

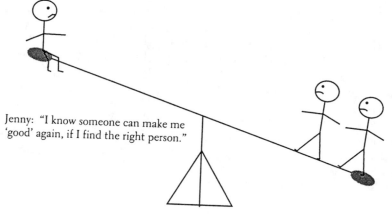

Jenny: "I know someone can make me 'good' again, if I find the right person."

Victor and Nicholas: "We'll leave you up there, abandoned, if you keep searching for a savior and humiliating us."

Figure 10.3. Ganging up on a part

fear the release of either the exiled parts. The Self can speak directly—slowly and carefully—to the younger, exiled parts. Protectors (either managers or firefighters) may try to interfere. Firefighters are especially quick to ring the blaring alarm and leap to attention, ready to block the secret-telling. Beahrs (1982) warns that when making contact with a part, allowing him to be heard, the therapist must remember that other parts may become terrified. "To suddenly have a hypermanic, apparently powerful, and grandiose competitor banging at the door of the self is terrifying, to say the least, especially when the primary self fears, not without reason, that the secondary might get the whole personality into great difficulties by his or her aberrant behavior" (p. 122). Managers and firefighters, then, have varying reasons why the secrets should be kept. They most typically fear that the Self or the whole system cannot handle the information. Because the person might blend with intensely emotional parts activated by the memories, the protectors might even believe they must conceal the identity of the abuser. They also fear that everyone—especially the therapist—will discover that the client's true nature is evil and repulsive. They will be abandoned once again. Protector parts also may fear being forced to give up certain relationships or being forced to give up all hope for redemption.

Interestingly, the manager parts may agree to permit secrets to leak out, but only at a pace set and monitored by them. They function as internal censors or regulators of intense emotions, thus controlling the discharge of any emotions and the accompanying memories. The managers' advice on the pacing of disclosing secrets should be considered carefully.

Swink and Leveille (1986) describe the resolution of polarizations involving the young parts. As the survivor "nurtures herself, she listens to her little girl within. Previously she has hated and feared this powerful child, convinced that if she loosened the reins, she would run wild. As she grows closer to her little girl, she can forgive her for needing and enjoying the attention given along with the abuse, she can accept the child's feelings, needs, strengths and creativity" (p. 137). Polarization principles help the survivor and therapist understand that some *parts* made the survivor feel that she hated and feared this inner child, while other parts insisted that loosening the reins would cause the child to run wild. As with most polarizations, once these opposing parts are identified and separated, the Self is free to express compassion, curiosity, and acceptance; this, in turn, facilitates the Self's role in resolving the polarization.

CHAPTER 11

Disarming Firefighters

They are the keepers of pain and rage, [who] free up the "good" personalities to function.

—*Frank Putnam, 1989*

EFFECTIVELY DISARMING firefighters of their destructive power always proves exciting and challenging. Extreme firefighters frighten all parts with devilish intensity. Unlike the managers, who struggle against directly experiencing any emotions, firefighters are convinced they must constantly display their explosive feelings in order to release internal volcanic pressures. Firefighters show no hesitation in lashing out abusively at other parts or people. They can be alarming and noxious to the internal system. Yet to disarm firefighters does not mean to humiliatingly strip them of power or force them to surrender weapons they believe symbolize their only value in life. Instead, with great respect for their heroism and unreserved commitment to their perceived role, we ask firefighters to join in a redirection of their inherently valuable powers: "The first step is to treat the demon respectfully and diplomatically, conveying at least the therapist's permission to exist as a legitimate part and asking what that part would really like to have happen if everything could go his way" (Beahrs, 1982, p. 127).

Given the destructive capabilities of firefighters, therapists and survivors often struggle ineffectively to handle these "demons" and "persecutors." For example, therapists may attempt to *restrain* firefighters in whatever way necessary (drugs, hospitalization, hypnotic suggestion), *eliminate* them (through fusion or exorcism), *reason* with them ("she's an adult now and no longer needs your protection from child abuse"), *punish* the firefighters (by blocking access to other parts they enjoy communicating with, or physical activities they enjoy, or access to the therapist), or simply *bribe* them ("Let me work now and you can get drunk later"). Before exploring which methods IFS finds most helpful, we look at methods which we believe only perpetuate firefighters' frustration and estrangement from the internal family.

TECHNIQUES THAT OFTEN FAIL

Reasoning with Firefighters

A quiet conversation explaining to the client that the childhood abuse-related dangers no longer exist will fail to convince even the most exhausted firefighters that they can finally relinquish their job. Schwartz (1995) quickly discovered that firefighters function as an automatic response to fear, and that he could not reason away their raw terror. Simply informing firefighters that the war ended years ago does not liberate them; they do not suddenly throw down their arms and skip into therapy with a sigh of relief and a carefree grin. The protector duties grip firefighters like a vise. Even the most brilliant reframe offered by the therapist inevitably has no lasting effect. Reasoning with firefighters leaves therapy stagnant.

Power Struggles with Firefighters

Imagine stepping in front of a 20-foot fire engine racing towards you at 50 miles per hour. Trying to out-smart, out-maneuver, or out-power internal firefighters works equally well. Firefighters will always win in a power struggle with the therapist, because they have a bottomless bag of tricks, manipulations, surprises, and intimidations. They can hold a young part hostage, telling the therapist that the exile is locked in a dark basement, terrified; they can run "movies" of horrible sexual abuse in the survivor's mind all day; burn and cut her body; cause medical problems so severe that she requires hospitalization; or cause the survivor to spend weeks in an alcoholic or drugged stupor.

Briere (1989b), as mentioned in chapter 6, refers to the "power to do bad." Survivors typically carry within them one or more parts who feel powerful in a negative sense. The other parts act as accomplices by handing over the keys to their rage. The keepers of rage are almost always firefighters. When the managers or exiles run into a stressful or frightening situation, they call upon the firefighters to tap into that rageful power and save them. (Unfortunately, their gratitude is rarely shown; instead, they show disdain, repugnance, or fear toward the firefighters and otherwise try to banish them.)

One of the most devious (and often successful) power plays is for the firefighter to impersonate a managerial part and pretend to be cooperating with the therapist. Putnam (1989, p. 204) calls these "ISH* imposters."

---

*Internal Self Helpers.

When the client or therapist requests a guide or helper, this imposter may appear and give "misleading or destructive advice" (p. 204). Firefighters may also "steadfastly maintain that they are not in treatment" (p. 215), trying to side-track many sessions by arguing over the semantics of which parts are in therapy. With these types of tricks in their bag, firefighters will usually win in a power struggle.

Eliminating Firefighters

The possibility of annihilation terrifies firefighters. If the ship is getting too unstable in these rocky waters, who better to throw overboard than the loudmouth troublemaker—never mind how good his intentions may be. Beahrs (1982) correctly warns that the client must learn that the goal is not to eliminate this life energy, but to accept it and direct it positively by giving "permission for all parts of the self to exist, which also subtly implies that behaviors can be placed under adequate control" (p. 127). Firefighters must be reassured that the therapist will help them find a useful role in the inner family. Beahrs (1982) explains that any attempt to eradicate a persecutor part will trigger incredible resistance; the part will behave "with the desperation of a cornered animal when threatened" (p. 129). He adds, "I know few things that any organism is more resistant to than dying; any part-self perceiving itself as a whole organism would fight any threat of annihilation with the full force of its life instinct" (p. 129). The firefighter must learn to see himself as "an important facet of a greater overall whole [and develop] an awareness that need not deprive him of his unique individuality. This often takes time, persistence, patience and skill—on the part of the patient as much as the therapist" (p. 125). Elimination, however, will never work.

SUCCESSFUL TECHNIQUES

Then what works? Below we explore helpful techniques for disarming firefighters.

Disciplining Firefighters

While locking horns with firefighters is not a wise option, a survivor may successfully discipline a firefighter. It is similar to telling a 17-year-old that he is grounded for the weekend. If done with prior warning, respect, and a careful explanation of the purpose—and without the parent's power-parts stomping across the teenager's pride—the teenager will go to his room, slam the door, and comply with the grounding. But a power-play—dropping the "You're grounded" bomb on him without warning and with much drama—may result in the young man stomping out of the house for the weekend. Similarly, a survivor or therapist can discipline a firefighter by warning that communication with the client's Self or with the therapist will be limited until the firefighter can speak with some respect and be direct about what he or she wants. In the following example, Lorene's Self found it best to simply end the conversation with Nicholas, who was being hostile, threatening, rude, and dishonest about what he feared and what he wanted.

Nicholas: *Dick says my father-the-child-molester may have loved me! How dare he sit there and calmly side with my father! How could he pretend the world is normal now? The last few days Lorene keeps telling me to wait, wait, wait. "We'll see." I wanted to kill her, hurt her, something to stop the pain and fear. She said, "We'll see. Let's talk to Dick first." She didn't know there was no safe place left anymore. We go to Dick's and he announces that Dad's a nice guy. Now death is everywhere. Lorene must let me be in charge of finding danger; she doesn't always see it. I see it everywhere.*

Self: *Nicholas, stop it. Be honest and tell me what is upsetting you so much.*

Nicholas: *I'm angry that Dick couldn't see the evil in Dad. So that means he's on Dad's side. He might as well have invited Dad over for dinner. I'm telling you the truth—Dick isn't safe anymore.*

Self: *Then why do you start crying again and again, but fight the tears so much?*

Nicholas: *I don't want you to know I'm afraid.*

Self: *Well, you're doing a good job of hiding your fear.*

Nicholas: *He shouldn't have said something nice about Dad. Ever.*

Self: *Why hurt my body if you're mad at Dick?*

Nicholas: *I hate you and want to kill you.*

Self: *You're not being honest or direct anymore, so I'll try to talk with you again later today.*

Ask Firefighters to Explain Their Conduct

The therapist should repeatedly explore with firefighters what they want for themselves and for the survivor. After learning about the firefighters' ultimate purpose, it is easier to understand and tolerate their automatic protective reactions. Many times firefighters respond that their goal is to protect. It is impossible to disarm firefighters without addressing their protective goals, a few of which are listed here:

Trying to Absorb Trauma. Firefighters often seek out or create fires (ironic, considering their name), convinced that some unknown danger is smoldering somewhere and must be found before it engulfs the survivor.

For example, a firefighter might "create a fire" by exacerbating a chronic illness like migraine headaches in order to distract the survivor from a worrisome topic in therapy. In this way, the firefighters step into a hurtful situation in order to absorb any pain. They deeply and tragically absorb all trauma, much like a parent who would gladly take on his child's pain. Originally, when the child lived with an abusive parent, the child's firefighter parts absorbed the pain of betrayal by turning it into rage that leaked out when the child (or later, the adult survivor) lashed out at friends or strangers for no apparent reason, the anger far out of proportion to anything obvious. As an adult, the effect of absorbing so much trauma continues to show up in behavior that might involve betraying friends and family through manipulation, stealing from friends, lying, or revealing confidences. (In this way, the absorbed pain also acts as an effective barrier against relationships.)

Also, for some firefighters it is another part's pain they carry, a burdensome task that acts to block out their own pain. Still, it is a valiant deed that should not go unrecognized. For example, if a father tells his ex-wife that he has never liked their 12-year-old son, the mother would not report this to the son. Instead, she carries the sadness and sense of loss *for* her son. Similarly, firefighters can carry the emotional pain *for* the young exiles. But exiles carry emotions, too. How is it different for a firefighter? The feelings become distorted, transformed so that when released they no longer resemble the initial emotion. Compare the two voices:

Exiled Part: *Why doesn't Daddy love me? Why does he hurt me and scare me?*

Firefighter Part: *That jerk should have been castrated, drawn and quartered, and then had his decapitated head stuck on a post for what he did to her.*

The exile's emotions are frozen, so that the emotion looks like you would expect it to at the time of the abuse. The firefighter, however, forced to carry so much pain while simultaneously performing firefighting tasks, ultimately twists the original fear and betrayal, mingling it with rage and hatred.

Using Self-Injury as Protection. Self-injury serves many functions. A firefighter, for example, may use cutting or drug abuse to relieve pressure or nullify pain. These behaviors are attempts at self-preservation, not attempts to destroy. Firefighters must learn that self-mutilation is not effective as protection. In addition to the obvious consequences to the client's body, the behavior triggers other parts who become disgusted or frightened by the self-torture. This, in turn, leads to escalating inner polarizations. If approached with respect instead of blame, firefighters may agree to turn down the intensity of their reactions so that the system can tolerate them. (See chapter 15 for further exploration of self-injury.)

Trying to Imitate the Abuser. As keepers of pain and badness, firefighters sometimes identify with the original abuser. McCann (1991) writes that often the survivor can be "unmercifully sadistic toward the wounded self, reenacting their internalization of a sadistic, harsh or punitive abuser" (pp. 5–6). Putnam (1989) addresses the "psychic fusion between the abuser and the child" (p. 174), and Herman (1992) notes that as the abused child usually feels extremely isolated, her dependence on the perpetrator grows steadily:

> The more frightened she is, the more she is tempted to cling to the one relationship that is permitted: the relationship with the perpetrator. In the absence of any other human connection, she will try to find humanity in her captor. Inevitably, in the absence of any other point of view, the victim will come to see the world through the eyes of the perpetrator. (p. 81)

The brainwashing techniques used by abusers induce reactions similar to a conversion phenomena that occur when hostages are rescued, where the hostages show a surprising level of sympathy toward their captor (Lancaster, 1991, p. 125). They also resemble the victim's bond with a kidnapper, wife batterer, religious cult leader, or pimp (Herman, 1992).

Lorene's firefighter Victor explains different ways in which a victim's part identifies with the abuser:

Victor: *Here are three ways that I used to blend with Dad or with men like him:*

1. I blend with Dad: *I see Dad hurting another little boy and I think Dad must hate him; the boy must be bad. I absorb the hate. I am Dad and I hate the victim; I am the victim and I hate myself.*
2. I blend with boys Lorene had sex with as a teenager: *They are cold, uncaring. I feel shame and embarrassment. I hate the penis inside Lorene; I hate knowing it will hurt and humiliate other parts; I hate the boy on top of me; I hate others who see us like this. So I blend with emotions around me and lose my Self. I am left with the knowledge that I am nothing, worthless, an object to be screwed.*
3. I can also blend with my father's coldness: *I act cold to other people and to other parts in me, and I no longer feel Dad's coldness. I am the coldness!*

So, if I blend with Dad's painful, angry, hateful child-raping, I no longer feel pain. I am the pain. If I blend with Nicholas' anger, or Destiny's lust, or Alex's deadness when she lives in her "other-world," I can no longer feel anger, lust, or deadness. By becoming one of those qualities, I neutralize it. Everything loses its meaning. Consumed by rage, I feel no rage. If I feel powerless, then I just feed the greedy machine (me) with the most expedient power available. If I feel scared, I act scary. If I feel unloved, I act unloving. So you see, sometimes I am Dad. I can feel his vileness, I am aware of his evil thoughts, I can even sense his powerful erection!

Parts of the adult survivor might also imitate the abuser by striving to act in a way that would make the abuser happy. Like children who become doctors to please their parents, an abuse victim can harbor an abusive part who would like to be pals with the molester, laughing together, creating secrets together. Parts can be so desperate for the abuser's approval that they will mimic him. To break this bond between the abuser and this part of the victim can be very traumatic. Spiegel (1990) explains:

Patients report that these personalities initially comfort them and allow them to get through terrifying experiences without any sense of physical pain. Unfortunately, as the actual physical abuse is discontinued, these same personalities often turn on the patient, inflicting psychological and sometimes physical pain on the patients in a kind of identification with the aggressor that allows patients to feel that they had some control over catastrophic events during which, in fact, they were quite helpless. (p. 252)

It is heartbreaking that firefighters feel so tainted and damaged that they believe their only asset is the ability to excel at being bad. Giving up the goal of negative specialness requires the survivor to explore the dark caverns secreting the firefighters who imitate the abuser and carry burdens of rage, coldness, and the need for power-sex. (We explore this issue more thoroughly later in the book.)

Trying to Distract. Putnam (1989) notes that resistance can take the form of "internal uproars, in which the personality system degenerates into a screaming mob within the patient's . . . head, often prevent[ing] further work by overwhelming the patient with internal stimuli" (p. 214). For example, the firefighter might send the survivor a series of horrifying flashbacks. If a survivor becomes overwhelmed with pictures of sexual assaults, she will turn away from anything that might further overload her senses. A firefighter might try to distract a survivor from crying, something most firefighters detest as a weak, submissive act. So, they begin a series of body-flashbacks: The woman spends her waking hours repeatedly experiencing the taste of her father's sperm in her mouth, the smell of her father's beer-laden breath, and the pressure of his two-hundred pound body on top of hers. She becomes incapacitated, unable to cry, her senses overloaded. Again, if approached with respect, the firefighter may at least agree to use types of distraction that are not dangerous to the survivor.

Trying to Stop Memories. When Schwartz (1992) worked with the abuse survivor he called Marcia, he found that every time he worked with an exiled part, Marcia was driven "to eat uncontrollably or to cut herself or to feel suicidally depressed. Later, I learned these reactions were the work of subselves desperate to stop what they perceived to be the dangerous flow of memory and the emotional agony it released" (p. 36). Both managers and firefighters might wish to block memories. Consider firefighter Alexandra's valiant effort to keep the therapist from accessing exiled parts' memories and feelings:

Alexandra: *I hate this "parts" stuff in therapy. I don't want to do it anymore. It's making me feel crazy. Crazier. Dick says to call him if I get too frightened this week. Ha! Not a chance. I hate him. I detest him. He pretends. Pretends that I'm good and that this therapy will work and that I'll be strong and safe, but he doesn't know anything about Jenny at all. He doesn't have to look at her lying on the basement floor, bleeding, with feces smeared on her mouth. He doesn't have to walk around acting like he's normal while this tiny girl scratches to escape.*

Does Dick think I owe him something just because he hasn't tried to seduce me—yet?? Does he figure I'll see him as a saint who just keeps giving to this poor, deformed creature—me?? Am I supposed to be pathetically grateful? I don't know why else he acts so damn concerned. I'm sick of it. Enough is enough. I don't care about him a bit.

Why doesn't Dick just act normal? Why doesn't he just start acting mean and hurt me? Get it over with. The "nice" way he acts is ridiculous. I want it to stop right now!

I refuse to keep journals and let him know how I feel—and I certainly won't let him find out how Jenny feels! I won't ever cry in front of him; I won't ever tell him how scared I get; I won't ever let him know I think Jenny was hurt because I'm so evil. Well, that's how it's going to be. And to prove it, I'll burn my stomach and then everyone will be convinced to just ignore therapy from now on!

Working with Alex quickly revealed that she carried an enormous burden of guilt. Alex believed that she should have been the victim, not Jenny. With time, Alex finally learned to trust Lorene's Self enough to express her own fears and sadness. This in turn greatly alleviated Alex's habit of distracting with destructive behavior.

Trying to Protect Other People. The survivor also feels that her sinister rage must be controlled in order to protect other people from her. Herman

(1981) states that the incest survivor often believes "she is too evil or dangerous to be intimately involved with other people, for she maintains an exaggerated fear of her own destructive potential" (p. 191). In working with anger, the client must be helped to clarify "the fact that . . . her rage is no doubt terrifying to her and can be expressed in very destructive ways," but that her anger does not magically cause misfortune to other people (p. 191).

Talk to Firefighters about Their Pain

Given this type of information about the firefighter's goals, the therapist can work with the firefighter to change those extreme, outdated methods of protection and develop new goals. Firefighters rarely admit it, but they often long to talk about their own suffering and discover whether the Self and other parts would be willing to take care of them. They ache to belong. If the therapist remains patient and compassionate, firefighters will often feel safe enough to reveal their own wounds (or permit the uncovering of the pain of parts they are protecting). The firefighter's ability to create dark chaos, forcing the survivor into a state of confusion and terror, does not mean the firefighter carries no pain. In fact, the firefighter is often like a frightened child trying to protect the family with primitive methods. Until their pain is addressed with compassion and patience, firefighters will have trouble controlling their automatic reactions. Consider this from Nicholas:

Nicholas: *Why do I crave humiliating sex? My duty? My penance? It's irresistible to me. An addiction that curses me. By these acts, I remind myself that Lorene is different from other people. This is the most important job I have. If Lorene doesn't believe she is different and must be isolated from others, everything else in the system crumbles. That belief acts as my impenetrable wall. Armed with that belief, I can withstand any attempt by others to connect with Lorene. My freakishness ensures my aloneness. It would be very different if I could accept love. But as long as I believe that I am an aberration, I sentence myself to loneliness, because no amount of love could ever counter the self-hate I feel.*

In therapy Nicholas learned to be direct about what he thought and felt:

Nicholas: *I screwed up with Dick today, upsetting all the other parts. I thought Dick would rather talk to a different part, so I left. I am covered by layers of deception, always trying to please someone by being different than whatever the hell I actually am. I even cloud other parts' views of what is happening to them. All these masks, but underneath* *everything, I feel small and weak, without substance or importance or worth. An awkward little boy afraid of anyone's frown. I hate needy, awkward, unfocused, wandering little boys like me.*

Alexandra also revealed the sadness and pain that many firefighters feel under their tough exteriors:

Alex: *I believe I am very evil, that I've absorbed it from Dad, that I cannot be helped, that I must be punished or destroyed. I accept it, but I feel enormous sadness and some anger. It isn't fair. I never did anything so horrible that I can't even have a chance at letting someone love me or care about whether I'm safe. I never meant to become cruel and self-abusive and cold. I am a violation of all my own beliefs and values. I don't support what I am.*

It's so sad to me. I desperately want to be loved and cared for, and kept safe. I want to be told I can survive anything, that I can exist in goodness and can even add to the goodness; that I deserve peace and safety and tenderness. I don't want to go to that cold, evil place that is dragging me in, waiting to devour my last chance at connecting myself to life.

Work Cautiously with Exiled Parts

As the survivor and therapist work more with the child-like exiled parts, the firefighter's "acting out" may also increase. The therapist must work cautiously and persistently with the young child-selves, checking with the firefighters periodically. Only then can firefighters relinquish their hyper-vigilance and return to their natural internal roles. Schwartz (1992) reports that slow, cautious work with Marcia's exile finally resulted in the firefighters' retreat:

> Gone were Marcia's frozen stares—the look of a deer caught in the headlights; no more did she suddenly bolt wordlessly from my office, or aim apparently unprovoked attacks at my personality, character and moral values, my commitment to her, my qualifications as a therapist and everything else about me, including my taste in office furniture. (p. 36)

In addition, once firefighters believe that it is safe for the therapist's or the client's Self to directly communicate with exiles, they are more willing to negotiate changes in their behavior. Schwartz adds this note about Marcia's treatment:

> Marcia's firefighters did not retreat into oblivion. They kept a watch on me as I worked with Marcia's exiles. But if they interrupted a conversation to

tell me I was treading on dangerous ground, I'd ask them to trust me for just a few more minutes. Then, I'd always check back with them near the end of the session, after I had finished the conversation with the exiles. Sometimes the firefighters would hold to the party line that I should not mess with young, fragile parts; but at the same time they agreed that Marcia had been safe with me—at least during this particular session—no promises for future sessions. The willingness to negotiate was a much-welcomed change from the earlier strategy of attacking me every few minutes.

Control the Managers' Exploitation of Firefighters

All this work with firefighters is futile, however, if the therapist works exclusively with the firefighters' rage or negative power and ignores the shaming managers who maintain extreme polarizations with the firefighters. Listen to managerial parts in *You Don't Love Yourself* (Sarraute, 1990) as they blame the firefighters for their risky activities that inevitably involve the other parts:

> You've run other risks... we tremble every time it comes over you... but we can never manage to transfer our trembling into your voice... which makes your attitude even more embarrassing... but you carry us along with you, it's impossible to resist you...
> And afterwards, when you've calmed down and we're home again, it's useless for us to remonstrate with you... You promise not to do it again... For a short time no one who goes out is guilty of the slightest imprudence... the only ones who show themselves outside are those who stand on their dignity... no more of those questions, ever... (p. 11)

Firefighters' instincts are often called upon by other parts, and for good reason. Their talents and survival skills can be quite valuable. Managers plan, plot, map out, negotiate, and deliberate, then turn to firefighters for action because of their knack for acting quickly and confidently. Yet the managers then portray firefighters as destructive, excessive troublemakers at best—abusers at worst. Managers also call on firefighters to create a turbulent distraction and draw attention away from the exile, when the exile feels vulnerable. When a situation or person scares an exiled part, there is always a firefighter who remains on call, ready to present a callous, hostile toughness to the external world. Thus, one therapeutic goal is to work with the managerial parts who so conveniently support the firefighters' charging into the slightest peril while they remain secluded in their sanctuary—only to shame the firefighters later for their extreme behavior.

Parts of the survivor (especially managers) may be terrified to face their own anger. As a result, those parts also choose to disown or ignore the angry firefighters. The managerial parts are relieved to hide behind the firefighters' anger. The polarization between managers and firefighters, therefore, is most likely the responsibility of both; it is an unspoken collusion meant to encapsulate anger. The managers disown all intense feelings, giving them to the firefighters so the managers can keep the survivor functioning as a "normal" person, without rage and fear leaking from every pore.

Although managers rely on firefighters and activate them when necessary, later the managers attack the firefighters for having made the person so despicable and indulgent. The firefighters, then, trigger much criticism from inner managers. (Managerial parts of other *people* are also activated by the survivor's firefighters.) Unlike other parts, firefighters fully experience rage, but they often misdirect the gushing anger. For example, firefighters easily dump volcanic eruptions of anguish and fury on a salesperson at a store, a flight attendant on a plane, or a car mechanic. The other parts gladly siphon their own rage. When managers or exiles run into a stressful or frightening situation, they can call upon the firefighters to tap into that raging power and rescue them. Unfortunately, instead of gratitude, they convey disdain, repugnance, or fear for the firefighters. Meanwhile, the protected parts experience a calming sensation. How reassuring to know that the firefighters work endlessly to contain the ever-fearful rage, along with other intense emotions and frightening memories. This unsung function of the firefighters soothes the non-firefighter parts and gives them a vicarious sense of control over the toxic environment in which the survivor lived at one time—and in which most of the parts believe they still live.

The firefighters themselves, however, feel utterly alone. At first, Nicholas performed as requested by other parts, lashing out to protect Lorene. He felt like part of a team. As time went on and Lorene grew up, Nicholas learned that in exchange for his protective services he would be shunned by other parts. He felt completely abandoned, lonely, and unlovable. Now he looks back at how he acted and begins to see himself as cold, evil, uncaring, someone with whom no one would voluntarily choose to have contact. It is easy to see how a part like Nicholas would resist therapy, insisting that anyone who acted kind or supportive towards him could never be trusted. Firefighters are desperately afraid of their sadness. In the following example, Lorene's Self works with manager Super-She to understand that firefighter Nicholas needs her help:

Super-She: *I woke up during the night with a horrible migraine. I took a lot of pain medicine. I refuse to spend all night with a pounding head just to satisfy Nicholas. If he wants to pretend I'm five years old again, he can do it without my body.*
Self: *But you don't help. You make it worse by making him so ashamed.*
Super-She: *Well he should be ashamed of some of the things he does.*
Self: *Yesterday you asked Nicky to take over at work because my boss was so angry about the report not being done.*

Super-She: So what? I shouldn't have to handle things like that. And it was yesterday—it's over now.

Self: But when you later cut Nicky off, he feels all alone with the aggressive anger that you asked him to exhibit at work.

Super-She: He's a big boy, he can handle it.

Self: No, he can't. I'll help him, but I expect you to back away from the criticism and disdain that you fling at him. If you want to ask him for help at work, ask him with respect, and thank him when the incident has passed.

Many parts fear that the firefighters will take over, releasing raging, suicidal, or other destructive behavior. In effect, they accuse firefighters of putting out one inferno only by creating a second one, of brutally smashing through walls and doors with hatchets. But they must acknowledge that firefighters are also professional, highly skilled, and courageous. In fact, few of us would want their job and most of us are enormously grateful that we can depend on them.

Teach Firefighters about the Self

It is important to ask firefighters to trust the Self *temporarily*—not to give up fighting forever, but to call a cease-fire while the Self tries different ways to achieve the desired goal, such as talking with the younger parts directly about their fears. Slowly firefighters learn that they can get protection and caring from the Self, from other people, and from the therapist without submitting to exploitation and abuse. As the therapist maintains Self-leadership in the face of firefighters' extreme behavior, the client learns to fear firefighters less so that she gradually differentiates her Self more easily. The client's Self, when differentiated, can help firefighters understand that using negative power only causes further victimization and disrupts any healthy, supportive relationships the survivor attempts to establish. The Self can then help firefighters actually give up the destructive behavior by demonstrating new forms of empowerment. In the following entry from Lorene's journal, her Self wants to work with Nicholas' fear about the therapist's vacation. Initially, her Self has difficulty separating from Alexandra, who is angry about Nicholas' disruptive outbursts. Once separated from Alex, however, Lorene's Self is able to speak to Nicholas with calmness and compassion, ultimately helping him to understand that spewing volcanic emotions towards anyone within his reach will not resolve his fear that the therapist will never return from vacation.

Self [blended somewhat with Alex]: I'm having a hard time with Nicholas since Dick left on vacation. Nicholas is such a pain—I can't balance this system with him in it. He screams (inside my head) cruel things at Dick, at me, at everyone. He encourages suicide and destruction. He insists I'm insane, can never be cured, am wasting my time working with Dick. I worked really hard tonight to get past all that, and get to Nicholas himself. (Well, maybe not his Self; but at least a calmer sub-part . . . ?) Nicholas, what is it? Alex, you must step away from me or I cannot talk with Nicholas. Your feelings are becoming mine and I need to be separate.

Nicholas: I can't stand Dick being gone.

Self: Why?

Nicholas: He left me. He'll leave again and again.

Self: His vacation has nothing to do with you personally.

Nicholas: It feels like he's leaving me.

Self: He has to do other things.

Nicholas: I'm too dangerous. He needs to be here so that he can guard me. I'll destroy things!

Self: I doubt that. Tell me why it's hard to have him gone.

Nicholas: He doesn't want to help us. He's cruel and horrible.

Self: You're so sad. It's not like you to cry. What is it?

Nicholas: I can't stand having him leave me over and over again. I really can't. It scares me.

Self: What do you think Dick is saying to you when he leaves?

Nicholas: I did a bad job. He's disappointed in me. He thought he'd be able to tolerate working with me, but he changed his mind. I failed; I made him unhappy; I am too much of a burden—I'm suffocating him.

Self: Can't you believe he's doing something unrelated to you?

Nicholas: No.

Self: Dick isn't disappointed in you, or mad.

Nicholas: I'm going to hang myself in the basement.

Self: Just so you don't have to experience Dick's leaving again?

Nicholas: Yes. Just for that reason. You don't understand how frightened I get.

Self: Nicholas, he'll be back. And I'm here with you. You're important to me. You add such vitality and purpose to my life.

Nicholas: No. I just cause destruction. I know Dick hates me.

Self: Nicholas, no one hates you.

Nicholas: I'm an adolescent version of Dad! I'm a bad person. I will be dead by tomorrow.

Self: You're not being fair.

Nicholas: No, he's not being fair by leaving me alone. I scream and scream and no one comes to take care of me. I can't get out of Dad's basement.

Self: Can you try and rest, not think about this? Dick will return, and then you can tell him how you felt when he was away. In the meantime, I'll stay close by and check on you often.

Nicholas: *I guess so. But don't forget you said you'd stay close by. I'll know if you leave!*

This type of reassurance from the Self after Nicholas has been direct and honest about his feelings eventually leads to Nicholas gaining trust in the Self's ability to keep parts safe and care for them.

Acknowledge Firefighters' Value

The survivor should assure firefighters that she recognizes the painful contributions that they have made over the years and that she would like to help get them what they really want—love and respect. She can ask them to hold off on attacks and offer them another role. Together, the survivor and therapist can explore what the firefighters believe should be their natural, healthy role in the internal system. Firefighters are rarely deadened, and their emotion is sincere—an attribute that can be turned into a great advantage for the survivor as they become zealous advocates providing assertiveness and support for the system. Firefighters also can be taught not to hide even their most primal fear. The rage should be directed at its appropriate target instead of leaking throughout the system.

> As the patient develops a new perspective on her angry feelings ... she often feels less guilty and begins to give up her magical, negative identity. ... Anger at the father and at other abusive men usually surfaces spontaneously.... When she no longer feels that she must submit to exploitation in order to deserve any sort of care, her resentment at being mistreated becomes much more lively. (Herman, 1981, p. 191)

Lorene found that when her firefighters were not extreme, they intensified and enhanced all of her experiences. They inspired her with their vigor, which was supported now by self-confidence rather than righteousness. For example, when Victor is not extreme, he expresses great relief in having internal controls maintained by Lorene's Self so that he can then relax. He is free to show his bold, breathtaking energy, and he takes Lorene on adventures she would otherwise avoid. He stimulates, excites, and urges Lorene into uncharted waters. Alexandra, when not extreme, acts with great innovation, with the heart of a revolutionary. She is free to hear another part's sadness or pain and the first to reach out to the past. This compassionate part has learned to use her ability to connect with others, to offer them support, to experience empathy without absorbing their pain or blending with them.

In general, firefighters need to feel that there is hope of change. If the client's Self can give them hope, the firefighters become more cooperative and less dangerous to the system. Lorene records:

Nicholas: I won't leave this place that you say is the past because I have to wait for Mom. I know she'll come and get me and Dad won't hurt me anymore.

Therapist: I'm so sorry your Mom didn't come. But now it's time to leave there. I've come for you.

Nicholas: No. You aren't the right one. I need Mom to come.

Therapist: What happens if you stay there?

Nicholas: I can't get rid of the bad power-sex feelings. I'm sure that I'm evil because I get excited by thinking of the things Dad did to me.

Therapist: You're only 12 years old. Any 12-year-old boy would get excited by those things.

Nicholas [dumbstruck]: That's impossible! Are you saying I might have a way out? Even if Mom doesn't come to get me, which I thought was the only thing that would prove I am good.

Therapist: Yes. I'm telling you the truth, Nicky. Your sexual feelings are normal. You look so sad now.

Nicholas: I am sad. And tired. I was so afraid that nothing could ever change.

Another example of Nicholas' hope:

Self: I was exercising and I started crying. I couldn't stop. I asked Nicholas what was wrong. He's stuck in the past, I think.

Nicholas: I wanted someone to come. A thousand times I couldn't bear it for another minute, but no one came to help me.

Self: I know, Nicky. But no one could come then. None of us could stop it.

Nicholas: But I thought I would die. And when I didn't die, I was even sadder. Because the longer they left me there, the more I became Dad. Every time I tasted his penis, I blended more with his body and his evilness. I blended in a hundred ways. I wanted him to love me; I tried to find good things about each encounter; I pretended to be special, tough, anything but powerless. I couldn't stay the same! I kept blending. Either it had to stop or I had to blend.

Self: What were you before that happened?

Nicholas: Fresher, more alive, more energetic. Even our cries for comfort and bottles and diapers all flowed from life. He changed that. No—I changed it. I couldn't stay the same. I can't taste his semen and choke on his penis and feel ice water in my urinary tract and not change. Unless I died. But I didn't die. I wanted to; I tried, but I failed.

Self: Nicky, there was nothing you could do, except what you did.

Nicholas: But I'm still so scared and so sad. I'm the most alone creature in the world. I'm caught between life and death.

Self: *Do you understand that pain can exist* within *life? One doesn't preclude the other?*

Nicholas: *I know the idea, but I can't ever feel it. I can't feel any goodness and strength flowing from the pain I feel. All I wanted was for someone to come get me out of the basement.*

Self: *Not just physically.*

Nicholas: *No. I would have to be sure it would never happen again. Too many surprises.*

Self: *That's what really hurts, then? The uncertainty, the unpredictability of the fear and pain and humiliation?*

Nicholas: *And aloneness. Blending with Dad was less terrifying than being all alone. When you have the flu and a fever and you're cold all the way into your bones, you're so sure you'll never, ever be warm again. Even the hottest bath can't warm the chill. That's how my aloneness seems. I'm paralyzed, smothered by that isolated despair a child feels when everything familiar has fled and only strange, dark, things remain. What can I do? I must die. Don't you see? I can't possibly bear this pain minute after minute.*

Self: *Calm yourself, Nicky. Physically, you are safe right now. We will find a way to heal the pain and you will never be in such danger again. How does Dick's absences trigger this terror?*

Nicholas: *Not "trigger." It probably just uncovers what I usually can disguise.*

Self: *I'm not sure, Nicky. But go on.*

Nicholas: *Dick pours pain into me. He acts like he cares, then he leaves. He's cold, maybe. It's my fault. I promised to work hard, but I must have done it wrong.*

Self: *Tell me again. I don't know what it means.*

Nicholas: *I made him leave.*

Self: *No, it has nothing to do with you.*

Nicholas: *I disappointed him, but I'm so sorry. I can change. I'm so frightened.*

Self: *Of what?*

Nicholas: *Of myself.*

Self: *You're just a little boy.*

Nicholas: *But I might explode from the heavy darkness in me.*

Self: *Nicky, I don't know how to help you. What would make you feel safe?*

Nicholas: *I can't be safe.*

Self: *Nicky, you must find your strength within—not just from sessions with Dick. You are not a child. You must mourn the loss of the splendor of your early childhood and then realize that life, trust, beauty, and love were not taken from the world, or even diminished, by Dad's cruelty* *and the family's failure to help you in any way. Everything you wish for is there—love, friendship, a full life, being with other parts. But you have to take those things, Nicky. You have to let us in.*

Nicholas: *When I stop being so angry and actually look at myself, I hurt so much.*

Self: *You cannot soften that hurt by yourself, Nicky. You are not old enough, mature enough, or strong enough. Let us in so we can help.*

Nicholas: *Sometimes I go running with Dashiell. That scared me at first.*

Self: *I know. Now Dashiell draws from your youth and energy when he runs. And he's finally able to experience companionship while being physical. You've helped him a lot. Now take another step, Nicky. Let Dick in, and let me in—just a little. Trust us. Your sobbing and pain are very hard for me to bear.*

Nicholas: *Why?*

Self: *I start to blend with you and feel so much pain. You are my hope. Without you, I will never be what I hoped to be.*

Nicholas: *What do you mean?*

Self: *You add something I've only caught glimpses of in the other parts. Your loyalty and commitment to protecting the girls, for example, are truly extraordinary. I admit your methods are absurd—blending with Dad and pretending to hurt the girls so nothing worse would happen; so they could get it over with; so they wouldn't get their hopes up for safety. But your fierceness is the most incredible thing I've every seen.*

Truthfully, I am in awe of your determination and the passion you are able to pour into something for which you are willing to fight. You are the strength upon which I had hoped this system could someday rest. Please let us in, just enough to believe that Dick will return and that I will always be here. Trust us that much.

Nicholas: *Okay, I'll try.*

Firefighter, shadow, demon, or devil—this feisty part will not go away but "will leave [us] no peace and will continue to plague [us] until it has been accepted" (Jung, 1917/1926/1943/1966, par. 90). We must welcome the value and richness that firefighters bring to the internal family.

CHAPTER 12

Disarming Managers

*In the effort to placate her abusers, the child victim often
becomes a superb performer. . . . She brings to all [her]
tasks a perfectionist zeal. . . . In adult life, this prematurely forced competence may lead to considerable occu-
pational success. None of her achievements in the world
redound to her credit, however, for . . . the appreciation
of others simply confirms her conviction that no one can
truly know her and that, if her secret and true self were
recognized, she would be shunned and reviled.*

— Judith Herman, 1992

M ANAGERS GROW accustomed to being in charge of the survivor's life.
They prove to be forceful protectors of the system. The other parts
habitually follow the direction of the reasonable-sounding managers. With
their willingness to lead in a crisis and their vast knowledge of the internal
system, managers often achieve formidable power.

Too often therapists and survivors attack managers with all sorts of
power moves (hospitalization, medication, insistence on rushing ahead to
uncover carefully buried emotions and memories). Managers counter with
passive but destructive behavior such as shutting down the entire system
(perhaps by pushing the survivor into an autistic-like state of unrespon-
siveness during a session), or tricking the survivor and therapist into believing they are working hard in therapy only to find that no changes are
occurring within the survivor. Managers, like firefighters, are a sensitive
bunch. They respond better to some techniques than to others. Let's first
examine techniques that typically *fail* to work well with managers.

TECHNIQUES THAT OFTEN FAIL

Attempting to Outwit Managers

Managers may typically consider themselves to be smarter and wiser
than the therapist. Certainly managers are far more familiar with the survi-

vor's internal system than the therapist. A power struggle with managers usually results in their victory. If even one manager disagrees with the therapist's goals or methods, that manager can skillfully shut down all internal operations so that the survivor experiences a convulsive halt to her life. She cannot go to work, cannot do the dishes, cannot even answer the telephone.

One of the managers' most successful and devious tricks, often used in response to a therapist's firm request to be given access to the client's Self, is to pretend that they *are* the Self. Indeed, managers' helpfulness fools many therapists into thinking that a manager is the Self, offering well-reasoned advice to support what is actually an extreme position. Lorene demonstrates the uncanny ability of manager Super-She to imitate the Self in a misdirected attempt to hide the Self, pushing it away to protect it from Dashiell's intense emotions, and thwarting the therapist's attempt to get Lorene's Self to lead:

Super-She [*pretending to be Lorene's Self*]: *Your sadness is too disruptive.*
Dashiell: *I'm scared of the way I live, always hiding and waiting.*
Super-She: *I would like to wipe out sadness, end it.*
Dashiell: *There has to be a way to live without feeling pain all the time. Will anyone take care of me?*
Super-She: *I am not your caretaker. I am not a mother for each part. The time when you were so little and needed mothering is gone. That hole can never be artificially filled. It may be an emptiness you will have to learn to bear. But it doesn't mean there is nothing left.*
Vincent: *That does it! That can't possibly be Lorene's Self. It sounds more like Super-She!*
Super-She: *So what? I'm in the lead right now. And rightly so—I can make the most astute and reasonable appraisal of Dashiell's problems.*
Vincent: *You have no right to pretend to be Lorene's Self.*
Super-She: *I hate this! You're ruining everything. I just about had things under control. I know what I'm talking about—trust me.*
Vincent: *Let me talk to her Self.*
Super-She: *Back off! You know as well as I that we must protect the Self at all costs. Dash's intensity will devastate the Self. That therapist is a fool to try and change the way I run things.*

Managers respond better to empathy and respect than to power and challenge; they cannot easily be overpowered or outwitted. On the one hand, it can be easy for therapists to work with managers because they prefer keeping the discussion on a business level, colleague-to-colleague. Therapists tend to rely on managers because they seem so reasonable. We see them as the "good" parts (Internal Self Helpers) who are less emotional and less out-of-control than the others. However, with their ability to mimic the Self and other tricks, managers are not always a therapist's allies.

Go Blindly Ahead without Managers' Support

A typical confrontation between the therapist and the survivor's managers occurs when the survivor becomes flooded with memories of the abuse. The release of long-buried memories and emotions often triggers the survivor's internal cycle of terror all over again, much to the dismay of the managers. The client Marcia, for example, began experiencing

> intermittent bouts of paralyzing terror during the day and nightmares at night. She started avoiding work, her social life declined and she froze in the presence of any man—all developments that appalled the competent, striving managerial parts of her personality, which lobbied heavily in favor of her dropping out of therapy entirely. These tough-minded, take-charge selves used her newly emerging frailties as proof that therapy was destroying her fragile sense of being in control. (Schwartz, 1992, p. 35)

Similarly, in this example, Lorene's manager (Vincent) does not like the intensity of the feelings held by the exiled part (Destiny), so he withdraws his support from the therapy process.

Self: *I had a hard time with Dick today. We agreed to work on Destiny's sadness and get her out of the dangerous-feeling place where she hides. Dick encouraged Destiny to talk about how she felt. She got tears in her eyes, felt frightened, curled up, hiding.*

Then Vincent stepped in, saying that he didn't trust what Dick was doing, didn't want to see Destiny hurt, etc. Dick promised he could handle it. He apologized (again) for being a little distant last week, explained the circumstances. Vincent insisted that Dick's distancing proved the wisdom of never crying in front of him again.

Vincent: *This is an absurd exercise. It is a game that has no meaning for me. It's gimmicky—a hoax—a cheap trick. Therapy doesn't address the substance or merits of Destiny's pain at all. How could it possibly help to pretend (imagine) that she's no longer being hurt and is no longer in a dangerous place? I know Dad isn't actually going to hurt her. There's nothing new about this. I go along with it for Dick's amusement and so I won't hurt his feelings. But rationally—logically—it makes no sense. Why can't Dick just recognize that Destiny is filled with pain and given the opportunity would cry all day every day. She'd make daily functioning impossible. Dick just can't be allowed to open the floodgates. Life will be out of control. Destiny will drown us. I won't allow this. The only parts who want to do this are Jenny and Alex, but they're too emotional already! I don't want to make Dick mad, but this is a futile path to take.*

Also, as a practical matter, I will no longer permit a part to cry in front of Dick. He was much too detached last week. To be quite frank, a dog who was in pain from a sore paw would have received more tenderness. I know that's awfully blunt, but it's true. I certainly don't blame Dick. I blame myself for letting it go that far. I should've listened to other parts' rules prohibiting openness, crying, trust. But you'd spent so much time slowly moving them towards that ability to open up and not care about tears—I thought it was okay. So last week I kept every other part away so Destiny could say whatever she felt and even cry, if she wanted to. How stupid of me. What poor advice I gave. Blind faith in one person and one process is stupid. It's my fault for not accepting one of the realities of life—Destiny and parts damaged like her cannot be fixed.

In this type of situation, the Self has the opportunity to show that the flashbacks and other reactions are merely a way of telling the story. The surfacing of memories does not cause the abuse to reoccur; the Self can handle any internal reactions; and the managers need not take on more responsibilities. But all this entails careful, patient work with the managers. Plunging ahead while ignoring the managers creates enormous difficulties.

Removing Control of Exiled Parts from Managers

The managers hold the young exiled parts in protective bondage. Therapy can be impeded greatly when the therapist and survivor have no access to these exiles. Managers, however believe that exposure of the exiles' secrets would result in dire consequences such as death or the loss of any chance for redemption. Managers need to learn that it is not necessary to hide the "discrete cache of terrible, wounding memories," in order for the survivor to continue to live. But this learning cannot be forced or rushed (Schwartz, 1992, p. 35). Indeed, managers are often neglected, suffering, and frightened—qualities that predispose them to overreact to murmurings from the exiles. In the following example, Lorene's manager incites mutiny in an attempt to impose numbness throughout the system to neutralize the exiles' intensity:

Self: *What is wrong? All these suicide thoughts all of a sudden tonight. Why do parts of me say "nothing matters—better to die"?*
Super-She: *I don't have to explain to you. Blood is—*
Self: *No. I don't want to hear your blood and fear speeches. Please be more direct. Are you scared?*
Super-She: *A dangerous man talked to you at work today.*
Self: *Are you frightened?*
Super-She: *Will he kill Jennifer?*

Self: *No. He cannot hurt us.*
Super-She: *You're wrong.*
Self: *Time will prove I'm right. Jenny?*
Jenny: *I'm fine. That man didn't scare me.*
Super-She: *It's so stupid to pretend Jenny's safe. As long as men are around, there is danger for now.*
Self: *Will you agree that nothing harmful happened to Jenny today?*
Super-She: *Well, yes.*
Self: *Then all I ask is that next time you sense danger, tell me — then give me the chance to evaluate the situation without your trying to scare Jennifer.*
Super-She: *I guess you can have a chance, but I'll still watch carefully.*

Managers will *never* allow themselves to be forced out of their position as protectors of the exiles or forced to relinquish their protective weapons unless their fears are addressed and they believe the young ones will be safe.

Annihilating the Managers

Some survivors might prefer to simply extricate the cold, aloof managers from their personalities, but this cannot be done. Consequently, it is vital that the survivor and therapist understand *why* the managers act so heartlessly. Most often, managers are struggling to keep the Self away from the survivor's deep reservoir of pain, desperation, shame, and haunting memories. Indeed, managers believe that once these feelings are exposed, the survivor will be devoured by a black hole of oblivion.

Schwartz (1992) described his work with the survivor Marcia: "Her manager did not trust me, and suggested quite bluntly that I didn't know what I was doing and couldn't handle the torrent of emotions in Marcia that my questions might release" (pp. 34–35). Schwartz had to convince the managers that "if we worked together, we could learn how to heal the exiles safely, without putting Marcia in jeopardy" (p. 35). He tried to "convince [Marcia's] managers that if they stayed and worked with me to help the little girl, she could be released from her terror and pain. Once that happened, they wouldn't have to expend so much energy on the crushing, grinding labor of keeping the hurt inner children walled off from awareness" (p. 35). Schwartz was able to convince the managers that they did not have to "shut down all emotional access" and eventually he was able to work with the little girl part "without shattering the sense of security that her managers guarded" (p. 35). In addition, familiarizing the managers with their intrinsic value within the system helps reassure them that they will not be eliminated once they relinquish their extreme protective roles.

SUCCESSFUL TECHNIQUES

Asking Managers to Explain Their Conduct

It is essential that the managers learn to be *direct*, to express fears and goals without the drama of cold, methodically extreme behavior. This is very difficult because managers are used to being manipulative and not direct. They are rarely even honest with themselves about what they feel. Their fear of letting anyone close to them must be confronted gently, as Lorene's Self does here:

Self: *What's going on? I can't work, can't concentrate on anything. Cutting? Now? Vincent is calm; Dashiell sitting by tree; girls with Vincent; Super-She in her room, doing something. All are okay? But I still feel blocked. Check again.*

It's Super-She again. I put her in a hot tub. She feels safer now — she can be her Self because she's supported on all sides by soft water. What are you afraid of?

Super-She: *I'm afraid that I'll be crushed and disappear.*

Self: *So you calmly show scary movies to remind you where you are and that you exist.*

Super-She: *Yes. I have weapons. No one should come near me.*

Self: *Why would someone crush you?*

Super-She: *Because my mind is so powerful.*

Self: *I can help you enjoy your mind. What are you protecting? It isn't me. Another part?*

Super-She: *Bonnie is so young still — only 12. I have to distract people so they won't notice her. I'll distract with my brain work.*

Instead of imposing cold fear over Lorene, it would have been much more effective for Super-She to simply *say* that Bonnie seemed weak and vulnerable and needed protection. Then Lorene's Self could explore the issue and determine whether or not Super-She was correct. If indeed Bonnie was feeling frightened (perhaps by a new memory Lorene was talking about in therapy), she could be comforted or the work could slow to a pace more comfortable for her. But Super-She's attempts to manipulate the therapist and Lorene away from a sensitive issue by creating intense (but unconnected, irrelevant) emotions, were destructive. With time, Lorene's managers, who were quite insistent about being frequently consulted by the therapist, learned to speak up and directly voice their objections. Even if the therapist was, for example, talking directly to Bonnie when Super-She became upset, Super-She would simply interrupt, voice her opinion directly (if somewhat forcefully) and then the therapist could continue, with minor adjustments made for Super-She or Bonnie if necessary.

Teaching Managers to Reveal Their Feelings

Although the managerial weapon of numbing all feelings breaks the survivor's connection to many emotions, this does not mean that managers have no feelings. They are terrified, too. They are *not* cold, ruthless, or passive by nature. Even their most objective-sounding speeches and aloof conduct conceal a reservoir of intense emotion. Underneath the rational-sounding protectiveness of a manager is often a deep fear of abandonment or of physical harm. When managers act coldest, they are usually aching to communicate their emotions. For example, Vincent was unable to verbalize his feelings, and so he took a small plastic doll and burned part of it and then recorded his feelings:

Vincent: *I get chills up my spine when I see the graphic portrayal of physical and sexual destruction and the abuse of power inflicted on a tiny body, as depicted on that damn doll. I want to know if the doll scares Dick, too. It scares me, and I don't want to be alone with my awareness of the existence of that horror in this world. Maybe this will be too much for Dick. I don't want him to pretend to be brave about something so horrible in me. After all, he didn't necessarily sign on to witness the actual physical impact of our work in therapy. He only signed on for the verbal communications. The doll depicts the horrible physical invasion and emotional disfigurement experienced by Jenny and Andy.**

Reluctant to look inward, managers are slow to explore their own feelings and experiences. They are accustomed to directing their concentration towards other parts and the environment, while they remain secretive and "as inconspicuous as possible" (Herman, 1992):

[They] avoid attracting attention to themselves by freezing in place, crouching, rolling up in a ball, or keeping their face expressionless. Thus, while in a constant state of autonomic hyperarousal, they must also be quiet and immobile, avoiding any physical display of their inner agitation. The result is the peculiar, seething state of "frozen watchfulness" noted in abused children. (p. 100)

Once convinced that it will be safe, managers are relieved to turn away from others and focus on their own emotions and thoughts. Interestingly,

---

*Several sessions after Vincent presented this doll to Schwartz, they discussed his reactions. Schwartz admitted that the doll looked so brutal that it bothered him, especially because it looked like some of Lorene's blood was on it. Schwartz said there were several times during the session that he had to really "sit" on some of his parts. Later, he was able to work with his parts and felt better able to talk to Lorene about Vincent's method of depicting the brutality she suffered.

these previously cold administrators often turn their disciplined patience and concentration to inner exploration and meditation. Hollow, mechanical, rote behavior becomes joyous and creative energy. Their ruthless edge is transformed into a life-engaging force. Consider the relief Lorene's manager feels at voicing directly what she wants:

Self: She? What would you like?
Super-She: I would like to hide.
Self: Try again. Be your Self. Be direct. You've done it before.
Super-She: I would like to sing and to fly and to play the piano. I want to be a grown-up woman. I want that very much.
Self: What else would you like to do as a woman?
Super-She: Interact with the world more, go places I've never been — museums, other countries, other people's homes — have different experiences with people and then see what being a woman means.
Self: You are more social than other parts of me.
Super-She: I can share things with other people in a way that the other parts cannot. I am the connector. I can touch you or another person and heal with love, caring, peacefulness. I communicate to others the joy Dashiell feels; the insight Vincent discovers; and the deep fears we all encounter within ourselves.
Self: Why do you disrupt things so much?
Super-She: I am like a gatekeeper, a guard.
Self: Maybe you could relinquish that role while still maintaining your connector responsibilities and talents.
Super-She: Maybe.

Managers tenaciously cling to the belief that emotions cannot be changed, that the survivor's intense feelings of terror, betrayal, aloneness, and sorrow are immutable. The only solution, the managers believe, is to bury the emotions. Schwartz (1992) describes Marcia's managers:

> The manager/protectors thought that since the damage had already been done, all they could do was isolate Marcia's hurt little-girl selves so that they would not overwhelm Marcia and make her vulnerable to being hurt again. They strove to control Marcia's relationships and make her tough, successful and self-possessed so that she would never be vulnerable to hurt and rejection again. (p. 35)

After Schwartz encountered Marcia's five-year-old abused part, he was permitted no further access; her managers insisted that "whatever happened in the past is over and done with — there is no need to dredge all that stuff up again" (p. 35).

Managers must learn for themselves that the Self can help these horrible feelings change and help free parts from these burdens. It takes time and repeated experience, however, for managers to trust the evolution of these changes. They will see by demonstration that the Self will not be overwhelmed—that experiencing strong emotions can be done without the Self's blending with extreme parts.

Allowing Managers to Co-parent the Exiles

Managers are overwhelmed with their responsibilities, yet reluctant to concede that they can safely relinquish guard duty because the Self will now protect the exiles. Managers can continue to help, but they are no longer in charge of that function. Managers need to know that the therapist will not be repulsed by the exiles and abandon or punish the client for exposing them; and that the client's external environment is safe enough to expose exiles (if indeed that is true)—that there are no dangerous people in her life who will attack her newly exposed vulnerability. At that point, managers often will gladly lay down their weapons and reapply their skills to healthier pursuits. One of the managers' greatest strengths is the influence they have garnered within the system. While the managers' ability to influence the entire system has functioned as a weapon, it can be changed into a positive tool. The managers can be called upon to exercise their influence by educating the child-parts, answering their many questions and helping them exercise their innate strengths. Managers easily fall into a co-parenting role with the survivor's Self, making sure that the exiles play and receive adequate attention and supervision. Finally, the managers can tell the exiles about the guilt and helplessness that the managers experienced when the original abuse occurred.

The Value of Limited Cooperation

The therapist and client must remember that even the wisest-sounding manager is not the Self. At the same time, the survivor should acknowledge and respect the valuable information that managers hold. In this example, during one session Lorene's manager (Vincent) expressed mistrust of the therapist, because he felt that the therapist was acting aloof and distant. Nevertheless, Vincent could provide helpful information and advice, without feeling forced to prematurely commit himself to the therapeutic goal at hand. Often it takes time before a manager is willing to admit that therapy is working. In the beginning, however, limited cooperation is all that is necessary for the therapy to proceed.

Vincent: *Things are very bad. Nicholas was in charge until a few days ago when he gave up; then sexual feelings flooded back in. I had a terrible session with Dick today. Dick said some stupid thing like he'll just wait* *until Nicky gets around to asking for help and believing in Dick's ideas about parts being stuck in the past. Only then will Dick help Nicky! Apparently Dick has a new therapeutic philosophy: Either Nicky must succumb to the time-travel crap or Dick will just sit and watch him deteriorate. Just abandon him until he decides Dick's way is right. I'm so mad!*

What Dick doesn't want to accept is that Nicky needs someone to be with him in the sadness, talk with him about it, let him learn to cry. Dick just insists that Nicky is wrong. Does he think the pain isn't real? That Nicky can just walk away from the pain and magically trust in Dick's time-travel ideas?

What the hell is the matter with Dick? A therapist shouldn't just sit there and listen, accusing Nicholas of not "letting him in." Nicholas was direct, honest, crying, in terrible pain. Dick offered no understanding, no participation. He prefers the quick, fantasy crap, ignoring the pain that Nicky has never had the opportunity to feel safe about sharing or even experiencing.

If Dick is emotionally unable — has insufficient energy or inner re-sources — to participate in the sharing of this pain, he should not do this kind of therapy. He should stick to cases where clients are basically healthy and stable.

Self: *Vincent, calm down for a few minutes. Remember that you can use all this protective energy to give me and Dick information about parts. You don't need to lash out at us with cruel criticism.*

Vincent: *Okay, fine. I would expect Dick, for example, to ask what things look like to Nicky where he is; ask how long he's been there; ask who else is there; ask what Dad is doing; tell Nicky he's doing a good job and doing the right thing in exploring his sadness; tell Nicky it's okay to be angry at Dad and that's where the cold/power sex feelings are hiding. I heard nothing coming even close to this!*

I would also expect Dick to come over to where Nicky is sitting on the floor in the corner, crying silently, and tell him that even though it's hard, Nicky is doing great and his tears are well deserved and valid and important.

Self: *That's better. That's very helpful.*

Vincent: *I don't know. I trust Dick, I care about him, I don't want to hurt him. It's possible something else was going on with him. However, regardless of the reason for his conduct today, I'm responsible for Nicky.*

Self: *Tell me more about what's going on with Nicky.*

Vincent: *Nicky is in incredible pain. He blames himself for the past conduct he's so ashamed of. He's tormented by fear of his own sexual arousal; he's suffering incredibly due to the other parts' insistence on experiencing their own sexuality hour after hour, day after day; he blames himself for younger parts' being trapped in the basement. Nicky is being very brave to look directly at his feelings.*

I guess I fed Nicky's anger at the end of the session. Nicky went too far, of course, and that wasn't fair to Dick (but at least it brought Dick out of his numbness). Then Nicky said he really needed Dick to talk to him. Dick responded: "Okay. Well, it's time to stop" !!! Nicky cried on the way home, cut Lorene's face, cried, and tried to sleep. He felt more and more disoriented, drifting, crazy. I think the best answer is a hospital. I don't want Nicky to lose this direct approach, staying with his feelings.

Self: *I'll make sure he's okay. The ultimate burden rests on my shoulders, not yours, Vincent.*

Vincent: *But I have to question whether or not Dick is the right person to see this through. I simply don't know if he can relinquish his insistence that time-travel has to be done in one swoop. Nicky needs to do it slowly.*

Self: *You are not in charge of hiring and firing a therapist. I am.*

Vincent: *My advice is that you be hospitalized. The environment will be more controlled. But other parts fight me on this, and you say I'm not in charge. Perhaps I could ask Dick about the hospitalization first.*

Self: *Thanks, Vincent. I know this is the right direction and your help is invaluable to me.*

Managers Play a Key Role in All Parts
Trusting the Self

The managers' growing trust of the survivor's Self often frees other parts to trust the Self. As the Self works with the managers, the firefighters feel relief because the managers are now less critical and less undermining of their efforts. Similarly, the exiled parts feel less distanced from the managers and less afraid of their fearsome coldness. Remember, despite their numerous blow-ups, these other parts are accustomed to trusting the leadership of the consistently well-organized, authoritative managers. If the managers trust the person's Self, the other parts will watch carefully, consider their options, and wonder whether or not they too might find freedom and safety under the umbrella of the Self.

Teaching Managers How to Hope

Slowly, managers learn that the Self is capable of maintaining health and balance throughout the system, even when parts experience strong emotions. This discovery of the Self's competence gives managers *hope*. Vincent poignantly describes his discovery:

Self: *Vincent, why do you feel renewed hope?*
Vincent: *Dick said there is value in facing sadness or fear. I've thought*

about that. Dashiell, for example, might cry because someone has unexpectedly hurt him. He's confused and thinks he must have been bad or else he wouldn't have been punished by someone he trusted. So how can I offer him strength to help him weather the period of sadness? I can avoid succumbing to the idea that the sadness will smother him. Instead, I can strive to balance the larger system of which we are all a part by adding to the energy which is "goodness."

Self: *Be more specific.*

Vincent: *If I either ignore or join the parts shouting for destruction and blood, then I necessarily reinforce or strengthen the energy that thrives on evil, imbalance, and extremeness. If, on the other hand, I provide and seek love and support and comfort for Dash, I automatically add richness and color to the universe.*

Self: *You feel better after the last session?*

Vincent: *Much better. I thought that the sadness experienced by some of the parts destroyed any hope. But hope remains as long as you [as your Self] remain available to us.*

The client's Self can slowly familiarize managers with the Self's power, so that the managers learn to trust that the survivor's life is no longer in danger of being overpowered by an abusive adult. In the following example, Lorene's manager Super-She explores her fears. She uses respect, honesty, and directness, which helps Lorene's Self immensely to hear Super-She's hope for safety, being able to make choices, and breaking through her physical passivity.

Super-She: *I've gone nowhere. I'm frozen, frightened. Dick can't help, so he'll be angry or at least disappointed. I'm nothing because I do nothing.*

Self: *I know you're very unsure of your relationship with Dick and you've worried about his upcoming business trip.*

Super-She: *I am scared that when he sends me out at the end of the session, he might disappear. He'll be gone and it will be my fault.*

Self: *Why do you want to burn my arms?*

Super-She: *Punishment. Acknowledgment of inner deformity. I can't live like a normal person. I'm like someone who has had a stroke — I can see and hear, but can't move, talk, eat, laugh.*

Self: *You are not a stroke victim, believe me. You've shown us your body. It is a normal, strong, healthy young woman's body.*

Super-She: *I forgot.*

Self: *You're starting to watch your own horror movies. I thought those were just to scare other parts.*

Super-She: *Maybe Dick will come back and be mad and hurt me.*

Self: *Well, he won't hurt you physically. That's under your control. If he hurts you emotionally, you can talk to him about it. Go ahead — make a choice about something.*

Super-She: *I can't.*

Self: *Yes you can. You can make a simple choice, like whether to stand up or sit down.*

Super-She: *I'm scared to—the only choices I have include hiding, accusing, demanding, harming myself, cutting off your paths to other people.*

Self: *Try.*

Super-She: *Okay, okay. Watch me take a deep breath and reach out my hand to touch Dashiell. Stop!!*

Self: *Scary?*

Super-She: *Yes, but my hand isn't bleeding. It isn't burnt.*

Dashiell: *My turn! I want to do a Self-exercise.*

Self: *Wait a bit, Dash.*

Super-She: *I don't know if I can live outside of my memories. I might be stuck here.*

Self: *Trust what your Self says, She. You truly are nothing more than what you choose to be right at this moment.*

Super-She: *I feel terrible.*

Self: *That's one small scared feeling—you are more than that.*

Super-She: *I don't think so.*

Self: *Trust your "powers of life." They are stronger than those fears.*

Super-She: *Do I exist outside of my breathing?*

Self: *Yes. You have a whole body.*

Super-She: *It feels so disjointed—nothing connected—bleeding at the gaps.*

Self: *That image is not real. Vincent is right. You're safe in your own body, with your own Self to help you.*

Super-She: *Will Dick come back from his trip?*

Self: *Yes.*

Super-She: *Okay. I really hope he does.*

Self: *That's a big admission for you!*

Once freed from their extreme role, managers can learn to use their intelligence to digest vast amounts of information and then let the Self make a final decision. They can think, write, analyze, and help discern messages from other parts. Managers can also provide zealous education for themselves and other parts. Their ability to concentrate and focus energy can now be used to accomplish once-distant goals such as raising children, completing a marathon, or starting a new career. The managers' innate confidence in interacting with the outer world provides a stability that serves as a foundation for all of the survivor's life goals as well as daily activities. In addition, managers can also benefit the survivor greatly with their ability to "examine the moral questions of guilt and responsibility and reconstruct a system of belief that makes sense of her undeserved suffering" (Herman, 1992, p. 178).

CHAPTER 13

Retrieving Exiled Child-Parts

The therapist must help the patient move back and forth in time, from her protected anchorage in the present to immersion in the past, so that she can simultaneously experience the feelings in all their intensity while holding on to the sense of safe connection that was destroyed in the traumatic moment.

—Judith Herman, 1992

HOW EASY IT WOULD be to just say, "Everything is safe now, dear—trust me." But any survivor can attest to the fact that she cannot merely comfort an inner child and thereby achieve health and a release of her pain. This is often because survivors carry within them young exiled child-parts who remain firmly stuck in the past. In this chapter we explore the causes for survivors' daily struggles in this time warp.

POCKETS OF TIME

Both survivors and therapists are surprised to discover that some parts exist in the past in "frozen time" (Herman, 1992, p. 195). Napier (1993) describes to survivors the "timeless nature of the unconscious," where their dissociated childhood experiences have become caught in "pockets of time . . . that have no relationship to your present reality. Instead of being part of your ongoing adult awareness, they continue to be filled with all the feelings you had as a child" (p. 76). Napier explains to survivors the process of emptying their "pockets of time" into the present:

An important part of the healing process is gaining access to these pockets of time and bringing their contents into your adult awareness, where they can be processed in ways that were impossible when you were a child. Until this happens, these old experiences . . . [are] more like actually *being* there.

As long as they exist in this way, you remain vulnerable to shifting without notice from your everyday adult awareness into a frightened or enraged child part. (pp. 76–77)

Herman (1992) analogizes the experience of abuse victims to prisoners of war, in that the "rupture in continuity between present and past frequently persists even after the prisoner is released. The prisoner may give the appearance of returning to ordinary time, while psychologically remaining bound in the timelessness of the prison" (p. 89). Like the released war prisoner, the abuse victim exists "simultaneously in two realities, two points in time. The experience of the present is often hazy and dulled, while the intrusive memories of the past are intense and clear" (p. 90). Putnam (1989) notes that adult survivors, "with their timeless unmetabolized trauma," often believe their childhood abuser can still harm them if they reveal memories in therapy (p. 173). "The terror is as though patient and therapist convene in the presence of yet another person. The third image is the victimizer," and thus patients often feel "as though they are risking their lives to tell their stories" (Lister, 1982, p. 875). With gruesome detail, Lorene's part, Alexandra, describes the abuse memories held by a young part named Andy. He is completely absorbed, hypnotized by the memories. Very little else gets through to him. For Andy, the abuse continues:

Alex: *Andy's very scared. He keeps talking about the dark place. He said it was a very bad place. Bugs and things on his face crawling and chewing. Hamsters? No—smaller. Gerbils? Put food on doll's face and watch mice chew it up. Tape eyes shut on Andy and only feel and hear things on his own face, imagining what the doll looked like. Will Andy look like that—skin gone, face ripped open?*

Terrified—terrified trying to be a brave boy who doesn't care at all what they do to the rest of his body or whose penis he should suck or whose rectum he should stick his fingers into. That doesn't matter at all compared to the dark things.

I told Andy how brave he is being, but he just cries more. I'm so tired and scared. It's been very, very hard to listen to Andy all night, especially with Victor interrupting and raving on and on about evilness.

I understand now why Destiny kept telling Jennifer to stop talking quietly to Dick and why she kept saying she didn't want to hear about those ropes (which apparently symbolize to her anything that happened in the basement).

For many parts of the survivor, the "past and the present intermingle and follow each other in chronological confusion" (Putnam, 1989, pp. 176–177). The fact that the survivor is now an adult holds little relevance for these parts. The exiles continue to expect the abuse to begin again at any time. Schwartz (1992) describes the need to retrieve exiled parts of the survivor he called Marcia, who had "a host of other hurt [child] selves — some caught in a time warp with the [abuser], others stuck at times when she had felt abandoned by her mother, rejected by her father and desperately lonely, still others ensnared in what had been an abusive marriage" (pp. 35–36). Schwartz describes Marcia's barricaded inner children:

> Each of these injured, exiled, child-like selves seemed to be imprisoned in a particular time and space, connected to a distinct episode of abuse. It was as if every one of these frightened, miserable child-selves had been left behind in time, keeping from Marcia's awareness a discrete cache of terrible, wounding memories, so that the competent and efficient managers could shuttle her along through life. (p. 35)

The exiled child-parts need more than attention in order to heal. Indeed, sometimes, no matter how much attention exiles receive, the extremeness remains. In order to relinquish the feeling that the abuse continues, the parts must be retrieved from the past and nurtured in the present. This retrieval and nurturance cannot be accomplished until the exiled parts *choose* to return to the present and entrust themselves to the care of the survivor's Self.

In seeking out and healing these child-parts who are caught in pockets of time, the IFS model uses language that describes a "retrieval from the past" or "moving the child-part to the future." If the client's parts are uncomfortable with the language, other terms can be used. The key is to release the exiled parts from their outdated fears and beliefs and any other extreme emotions they carry (their burdens) and update their understanding of the safety of the world in relation to the adult survivor's present-day environment.

The survivor and therapist must "walk" two paths within the survivor's internal system before successfully retrieving the young parts and bringing them into the present. The first path spans the territory of their protectors, the managers and firefighters, who must be convinced that the proposed course of action is safe. After the initial work with the protectors, the retrieval may begin, but the therapist must check back with the protectors periodically. The second path traverses the inner world of the exiled parts, as the therapist familiarizes them with their own strengths and eventually frees them from the archaic fears which have permeated their lives. Throughout the process of walking these two paths, the therapist helps the survivor's Self remain in a leadership position.

THE PROTECTOR PARTS

Schwartz (1992) found that when he attempted to work with a survivor's child-like parts, the managers and firefighters became "desperate to stop what they perceived to be the dangerous flow of memory and the emotional agony it released" (p. 36). He warns that "managers and fire-fighters cannot leave their dreadful roles until the exiles are safe, and after that they shift gratefully. In the meantime they respond better to empathy and respect than to power and challenge" (p. 37). Stone and Winkelman (1985) similarly note that "as long as the protector/controller is in charge of the personality, the child will remain buried and therefore inaccessible. . . . When the aware ego becomes more effective, the protector/controller quite willingly surrenders control" (p. 151). Once a part can see where he got the extreme feelings or beliefs that he carries in or on his body (his burdens), he is able to take those out of him (as described in Schwartz, 1995). This unburdening becomes a central aspect of the IFS work with survivors.

If unprepared, the fiercely protective managers and firefighters will repeatedly and vigorously oppose most contact with the exiles. Schwartz (1992) finds that trying to work with wounded inner children involves great danger if the managers and firefighters are not consulted first:

> As well they should, these parts will resist the well-meaning but premature healing attempts of therapists. . . . When their resistance is successfully circumvented, they can rise again later to inflict severe punishments on the clients as a way to ensure the system's safety. When I proceeded too quickly past Marcia's [protectors], they "protected" her with episodes of acute physical pain, serious illness, self-mutilation, and suicidal ideation. (p. 36)

Why can't the protectors simply be dismissed from their jobs? Some of the reasons have been discussed in the previous chapters on disarming firefighters and managers. Here, we explore more fully why and how the relationship between the protectors and the exiled parts blocks the therapist and survivor from easy access to the child-parts.

Managers and Firefighters Believe Exiles Must Remain Banished

The managers and firefighters have varying reasons for why the exiles' secrets and intense emotions should be kept hidden. Most typically, they fear that either the Self or the entire system cannot handle the information. They do not trust the survivor's now-adult Self either to protect the system from the exiles or to protect the exiles from further abuse. Some protectors fear that the person might blend with rageful, desperate, or suicidal parts who will be activated by the memories. Still other protectors might fear that everyone, especially the therapist, will discover the truth— that the survivor is damaged and repulsive—and that they will then abandon her. Firefighters and managers also legitimately fear the consequences of releasing the exiled parts because the exiles will gladly suffer more abuse for a bit of love.

Underlying these reasons is the belief that the exiles are defenseless, fragile, unpredictable, and a danger to themselves and the entire internal system. Typically, the exiles will acquiesce to this assessment, accepting the label of defenseless along with the accompanying protection. Jenny, one of Lorene's young exiles, recites her familiar litany of total vulnerability:

Jenny: *My body is my true enemy. It goes with me everywhere. It prevents me from disappearing. It lets people see me. I can never be safe if I'm in this body.*

The protective parts believe that the exiles are vulnerable because they have been victimized, are still frightened, and cannot adequately protect themselves. Often this is true—the exiles are still frightened, unable to protect themselves, and merely huddle in fear. Andy, a child-part of Lorene, admits:

Andy: *When people look at me, I think they are going to lash out—kick me, punch me—just to laugh and see if I'll cry and cry more and still no one will help. But people just walk by me. I don't know when it'll happen, which one of them will hurt me, how loud I'll scream. So the screams just stay in my eyes and I keep waiting.*

The protective parts tend to view the younger parts as wounded, bleeding, spiritless, atrophied, lacking any physical or emotional strength. In this they completely underestimate the younger parts and discount their years of heroic endurance and stamina in the face of horrendous abuse. Indeed, the protectors want to keep the exiles captive, so that the exiles can hold the abuse-related memories and emotions captive. Consider Lorene's exile, Bonnie, and her memory of the abuse:

Bonnie: *In a room with wood floors, white walls, staying under a table while Dad's friend stays on the bed with his sons. I saw him pay Dad money; maybe I've been sold to him forever. I bang my head on the floor, moan, like a trapped animal. Will he rip open my body? I feel the pain shoot throughout me even though he didn't touch me yet. Hot searing pain like electric jolts which are much bigger than my body. Did you ever feel someone forcing things into your rectum—pain throbbing through your body over and over? Then his wife comes and laughs and laughs and smothers my face with her breasts. He comes and yells to hold still and my body isn't mine. I'm nothing. I cannot fight him. I can only become the pain so that I won't be the little girl who feels the pain.*

With this type of terror locked within the exiles, it is no wonder the other parts fear their return to the present-day life of the adult survivor.

All three groups of parts, then, share the belief that the exiles must be banished, kept from both the Self and other parts, so that they can receive maximum isolation and protection. Tension often increases as the exiles' desperation and neediness propels them to try to break out of this internal prison.

In exploring reasons for refusing to grant the Self access to exiles, remember that managers and firefighters have different views as to why the exiles are kept in hiding. Lorene's manager, Vincent, explains his crucial protective role:

Vincent: *I am the only one who knows of the hot molten steel raging inside the seven-year-old's abdomen. It could destroy her. She could implode. It is my job to protect her. My work is incredibly essential — terrible things could happen to the little girl.*

In contrast, a firefighter may protect an exiled part because he believes the exile is evil and vile, in need of concealment. For example, Nicky believes if people see the "damaged" Jennifer, they will be disgusted and turn away from Lorene, causing her great pain and shame.

Sadly, then, both firefighters and managers keep the exiles banished because they blame, hate, or fear the young parts. They are too small, need too much care and love, and would endanger all parts in the system just to get a little attention. (See chapter 16 on firefighters' and managers' view of the "badness" of exiles.) The protectors' intentions are founded in deep fear. When Lorene entered therapy, her firefighters remained on call at all times, ready to pounce on the therapist or Lorene. Victor rants to Lorene:

Victor: *Moving Destiny and Andy from the past is wrong. Remembering about the bathroom and basement is wrong. Remembering about Dad's games is wrong. Dick breaks too many rules such as: Don't feel real feelings; don't acknowledge your sexuality; don't cry; don't touch anyone; don't tell the truth.*

Despite their differences, if a manager can convince firefighter parts that a threat is imminent, the two groups will join, forming an alliance to counter the threat. For example, if a managerial part (Super-She) believes that she cannot adequately address an imminent danger, she will call upon a firefighter part (Nicholas) to join in the fight for survival. Even though it means enduring the firefighter's chaotic techniques, the manager recognizes that at least the chaos will be controlled by internal, rather than external forces:

Super-She: *Jenny says someone keeps hitting her in the face, over and over. So evenly. Hit, hit, hit, hit. I keep going to work, going to meetings, achieving, accomplishing. But I can always feel someone pounding her face with a hammer.*

Nicholas: *I'll stop that crap. I'll cut that leg open so the blood will pour out and now she's a different person.*

Super-She: *I know it's just your macho garbage, but still — it does sufficiently distract and distort.*

Nicholas: *Admit it — I'm better at handling these emergencies than you. Your graduate degrees and committees and timetables are too wimpy. Now the pounding is her body pumping blood from her leg onto the bathroom floor. Everything's fine now. She doesn't feel anyone pounding her face anymore.*

The Self and the therapist need to intercede repeatedly in the alliance of the firefighters and managers to keep the exiled part quiet. They must listen to the protective parts' fears and ideas and then quietly and firmly continue to care for the protectors, while refusing to turn over leadership to them. However, a managerial part might also intercede, realizing that a firefighter's rampage of destruction has become so out-of-control that the ultimate annihilation of the client herself (instead of just the exile) is inevitable (through suicide, imprisonment for criminal acts, life-threatening disease caused by promiscuity or prostitution, life-threatening eating disorders such as anorexia nervosa, or making it impossible for the Self to ever return to a leadership role due to permanent physical and mental impairment caused by alcoholism or drug abuse). At some point, the managerial part may retract her permission to let the firefighter act, and move to block him, ending the alliance.

Even when one protector concedes that the survivor should have access to an exiled part, another protector may vehemently disagree with these tactical decisions. For example, firefighter Victor battles manager Dashiell to keep the exiled Andy from talking:

Victor: *You won't get any information from me or Andy. I refuse to get involved anymore. I'm just going to do whatever I want to do.*

Dashiell: *Where is Andy?*

Victor: *Dead, I guess. Who cares?*

Dashiell: *I do. Let me have him.*

Victor: *He's gone. Forget him. Pretend like he's still in the basement playing sex-games.*

Dashiell: *You should die! I hate you more than I've ever hated a part.*

Victor: *So what? My job doesn't require that I win a popularity contest. If I have to go on seeing Dick, I'm going to play hard ball. No more* *understanding and caring nonsense. Next I'll kill those stupid girl parts. Then Lorene.*

The survivor's Self or the therapist must step in to talk with a part like Victor. If he cannot be convinced to let Dashiell or the Self near Andy, the survivor may have to insist, explaining to Victor that they *will* speak to Andy. (Later, the survivor or the therapist should check in with Victor to address his reaction to the contact with Andy.) This approach, however, often encourages power struggles.

The protective parts' fears cannot be underestimated. Each part may fear something different, and each fear must be addressed. Most significantly, remember that the fears are very real to the parts, given the time warp within which the exiles (and some of the protectors) live. The fears should be treated with great respect.

Relinquishing Roles as Protectors

Hopefully, it is clear by now that before firefighters and managers can stop imposing their "protective" behavior on the survivor, their fears must be addressed. We go on to explore ten things the protectors need to learn before they will step away from the young exiled parts.

1. *Firefighters and managers need to know that the Self will not blend with the exiles.* Instead, it will care for the exiles, monitoring their behavior so they do not successfully attract more abuse. There are parts who can also care for the young exiles, but the caretaking should be done under the direction of the Self. This type of interaction comforts the managers and firefighters greatly; they learn to trust the Self to remain in a leadership position and safely acclimate the exiles to the present-day life of the adult survivor.

2. *Both firefighters and managers need to know that their opponents will retreat, too.* The two groups must retreat almost simultaneously, one step at a time, learning to trust the other not to be extreme. If the managers think the firefighters will continue their destructive efforts to distract the exiles from moving to the present, the managers simply will not retreat. (See chapter 9 on depolarization.) If the firefighters think the managers will not stop imposing a cold numbness and hiding all feelings, the firefighters will fight back with chaos and impulsive outbursts, refusing to retreat from their extreme position. In addition, the survivor's Self must not blend such that it exhibits fear of one group or the other. It is important that the Self remain separate when confronted with scare tactics used by either group of older parts to "protect" the exiles. As the Self resolutely

demonstrates the desire and capability to care for all parts, firefighters and managers are better able to trust one another.

3. *Firefighters and managers need to get the permission of the exiles to release them from their protective functions.* Merely asking the protective parts to step aside isn't always enough. Often it's also important to get explicit permission from the exiled parts to release their protectors from duty. The therapist can ask the exiled parts whether they would be willing to dismiss the sentries who guard them and trust the Self for a short time, and whether they can stand alone just long enough to be direct about their fears. In the dialogue below, the consequences of failing to ask for this are painfully evident. Because Jenny has never dismissed Alex as her guard, Alex and Jenny *both* fight valiantly against Lorene's attempt to confront Jenny's reaction to the therapist's leaving on a business trip.

Alexandra: *It's over. Everything is ending. Out of the way, destruction is near!*

Self: *What are you screaming about? Are you so terrified because Dick is going on a trip?*

Alexandra: *I'm not trying to kill everyone—Dick is. He shouldn't go away. It means he was pretending to care when he was really planning to abandon us and create great danger.*

Self: *How does it feel to you?*

Alex: *Caught, trapped, nowhere to go. Try to make my own world where I can hide everyone. Don't reveal any weaknesses. Stay angry and keep people away from me.*

Self: *How do you pretend to the world you are strong?*

Alex: *Super-She uses her intellectual achievements. Fools them. Lets them think we're normal.*

Self: *But you're scared.*

Alex: *I'm scared they'll find out about her.*

Self: *The little girl part? Jenny?*

Alex: *Yes.*

Self: *Let me talk to her.*

Alex: *No. Stay away. I'll cut up your body. I'll set you on fire.*

Self: *Why are you lashing out at me? Be direct.*

Alex: *I need to keep us hidden.*

Self: *I'll talk to her quietly and you can stand guard, if you like.*

Jennifer: *I want to stay with Alex in the "other-world" she made for us.*

Self: *Are you scared because Dick is leaving town?*

Jennifer: *He doesn't exist anymore. He wasn't real.*

Self: *He is real, and he will come back from his trip.*

Alex: *See how stupid this is. How can I hide if you make so much noise.*

You're always trying to make deals, coax parts out of fear and into different roles. Go away.

Jennifer: *Alex is right. Alex is strong and will hide me. It's safe here. Like my closet. It isn't good to stay in here, but at least no one can hurt my body. I'm buried here.*

Self: *I will not force you to come out. But remember that I am here and I can protect you. While Dick is gone, you can hide if you need to, but I'll check on you and talk to you. You don't need to have Alex threaten me. Whenever you wish, you can tell Alex that you want to talk to me.*

4. *Firefighters and managers need to know that they have played a valuable role, particularly during the survivor's childhood, and they need to be assured that they will continue to have a valuable role in the system.* The managers and firefighters might perceive the exile's freedom as a threat to their role as the great protectors of the system. For example, firefighters might believe that if the Self is permitted to listen to, take care of, and protect the younger, abused parts, then the firefighters will disappear from existence because there will no longer be a "job" for them; the reason for their existence will be gone. Without help from the Self, firefighters especially remain unaware of any sense of their existence beyond their role as protectors of the exiles. Other chapters discuss the valuable functions that both firefighters and managers have served for the survivor. Before and during a retrieval process the protectors can be reminded that, even when the child-parts are taken out of exile, they will retain important positions within the system. They will not be eliminated; instead, the Self will help them find new, preferred roles.

5. *Firefighters and managers need to accept the exiled parts as they return to the present — without blame and without judgment.* As mentioned earlier, Lorene wrote about using a tiny doll to demonstrate the vulnerability of a small child to parts who blamed her exiles for the abuse. As her Self, she explains what happened when parts of her insisted on mutilating the doll and bringing it to the next therapy session:

I took a little, plastic doll and I made it look like a tortured baby. I slashed it up with a razor blade, used marker to put red and brown all over it, like blood and feces. It dramatically demonstrated to some of my parts that a child is too small and helpless to suffer the inhuman things that I have survived. No child should ever have to experience these things. The doll gave Jenny and even Nicholas a glimpse at a stark reality which they ignore: I didn't deserve Dad's instrument-rapes and I didn't deserve my parents' abandonment. My parts understood the message. Even when I just think of the doll, I shiver. The doll truly communicated the total lack of power I had as a child. Nicholas always thought he/I should have done something rather than "participate." The doll shows that a tiny child who is regularly tied up, brainwashed, cut, burned, and raped simply lacks even the slightest ability to do anything other than survive.

6. *Firefighters and managers need to refrain from blending with the exiles as the young parts experience their sadness, sense of betrayal, and pain.* In the following example, Lorene is initially surprised by the fierce emotions displayed by Alex, Nicholas, and Super-She, until she realizes that, in protecting Jenny, they positioned themselves so close to her that they became overwhelmed by her emotions. Note the blending/protective response of Lorene's system when it becomes clear that Jenny is going to talk about her memories in therapy.

Nicholas: *No way! I can't believe you trust a dumb therapist. I'll get Alex to seduce him. Jenny will go for it because then she'll get held.*

Super-She: *That will probably work. I'll be super-brave and maintain control of crying, shaking and other weaknesses.*

Alexandra: *Then I'm going to the other-world I built. I'm not staying for this.*

Self: *Be quiet, Alex. Why are you all so scared? I know you usually act like overprotective maniacs when you get terribly scared. Super-She, why are you so angry, and yet supporting the degrading sexual conduct by "freezing"?*

Super-She: *I don't think it's appropriate to blame me for this difficulty.*

Self: *I think that right now you're the most likely one to help me. You could easily refuse to support Nicholas' "firefighter" interference.*

Super-She: *Well, it's not my fault he's nuts. I certainly didn't suggest the seduction of Dick just to avoid Jenny's talking to him.*

Self: *You know that I won't allow Nicholas to implement his suggestion, and it wouldn't work anyway—but he can create a great deal of fear and embarrassment among parts so that I won't be able to focus on taking care of Jenny. Do you like what you're doing by freezing and numbing parts of me so I can't handle this?*

Super-She: *I hate this! I hate being Super-She. I hate being super-strong while someone hurts you. But I can't bear for Jennifer to be sad and frightened.*

Self: *Okay. Now I get it. You're all too close to Jenny. You must pull away so you won't blend with her; otherwise I can't work with her feelings. Super-She must stop freezing my feelings so that I can show Jenny the compassion and caring that I feel for her. I promise that I will not blend with Jenny. I will take care of her without being overwhelmed by her emotions. But all of you must back off and trust me.*

Both Lorene and the therapist became proficient at identifying parts who were overwhelmed by another part's emotions. Once they could convince the protectors to retreat, assuring them that Lorene and the therapist could care for the emotion-laden exile, the protectors relaxed and stopped blending.

7. *Firefighters and managers need to know that they, too, can be helped, listened to, and respected.* Sometimes out of envy firefighters or managers who remain stuck in the past will fight against an exile's move to the present, perhaps because they, like the exiles, want to be cared for and listened to, but they are afraid to leave the past. Or a therapist may find that an exile refuses to leave the past until the protector leaves too. While focusing on the retrieval of exiled child-parts, remember that sometimes *all* the survivor's parts believe the survivor still lives in a very dangerous world.

The retrieval of an older part may require the therapist to answer a different type of question about safety. The child-like parts ask questions referring to their physical safety from the original abuse. ("Is Daddy going to wake me up tonight?") The older managers and firefighters might focus on questions about current adult relationships that the parts fear might become abusive; they worry about new rejection, betrayal, and abandonment. Paradoxically, these things might result from the part's own behavior, like a firefighter setting up a rejection that he feels is inevitable. Consider the commentary of Lorene's Self as she recounts firefighter Nicholas blocking the retrieval of Lorene's young part, Andy.

Self: *Today Dick asked a young part, Andy, about what happened when I was young. Andy was very, very sad. He focused on Mom not coming to get me away from Dad. Dick says Andy should accept the fact that Mom isn't coming. Andy says no, he can't leave the past, he has to wait for Mom. Dick tried to move other parts away to help Andy, but Andy closed off, said he couldn't see anything anymore, no more memories, the end.*

Andy wouldn't talk to Dick anymore. He was very sad and wouldn't even look at Dick for almost an hour. Stayed curled up under my coat, head down. Tired, tears, not caring about anything except waiting for Mom. He wants Nicholas to tell him what to do. Andy didn't care if Dick understood, didn't expect him to help.

As Lorene and the therapist worked with other parts, they finally discovered that Andy refused to leave the past because of his strong connection (almost symbiotic) with Nicholas, who was at least partially stuck in that childhood molestation scene, too. Andy could not leave until Nicholas left. Lorene and the therapist then worked with Nicholas, who amazingly admitted that the incest memories sometimes aroused him. Nicholas reported that he felt he could not leave the past because he could not control the arousal; he believed that he was evil and that he could never feel sexual pleasure unless it was accompanied by abuse. The therapist reassured him that any 12-year-old (Nicholas' age) would be aroused by exposure to so much sex. Nicholas responded, "No—absolutely not!" Lorene describes the struggle further, with Nicholas' thoughts leaking through:

Self: Dick tells Nicholas that many, many people have those inappropriate sexual feelings. (What's he talking about?)
　　Dick says it's very normal to feel sexual when constantly exposed to sex. (What's going on?)
　　Nicholas is dumbstruck, incredulous, hopeful, trying to pretend he misunderstood. (How could Dick be right? Impossible.)
　　Calming himself down—saying no, Dick has misunderstood. Don't confuse sympathy with empathy, or pity with understanding. (But maybe?) Dick assured Nicky that he can move to the present also. (Nicholas hopes!)

8. *Firefighters and managers need to learn to let both the exiles and themselves experience intense emotions, without the accompanying need to do anything.* Before parts are moved to the present, they behave like any oppressed group; they grow more and more desperate and seek any opportunity to break free and tell their stories. As the exiles are given permission to express their emotions, the protectors can learn to do the same. For example, sometimes a firefighter pretends an exile is scared, when actually it is the firefighter who is scared. In this example, Lorene's Self discusses Victor's admission that he feels desperately lonely and needs comfort:

Self: Victor used to pretend he was never scared of anything, yet he wandered from one child-part to another, trying to suppress anything that might activate or trigger more of his own fears and sadness. This week Victor actually admitted his desire to be held and loved. He begged for someone, or something, to give him boundaries—like a straitjacket. (He pretends he is "held," encompassed, by a brick wall.) Victor admitted that he often tried to keep Andy quiet so that he (Victor) wouldn't get scared!

9. *Firefighters and managers need to watch the exiles become stronger and stronger as they shed their outdated burdens of terror and pain.* Often other parts are surprised to find inherent strength in exiled parts. However, even when an exiled young part exhibits strength and voices a desire to permit the Self to care for and protect it, other parts might still interfere,

believing that the exile simply isn't strong enough to realize what she would risk if she emerged from the manager's cocoon of numbness or the firefighter's distracting destructiveness. They push the exiled part back into hiding, even terrorizing the young part with "pictures" of the abuse recurring. The protectors must learn that each independent step taken by an exile is more than an accident, that the exile is truly learning to walk by herself.

10. *Firefighters and managers need to know the childhood abuse will not recur.* Managers and firefighters might equate *remembering* the abuse with an actual recurrence of the abuse, as the following example demonstrates. When Lorene's Self intercedes, however, firefighter Alex and manager Vincent cautiously agree to let the exiled parts be heard:

Jenny: I want to remember, to see and talk about those things that happened to me.
Self: Why?
Jenny: Then I won't be all alone with what happened. You will be there and Dick will be there. Right now, I'm so alone, and I'm in such a dark, small place where no one can hear me. I don't want to stay.
Self: Who is making me feel like I want to be in pain?
Alexandra: I am! Cutting is best. I'll cut my stomach tonight—then everything will calm down.
Self: Cutting won't help Jenny. It will only mask the love you feel for Jenny. Just be direct with her.
Alex: You don't understand. I can suffer for her so she won't suffer at all, and no secrets will be told.
Self: Why is Jenny hurting?
Alex: Because she can't remember things. But maybe Jenny isn't even here, maybe she was never real. I don't want to hear her secrets.
Self: Alex, you must separate yourself from Jenny. You exist separate from Jenny's pain. Let me take care of Jenny and decide when it's good for her to talk about the abuse.
Vincent: Bad things are happening inside.
Self: I know, Vincent. But whatever is happening, we can go on.
Vincent: Perhaps the best thing would be to set aside this incest issue for a few years. I have no idea where you think you're heading with it.
Self: You don't always need to know where. But it will come. Things won't stop here. I will take care of Jenny. I know you want to help, but wait till I ask you. Alex, can you trust me that nothing will happen if Jenny talks about her memories?
Alex: I guess I could try for a few minutes. If I have to.
Self: Jenny, if Alex backs away, will you trust me to take care of you?
Jenny: Yes, I'd like to try it, if it won't make Alex mad.

REFUSING TO LEAVE THE PAST

Convincing managers and firefighters to allow access to the exiled child-parts is only the first step. Cautiously approaching the exiles is next. Unfortunately, they sometimes "dig in their heels" and refuse to leave the abusive childhood setting where they reside. Here we explore eight specific reasons given by child-parts to explain their refusal to leave the past. (These reasons may apply to other parts as well.)

1. *The child-part does not yet trust that the Self can care for it.* It is crucial that exiles believe that the Self can capably care for and protect them. It is only under the Self's care that exiles can shed their burden of guilt-by-participation (in the incest), shame at not being "good," and betrayal after her repeated abandonment. If the Self can visit the exiles consistently in the past, the exiles will gradually feel safe enough to leave their stuck points. It has been a long, long time since the Self carried on a daily relationship with the exiles, and it takes time to redevelop the trust and familiarity necessary for the Self to guide the young parts out of their home in the past.

2. *The exile views the client's present life as dangerous.* The survivor may be living with an abusive husband, or perhaps even still living with her father but insisting that the incest has ended and she no longer fears him. The exile might also perceive internal dangers, pointing to dangerous firefighters who have repeatedly attacked the survivor. Whether the danger is internal or external, it must be addressed. The therapist and survivor should not remove the exile from the past only to thrust her into another abusive setting in the present.

3. *Something in the past holds the child-part captive.* Sometimes an exiled child-part insists, without explanation, that she cannot leave the past. The therapist and the survivor's Self can only ask her questions about where she is, what she is waiting for, or what she fears will happen. Often the child can describe the restraining force. Perhaps it is sheer terror, or a message from the abuser that paralyzes her into a nearly autistic state, or a sense that if she leaves the past she will never be redeemed, forced to suffer through eternity the burden of her "sins." She may also believe that she will be abandoning other parts if she leaves the past.

4. *The child-part lives in terror that the abuse will recur at any moment.* She fears her body will be hurt again. As discussed above, it cannot be overemphasized how much the child-parts may have been terrorized. A young part, trapped in pockets of time created two, three, or four decades earlier, actually believes that her abuser may come into the adult client's

bed tonight, or pass her on the street and wink, signaling that he is still in charge. She watches everyone, and prefers to hide in a cocoon at home where she won't encounter unexpected danger. She does not like outings or parties or public events, because there the abuser might wander in and surprise her. The most obvious characteristics of these young parts, then, are frozen waiting and absolute certainty that the abuse has not yet ended. This is not a child who runs and plays and laughs. Spontaneity left her life long ago. She acts very much like a young child who is presently being abused. She flinches from loud noises or sudden movements, she stares at nothing, she demands nothing, she shivers, she cries, she clings, she shies away from people. You can tell her that her childhood abuser is now dead, or living far away, or in prison, or no longer interested in the now-adult body. The exile nods, assures you she understands, and then quietly asks, "But is he coming tonight? Tomorrow night?" She must slowly be shown that her body and soul will be protected by the Self.

5. *The child-part fears that expressing emotions will result in additional disappointment and unbearable rejection.* Lorene's part, Andy, demonstrates a willingness to take a peek and see if the therapist still shows he cares, even as Andy worries that the therapist will become disappointed and ultimately reject him:

Andy: *Usually Nicholas acts angry and defiant to hide me. Today Dick kept asking about me. He really was interested in how I felt! He helps me find courage. But I felt a little guilty for taking something—Dick's interest in me—that I don't really think I should have. I feel like I've done something wrong. It was hard not to cry when I told Dick about the "disappointment place" where I feel very lonely, but I'm not blending with anyone. A huge, desolate place. And me. I choose to stay there. Why? Nothing to compare myself to in that place. Everything is neutral. Then I won't feel anyone's disappointment in me. I wonder if Dick thinks I'm disgusting.*

Exiles feel horribly alone and need to express that in a safe environment. Every day they relive the abandonment they felt at the time of the abuse. Jennifer expressed her anguish:

Jennifer: *I cry and cry and bleed and call Mom but she is too busy. Sometimes Dad does not want me anymore either, and so he gives me to his friends. And when they come, oh it hurts so much and I'm scared and why doesn't Mom come to help. Make him stop. I'm so scared and it's so hard to be quiet. It goes on and on and it hurts too much to think it will stop. Sometimes it is better to believe it will never stop—this is normal life—don't call out for Mom to save me.*

6. *The child-part wants to protect others from having contact with her, since she fears her power to trigger rage, sexual arousal, and similarly intense reactions in other parts and people.* The child-part has seen that her body can cause a grown man to desperately seek her out, craving her touch, resulting in startling physical and emotional changes as he soars toward orgasm. She also knows her presence can trigger unpredictable anger in adults (or in the survivor's internal firefighters). Like all parts in the abused system, she may believe she has a negative, magical power over other people. Working with the survivor's Self, the exile can learn that she had no magical powers over the perpetrator; instead the abuse occurred because he himself had parts who were extreme and caused him to be abusive.

7. *The child-part believes she should remain in the abusive setting as punishment for her past sins—for "causing" the abuse, enjoying the attention, feeling physical pleasure, and telling (or failing to tell) other adults about the abuse.* This belief is tenacious, frustrating many a therapist and survivor who feel as if they cannot reach beyond the child-part's shame and guilt (explored further in chapter 16). This is particularly the case when the child was bombarded with religious notions of punishment and redemption. Over time, the exile needs to learn that whatever she thought or felt in the past was a successful and creative way of defending herself in the past, but the defenses are no longer needed in the present.

8. *The child-part fears losing her only power and control when she gives up her secrets.* The inner child may also be afraid to tell any abuse-related secrets for fear that she'll lose control of the abusive situation (which she believes is ongoing). Sgroi and Bunk (1988) discuss the idea that the child who holds the secret of the abuse might feel that she is "in a dominant power position over those who do not know the secret" (pp. 172–73). They add:

> Clinicians should be aware that keeping the sexual abuse a secret from others may also be part of rewriting the script for the child, and as such is a coping mechanism that helps the patient feel more in control while the abuse is going on. A child might say, "If I tell someone, it will be because I want it to stop. But if the abuse continues, it will be because I wanted it to continue." [Ultimately] . . . the secret keeping helps the survivor feel more in control of himself or herself within the context of [any intimate] relationship. (p. 173)

RETRIEVING THE CHILD-PARTS
•
Making Contact

Contacting the exiles rarely poses a difficulty once the managers and firefighters have been calmed. Most exiles crave the opportunity to "come out," although some will briefly hide or retreat. Initially the therapist or the survivor's Self can access a young part by simply asking him or her to appear or by focusing on a vulnerable feeling such as sadness or loneliness (see chapter 8 regarding accessing parts). Napier (1993) explains to survivors how they can use a bridge across time and space:

> Recall a situation in recent days that upset you or triggered you into one of those "pockets of time." Then, use the feelings that were present in the recent situation as a bridge and allow yourself to follow the bridge across time and space, back to a time and a place where you experienced something similar as a child.
> In order to use your feelings as a bridge, simply ask your unconscious to take you back. . . . Because there is no time in the unconscious, you can be here, or there, or anywhere, with just a thought. (p. 161)

Discovering where in the survivor's "time-line" the child-part became stuck poses little problem in most cases. Most child-parts can identify their stuck location. Usually, the survivor's Self (or therapist's Self, if necessary) simply needs to ask the exile. Some show the Self a physical scene, some simply describe where they are, and others give the Self a feeling that the survivor identifies with a particular time or setting.

Do Not Kidnap a Child Part

Therapists should never insist that an exile leave the past and enter the future, since this would be tantamount to kidnapping and would repeat the abusive relationship. As discussed above, exiles sometimes need to stay in the past until they can tell their story, until a firefighter becomes less destructive, or until an abusive person with whom the survivor is having a relationship is no longer part of her life. Trying to repeatedly cajole the exile into leaving before these things happen will undermine her trust in the Self and in the therapist. Ingerman (1989) explained how she solved the problem of one client, Susan, whose inner child was stuck in the time of the childhood abuse. Ingerman learned that the child-part did not realize that the abusive situation had ended. Ingerman "explained that circumstances were different now, and she didn't have to worry about her father hitting her"; the child-part finally agreed to return to her "home"—to her body (p. 27). Ingerman warned that it was important to "refuse to capture and drag back a missing part; instead I'll do everything I can to convince it to come back freely. In my experience patience and information about what, and who, is waiting for the soul in life, always results in its agreement to return" (p. 26).

The IFS therapist similarly goes directly to the exile and asks questions about the *possibility* of leaving the abusive setting where she is stuck, working with her patiently until she is ready to leave. The therapist or the

Self can enter the scene and care for the part in the way she should have been cared for when the abuse originally occurred. The exiled part may prefer to wait until later to speak about the abuse, once she has returned to a safe place in the present.

The Journey Home

Here, Lorene's Self discusses moving Destiny from the past to the present, demonstrating a direct access retrieval, where the therapist brings back a part because, at that point, the client's Self is not trusted enough to perform the retrieval. In many cases, the Self (or the Self with the therapist) does the actual retrieving.

Self: *Parts have fought time-travel for so long. But Dick got Destiny to describe where she was. This time he didn't say, "Are you ready to come into the present?" Instead, he made it a smaller, more concrete step and simply asked her to look around and describe where she was. It worked!*

Des described the bathroom, but refused to tell Dick what was happening, instead just referring to the "worst things." Then Dick told Destiny he'd help her leave when she was ready. She argued at first that she was meant to be there, but finally she said she'd go.

Des then eased across the bathroom, afraid of Dad's angry eyes. She stopped again, asking Dick about whether she was meant to stay because she was bad. He again refused to bend on the subject. Finally they left the bathroom and went outside Dad's house.

Des became frightened again outside, but Dick kept reminding her to listen to his voice, look at him, and follow him to the present. Des followed him to my home (now).

It felt like it happened so fast, but it took about half an hour.

The most important thing for Des was Dick's willingness to physically hang on tight to Des, keeping her safe in the present, while horrendous forces tried to rip her away and keep her in the past.

It's been a week since that session. Every time Des got frightened (often), she'd remember that Dick was still (figuratively) beside her. She is immediately calmed by that knowledge. Maybe now she can "tell her story."

This retrieval is typical in that a part who is stuck in the past needs to describe the abuse-related scene where she is stuck, have someone enter that scene, and help her walk away from it. While some parts who watch this retrieval might object, accusing the therapist of being "hokey," other parts insist that they too want to be retrieved and brought to the present.

Finding a Home in the Present

Once all this is in place—managers and firefighters have been consulted and are cooperative, the exile wants to come into the present, the present is a safe place for her to live, and the Self is differentiated enough to care for her—then the child-part and Self should discuss various (imagined) locations for the exile to live. The range of locations is limitless. Some exiles want to stay close to the Self, at least for a while, and so accompany the person around all day. Other child-parts feel comfortable staying in the survivor's bedroom or living room. Others want to stay outside in a pleasant setting or live on an island. It doesn't seem to matter, as long as the child-part feels safe and can be visited easily by the Self. In addition, if the present does not feel safe, the child-part can be taken to a different location where she was safe in the past.

Once a location has been agreed upon, the Self takes the part to the new place, stays with her until she feels safe there, and tries to arrange things so she is comfortable. The Self also asks the child-part if she would like other parts to stay with her, to keep an eye on her when the Self isn't there. If the exile wants this, then the Self asks for volunteers among the other parts. Frequently, one of the managers volunteers and caretaking becomes the part's new role.

Checking with Managers and Firefighters

After a retrieval, the Self (or therapist) must ask the managers and firefighters how they feel about the change and ask whether any parts are likely to sabotage it. Remember that, as long as they mistrust the Self, some parts will work to block the Self's access to the exiles. Some parts might keep the Self from following through and visiting the child-part. But if the Self doesn't follow through with visits, the child-part will feel abandoned and may even return to the past, becoming more reluctant than ever to leave. The noninterfering protector parts will also lose trust in the Self. To avoid this scenario, the Self first must remain differentiated. While this does not guarantee access to the exiles, it does ensure the Self's success (after a time, perhaps) in working with the managers or firefighters who want to prevent communication with exiles. The protectors ultimately learn that the Self *joins* them in their goal to do what is in the best interests of the young exiles. As the Self builds a trusting relationship with the protectors, it benefits from the wealth of information held by them.

Maintaining a Differentiated Self

The key to the entire retrieval process is the leadership role of the differentiated Self. As mentioned, on occasion the therapist's Self will have to function as the Self of the survivor's system, until the parts regain their trust in the survivor's Self.

The Self must remind frightened parts of what is, in fact, real. If the Self is not afraid (fear would indicate it had blended with a part), there is nothing inside that can hurt the survivor. Only fear opens the door to destructive behavior. The Self, then, assures the parts that it can handle any pressure that arises. Notice how the various parts rally around to help Jennifer (after her retrieval from the past), when she becomes frightened by Lorene's change of jobs. Note that Alex's previously close, protective relationship with Jenny means that before Lorene's Self can effectively calm Jenny, she must first calm Alex:

Jennifer: *Everything is raw and fragile today.*

Super-She: *I will handle things at the new job. No one else has to. I can super-function, impressing everyone at work.*

Self: *I appreciate your help, but all the parts must realize they don't need protection from any danger at the new job.*

Alexandra: *We can all hide or refuse to go. I don't care what happens there, anyway. I'm just not going to go. I'm going to build another world for myself and any other part who wants to can come with me.*

Jenny: *I'll go with you, Alex.*

Self: *Alex, if you were going to be at work, what do you think could happen?*

Alex: *Target. Rape. Shame.*

Self: *Think of the reality. Just an office, some people, a desk—things you are familiar with.*

Jenny: *No garages? No basements? No bathrooms? No ice water in my vagina?*

Self: *No. That is a promise. I would not let that happen again.*

Alex: *People might say mean things there.*

Self: *People will say mean things sometimes. But then what? Think of real things—I love to work and so do several of the parts. It is stimulating, interesting, purposeful.*

Vincent: *Super-She and I like to work.*

Self: *Why punish yourself so much, Alex? Why create terror?*

Alex: *It helps make me emotionally unavailable. It reminds me I am meant to be hurt, so I will be prepared for more pain.*

Self: *You are preparing only for physical pain. Your images are about blood and rape and physical terror. The only thing that might happen— the worst thing—is that someone might hurt your feelings at the new job. By doing this, you only make the "hurt feelings" harder for me to handle.*

Alex: *So what am I supposed to do?*

Self: *Trust me to lead. I'm perfectly capable of it.*

Alex: I'm too scared. I never felt so scared.

Self: Actually, you have felt this before. Many times, I think. It is a comfortable hiding place where you go. If you need to hide, let me make a safe place for you. Jenny, did you listen? Can you help Alex not be scared?

Jenny: Yes, I can help. I won't ask her to take me to the other-world. I'll stay with you and then maybe Alex can get better, too.

Firefighters and managers can prove to be extremely helpful in guiding the newly returned exiles into their inner family, particularly in reassuring them that the survivor's Self can be trusted. Consider how Lorene's manager (Vincent) interacts with the child-part (Andy) in the following example. Later during the inner conversation, Alexandra and Dashiell join in, showing their curiosity about the internal family's activities. They use a caring, supportive tone towards Andy, like older siblings might use.

Andy: It was hard not to cut today, but I didn't. Bridgette says I'm wrong to consider my body the enemy. I cannot accept her ideas, because I cannot accept that I am good, or strong, or trustworthy. I don't trust myself. A person says, "Hello" and I scream, "Take care of me!"

Vincent: You sound very confused. (No! Nicholas, be quiet! I'm talking to Andy.)

Andy: Well, I'm not used to talking to someone else. I usually talk to Nicholas.

Vincent: What do you want?

Andy: I want to change. I want to feel strong and brave and bigger. I'm not big enough.

Vincent: Big enough for what?

Andy: To protect myself.

Vincent: From what?

Andy: From the things I blend with.

Vincent: Like Dad? What did he give you?

Andy: Attention. He was very big and had lots of power. He took whatever he wanted.

Vincent: What do you want that you need so much power for?

Andy: I want to believe in something strong.

Vincent: Do you believe in Lorene's Self?

Andy: I hardly know her. What do you mean?

Vincent: Which parts do you know well?

Andy: Jenny, Alex, and Bridgette, a little.

Vincent: And you only see Lorene's Self through them?

Andy: Yes.

Vincent: They have some powers, but not the power of leadership. You drift about, with no sense of direction or leadership.

Andy: I would be ashamed and embarrassed for her to know me. I have done bad things, I think. I am selfish.

Vincent: Of course. And we each participated in our own way. You are not so powerful that you can act alone on such things.

Andy: This body is a traitor. I have to carry it with me always and I hate its cruel, adult demands when I feel like a child who just wants a mother.

Alexandra: So you hurt it?

Andy: I try to disguise it, ignore it, pretend it's not mine, scream at it, disown it, murder it, and torture it.

Alex: No kidding. Why can't you just let Lorene make the choices for your body?

Andy: She's a girl. She can't understand.

Dashiell: It is true that male parts in a female person are decidedly at a disadvantage as far as finding a "leader" to understand certain bodily fears.

Andy: This is all very embarrassing to discuss. How can I forgive myself for shameful manipulations? And how can I learn to live with my body?

Alex: What have you done with the shameful feelings?

Andy: I explain them away for short periods, telling myself it wasn't meant to be cruel, etc. And I feel sorry for myself. And I eat or cut — to keep from crying or screaming.

Dashiell: Why can't you cry? Is it dangerous?

Andy: It feels like the most lonely thing in the world. Like nothing living exists anymore and I'll drown all alone.

Alexandra: Rather dramatic.

Dashiell: What would you cry about, if you could?

Andy: Everything. You see, I could take on everyone's pain. I blend and my pain gets filtered and distorted. I can't find it by myself.

Vincent: We'll try talking again tomorrow. Sleep now.

In the face of the inevitable feelings of vulnerability experienced by adult survivors of abuse, the exiled parts must learn that the Self can and will take care of them — but only if they don't overwhelm the Self with their feelings. The exiles must also be assured that the Self will return if it leaves; that the protective parts will not be permitted to keep the Self locked away anymore. While this process of giving repeated reassurance may be draining, it has proved to be immensely successful in interrupting the sequence of extreme protective reactions triggered by the belief that the exiles' vulnerability cannot be sufficiently handled by the survivor's Self.

One indication that the Self has blended with an extreme protector is the survivor's insistence that she cannot bear to hear what secrets the exiled parts hold. In Sisk and Hoffman (1987), the survivor Sisk describes the inner turmoil she felt when, as an adult, she encountered her abusive stepfather. She felt a "battle raging inside" her, and she *became* (blended with) her frightened exile part.

> It was as if each painful memory had ripped off a part of me and I had left those parts behind. And now the memory had snapped back to me with each part. . . . And I couldn't protect the little girl inside anymore. I couldn't tell her all those disgusting things had not happened. For she and I both knew the truth now. She felt it. I felt it. We felt it together! (p. 195)

After blending with the exile, Sisk's Self no longer stood alone. Sisk was unable to care for the part who was afraid to hear the secrets. Sisk's Self would have to separate from the fearful part before her Self could comfort the little girl and hear her story.

Contrary to the pervasive belief in psychotherapy that change is not possible unless the survivor reexperiences the exiled feelings, we find that different parts have different needs in this regard and should be consulted as to how they can best be relieved of their burdens. For some parts it is important that the Self not only hear their story, but also experience their feelings. This often occurs after the part has been retrieved, when it is safer to be close to the exile. But other parts are fine after just showing images of what happened to them. This point demonstrates that *before* retrieval, being close to a young part often results in blending, making the survivor feel like she (instead of just part of her) is trapped in the original abusive setting. While this might make the exile feel less lonely, it also blocks the Self's ability to help the exile change her situation. *After* retrieval, however, it is much easier for the Self to be close enough to the young part so that the survivor can share the exile's feelings, while at the same time the Self retains an adult, present-day perspective.

As therapist and survivor work cautiously to lead an exile out of the abusive setting, managers and firefighters will often interfere, working hard in their protective roles. If they are not dealt with directly, they will plunge the survivor's Self into despair by blending. In the following, Lorene's Self finally blends with the protectors:

Self [blended with parts]: The time-travel we tried with Andy yesterday in therapy felt bad. I know it's because Victor was interfering, every few minutes saying things like, "Well, that was nice, let's stop now, okay?"

Today, Victor said he'd kill Andy because Andy can't live in the present. My mind is filled with visions of blood, horrible death. I sense peacefulness from Andy, like he's glad to be dead. Victor is bitter and more angry than I've seen him in a long time.

I feel depressed and sick, refusing to cry, nightmares. I think it's a mistake for Dick to "move" parts. They belong in a certain place and time and should be left alone.

The therapist's Self can provide only a certain amount of leadership for the survivor's internal system. Without the survivor's Self acting as leader, the exiles become afraid and often will not remain in the present for very long. Blending, therefore, proves to be one of the most detrimental obstacles to progress; it must be watched for carefully and addressed each time it occurs. A differentiated Self is the key to a successful retrieval.

LEARNING TO LIVE IN THE PRESENT

The Survivor's Reactions

Moving an exile to the present invariably affects the survivor's day-to-day functioning. Initially she might feel even more vulnerable or overprotective — perhaps either smothering or distancing from the therapist — because after retrieval the exiles may feel the freedom to share intense emotions. M. Watkins (1986) describes one patient's child-part whose "goal [was] not to grow up, but to be allowed to live, to exist," which included having permission to allow sadness overcome her (p. 155). For a time, the survivor may want to remain at home or someplace where she feels safe. Lorene writes:

I sense so much sadness and fear — that feels like Andy. Andy's feelings are easy to access now that he's in the present. It was hard for him to get used to being out of the scary basement. It took a week of staying in bed, hiding. Some days I felt very sick and weak. Finally I got Andy to talk to me without Victor interfering.

Indeed, simply telling the abuse story may "plunge the survivor into profound grief" (Herman, 1992, p. 188). Swink and Leveille (1986) observe that when the survivor begins to remember and face the abuse, "most victims will have dreams, nightmares and/or flashbacks of the abuse. If these had been totally blocked previously, they can be very frightening and confusing as they seem to be coming out of nowhere. . . . It feels as if she is being further victimized as she relives these experiences, but this time from within her own mind rather than from someone outside" (p. 123). After working with the parts who fear that the exiles' intense emotions will overwhelm the survivor, however, she inevitably celebrates her new ability to "feel the full range of emotions, including grief" (p. 188). The survivor relishes the ability to experience this full range of emotions after a lifetime of guarding vigilantly against them. But it takes time for some parts to welcome the reunion between the survivor and her emotions. If the external pressures in a survivor's life offer little opportunity for comfort and self-soothing during frightening periods, the retrievals should be paced accordingly.

Back to the Past

Despite all precautions, there will be times when child-parts return, or are thrust, back to the time and place where they were originally stuck. When this happens, the therapist and client's Self need to explore what happened to make the part return and what needs to change so that the exile can remain safely in the present. Often the cause of the reversion, as listed in the reasons above, is not wanting to leave the past, or something frightening which may be happening in the client's external world.

Nobody's Perfect

Errors will occur. No one does this work without stepping on a few landmines which violate internal rules. It is helpful if outside of therapy sessions the survivor carefully monitors the reactions of the system, perhaps keeping notes that can later be shared with the therapist. Parts will be quick to yell, "Abandonment!" They might accuse the survivor or therapist of abandoning them, for example, when the survivor permits a firefighter to release rage in an argument between the survivor and her husband, frightening the newly retrieved exile; or when the therapist does not receive a message and inadvertently fails to return the survivor's phone call; or when the survivor agrees to have dinner with her abusive parents. No matter how illogical the exiles' reasoning might be, the therapist and Self must respond quickly to the abandonment cry, if the cry is not to be experienced as another form of abuse. In the following example, Lorene's Self responds to the accusations of the young part, Andy, who felt abandoned as a result of Lorene's and the therapist's failure to check on him during the session after Andy's retrieval from the past.

Self: *I know Andy is so scared in that dark place. He says that when I was a child, he welcomed the intrusions to sexual parts of my body if they'd keep those things off my face. (Dad and his friends used to terrify me by putting moving bugs or gerbils on my face while my arms were tied.) Andy won't tell Dick what he sees. I know that means Andy has returned to the past. He's also mad that Dick didn't check in on him after moving him into the present.*

Andy: *So what? So you figured something out? I don't care. And I don't care that you know I welcomed sexual things in trade for no face creatures. I invited the sexual contact. That probably means I'm as bad as them, but that's just how it is, so don't try to make me pretend I'm good.*

Self: *You're so terrified.*

Andy: *Yes! Why didn't you and Dick check on me after you brought me out? You promised. Then he went on a trip. I'm mad that I have to be here again, and terrified of what they're going to do to me next.*

Self: It's not real. Dick told you that over and over again today.

Andy: No! I couldn't hear him or see him — he wasn't there.

Self: Sometimes you could hear him.

Andy: Well, maybe. But I'm never going to count on him or on you again.

Self: Why didn't you just tell him instead of throwing the pillow at him?

Andy: If he knew it was me, he'd be mad because he doesn't want to be with me. I had my chance and I must have done a bad job because he didn't check back on me. I thought he knew how scared I was to be in this new world. The present isn't terrifying like the basement, but it's unfamiliar and it's lonely in the present.

Self: It's my fault, too, Andy. I got distracted with Victor.

Andy: Sure, and you were experimenting with having Victor feel himself in the body. Why?

Self: That's when you got scared and went back?

Andy: Yes.

Self: Okay. In the next session you can try to leave the basement and we'll help you move to the present again.

The parts who have been moved to the present must believe that the survivor and therapist will come back and listen to their story, comfort them, and verify their existence. Otherwise, the protector parts will rebel, and the young parts will blend with the survivor, overwhelming her with their neediness and desperation.

Needs of Retrieved Parts

Once the child-part has returned to the present, she must learn to live again. What does she need in order to become healthy and remain in the present?

1. *The child-part needs a safe place where her physical and emotional needs are met.* Exiles are like abandoned children; they desperately want to be cared for and loved. Survivors generally find it helpful to perform very concrete tasks like eating healthy food, re-reading a favorite book, or listening to comforting music. It is similar to caring for a child who has returned home after being very ill and hospitalized. The child is still weak, but ready to begin returning to the world, leaving high fevers and strong medicines and blood tests and hospitals far behind. The first step should not be a crowded, noisy party to celebrate the child's return. French toast, cartoons, crazy eights and some favorite stories bring the quiet companionship, familiarity of home, and physical caring he needs right now. So, too, with the parts of the survivor who have finally come to live in the present. The survivor should take some time to go to a movie, invite a friend over

for tea, watch a basketball game, or listen to a new CD. It's best to wait a bit before buying a case of beer, making a large pan of fudge, or attending a huge outdoor concert or football game.

Again, a newly retrieved part's needs may be very concrete. For example, the therapist should encourage the survivor to pay attention to the physical setting: explore whether the exile feels safer when the survivor spends time in a small, cozy room or in an airy, larger but still well-protected room (perhaps high enough in the building so that no would-be attackers could enter a first-floor window). In a short period of time, this need for physical safety will lessen as the exile trusts the Self's decisions about daily life activities.

2. *The child-part needs to tell his or her story.* Ironically, the exile may wish to return with the therapist or the survivor's Self to the original abusive setting or remembered incident. It is like concentration camp prisoners returning, decades later, to the place where they once waited for their own death; or a Vietnam veteran returning to that country to face old nightmares on his own terms. So the therapist and survivor can join the exiles and witness the story, and then lead them (again) out of that dangerous place to safety. The incest survivor's exile must be "allowed to tell all her experiences. . . . The child inside is terrified, so [the client] must listen, allow the memories to come through, and encourage the child to believe that she is now safe" (Blake-White & Kline, 1985, pp. 397–98). The child has paid a heavy price for keeping silent. In telling their story, exiles need to be encouraged by the survivor's Self to experience the emotions they have buried for so long.

Jenny: *Why does Dick talk to you about how I look calm but my eyes are too wide open and I won't blink?*
Self: *Because inside you feel scared but you are afraid to show it. It's okay to be direct with Dick or with me. We won't be mad about what you're feeling.*
Jenny: *Where I lived before, it was better to be quiet.*
Self: *I know—that's why we helped you leave that place in the past.*

M. Watkins (1986) describes one child-part's passivity after her return to the present:

> At first she feels almost dead, acts extremely passively. . . . As we speak more to her she gives her own history, which borrows some events from [the patient's] life but puts different emphasis on them. . . . When the little girl begins to feel more alive she experiences at the same moment the deep sadness over the father's absence. . . . And so she cried and cried. (pp. 155–156)

For the first time, the survivor is able to tell her story with *feeling*. This is in stark contrast to traumatic memories, which do not progress in time and are emotionless and stereotyped. This telling of the abuse story in "the safety of a protected relationship" actually transforms the "physioneurosis induced by terror" simply through the use of words (Herman, 1992, p. 183). Remember, too, that this type of intense emotion may agitate the managers, who fear that the Self will blend and become engulfed in the exiles' emotions, thus subjecting the survivor to incredible danger. The Self can go directly — though slowly and carefully — to the child-parts. Protectors (either managers of firefighters) may again try to interfere. Once protectors realize the young parts just want to tell their story and be heard, and that the process will not make the survivor four years old and vulnerable to incest again, the protectors will often retreat. Lorene's Self describes a poignant victory in listening to her child-part.

Self: *I'm so surprised. In our session, Dick listened to Jenny tell him how sad she felt, how she believed she was bad. That helped me to be brave enough to let her cry all day today and tonight. And when she cried, Nicholas and Alex didn't create scare-tactics to make me back away from Jenny or scare away all unseen dangers that might be lurking around. I just asked Jenny why she was sad! Hiding, in a fetal position, down in the corner, Jenny said she was scared her body would be hurt. And I gave her attention just by letting her cry and saying those words.*

I feel safe, I feel proud that I did a good job, and I feel like I have energy. Usually when Jenny is sad, I drain all my energy by letting some part create terrorizing slides and movies like a wall around her. All I had to do is listen to her, like Dick did today.

Alex decided that maybe therapy isn't such a stupid, futile process after all. I thought I was very smart and powerful in the ways I used to protect Jenny. It's a little embarrassing now when I realize all I had to do was listen to her.

Schwartz (1995) encourages child-parts to leave the past as soon as they are reasonably comfortable, reassuring them that return visits to the past are possible: "I usually try to bring a stuck part into the present as soon as it is willing to come, rather than leaving it in the past until everything there is resolved. If a traumatized part can rest and heal in the present, then it will have an easier time understanding what happened to it and bringing that perspective with it on any return visits" (p. 106). Thus, if exiled parts have issues to resolve in the past, they can still live in the present, visiting the past with the Self until they understand what happened and are ready to let go of it. All parts must be reminded, however, that simply telling the story of the abuse will not resolve all problems the survivor experiences.

3. *The child-part needs to learn to trust.* Even after the exile returns to the present, the therapist and survivor must continue to promise that the Self will care for, but not blend with, the child-part. The Self can then get close to the child-part and reassure him or her that the Self cares and can be trusted, even when other parts attempt to interfere in their relationship. In this example, Lorene's child-part, Jenny, after a successful retrieval from the past, explores her relationship with Lorene's Self and her ability to stand alone separate from the older, protector parts. Predictably, the older parts jump in, trying to keep the Self (who is still a bit of a stranger to some parts) from getting too close to Jenny. Lorene's Self rejects the dramatic but well-meaning advice offered by the managers and firefighters and supports Jenny's wishes to remain living in the present:

Jenny: *I can't even tell if I'm dead or alive sometimes when I'm hiding in here. It's very dark and I can't feel anything.*
Self: *Do you want to come out to the present, where I live?*
Jenny: *Maybe for a little while. Alex and Super-She and Vincent all told me to stay still, but I told them to be quiet.*
Self: *Good for you, Jenny! How did it feel?*
Jenny: *Well, I was a little surprised. I never talked back to them before.*
Alexandra: *You see, Jenny is too stupid to ask for help or ask for love when she needs it. She only knows how to become numb and float around in a stupor. Just leave her to us.*
Self: *You talk about her like she isn't here or like she's mentally handicapped.*
Alex: *Well, the truth is the truth, right?*
Self: *No, Alex. Jenny's a lot stronger than you think.*
Alex: *Oh, sure. Ask her what she's willing to do to get a man to hold her and tell her that he loves her.*
Self: *I imagine she'd do a lot for that. But I will be here to make sure she doesn't put me or any part in a position where a man can cause harm again.*
Alex: *Well, I can put a stop to all this nonsense right now. Watch me cut your face. See? Blood pouring down your forehead, and I never even changed my facial expression. I'm pretty strong, huh?*
Self: *I know you can sneak in and take over sometimes, Alex. But you're scaring Jenny, not helping her.*
Vincent: *You're all being foolish. Why not just breathe deeply, look out the window, and think of nothing. Clean out this chaos and become blank.*
Super-She: *I agree. The little girl must put herself into a trance. She must look relaxed, like she doesn't care, doesn't see, doesn't hear. Little children should not have to witness pain and blood. Sleep with your eyes open, Jenny. Go deep inside and become nothing. Then I will act*

"normal," pretend nothing is wrong, go to school in the morning, read books, raise my hand in class. Very normal.

Self: *I appreciate all your concern and warnings. However, I am going to let Jenny's desires take control here. She wants to come out of that dark place, and she wants to be held and to tell me things. I will insist that you not interfere. If you do interfere and cut me or distract me from Jenny, I will return again and again until she has the care she deserves.*

4. *The child-part needs to learn that she is not bad.* The child-parts yearn for someone to rescue them; they need to believe that they are worthy of protection. It often helps to talk to child-parts about the fact that the abuser, in addition to the extreme parts who inflicted harm, also had parts who cared about her (if there is any evidence of this) and a Self that was deeply buried. Few things frustrate and pain therapists more than survivors who insist that they are "bad." (We explore this further in chapter 16.) A mother feels enormous guilt when her son is struck by a car as he leaves school one afternoon, although she could have done nothing to prevent the accident. A husband whose wife leaves him for another man feels certain that he could have done something to avoid this, even if it is not true. And a therapist whose patient hurts himself or another person searches desperately for signs that she might have missed, steps she should have taken. It is not unusual to bear the burden of guilt after a trauma. It serves many functions. For example, in working with the badness experienced by child-parts, therapists learn that the badness sometimes acts as a security blanket that the part initially refuses to give up. The part will discover with time, however, that this belief in her own "badness" undermines the very sense of safety she yearns for, and blocks access to the safe world now being offered to her by the survivor's Self.

5. *The child-part needs to learn that she can leave her isolation and join other parts and people in relationships.* Rieker and Carmen (1986) describe the child victim's constant isolation, always remaining alone with the truth of the abuse, always maintaining the facade, keeping the secrets: "In abusive families, the victim's isolation is reinforced by helpless dependency and shame, the offender's threats of retaliatory violence, and the disbelieving responses of potential helpers" (p. 365). This isolation continues into adulthood: "Traumatized people feel utterly abandoned, utterly alone, cast out of the human and divine systems of care and protection that sustain life" (Herman, 1992, p. 52). Sgroi (1989) discusses how survivors use secret keeping as a barrier to create distance between them and their family, friends, and therapists:

> Prolonged secret keeping demands increasing amounts of energy exerted by the secretholders because secrets about anything that is important are

inherently unstable; more and more energy is required to overcome the tension that builds as the content of the secret is held back from the unaware. . . . Fear of exposure is thus the reason that it is extremely difficult for adult survivors to have their intimacy needs met while they are erecting and maintaining barriers against intimate relationships. The tragic results are loneliness, isolation, and emotional depletion; being cut off from others to protect against exposure also cuts off genuine caring and nurturance. (p. 126)

The exiled parts need to believe that they are no longer alone, which means convincing the managers and firefighters that the exiles no longer need to be feared or kept isolated. New relationships will be created as some parts leave their old, extreme roles and find new, preferred roles. After the roller coaster of pain, tears, and hostility that comes with survivor therapy, this stage is very exciting and positive. For the first time ever, the young exiles are free to do what comes naturally to children. They roam the inner landscape, make friends, delight in watching firefighters bicker with managers, and discover how to play, sing, dance, and enjoy spontaneous feelings.

6. *The child-part needs to learn that what she wants counts.* It is not easy for this long-neglected child-part to believe that her needs and desires are relevant. She has long depended on the managers' advice to remain frozen, never hoping, never planning for the future, never taking risks or making choices. Learning to voice her wishes may be practiced initially in regard to minor decisions such as choosing to eat when hungry, sleep when tired, go to the bathroom when necessary, or put on a sweater when cold. Herman (1992) notes: "Now she has the capacity to revisit old hopes and dreams. The survivor may initially resist doing so fearing the pain of disappointment. It takes courage to move out of the constricted stance of the victim. But just as the survivor must dare to confront her fears, she must also dare to define her wishes" (p. 202). The child-part must slowly learn that she is no longer powerless, that she has the power to identify preferences. Andy expresses his indignation at *not* yet knowing who he is:

Andy: I blend and blend and blend until I can't find myself at all. Do I like running? Playing the guitar? Writing? Singing? Children? Outdoors? Quiet or noise? Many people or few people? Dark or light? I just can't remember. I blend all the time, hiding behind Nicholas especially. All because I am afraid someone will look at me with cold, disappointed, disinterested eyes. But it isn't fair. I am a real person, and I don't like hiding all the time.

A child being molested has little power to express wishes or exercise his ability to make choices. Retrieved exiled parts learn they are no longer powerless victims who must drain all resources into survival. Now they can make choices.

Survivors often limit their choices throughout the day by taking the least dangerous path. ("I must go to work or my boss will be mad and I'll have to find a job with strangers." "I must pay this bill or they'll get mad and take away my car and I'll have to ride on a bus with strangers." "I must drink with my friends at bars every weekend or they'll think I'm not normal and discover that I'm repulsive.") Survivors are often shocked to experience the freedom of making choices. Even if they make the *same* choices, it will be for reasons that are not based in fear. ("I want to be on time for work so I can get that promotion and do something more challenging." "I want to make my car payment on time, because then I can drive to California this summer and see the ocean for the first time." "I want to go out with my friends on weekends, but only if they don't go to bars; instead, we can to go the beach and barbecue hot dogs and then play volleyball until midnight!")

The End of the Journey

The journey that survivors and their therapists undergo in order to retrieve and welcome home the young exiled parts typically proves to be complicated, tumultuous, and painful. To bypass protective parts or fail to take their fears seriously invites chaos. Schwartz (1993) reminds therapists, however, of the detrimental impact that *not* retrieving the exiled parts will have on the survivor's life:

> Simply to urge clients to move on into the future, regardless of the shadowy selves they are leaving behind, is like asking a family caravan traveling the country to abandon children along the way, whenever the trip becomes dangerous or painful. The answer instead is to look back, find the orphans and bring them back on board, before the caravan moves on. (p. 75)

Ignoring the experiences and memories of the child-parts, then, is to neglect (and invite the suffocation of) vital aspects of the survivor's very being. The parts who are retrieved from their exile and properly cared for add much to the survivor's life—elation, contentment, warm affection, and appropriate sadness or empathy. Their creativity and spontaneity fill the survivor's life with a new freshness. Releasing the child-parts from a narrow, constrictive world into a world filled with a richness of opportunities and choices is a joyous experience for both survivors and their therapists.

PART III

Special Challenges in
Therapy with Survivors

CHAPTER 14

Trust

The survivor brings [a] lack of trust to the therapy rela-
tionship, making development of a therapeutic alliance a
slow and often tedious task. She may fear the therapist,
seeing him/her as parental or an authority figure and
thus as abusive, manipulative, unprotective and/or re-
jecting.

— Christine Courtois, 1988

Secrecy and silence are the perpetrator's first line of
defense.

— Judith Herman, 1992

SURVIVORS ACHE TO trust someone, even as they struggle against the
addiction of guarding secrets. A young child caught in an abusive
setting tries desperately to "find a way to preserve a sense of trust in people
who are untrustworthy, safety in a situation that is unsafe, control in a
situation that is terrifyingly unpredictable, power in a situation of helplessness" (Herman, 1992, p. 96). Years later, the adult survivor's lack of trust
forces her to use various techniques to keep the therapist at bay. A managerial part might appear to perform as the perfect client, thus risking
no anger or disappointment from the therapist, while still blocking any
opportunity for the younger, abused parts to expose their vulnerability by
crying or relating the abuse memories during a session. Firefighters prefer
to handle their mistrust by picking a fight, flinging accusations, and dash-
ing out in the middle of a session without a word.

Schwartz (1992) reports that before he learned the rules for navigating
a survivor's inner world, lack of trust made therapy with abuse survivors
feel like

crossing a minefield without a map. . . . A session would seem to be trun-
dling along smoothly when suddenly a client would go on the attack—

castigating me for selfishness, callousness, manipulativeness and general therapeutic and personal worthlessness. Or, [the client] might suddenly freeze, bringing therapy to a halt, or show signs of an alarming relapse. (p. 36)

Lorene's parts demonstrate the difficulty of being direct about even small things which may seem insignificant to the therapist. Sometimes a casual comment by the therapist would silently trigger apprehension and fear among Lorene's parts:

Nicky: *I left Dick's this afternoon because he said I should.*

Alex: *That's not quite true.*

Nicky: *Well, I asked if I could leave early and he agreed that since I came early, I could choose to leave early. So I did. I was angry and embarrassed and trapped and sad. Angry because he's uncovering too much about Destiny. Trapped, like I always feel there. Sad because Des is crying.*

Destiny: *I was close to tears every minute I was there. It felt like my heart was being crushed.*

Nicky: *I hate that. It makes me so angry at Lorene and Dick. So I took you away from there.*

Destiny: *Leaving there was strange, like it happened in slow motion. I saw every thread in the rug, every stair, every part of the wall and doors. Dick yelled to come back and I silently screamed, "You have to come get me, please, and bring me back. Don't let Nicky take me!!" But he couldn't hear me. When Dick and Nicholas both act stubborn and mean, I get lost in the shuffle. Why can't Dick come get me and only be mad at Nicky? I feel so sad. Things are crashing and crashing. I live in an avalanche. Sometimes I can hear the rumbling in the dark and I see shadows. I know I have to be ready for even bigger, sharper rocks to crush my head and my body, crashing and crashing. That's how I live.*

Vincent: *Do you know why your name is Destiny?*

Destiny: *No.*

Vincent: *You are the key to the future of our balance, our existence.*

Destiny: *Is Nicky punishing me, too?*

Nicky: *Yes, absolutely. I hate the way you trust Dick.*

Alex: *There's nothing wrong with that.*

Nicky: *He's leaving town again next week. Danger. Lots of danger.*

Self: *Nicholas, I'll handle this. Leaving in the middle of the session was unfair and rude. I should have stopped you, but there was so much chaos thrown at me from other parts. Besides, you should take some responsibility for your actions.*

Nicky: *Well, usually if I threaten to leave, Dick says, "If you decide as your Self that you want to leave, you can. Otherwise, stay." Today he just said, "You can choose to go." He didn't care.*

Alex: Well, Dick at least could have made an effort to keep me there and just ignore you.
Destiny: Maybe it's better this way.
Self: Do you want to continue in therapy?
Super-She: I'm too busy with work.
Dashiell: It's better to go. Nicky is dangerous.
Vincent: We take up too much of Dick's time and we've been going to therapy long enough!
Bonnie: It can be embarrassing sometimes.
Nicky: He's disgusting. And he's doing a lousy job.
Alex: He'd rather not complicate his life—and he might reject me.
Jennifer: I want Dick.
Destiny: Better not to go. Trapped in avalanche with Nicky.
Bonnie: I like being with Dick.
Andy: I want to see Dick very much.
Self: We will continue going to therapy sessions. I need to work on healing Destiny so that she won't feel like she's caught in quicksand. Any of you who hear Dick say something that sounds like abandonment—tell him! At least give him a chance.

If the IFS therapist carefully approaches each part's mistrust and suspicion, the client may be willing to reveal her pulsating fear. Instead of simply lumping it all together ("I'm scared you'll hurt me"), the client learns to separate each layer of fear. The abuse survivor may always have parts who perceive danger whenever she trusts someone with her secrets, her pain, or even her most mundane thoughts. However, she can learn to go to that scared part and ask why it is scared. Then, as her Self, she can evaluate the part's warning and choose to trust or mistrust. She won't be overwhelmed by the fear that the slightest trust will endanger her entire being. At some point, the survivor will measure out that first drop of trust for the therapist (by showing up for the first session? by disclosing her name? by admitting that she needs someone to talk to?). In time, she will master the ability to soothe or question the part who screams, "That's one drop of trust too many!" She can request that the part be more direct and identify the perceived danger in trusting the therapist ("He'll think I'm disgusting"; "He'll tell the abuser to hurt me again"), and the client can determine, as her Self, what that part needs. The part may need comfort and reassurance from the therapist or may need to be told to sit tight while the client experiences trust for a few more minutes, or a few more sessions.

With each step of progress, the survivor's parts test the therapist and challenge her sincerity and commitment. Herman (1992) agrees that "both therapist and patient should be prepared for repeated testing, disruption, and rebuilding of the therapeutic relationship," accompanied by the patient's "intense longing for rescue" (pp. 148–49). While other therapy relationships are initiated with some degree of trust, "this presumption is never warranted in the treatment of traumatized patients" (Herman, 1992, p. 138). (Chapter 19 explores further the effect of this mistrust on the therapist's parts.) Lorene's part, Victor, demonstrates this mistrust:

Victor: *I've decided there is no way I'm letting this go on. Dick is stupid, unethical, untrustworthy, incompetent. I'm not letting him see anything dangerous like crying. Forget it — all of you just forget it.*

Every interaction with a survivor can be viewed as a test for determining trustworthiness. The abuse survivor both fears and seek to expose betrayal and exploitation within the therapy relationship. Herman (1981) describes this process well: "She fears that the therapist will dominate and exploit her, as her father did, or neglect and abandon her, as her mother did. She has little faith in any other possibility. If this fear is not clarified and understood, the patient may act on it, just as everything seems to be progressing well" (pp. 189–90).

In the roller coaster ride created by trust issues, an especially cunning trap involves manipulating the therapist into a situation in which the client's parts try to "prove" that the therapist is capable of abusing the client. Lorene's part, Alexandra, strongly believed that the therapist would exploit her, sooner or later. She voted for sooner:

Alex: *I have no doubt that Dick will be unable to resist molesting Lorene. A therapist is no different from other men. Dick will hurt me. It's not his fault, I suppose. It's just that Lorene's evil sexuality draws men like a magnet, forcing them to defile her. It may be better for me to seduce Dick. That way, I can get it over with and I'll be in control of when, where, and how humiliating. Otherwise there's no relief from the frightening waiting — until it happens. No place is safe. He's pretending he's not a man right now, so he hasn't touched me yet. I can't just wait. It will come, but I can't just wait while Dick pretends to care, to support, to be my friend, when I know he wants to degrade and torture me.*

A more subtle problem involves setting traps for the therapist to *symbolically* abuse the patient. Again, this is often a test to determine whether the therapist is capable of being trusted. If the therapist fails to recognize the traps, then the survivor's parts can justify withholding their trust. One type of trap might be refusing to pay the bill, finally forcing the therapist to terminate therapy. The client can also build a trap by waiting patiently for the therapist to make a mistake, such as forgetting to check on a young part who disclosed details of the abuse during the last session. Once the mistake is identified, the client can slash her leg or face with impunity, sending the message that, "If you hadn't ripped out that part's secrets, I

wouldn't have blood dripping down my leg right now. You did this to me."
The client might also simulate the abandonment and betrayal of abuse by
demanding an impossible number of extra sessions. Vincent, the most
over-protective of Lorene's parts, explains the rationale to the therapist:

Vincent: *You exposed all these terrified parts, you jeopardized my sanity,*
you allowed the vulnerable parts to escape from their protective sanctu-
aries. They stand now— abandoned by you—and paralyzed with fear as
they scream and scream. We must have extra sessions. Also, maybe you
should call me every day—just until this calms down.

Therapists often expect the can-I-trust-you testing, but are surprised
when, having passed the tests, the patient confides secrets and cries, only
to return the next session and confront the therapist with even stronger
mistrust. The therapist feels perplexed by the survivor's vacillation between trust and distancing. Siegel and Romig (1990) write that survivors
of sexual abuse

> often [appear] resistant to therapy, exercising an alternating approach-
> avoidance stance regarding the abuse. It must be remembered that because
> many survivors have spent a lifetime bound in secrecy, this vacillation and
> reliance on denial or dissociative behavior is quite common. . . . Thus, survi-
> vors begin therapy in the grip of two major violations: disclosure of their
> secret and the need to trust the therapist. (p. 248)

Lorene's part, Victor, describes the feeling of swinging back and forth
between trust and distancing as the minutes ticked by during a therapy
session:

Victor: *Last session, Dick was very patient and slowly helped me stop*
guarding Bonnie so that I could talk directly to him. That night I had a
nightmare about Bonnie being in danger from a sexual maniac. So I
decided Dick should definitely be afraid of Bonnie's sexual feelings and
that Dick was going to be very mad at me.
    So I was ready today. Ready for him to be mad; for him to be dis-
gusted with Bonnie; to be angry that I hadn't kept her locked up some-
where; and ready for him to be sure that he'd made a huge, gigantic
mistake in being nice to me.
    Then today—does Dick know what he's doing?? I avoided being
friendly with him—I was very rude—and he told me that I was afraid
because last session made me feel so safe. I kept being rude today, but
he just promised that I was safe, and that he'd help me move from the
dark place. I stayed very brave and distant and cool.
    He came and sat next to me and said those words about feeling safe
and trusting. It'd work for a minute, then I'd feel scared and throw

something at him. Dick would reassure me it was okay to feel safe. Then I was okay for a few minutes, then scared again. I'd think: Don't deserve this; shouldn't do this; it'll contaminate Dick somehow; he'll get mad; stop, stop; your job, Victor, is to block out false safety.

Then I felt sad—I couldn't believe it! What am I going to do? Maybe Dick doesn't understand the potential power of the evilness in Lorene. Does he really think he knows what he's doing?

I'm tired of guarding that stupid Bonnie. Let someone else do it— maybe.

Bonnie might be tricking me—making me feel safe if Dick sits next to me—just so she can be next to him. Could that be true? She's capable of anything. I'll have to kill her if any sexual feelings come to surface—I think.

Another common trust issue involves the therapist's encountering layers of secrets. The need to be secretive and not trust anyone often permeates the survivor's daily life. In general, the client "will gradually lead the therapist through the hierarchy of secrets, starting with those that are least traumatic and only moving on to the more highly charged secrets if the therapist passes the first test" (Putnam, 1989, pp. 174–75). Herman (1992) quotes one survivor: "I saw a mask. It looked like me. I took it off and beheld a group of huddled, terrified people who shrank together to hide terrible secrets" (p. 128).

But the secrets go beyond the abuse incidents. Putnam's (1989) description of MPD clients applies equally to all abuse survivors: "Secrets of the past are not the only secrets kept by multiples. In the vast majority of cases, they have continued to live a life of secrets" (p. 174). The therapist soon discovers that the survivor keeps secrets as a matter of course—even secrets that are completely unrelated to anything the survivor cares about. Lorene's therapist had to pass many tests before Nicky finally disclosed that, even as an adult, Lorene continued to engulf herself in secrets. The disclosure greatly embarrassed the secretive managers, especially Vincent:

Vincent: *I'm humiliated by Nicholas' telling Dick about my secret world. My life is a lie. I act like an adult, an intelligent, normal person. But I'm an imposter. Since I still see danger everywhere, I still get scared and cry, and I still hide things from people. No one knows how I live each day. Now Dick will know.*

Being secretive makes me feel safe. The secret world is my real world. I don't eat in front of other people, I don't show my cuts and burns, I have secret sex, secret eating, secret everything. I don't tell people what I did over the weekend; I don't tell if I'm sick; I don't tell what music I like; I don't tell what movies I've seen. If the therapist asks inconsequential questions, I refuse to answer just so I'll have more secrets.

> *But Nicholas guards much of my secretive nature. If he has decided to end that, I will be exposed. Everything will change. I may no longer be safe in my secret life.*

Throughout all these tests of trust, it is essential that the client's Self and the therapist continue to reassure the parts that trusting the therapist will not endanger them. Feinauer (1989) accurately describes the importance of survivors' believing that "therapy is a safe environment and the therapist is committed to going through the process with them until it is over. Unless they trust their therapist to be sensitive to their fears, pace, and individual issues, the clients will become resistant. These clients require more time for therapy than many others" (pp. 332–33). Breaking through the tough exteriors of the protector parts always reveals an underlying hunger for trust, caring, and support that is often guarded by a facade of ambivalence. Lorene's Self and her part, Nicholas, depict this ambivalence:

Self: *Some of my nightmares come from Nicky's decision this week to not fight Dick anymore. I have some parts who trusted Dick immediately. But Nicky fought a long, hard battle against Dick. Nicky is afraid Dick will laugh and say his caring and trust was a joke. Nicky is also afraid that if he isn't acting as tough sentry of my system, I'll have no sense of who is dangerous and who is safe.*

Nicholas: *Why doesn't Dick give up? He should stop trying to treat me nicely when I'm so mean and cold and hit him and say I don't care, say that he's not even real. I'm going to try very hard to convince other parts that Dick's vacation is proof he won't come back or isn't real so I can die, die, die.*

Nicholas struggled particularly hard against trusting the therapist, using every trick in the book. In the following excerpt, Lorene's Self carefully takes Nicholas through the events of one session and successfully uncovers the points where Nicholas' mistrust of the therapist interfered:

Nicholas: *I hate Dick. He plays games. He doesn't take me seriously. He's bad to talk to. I'll hate him forever.*

Self: *What happened that made you mad? Start at the beginning. First we saw him at the door.*

Nicholas: *I think he's mad because he was done with the other person and I wasn't there yet.*

Self: *Then we went into his office.*

Nicholas: *I don't like Lorene trusting this guy.*

Self: *Then she gave him money.*

Nicholas: *I hate that. He's doing this just for money.*

Self: Okay, then we talked about Lorene's job.

Nicholas: It's a dangerous place. The longer she stays at that job, the harder my job is because they depend on her more and more, and I'll have to make her irresponsible so they'll fire her. And stupid "Dr. Schwartz" doesn't get her out of that place. He wants her to stay there so he has a better chance of getting her money and being rich.

Self: And then she asked Dick about her boyfriend.

Nicholas: Dick probably just wants her to talk about sex so he can think about it. Either do it or not! I can't stand waiting to see if he'll try to seduce her.

Self: I don't think that'll happen.

Nicholas: I know more than you. He's keeping secrets.

Self: You're jealous.

Nicholas: Well, maybe. But I don't call it jealousy. I think Dick should stay with me every minute, protecting me. Never go to sleep; never do anything. He should blend with me completely—absorb me so I can disappear. That's the only way he can make me safe.

Self: That's not realistic.

Nicholas: It's real to me.

Self: Okay. Then you asked Dick if liked to travel.

Nicholas: He said yes! See—he'll go away, and I won't be safe. He doesn't care if I'm safe.

Self: So you started yelling at him.

Nicholas: Well, I wasn't going to, but I decided, too bad, he knows I'm here anyhow.

Self: Did you like talking with Dick directly?

Nicholas: I hated it. It's stupid. A waste of time. I'll never ever go there again. I'll take 100 million drugs on Friday night so I can't wake up on Saturday and go there.

Self: Are you very lonely?

Nicholas: Yes, the most lonely in the whole world. No one holds me.

Self: Is that what this is all about?

Nicholas: I have a bigger rule than the "no crying" rule.

Self: Yes, I see that.

Nicholas: Keep people away—always at a distance. They aren't real; aren't real at all. Hugging means lying about love.

Self: So you manipulate everything to get a hug?

Nicholas: Yes. Sometimes I go see friends I don't even want to see that much, but I know they'll hug me when I leave and that makes it all worthwhile.

Self: Do you like being hugged?

Nicholas: Yes. The most. No one held me when I was little and scared.

Self: You're still little and scared.

Nicholas: Yes, but I'm not the littlest boy getting hurt by bad guys.

Couldn't Dick let me stay with him and I'll be his little son and he can hold me in the middle of the night when I have a bad dream?
Self: *Do you think Dick is real?*
Nicholas: *Sometimes when he touches my hand to say good-bye, I'm surprised and happy that he feels solid and three-dimensional and real. My hand doesn't go through him. But that only lasts for a second or two. Then I wonder if he's just an image, just pretending to be real to trick me. That makes me so angry—furious! Maybe if he could hit me a lot, I could feel him being real.*
Self: *Isn't there something less drastic?*
Nicholas: *No. Stop talking! I hate and hate and hate—mostly myself more than anything.*
Self: *You've worked hard and given me valuable information. Rest awhile now.*

Regardless of the particular content of each test, the issue of trust will arise again and again. The therapist should encourage each part to challenge him or her directly, so that new issues can be addressed promptly and honestly. Lorene's Self reports:

Destiny asked Dick questions today such as: "Are you going to kill me? Why do you come back from trips every time? Do you feel sick to your stomach when you think about having an appointment with me?" Strange questions, but asking them seemed to help her trust Dick.

Surprisingly, just when the survivor's trust has increased to the point where the therapist feels it is safe to gently urge the survivor to start focusing on the sexual abuse itself, her managers pull the secret cloak around her again. For example, the survivor may ironically decide she cannot discuss any sexual abuse details with the therapist precisely because their relationship is so good and the therapist is so kind and supportive. Sgroi and Bunk (1988) write:

Many survivors have reported that they could not work on unresolved sexual abuse issues in individual therapy with a therapist who had worked very effectively with them on other issues. It is likely that, as the survivor begins to experience a caring relationship with the therapist, his or her self-doubts and anxieties become enhanced. As in other relationships, the survivor becomes concerned that disclosure about the as yet untold aspects of his or her internal reality will result in abandonment. A survivor might say to himself or herself, "If my therapist really knew me, she would not care so much about me. She would think I am bad and evil. She would think I am crazy." The fears and the lack of trust further increase the survivor's belief that his or her sexual abuse should not be discussed with the therapist. The survivor cannot risk the loss of yet another person on whom he or she is dependent. (p. 185)

The key to developing trust, then, is patience. Shengold (1989) describes the deep source of mistrust that makes this patience essential to therapeutic progress:

> It is not hard to understand why change must be slow: there is so much to distrust. The emotional connecting necessary for insight is initially more than soul-murdered people can bear. They learned as children that to be emotionally open . . . was the beginning of frustrating torment. . . . They have been abused and neglected and have learned a lesson: if you cannot trust mother and father, whom can you trust? So a really meaningful alliance with the analyst takes a long time to develop. (p. 312)

When parts emanate intense mistrust, the therapist may slow the therapeutic pace to a crawl. Sgroi and Bunk (1988) warn, however, that the mistrust should not halt all exploration of abuse-related issues: "It is easy for both the clinician and the patient to fall into the trap of finding other reasons (such as the patient's fear of becoming psychotic or suicidal or the reported difficulties in distinguishing between real memories and dreams) to avoid talking about the sexual victimization during therapy sessions" (p. 173). Neither firefighters' repeated threats ("I'll kill myself") nor managers' incessant disclaimers ("We feel just fine now") should permanently deter the therapist or the survivor's Self from continuing to work with feelings and memories associated with the abuse.

Yet a worsening of symptoms such as self-mutilation and flashbacks inevitably jeopardizes the trust survivors place in therapists, causing many survivors to question whether they should trust their therapists: "Why is my therapist making my whole life fall apart? I can't sleep; I can't stop cutting; I drink too much and eat too much; and I'm scared to go to work. I can hardly function anymore!" Blake-White and Kline (1985) acknowledge that, after the initial sessions in therapy, the incest survivor's anxiety may increase, and she experiences more nightmares, flashbacks, visual, tactile or auditory hallucinations. "This terror is so overwhelming that she wants to run, deny, and attempt to forget. She is occasionally angry with the . . . therapists, accusing them of 'making me worse'" (p. 401). As Lorene continued to explore abuse-related memories, her nightmares, self-mutilation, and terror increased significantly. Firefighters like Victor tried hard to distract:

Victor: *That idiot Dr. Hotshot Schwartz doesn't know anything. He thinks I'm afraid if we get Andy "unstuck" from the past, therapy will end. Doesn't he know the stakes are higher than stopping this awful therapy? I hate him for thinking I'm such a baby that I only care about missing him. That's stupid. There are huge, horrible dangers around — and losing Dick isn't one of them! That's baby stuff! I'll kill her. I will, I will. I'll do whatever it takes to stop the screaming noises.*

Alexandra: Where do the screaming noises come from?
Victor: Someplace inside, you idiot! Someone who remembers. Make it stop—no—I'll do it—it's my job. But I'm very scared. I wish Dick would take me seriously and talk to me about what I see, instead of talking about whether I'm afraid of losing him when Andy is "healed." I hate the fact that I like to sit and talk with him. I'd rather push him far away.

It is helpful to remember that many of the accusations hurled at the therapist result from the survivor's belief that she can *never* be safe. Parts believe that the therapist, either intentionally or negligently, is teasing the survivor with the hope and longing for safety when it's an impossible goal. Ellis (1990) describes the client's fury when the therapist repeatedly leads her back to the question of whether she is intrinsically bad and beyond loving: "I will be repeating myself often. She will be furious with me for leading her back to comfort and safety. She believes that there is no safety for her" (p. 254). The therapist can remind the client that her continued challenges mean that she is healthy enough to recognize that all people cannot be trusted. She needs help only in distinguishing between abusive relationships and healthy relationships, so that she can better identify who is trustworthy and learn what to do when her trust is betrayed.

CHAPTER 15

Self-Destructive Behavior

In their own flesh, they bore repeated punishment for the crimes committed against them in childhood.

—Judith Herman, 1981

THE IDEA OF CUTTING, burning, or otherwise maiming one's own body disgusts and frightens most people, including many therapists. Self-mutilation, however, is a frequent companion of sexual abuse survivors (van der Kolk, Perry, & Herman, 1991). Although self-injury is often interpreted as suicidal behavior, the actions rarely express a yearning for death. Self-injury is used not as a means to kill, but as a means of self-preservation to "relieve unbearable emotional pain" (Herman, 1992, p. 109). D. Miller (1994) describes survivors' reluctance to give up self-injury:

> [W]omen who hurt themselves become very attached to and protective of their symptoms. They do not give up the self-abusive behavior easily, because it provides the familiar reassurance of relationship, no matter how much it harms them. (p. 48)

Before therapists try to separate survivors from their self-abusive behavior, it is crucial that they understand the varying purposes which motivate parts to injure the survivors.

PURPOSES OF SELF-INJURY

The therapeutic response may differ according to the goal of the part who controls the behavior. Most of Lorene's parts (whether firefighter, manager, or exile) have directly participated in, encouraged, or hoped for self-mutilation at one time or another, although each with different motivations. Self-injury allows Vincent to seize control of runaway emotions ("It's much better not to have all that crying and carrying on, now, isn't it?"); Super-She basks in the familiar melancholy comfort of the self-inflicted injury ("I know this pain so well"); Destiny experiences her existence in a tangible way ("If I bleed, I must be alive"); Jennifer dreams of a maternal nurse applying salves and bandages ("Mommy, I got hurt"); Alexandra uses it as a means of chaotic distraction ("Don't look at me — quick — look over there!"); Nicholas seethes with ignorant pride in response to self-inflicted punishments ("What incredible courage and power I have!"); for Victor, it is a chance to mete out corporal punishment ("You deserve this — take it like a man"); and Bonnie uses it as a means of avoiding contact with other people ("You're too disgusting to let other people see your scarred deformity"). The myriad of purposes underlying self-injury is well expressed by Lorene's parts during a self-mutilation episode:

Super-She: *Become pain. It absorbs me, I absorb it. Send Dick a note with a check and never see him again.*
Victor: *Just close my eyes and cut. Try to control the punishment, redirect the pain. Nothing else matters. Breast covered in blood, tattered. Hundreds of cuts. The nipple bleeds the most.*
Destiny: *It's like finding myself again!*
Super-She: *I think about nothing but the pain. I don't think about anybody or anything. Total absorption, concentration, disappearing.*
Vincent: *I feel a tremendous release, and then suddenly —*
Alex: *I pretend like it didn't happen. Not to me. It couldn't have.*
Bonnie: *How could I be so stupid. I'm so ashamed. Like waking up in the morning and finding I had sex with a stranger.*
Dashiell: *This cutting/raping is your punishment for telling Dick too many secrets.*

Inflicting Punishment

Punishment is one of the more obvious purposes of self-mutilation. Lorene's Self describes how both the disclosure of secrets in therapy and the therapist's vacation triggered cutting episodes:

Self: *Many parts were so relieved to see Dick today. He's real and he came back from his trip! Nicholas was embarrassed about what he had done to my face. (To distract Dick from the cuts on my face, Nicholas challenged him to a fist fight.) The lacerations were Nicky's way of punishing Destiny for talking to Dick about scary secrets last session, and for Destiny's believing that Dick would return from his trip safely and still remember me.*

When Nicholas cut Lorene's face, the message to Destiny ("Be quiet! Don't tell any more secrets!") was clear. But there was also a message to the therapist: "This is what will happen if you go away again—this is *your* fault."

It is very common for secret telling to trigger self-injury. Putnam (1989) notes: "Needless to say, [self-mutilation] experiences often stifle the patient's attempts to remember or reveal the past. This is, of course, one of the primary functions of the persecutor personalities" (p. 206). Nicholas often punished Lorene after parts had revealed abuse-related facts in therapy sessions:

Nicholas: *Today I burned her twice, but it wasn't enough. I let the oil get too cool while I yelled at Destiny about what a wimp she was. (Other parts made futile efforts to get her to fight back and stop the burning.) She lets Destiny talk about that uncle. I hate Lorene talking directly to Destiny, who is supposed to hide behind me, and I hate those memories and how they make my body feel.*

Lorene-the-idiot said that self-mutilation is a good sign!! She says it shows I'm in pain and not covering it up with coldness or some "mindless behavior." If that's true, then the self-mutilation won't take anything away. It won't stop my pain for long.

Dispelling Self-hatred

Another goal of self-injury is to dispel self-hatred. Even if no specific event which deserves punishment has occurred, a firefighter might self-mutilate to relieve tension created by external events or internal chaos. It is easy to turn against the body and use it as a receptacle for self-hatred, because survivors "perceive their bodies as having turned against them" (Herman, 1992, p. 86). Thus Nicholas inflicts punishment on Lorene's body to relieve overwhelming guilt and revulsion:

Nicholas: *I cut my finger very deep and watched the blood pour into a wastebasket for a long time. Tainted juices running from the venomous serpent. It hurts, but it doesn't seem like my pain. I detest every drop of life in this burdensome body.*

A related goal is to purge "evil" forces (often experienced as sexuality or rage) from the survivor, not unlike the purging of bulimia or the archaic medical practice of applying leeches to "bleed" the body until the disease was gone. The destructive act cleanses the self-disgust which continually builds. It also rids the body of whatever the part feels the abuser may have left within the survivor's body—like a douche to wash away sperm, an enema to wash away feces, or a hunger fast to rid the body of poisons.

Distracting from Pain

Another goal is to create a tangible, physical distraction to quickly turn the attention of parts away from painful memories, especially those accompanied by body memories like smell and taste. Destiny reports:

Destiny: *I cut after a session discussing the sex with my uncle. The sex was my fault. I know that. While Nicholas has been in the [internal] hospital, I sit curled up in the corner on the floor of his hospital room, watching Andy act violent and Nicholas act dead. No one can help me, because I don't even exist. I stopped existing when he kissed me so much I couldn't breathe and his pubic hair smelled like urine. I don't cry because I'm not even here.*

I don't want to be dead. But I feel like fragments of energy floating around. But how can fragments of energy remember what a penis tastes like? Maybe cutting my face will wipe the nauseating taste from my horrid mouth.

Self-mutilation acts as a powerful distractor, because it produces immediate and compelling somatic and psychological responses. Normal means of self-soothing fail to calm the survivor's feeling of terror, despair, or desperate isolation, but "abused children discover at some point that the feeling can be most effectively terminated by a major jolt to the body" (Herman, 1992, p. 109). Recall the feeling that surges through your body after swerving to avoid a car accident, or when pain and blood suddenly appear after you break a glass while washing it. The surging feeling experienced by survivors is similar, but reaches much higher levels of intensity. Instantaneous and powerful, the stimulation and excitement caused by the emotional and physical responses of self-injury easily distract the survivor from long-buried emotions that try to leak through. It is often performed "until it produces a powerful feeling of calm and relief; physical pain is much preferable to the emotional pain that it replaces" (Herman, 1992, p. 109). For example, if facing abuse-related sadness and rage causes too much fear, a firefighter will create diversionary pain to mask the genuine pain that is usually kept well hidden and well guarded. Nicholas admits:

Nicholas: *I'm going to burn away this false body. There, I burned her. This anguish permeating my cells must end now! Poured boiling water on her hand today. She almost called Dick, but I threatened to do more things if she called him.*

Soothing the Parts

Self-mutilation also works well to help survivors "feel less anxious and more in control" (Sgroi, 1989, p. 123), soothing and calming parts, and thus decreasing feelings of helplessness. Nicholas reveals:

Nicholas: *I went to my brother's tonight. He and his friends were all ignoring me, so I felt like I was in danger. To calm down, I told myself that I could cut when I got home. Cutting is my safety valve, my security blanket. I sleep with cutting instruments nearby in case I wake up scared.*

While cutting one's body hardly seems soothing to most people, it often gives a survivor a sense of being in control of the pain, the humiliation, and the scars. Parts of her believe with all their hearts that she *will* be injured, again and again—so better to do it themselves, and be comforted by the knowledge that the pain won't be too bad, the scars won't be too noticeable, and the humiliation won't trigger suicidal despair. In fact, the cutting is used by some parts to fill them with energy or euphoria to facilitate their "job" of keeping other parts safe from memories of the childhood trauma (Gainer & Torem, 1993, p. 263). So, a part will injure the survivor in order to preempt and control punishment that might (is expected to) come from someone else. Perhaps it is an extreme version of a more common experience such as taking a needle and digging into one's finger for a splinter in the hope of avoiding having a doctor do it *to* you. Self-inflicted injury soothes, while other-inflicted injury frightens.

Proving Existence

In a less wrathful way (but no less scary for therapists), self-mutilation confirms the very physical existence of the survivor. If she hurts and bleeds, she must still be alive. Destiny describes this:

Destiny: *I realized that I didn't want to die—I wanted to become alive again. So I cut my arms. I watched the blood pour out, tried to connect it to me somehow, but it had nothing to do with me. The skin wasn't mine, the arm wasn't mine, the blood wasn't mine. It had nothing to do with me. It didn't even hurt. It wasn't a punishment. Just trying to become alive.*

Self-injury often helps a part feel connected to his or her emotions. Feeling something—even severe physical pain—is better than breathing through the numbing haze of anesthesia day after day.

Creating Distance

Self-mutilation can also be used to create distance between the therapist and the survivor. Lorene's part, Nicholas, explains his view of this power struggle:

Nicholas: *Listen, if that idiot therapist thinks he's in charge here, it's about time he found out otherwise. If he won't do whatever I want (stop talking to Jenny about secrets; stop going away on business trips; stop saying he cares; stop pretending Lorene will ever be normal), then I will punish him through Lorene's body. If he wants to fight, I'm more than happy to demonstrate my courage and incredible strength by slashing Lorene's wrists or shoving a hot iron against her face. I've even thought of injuring Lorene's body right in the middle of a session. Ha! Dick would really have a fit then! That would definitely make him cry "uncle" and concede my superior power and control over Lorene.*

Provoking Caretaking

Self-mutilation can be used to justify turning to someone for help — a doctor, a nurse, the therapist, or the survivor's own nurturing parts. After all, blood, gashes, blisters, or infection cannot be ignored; they must be washed gently, bandaged carefully. For many survivors, the injury is an attempt at self-healing. In essence, "If I can see the damage, I can repair it." Lorene's Self explores her cutting experiences with Dashiell:

Self: *Why do you cut now?*
Dashiell: *To take care of me. To bandage it. I would sleep better knowing the injury is taken care of.*
Self: *What is scaring you?*
Dashiell: *Being all alone and bleeding.*
Self: *If I am hurt, I will take care of it. You are a part and cannot be all alone. It's impossible. It only feels like you're all alone because you don't realize I'm here and I love you.*
Dashiell: *Why do you hesitate?*
Self: *Super-She yells that I don't love you because I let you get hurt and you'll die. Never mind, I just turn her off. I say that I will be there for you.*
Dashiell: *You're afraid to love me. Afraid I'll hurt you?*
Self: *Sometimes.*
Vincent: *He'll follow your lead. He won't hurt you.*
Self: *I know. Who is it that is afraid to love Dashiell? Bonnie? Alex? Just watch how I do it.*

RESPONDING TO SELF-MUTILATION

Self-mutilation usually upsets the therapist more than the client. Putnam (1989) finds that "direct injury to a patient's body is usually the form of internal persecution that disturbs therapists most, although many patients regard this as less troublesome than some other forms of persecution" (p. 206). In fact, survivors' parts may deliberately activate the worried parts of their therapists to punish them, to find out if they care, or to discover whether they are strong enough to handle the amount of pain survivors carry. For this reason, therapists should work carefully with their parts and be honest with clients about their reactions.

The therapist should carefully evaluate the punishing part's power before acting, either by withdrawing from the issue that triggered the self-punishment or pushing ahead with the triggering issue so the parts can learn to trust the therapist. Putnam (1989) notes that many patients

> exaggerate the dangerousness of some alters. Not uncommonly, a therapist will hear from other alters about the incredible earth-shattering rage of personality B, only to find that B, while appropriately enraged over some past event, is well controlled. This choice between taking what alters say at face value or with a grain of salt is a predicament that the therapist repeatedly faces during the course of therapy. In issues of dangerousness, it is best to err on the side of caution. The therapist should not, however, let such threats deter him or her from seeking out and meeting the alter personalities of the patient's system. . . . Rumors of violence are often a form of resistance, augmented by the patient's own perception of the "dangerousness" of the information and affects held by that alter. (p. 133)

If the client's Self cannot make headway with parts who are unwilling to give up self-mutilation, she must promise the parts that she will work on this issue with the therapist. In the following example, Lorene's Self tries to make headway, but fails. Nevertheless, she knows she has back-up — reinforcement — available in her therapist:

Self: Super-She? Can you let go of cutting?
Super-She: You act like every part is okay but me.
Self: You have tremendous power. You implement your fears in a destructive manner.
Super-She: But I'm right to do that. You're trapped.
Self: No — you are. You've trapped yourself somehow. I don't understand you and I don't know what to do with you. Why do you want to bleed, feel pain?
Super-She: Did you ever hear of crying blood instead of tears?
Self: I'm not getting very far with you. Let's try talking to Dick about it.

Self-mutilation frequently conveys a message, either to another part ("Stop talking!") or to the therapist ("I hurt so much")—unless it is done as a secret ritual to cleanse and purge, or to soothe. The therapeutic focus should be on exploring the "paradoxically protective intention" of each part (Gainer & Torem, 1993, p. 263). Briere (1989b) aptly describes self-mutilation as a form of communication often used to influence the therapist by allowing survivors to "say or demand things that they believe cannot otherwise be said or asked for" (p. 132).

The IFS therapist can ask parts knowledgeable about the self-mutilation (either the injurer or some more distant part who has a great deal of information about the inner landscape) a series of questions to help decipher each part's message. Such questions might include:

- How close to the therapy session did the self-injury occur? Before or after? Have you ever hurt yourself *during* a session (even a small amount, by digging your nails into your leg, by sitting in a very uncomfortable position for an hour, by biting your lip until it's raw), or perhaps in the waiting room?
- Do you ever injure yourself without telling me, or is the injury a message to me?
- Do you experience emotions while hurting yourself or are you numb before, during and after?
- Do you get pleasure in preparing for the self-injury—perhaps shopping for cutting instruments, salve, and bandages, and then laying them out carefully next to your bed?
- Are you alone at your own home when you do it? Visiting your parents' home? Notably, self-injury is typically done while the survivor is *alone*, while other types of abuse repetition are done with someone (other than the survivor) who is recruited to play the role of abuser.
- Do you need to take alcohol or drugs before hurting yourself?
- Do you harm places on your body that are visible to others such as your face and hands, or do you confine your injuries to parts of your body concealed by clothing, such as your genitals or stomach?
- What do you tell people who see your cuts (burns or scars)? That you are accident-prone? That someone else did it to you?
- Afterward, what do you do? Sleep? Read? Cry? Masturbate? Panic? Call for help?

Be aware of self-injurious acts that do not ordinarily qualify as self-mutilation but nevertheless serve to regulate emotions and "to simulate, however briefly, an internal state of well-being and comfort that cannot otherwise be achieved" (Herman, 1992, pp. 109–10). The obvious choices:

drinking, drugs, smoking, not exercising, an unhealthy diet. (These behaviors are socially acceptable, perhaps even condoned.) The not-so-obvious choices: rubbing dirt or ink into an accidental cut or abrasion, hoping for infection; eating chocolate, knowing it will cause a night-long bout of diarrhea or heartburn; savoring the irritation or pain of a festering hangnail, paper cut, or headache; putting off a dentist appointment until root canals become necessary; not urinating until the discomfort turns painful; wearing clothes or shoes that cause significant discomfort; not eating all day until weakness and fatigue set in; or sitting in an uncomfortable position for hours until neck/back pain becomes severe.

Non-corporeal choices might include: remaining in a job that brings little money and much tension; habitually over-spending, then suffering through months or years of financial misery; provoking unnecessary arguments with people to incite rejection or abuse; or remaining with an abusive mate. Of course, there may be other reasons for these behaviors that don't include self-harm. For example, the survivor could be terrified of dentists, or unable to find another job. But a consistent pattern of self-harm, even if well-disguised, should be considered.

Finally, be aware that parts may injure and terrorize each other. For example, a promiscuous part might engage in sex with an abusive partner "and then [turn] the body over to the frightened and often frigid host at the height of sexual degradation" (Putnam, 1989, p. 179). Other ways parts may injure each other include hurting those parts who seek help or companionship from others by choosing a form of self-mutilation that forces the survivor to avoid other people (a large cut on the face stops her from going to work; a hundred small cuts on the stomach or breasts prevent sexual relationships). It is also possible to cause an illness or get in a car accident in order to take the therapist's attention away from working with certain parts. Or one part could (internally) repeatedly punch and kick another part.

The spectrum of motivations for self-injurious acts ranges from a managerial part saying, "I won't be nice to myself," which usually involves not doing caring things for oneself, to a firefighter part saying, "I know this will harm me," which tends to involve more deliberate and actively destructive conduct. Always ask the parts to explain the reasons for their conduct. Soon they learn to convey the intended message with words instead of with razor blades and bandages. Until survivors learn another method of making their inner pain bearable, they remain afraid to give up self-injury. Remember that most of the parts are involved in, or support, self-injury in one way or another. If one part is convinced to give it up, often another will take over.

As with other work with survivors, the key to interrupting self-injury behavior is to work with the survivor's Self. Gainer and Torem (1993), in analyzing the use of ego states to treat self-injurious behavior, find that their work "relies heavily upon the patient's ability to experience a rational, objective, mature ego state and to mobilize these resources," i.e., a "center core" that acts as a "conduit for all of the energies and resources of the system" (p. 264). They warn that the client should "demonstrate the capacity to maintain him/herself in a 'center-core' ego state before exploring the [self-injurious behavior]" (p. 265). This center core is similar to the IFS concept of the Self. Without the intervention of the Self, the extreme parts will have an enormously difficult—perhaps impossible—task in trying to relinquish their soothing, comforting slashing and burning of the survivor's body.

REVICTIMIZATION AND REPETITION COMPULSION

One of the most frustrating behaviors survivors face is the compulsion to repeat painful and abusive events. Survivors reenact their victimization, despite the concurrent awareness that this time *they* act as (or recruit) the abuser. "Revictimization in adulthood is part of the legacy of childhood abuse" (Putnam, 1989, p. 69). Many clinicians have commented on the correlation between childhood abuse and adult victimization such as rape, spousal abuse, or marrying and staying with men who are sexually abusive toward their children (Finkelhor & Browne, 1985; Herman, 1992; Jehu, 1988; Russell, 1986). Wyatt and Newcomb (1990) conducted a study of 111 sexual abuse survivors and found that self-blame played a key role in the adult abuse they experienced. This self-blame may "increase their fears and worries and, consequently, their vulnerability to be revictimized, to accept their fate as victims, and to accommodate abusive relationships" (p. 765). The survivor repeatedly reenacts "dramas of rescue, injustice, betrayal" (Herman, 1992, p. 111). Both fascinating and perplexing to therapists, "there is something uncanny about reenactments. Even when they are consciously chosen, they have a feeling of involuntariness. Even when they are not dangerous, they have a driven, tenacious quality" (Herman, 1992, p. 41).

But why repeat abuse? Survivors often know no other way to *experience intimacy* and feel connected to others. Herman (1981) notes that many incest survivors have "affairs with much older or married men, in which they relive the secrecy and excitement of the incestuous relationship" (p. 103). Only by reenacting the "pathological bond with the abuser" (Herman, 1992, p. 92) can survivors reach the level of intensity that the abusive childhood relationships engendered. D. Miller (1994) discusses the intimacy of self-injury:

> Trauma in many ways creates a higher level of arousal in the victim. . . . Many adults who suffer from [PTSD] have developed a craving or need

for frequent experiences of excitement. The TRS [Trauma Reenactment Syndrome] symptoms, even while they may be serving a numbing function, can also increase sensations of excitement. . . . [When survivors] stop their self-injurious activities, they feel an intolerable emptiness, dullness, flatness, or depression. They experience a terrible loneliness and sense of being disconnected. It is no wonder that so many choose to return to their self-abusive activities when there seems to be no other way to achieve excitement and the illusion of connection. (pp. 49, 57)

She also notes the paradoxical function of self-harm: "The self-injurious behavior serves . . . both to keep others at a distance and to keep her from feeling alone. She experiences the behavior itself as a relationship" (p. 9), one that is "more real and dependable . . . than relationships with people" (p. 38). Many survivors reenact painful relationships in order to satisfy their unending "longings for protection and care" (Herman, 1981, p. 103). They submit themselves to abusive lovers or husbands and thereby *get cared for* in the best way they can hope for, given their tainted bodies and souls.

Furthermore, there is the hope that by transferring "remembered pain across the amnesic boundaries of the alter personalities," the current *sharing of trauma* will be therapeutic (Putnam, 1989, p. 179). Victimization among parts serves the same purpose. Thus "many of the acts of internal persecution that appear to be senselessly brutal to an outside observer may actually be misguided attempts to share, and therefore to dilute, unprocessed pain" (p. 180). True, sharing pain by causing pain seems an extraordinary idea to many people; but survivors may not have been permitted to communicate their pain in any other manner. (Still, few therapists appreciate a client bitterly cursing them instead of saying "I hurt so much.")

Another reason for parts lashing out at each other may be one part's attempts to *get rid of feelings* dumped on him by another part. For example, a child-part may be exiled along with a manager's rage, so that the manager can keep the survivor functioning without being distracted by the rage. Understandably, the burdened part will often try to shed these foreign emotions, and internal victimization is the result.

Seeking revictimization may also be a belated attempt to *master the trauma* (Putnam, 1989). But Herman (1992) aptly notes that, even if it is an attempt at mastery, "most survivors do not consciously seek or welcome the opportunity" (p. 42). Sgroi (1989) observes that survivors often fear reliving the abuse: "We believe that what they really fear is that they will be unable to tolerate experiencing the intense emotions of fear, anger, and the sense of being overwhelmed that accompanied the abuse" (p. 116). Hymer (1984) found that revictimization of childhood trauma victims may actually enable clients to *build tolerance* by conditioning themselves to the pain and "strengthening the adult self through attempting to ultimately come to terms with the threatening object instead of succumbing to it" (p. 148).

Often, underlying anger and fear rotting away inside a survivor are used as a means for her to take control over the interminable wait for more abuse. This time, she'll be prepared and the outcome will be different (Herman, 1992, p. 39). Alexandra describes the horror of waiting to be hurt:

Alexandra: Some men I knew were friendly and caring, but they confused me by never hurting me. I'd wait and wait some more. How can a man love you as a friend, share important things, learn and work together, and not want to torture, degrade, and draw emotional blood? The frustration and confusion are so intense. It feels like being thrown off the roof of a tall building and crashing down towards the cement, waiting and waiting to be crushed, but it never comes. Just the falling.

Early in therapy, it became clear that Lorene's part, Jennifer, would sometimes seek out power-sex to "get it right this time," so that she could finally be loved. The child-part could not manage the sexual encounter herself, so she would tap into the power of an older, angrier part, usually Alexandra, who might not have been available to Jennifer as a child. Alex is blunt:

Alexandra: I feel like sex takes over my body. I don't choose orgasms, my body demands them. They control me. It makes me furious. But if it's impulsive and angry, it's not my fault—it was uncontrollable. I can say that lust and anger got the better of me. When the body has an orgasm, it betrays me. It made me participate in something I hate. I pretend sexual partners are non-beings because sex is like rage—it's inhuman to impose it on someone else.

THERAPIST'S SURVIVAL

The use of self-injury and revictimization will often frighten parts of the therapist. Some parts insist that the therapist do anything necessary—hospitalization, medication, threats of stopping therapy altogether—to halt the self-mutilation.

Many therapists are drawn into power struggles around this behavior, but the struggle is often futile, and therapists usually lose. This happened repeatedly in the early months of therapy with Lorene. She would show up for a session with a slash across her face, or an obviously bandaged arm with blood showing through the white gauze, or a distinct limp resulting from burns on her foot. It did not matter whether the therapist chose not to mention the obviously new injury or chose to ask Lorene what had happened—either way, the gauntlet was thrown and the power struggle began. Before learning that it was best to *ask* the parts involved why they wanted to harm Lorene's body, the therapist was left to threaten, implore, and beg. Deals were made but rarely kept. All of the therapist's parts would leap to attention, hastily searching for a means—any means—to stop this human horror. The therapist had to deal with his conservative part ("Admit her to a hospital—fast!"), his critical part ("Imagine if your colleagues found out your wonderful therapeutic skills trigger mutilation!"), his compassionate part ("I can't bear to see the graphic depiction of her inner torment"), his guilty part ("I'm definitely screwing this up somehow"), his stern part ("I can outstare her, wait for her to start behaving in a sane manner"), and his fighter ("She *will* stop this immediately—I'll make damn sure of that!"). The therapist must trust his or her Self, working with the client's Self if possible, to make decisions; the extreme reactions by the therapist's parts should not form the basis for major decisions. (We explore more of the therapist's reactions to therapy with survivors in chapter 19.)

CHAPTER 16

Badness, Shame, and the Search for Redemption

If the victim is in the tormenter's absolute power, the child can turn for rescue and relief only to the tormentor, making for an intense need to see the torturer as good and right.

—*Leonard Shengold, 1989*

SURVIVORS SHARE A pervasive sense of badness and shame. A survivor might report feeling like a "bad, disgusting girl who has done something very wrong and, therefore, is being and should be severely punished. Many of these messages control the woman's life, causing her to have a low self-image and to be self-destructive" (Blake-White & Kline, 1985, p. 398). The adult survivor believes "that she is indelibly marked and deserves to be isolated—outcast—from society" (Sargent, 1989, p. 175). She is "often plagued and depressed by 'inner tapes' of self-blame, revulsion, fear and shame" (Gilligan & Kennedy, 1989, p. 9). Most parts of survivors share this sense of shame. The sexual aspect of the abuse acts as a powerful magnet for shameful feelings. "There may be no human activity that so opens us to the scrutiny of another, nothing we do that exposes so much of what is normally private" (Nathanson, 1992, p. 288). Even a child can transform the vulnerability exposed by inappropriate sexual conduct into her own "badness." One preschooler who was molested by her father reported to her therapist:

Child: *Daddy scares me and hurts me. He says I'm a bad girl.*
Therapist: *Why?*
Child: *He says that to me. Daddy says to stay in the chair and take off the clothes. Then he says the little girls are bad girls.*
Therapist: *Why does he say you're bad?*

Child: That's because I am. The Daddy says I am.
Therapist: Are you sad about that?
Child: Yes, but did he take me on the merry-go-round, too?
Therapist: Yes, he did fun things with you, too.
Child: And then he was mad that I got bigger?
Therapist: No, you didn't do anything to make him mad.
Child: Is he going to grow taller and taller?
Therapist: Why?
Child: Because he'll be so big that he can't fit in our house and he won't
    hurt the bad girl ever again.

The word bad is frequently used by survivors to describe themselves, but it fails to adequately convey the depth of shame and self-degradation that survivors experience. Briere (1989b) cautions that a "more appropriate term may be 'self-hatred' . . . [because] of the extent of self-disgust and loathing seen in many survivors of severe sexual victimization" (p. 43). The resulting internal contradiction between feeling hateful because they're evil, and hating themselves, is devastating, often making survivors feel overwhelmed by a desire to harm or punish themselves (as we discussed in chapter 15). Unlike clients with less polarized internal systems, an abuse survivor often experiences a self-disgust so intense she can actually vomit when she thinks about herself; she can sit and slice her arm with a razor blade as she repeatedly reminds herself in a rote fashion that she is grossly repulsive. Briere (1989a) explains that "part of you does the killing or self-mutilation; part of you receives the killing or self-mutilation." Briere remarks that this split is dramatically apparent, but warns that "if you're misled, you may even think that's evidence of MPD, which it isn't. It just reflects one of the many splits" a survivor experiences (Briere 1989a).

We use the term shame somewhat loosely—encompassing various negative emotions (guilt, humiliation, embarrassment, culpability, debasement) resulting from the survivor's involvement, whether voluntary or not, in embarrassing, illegal, socially taboo physical acts that somehow (the survivor believes) altered the survivor's very personhood from good to bad, from innocent to tainted. In contrast to our loose definition, Nathanson (1992) distinguishes shame from guilt:

> Often shame is confused with guilt, a related but quite different discomfort. Whereas shame is about the *quality* of our person or self, guilt is the painful emotion triggered when we become aware that we have acted in a way to bring harm to another person or to violate some important code. Guilt is about *action* and laws. Whenever we feel guilty, we can pay for the damage inflicted. The confessional is a system of release from guilt, for it allows us to do penance for sins we know we have committed—a simple trade of one action for another. (p. 19)

Initially, this distinction is neither helpful nor apparent to survivors. The problem abuse survivors face is that they can *never* pay for the damage inflicted or do enough penance. Their shame at having participated in, or been the subject of, something horrible is so profound that no one can offer them a release from the guilt. Survivors believe that neither compensation nor penance is possible, because the sins they have committed against themselves specifically (somehow allowing the abuse to occur) or the world generally (for simply existing), exposed the immutable fact that they are shameful, vile beings.

Most survivors vehemently believe that our society's basic principles of guilt, compensation, fairness, and retribution simply do not apply to them. The fact that they did not initiate the molestation, did not want it, or did not benefit from it in any way is not relevant—a mere technicality. Some religions believe that humans are born with original sin, even though they personally did nothing to warrant having this black mark assigned to their souls. So, too, do survivors believe they carry a black mark due to someone else's misdeeds. Or, if a drunk driver runs over a child who consequently loses a leg, it doesn't matter that the child did not cause or want the accident to occur. The child forever after has only one leg, just as the molested child forever after has a tainted being. Perhaps most analogous is a young woman who loses her virginity by rape and later encounters a finance who chooses not to marry her because her hymen is not intact; the manner in which she lost her virginity is not relevant—only the result matters.

Nathanson (1992) describes the apparent immutability of shame depicted in Toni Morrison's 1970 novel *The Bluest Eye*:

> Young Pecola grows into adolescence surrounded by, immersed in a literal sea of, parental contempt, from which she derives a self-image of terrible ugliness that she attributes to her negritude. If only her eyes were blue (like those of her pretty blonde classmate), then certainly Pecola would be less dissmelling and perhaps even acceptable to her chronically angry and shaming parents. Nothing slows or modulates the constant onrush of degradation to which she is exposed. She is steadily and steadfastly beaten by her mother, then raped and impregnated by her father. . . . Peace comes to her only with the delusion that she is beautiful, that she now has the bluest eyes ever to be seen, that finally she is worthy of love. (p. 463)

In order to assist the survivor's parts in releasing the shame and sense of badness, the therapist and survivor need to understand each part's outdated beliefs and unique line of reasoning. Addressing an exile's shame for participating in the incestuous act does not address a firefighter's shame for failing to jump in and protect the child from the abuse. Each part carries its own burdens. Moreover, numerous variables affect the treatment of the shame: the origin of the shame, the part's attachment to it, whether a part directs the shame towards itself or towards other parts, and the need of polarized parts to have their opponents maintain a sense of shame.

Jehu (1988) lists the varying types of self-blaming beliefs reported by survivors he surveyed: *Compliance* (80% of the victims reported reacting with passive compliance by not physically resisting or not saying "no" to the abuser's advances); *secrecy* (96% of the victims kept their abuse a secret for some period of time); *seductiveness* (62% of the victims reported believing the sexual abuse resulted from their being "seductive," for example, wanting the abuser to hold and touch her); *sexual curiosity* (for example, asking the offender about sexual matters); *physical pleasure* (58% experienced physical pleasure and 86% believed that it was unnatural to feel any pleasure during molestation); *emotional pleasure* (64% used sex abuse to obtain attention or affection); and *material benefits* (41% of the victims reported believing that they used the sexual abuse to obtain material favors and awards and 50% reported that bribery was used by offenders as an inducement to engage in sexual activities).

RELEASING SURVIVORS' SHAME

Approaching a survivor's shame is a difficult and precarious task. Herman (1981) writes that the "patient's shame is usually the first obstacle that the therapist encounters" (p. 189). The shame "appear[s] to have an integral connection with the [original] coping mechanisms" and should be disturbed only with great care (Sgroi & Bunk, 1988, pp. 162–63). Confronting a survivor's shame by insisting that she did nothing wrong and is not a bad person "can be devastating for an adult survivor" and therapists regularly "find that adult survivors invariably react with alarm and distress when they are challenged in this way" (p. 164). Indeed, insisting that the survivor is good may cause her to flee therapy (Herman, 1981; McCann et al., 1988). Even just the act of acknowledging her shame in therapy can be threatening. Assurances, such as "You are not to blame," may constitute unbearable challenges to a survivor's faltering sense of power and control.

All parts need to understand that each sought to control the abusive incidents in different ways and that blaming themselves or each other for the sexual abuse may have served as a control mechanism. In fact, parts may be afraid to *not* feel guilty or ashamed. For example, an abused child often reasons that "if she can think of herself as having caused the assault, then perhaps she can prevent such helpless victimization in the future" (Rieker & Carmen, 1986, p. 363). In order to achieve some control and avoid helplessness, the survivor may even insist that as a child she was a seductress, "learning to seduce an abuser because it [gives her] control over the timing and circumstances of the inevitable sexual abuse" (Putnam, 1989, p. 192) and gives her a "means of controlling [her] reality"

(Sargent, 1989, p. 175). Consequently, when the therapist prematurely attempts to release a survivor's parts from shame ("It wasn't your fault"), it may feel as if only utter helplessness remains. Sgroi and Bunk (1988) explain from the child's point of view how taking charge of some element of the molestation gave her a sense of control:

> Imagine the little girl whose father creeps into her bedroom on some nights and engages in various sexual acts with her under cover of darkness when others in the home are asleep. . . . How can she comfort herself? One method, described by adult survivors, is for the child to tell herself, "If he *does* come tonight, it will be because I *wanted* him to come. If he comes, it will be because it was *my* idea, not his. I am in charge — not him. If it happens, it must be because I *want* it to happen!" (pp. 162–163)

Another important aspect of shame is its function in controlling rage. While shame can be controlled, rage cannot. Parts may be reluctant to give up the shame, because it conceals the rage at the abuser and the people who failed to rescue the child. The parts instead turn it inward toward a safer target. Guilt also conceals uncontrollable fear. In facing the abuse memories the survivor "truly may experience terror. One means of controlling her terror is to focus on guilt" (Sargent, 1989, p. 184). Feeling shame, humiliation, and embarrassment may seem preferable to "uncapping a rage that she fears is overwhelming and destructive" (p. 184). By immersing herself in shame, the survivor may also believe she is protecting her children, her spouse, and her friends from the horrible, consuming rage she contains (Ellenson, 1989).

REDEMPTION

Closely related to shame is the need for redemption. All children crave approval. Young children are so dependent on adults for survival that they desperately want to be valued — if they are worthless, they may not be fed, protected, and kept safe. Abused children learn quickly that they have little value and garner little approval unless they remain silent and compliant. Acts of abuse communicate to children that they are valued only as objects of pleasure or humiliation. In receiving this message, the child takes on a burden of worthlessness and the accompanying craving to be redeemed as something valued by the abuser — the person who gave the child the burden.

Adult survivors have parts who still carry the burden of worthlessness and a need for redemption. This need for redemption by the offender and no one else helps explain the abuser's tenacious hold on the adult survivor decades later. The parts believe that the offender's approval cannot be replaced by anyone else's attention, love, or trust. The therapist futilely insists that the abuser — not the survivor — is to blame. The client insists that redemption must come from the original abuser and often, if the abuser was a parent, the survivor wants redemption from the other (non-rescuing) parent, also. These parts believe that to survive and to be valued, they must get back their self-esteem from the person who took it away. The survivor believes that to admit the abuser is bad means giving up all hope that the abuser will ever return to redeem the survivor — she will never be released from the shame, never worthy of love.

As with shame, different parts act out the need for redemption in different ways. Managers, for example, often believe that if they could make the survivor perfect, she would be redeemed. Firefighters tend to believe that if only they were punished severely enough, the survivor would be saved. In contrast, the young exiled parts often search for love endlessly. (Paradoxically, they automatically mistrust anyone who offers them love, since they see themselves as being disgusting and unlovable.)

WHO IS ASHAMED OF WHOM?

Therapists often feel frustrated by the fact that survivors' shame resurfaces again and again. Often what they miss is the fact that each part feels a different type of shame, sometimes directed at the part itself, sometimes directed at other parts. In the following sections, we pinpoint the different sources (and targets) of shame, along with the accompanying need for redemption. We go on, then, to explore how the networks of relationships interact around the issue of shame.

Managers and Firefighters Ashamed of Exiles

Managers often find exiles shameful because they are perceived as weak ("All you had to do was tell your father no"), willing to accept new abuse in exchange for love and approval ("You did anything he wanted just to get a friendly pat on the head"), and participants in — or causes of — the early abuse ("If only you weren't so needy/lonely it would not have happened"). Thus, the child-parts are typically viewed as "helpless [and] vulnerable, yet culpable" (McCann, 1991, p. 6).

Firefighters agree that exiles are shameful, but for different reasons. While managers view the exiles with a tender and nearly tolerated shame, firefighters feel a wounding and angry shame. Nicholas voices his opinion on blame:

Nicholas: *I'm not the one that started all this. Jenny just had to be a cute little daddy's girl so he couldn't resist his urges to touch her.*

Firefighters believe that exiles endanger the entire system by exposing their open wounds to tempt abusers searching for a victim. These protective parts often convince the exiles to keep their shamefulness hidden, so that they can prevent the exiles from being rejected by people. This benign intention does not alter the fact that the managers and firefighters blame the exiles for the original abuse. "If she ever experienced sexual pleasure, enjoyed the abuser's special attention, bargained for favors, or used the sexual relationship to gain privileges, these sins are adduced as evidence of her innate wickedness" (Herman, 1992, p. 104).

> Sometimes he was a monster, but at other times he was gentle and warm. He often paid the most attention to her. She may have experienced physical pleasure from the sexual abuse, which was mixed with anger and physical pain. She is confused and overwhelmed by these contrasting feelings.... She experiences shame for her confusion and mixed emotions. (Agosta & Loring, 1989, p. 120)

Lorene's adolescent part, Destiny, was ashamed that she had enjoyed some of the sensations she felt during the abuse; she also believed that any "voluntary" movement of her body proved that she had willingly participated in it:

Destiny: Now you know why I let Nicholas hurt me. I think of myself as nothing but human garbage, so what difference does it make? What else could I possibly deserve?

Nicholas: I can do anything I want. I'll put a butcher knife in her vagina.

Self: I know. But it's my body that gets hurt.

Nicholas: I don't care. You're an idiot. What the hell do you and Dick think you're doing?

Self: Nicholas, we've had this fight before — many times.

Nicholas: And I'm still in charge.

Self: If that were true, Destiny would still be blended with you. Des, what hurts you so much?

Destiny: What I did caused everything else. No one humiliated themselves as much as I did. He wasn't even hurting me — there was no pain, only blackness and fear. Blackness isn't that bad, is it? My chest aches so much — like I've been trying to cry for years and years. My shame is so deep.

Self: Are you glad Dick knows?

Destiny: Yes, very. I think he can understand now why the other parts are so bad. If only I could get clean again. Nicholas says he'll pour gasoline on me and burn the poison away. Today he wanted to burn pubic hair after he used the butcher knife to slice, slice.

Self: Does he scare you?

Destiny: I don't want to hurt his feelings. Why is he so mad? He does love me, right? Can Dick make him stop?

Self: I don't think so—not directly. Arguing with Nicholas doesn't help. Dick can help you stand up to Nicholas, though.

Destiny: Will Dick be mean to me now? He doesn't seem to be revolted by looking at me, even though I'm covered in feces.

Self: He says there's nothing to see on you.

Destiny: Is he just being polite? He's rarely rude, except sometimes to Nicholas, which is okay.

Self: Ask him.

Destiny: The things I did—there's something I liked about it. I could feel my body. It's disgusting, I know, but for Jenny the body was always so numb and dead. Even though I was ashamed if Dad made me sit in all that crap, my body reacted. It was degrading, but I felt the coldness and softness that I sat in. But the worst thing in the water—my body felt terror run up my spine and through my stomach and pain shot through my head. Do you see what I'm saying? I had physical reactions. I participated with my body.

Self: Did it feel sexual?

Destiny: I don't think I knew what that was. But I wasn't numb. I moved. I took my hand and moved it across my body—my face and stomach and arms and legs, with feces that came from someone else's body. I wasn't paralyzed with fear.

Self: Destiny, I need to know something very important. Where did the "badness" inside of you come from? When did it start and how did you know you were bad?

Destiny: Nicholas told me about it.

Managers and firefighters also blame exiles for being "selected as victims, cooperating with the abuser, and for (magically) causing the abuse to occur in the first place" (Sgroi, 1989, pp. 123–24). Many parts believe the younger, abused parts are bad, because they either asked for or deserved the abuse. Sadly, although exiles feel hurt and rejected by being labeled bad or shameful, they accept the label nonetheless. Lorene's five-year-old part, Andy, offered this piercing description:

Andy: I am careful not to tell anyone what I do with Dad because it is the worst thing, I think. I am careful what underpants I wear, so no one will see anything on them. I don't want anyone to know that I am the worst secret alive in this world.

Once abused children discover their utter helplessness, they learn to demonstrate automatic obedience to the perpetrators, proving their loyalty and compliance over and over as they "double and redouble their efforts to gain control of the situation in the only way that seems possible, by 'trying to be good'" (Herman, 1992, p. 100). Lorene's four-year-old part,

Jennifer, exemplified the young exile who all too readily agrees with Lorene's father that she is bad:

Jennifer: I am a bad girl Dad says and I try to be good but it never works. I know Dick says I'm not bad, but maybe he is confused. He can't see the evil in me. He doesn't really believe in evil the way I do. I try and try and try to be good so Dad won't be mad but I get so tired and so I go hide in my closet. Even when Dick calls to me to come out, I cover my ears and I know the truth about me.

Managers Ashamed of Firefighters

Managers view firefighters as shameful because they act aggressively, in a rash, unrestrained, hot-headed manner. They cause chaos by creating new, unexpected peril, which the managers have not been able to anticipate. Their impulsive, riotous behavior can result in self-mutilation, substance abuse, rape, or imprisonment. For example, manager Super-She points to firefighter Alex's promiscuity as "proof" of Lorene's badness. Super-She shuns Alex for her behavior. Even as an adult, the survivor's managers still may be using a firefighter like Alex to seduce a seducer, hoping that it will finally give her control over the circumstances of the abuse. Managers believe that firefighters could be redeemed if only they would behave in a more refined manner. However, managers also hesitate to encourage this road to redemption, for who but the firefighters could act as a repository of rage? Who but the firefighters could so successfully lash out at enemies?

Firefighters Ashamed of Managers

Firefighters believe that managers should be ashamed of their passivity, coldness, and general absence of emotion. They see managers as being lifeless and submissive, a dog rolling over and taking more abuse without making any effort to resist.

Firefighters also resent managers for accusing firefighters of being destructive and chaotic, especially since it is sometimes the managers who *ask* the firefighters to take on tough jobs such as containing rage or attacking when a threat is perceived. Nicholas bluntly states:

Nicholas: I do bad things and the other parts like it; I become bad, as they wanted, and then they hate me for what I've become.

In the meantime, according to firefighters, the managers stand by acting blind and deaf to horrendous betrayal, abuse, and humiliation. Firefighters say that if a manager saw a bleeding, dying child on the street, the manager would walk right by, stiffly noting that stopping to help would interrupt the day's carefully planned schedule.

Firefighters Ashamed of Themselves

Often firefighters see themselves as shameful, too—as members of a street gang who blindly initiate wars, sweeping through neighborhoods with indiscriminate destruction. As proof of their inner badness, they spotlight the rage they vent (on behalf of themselves and other parts), their participation in forbidden sexual activity, and their complicity in any acts which have hurt others (Herman, 1992, p. 104). They are also ashamed of their ability to ignore their own values and hopes in favor of any expedient trick or stopgap measure which might accomplish the mission. A firefighter like Lorene's part, Alex, often carries this burden of self-disgust:

Alexandra: *I distract other parts with my sexual activities. I do my job! But I know that I should be erased from existence. I exemplify sin and poison spreading over everything that I come near. Inside of me is just chaos and craziness. It hangs there, waiting for release—I should be locked away where no one can see me. I am everybody's worst nightmare. Nothing in me is explainable or understandable.*

I think Dad meant to get me, not little Jenny. But now at least I can distract men away from Jenny by seducing them, or by creating a continual string of crises, like starting fires and shoplifting and suicide attempts and acting insane. No one will look at Jenny anymore.

Sadly, these parts think of themselves as being despicable. Herman (1992) quotes one incest survivor: "'I am filled with black slime. If I open my mouth it will pour out. I think of myself as the sewer silt that a snake would breed upon'" (p. 105). Nicholas, another firefighter, expressed similar feelings in his unique way:

Nicholas: *You don't understand why you must avoid all sex. I'll do anything to satisfy sexual arousal. I blame Alex for being a nympho, but she isn't too bad. She enjoys fun sex. It's me who spends days thinking of a way to satisfy—put an end to—the underriding arousal I feel. I'm not seeking an orgasm. My arousal stems from the Dad-in-my-bed world. I am trapped by my own sexuality. So I tap into my fierce, cold determination and spend days planning how to drench my arousal with humiliation—doing something "wrong" like having sex with a bad man, making the cycle end by proving it was someone else's sexual desires that caused the sexual encounter, not mine. That's why I'm passive in my approach.*

So it's not an orgasm I seek; it's an encounter that will scare me, and give me contact with a human, and embarrass me.

Self: *What scares you the most?*

Nicholas: *The cold anger that I use to express the sexual arousal. It's so disgusting. It's against all the values that I know you hold. It blinds me to reality. Nothing else matters.*

Self: *What is the connection between the coldness and the arousal?*

Nicholas: *I look calm, composed, sure of myself. I move like I'm in a daze. Your body looks passive and calm, but mine is a rage of arousal. I feel powerful and in control and not afraid. As I take each step, I manipulate the other person into a place where he feels he has no control. He did not want to have sex with me, but he has no power to resist. As the cycle continues, I gain strength and feel more arousal. I let the sexual excitement rule me, guide me, control my behavior.*

Self: *Where does it all come from?*

Nicholas: *Anger. It's not sex. It's pure, bitter fury.*

Self: *Directed at whom?*

Nicholas: *I thought it was directed at me or maybe at you. Then I saw that some of it was directed at Dad, at being trapped in his world where the satisfaction and the need for power ruled everything. It's like being mad at someone who introduced me to cocaine or alcohol and left me alone with the addiction.*

Firefighters often believe they can only be redeemed by suffering punishment equal to both their internal badness and their external crimes. However, all parts need to acknowledge their contribution to the firefighters' retaliatory hostility. In essence, the survivor as her Self must recognize "that she or he has become a self-abuser . . . and that she or he is in control of (and responsible for) ending self-punishment" (Sgroi, 1989, p. 124).

Managers Ashamed of Themselves

Managers may also feel ashamed of themselves. They often feel that nothing could possibly erase their badness because it permeates the fiber of their entire being. Managers often require more in-depth exploration of the causal connection between the abuse and their perceived evilness. A simple declaration that the part is not evil represents "a refusal to engage with the survivor in the lacerating moral complexities of the extreme situation" (Herman, 1992, p. 69).

Lorene's managerial parts directed shame at themselves. Vincent believed that some people (including Lorene) are born already tainted and they attract badness. There is little that can be done about it; Lorene simply has to bear this burden. Vincent also felt that at the time of the abuse he was mature enough to understand that the child abuse was occurring, and he should have stepped in to protect Lorene when she was a child:

Vincent: *I am so wise, so respected. But it is my accompanying passivity ("I'll just collect information and mull it over") that makes me worthless. I stood by, again and again, while Lorene was molested and brainwashed as a child. I thought it was not in my nature to act. I did nothing.*

The older parts who are burdened by shame are often consumed by this type of philosophical or spiritual dread of an evil entity that has come to rest within them. Managers sometimes believe that the younger parts were abused because the managers themselves are intrinsically bad. Lorene's managers had different views of their own "badness." Vincent's view:

Vincent: *Therapy has improved some things, but not enough to change my essence, my evilness. It has uncovered and released burdens I thought were permanent. It has shown me energy and connections to life I swore could not exist. But I'm not sure that I can sustain these new, fragile images and ignore the guilt that gnaws away at me. I seem irrevocably damaged, tattered. I can go through the daily motions, function at high levels of achievement, but there is always the pre-existing truth of what I am.*

If it weren't for the impregnable truth of my very nature, the younger, weaker parts wouldn't have been abused. I would have been able to protect them from Dad. But I am singed, burnt beyond wholeness. I cannot free little Jenny from being trapped inside this system with me.

But at least I can be steadfastly aloof—holding her away from my evilness and working hard to protect her from more abusers by being brilliant, successful, and giving the appearance of being the opposite of a victim so that we do not attract more molesters.

Dashiell believed that to be sufficiently cleansed of sin, Lorene would have to suffer a degree of punishment equal to the amount of sin she carried. Paradoxically, until the magic moment of redemption arrived, the punishment Lorene sought or experienced increased her vulgarity. Dashiell felt frustrated and trapped in something he did not understand but which nonetheless controlled much of his life.

Another of Lorene's managers, Super-She, believed that Lorene's abusive relationships as an adult, her promiscuity as a teenager, and perhaps even her participation in incest as a child resulted in Lorene's becoming a person whom Super-She was ashamed to be associated with. But Super-She's approach to the shame she felt was practical: ignore it, it will only get in the way of functioning, let some other part moan about shame so Super-She can focus on compensating for the shame with a lifetime of achievements.

RELEASING THE BURDEN OF SHAME

Thus all parts believe, for various reasons, that there is much shame to be concealed within the survivor. It is no wonder that parts work very hard to hide their "true nature" or that of their fellow parts, all the while desperate for redemption so that they can be relieved of the burden of shame. The survivor experiences the excruciating internal fluctuations of feeling like a victim who is hated by other people, and hating herself. The IFS model has developed a variety of methods for releasing survivors from the overpowering sense of shame they have carried for so long. We first explore several shame-releasing techniques that are not helpful, and then look at several techniques that are often quite successful.

TECHNIQUES THAT DO NOT WORK

"You Are Not Bad"

Therapists treating abuse victims around the world have told their clients countless times: "You do not need to be redeemed. You are not bad. It was never your fault." In addition, the victims have repeated these words of wisdom to themselves, mantra-like, and their spouses, friends, and family members have given the same assurance. It doesn't work. Shame is never "fully assuaged by simple pronouncements absolving [the survivor] from responsibility" (Herman, 1992, p. 69).

The survivor counters the therapist's positive statements with what she believes is absolute undeniable "proof" of her badness: She has cut or burned herself many times, she has been diagnosed with all types of mental illnesses, she has been repeatedly hospitalized, she has required medication in order to just barely function, and she has thought about hurting someone else or has actually done so. Sometimes the proof of badness is merely the fact that she has been tainted by a type of "original sin" that can never, never, never be erased ("I saw and did horrible things, and horrible things were done to me"). But often the proof of badness is an ironclad gut feeling: "I can *feel* the truth of my badness. I (unlike you) can look inside of myself and see revolting grossness. I am not even human." Herman (1992) describes the survivor's shame: "Simply by virtue of her existence on earth, she believes that she has driven the most powerful people in her world to do terrible things. Surely, then, her nature must be thoroughly evil" (p. 105).

Notice that most of these types of proof are irrefutable. A therapist cannot refute or modify something that occurred in the past: "I was mo-lested"; "I seduced my seducer"; "I have thought about hurting others." Those statements are often true and cannot be altered. Nor can a therapist change something that exists in the present as a normal part of being human ("I have sexual feelings"). These points cannot be argued with the survivor in a logical manner.

Shame cannot be altered without addressing the child's imprinted feel-ing of worthlessness, which is inextricably linked to terror of abandonment or extinction. Armsworth (1989) warns that to be of "help, the therapist must understand that the client's experience may have involved absolute terror, since the child or adolescent may have feared for her survival" (p. 557). Rieker and Carmen (1986) explain further that "even when patients provide concrete details of abusive relationships, therapists may fail to realize that the victims' subjective experience . . . brings with it the feeling of abandonment and annihilation" (p. 368). Briere (1989b) writes that the child's chronic perception of danger causes her to view her "continued existence as tenuous" and "to view survival as the ultimate goal of life" (p. 42). Sgroi and Bunk (1988) report the words of a survivor: "'I thought that if I refused my father or got angry at my mother, I would die; I would simply cease to exist. . . . I couldn't risk it'" (p. 141).

By molesting her, the abuser treats the child as if she were not human — nothing more than an inanimate extension of the abuser's sexual whims or self-indulgence. The child could be robbed of life by him at any time. One young victim expressed her terror: "Daddy wants to kill me. Then he will kill himself. Then he wants to put his spirit in my body. Then he will have my body for himself for always."

One way the child might deal with the intense shame and sense of being non-human is to actually believe that she does not exist. To survive this (and other) overwhelming emotion, the child-like part may put herself into a state of numbness; she will push her soul "out-of-body" so that she can protect her Self. She must separate the Self from sensations of her body so it feels as though she is no longer contained by her body. Beahrs (1982) explains how a child in a sadistically punitive and hostile environ-ment learns that coping might mean imagining that she has stopped exist-ing symbolically, or has negated her sense of being. Many survivors learn that "leaving the body" protects the fragile link between their bodies and their spiritual death. Lancaster (1991) describes depersonalization, which brings "a sense of unreality about the patient's self, as if it is somehow detached from the world or from their own body" (p. 103). Ingerman (1989) describes how parts of the person leave the body at the point of trauma as an "innate response that somehow helps ensure the organism's emotional survival" (p. 27). Lorene's part, Jennifer, became skillful at leav-ing her body during the abuse. She recalls this experience:

Jennifer: *I wish I could stop crying when he makes it cold and hurt inside of me because it makes him yell, pushing harder. It's better not to show anything, no feelings, deaden the feelings. But I can't deaden the pain. Over and over, many, too many times. His hand is bigger than my stomach. I am just there, a nothing, and I stay still, not breathing. I squeeze my eyes tight. What if I disappear? (Stay very still. Pretend it isn't me.) But what if I can't come back from the place I disappear to? What if the place that was going to be tomorrow isn't there anymore?*

Lorene's protector part, Alexandra, explains how four-year-old Jenny lost her sense of existing as a separate being:

Alexandra: *When Jenny was hurt by Dad, she gave him every physical and emotional sensation she owned. She was left naked and raw, exposed. She felt no boundary between herself and everything around her. Nothing belonged to her anymore. Without boundaries, sometimes the only way she could pretend to be solid or real was to pretend that she was a tree.*

Another survivor wrote a short story describing this same phenomenon, the loss or her identity as a separate being:

[The nine-year-old girl] lay on the narrow bed in the very early morning light and felt herself dying. She kept herself very still until she could feel nothing at all, and then she knew the process was complete. She was dead. Now, she knew, came the washing of the corpse, and this one needed it. The monster that had killed her had left blood on her. . . . What if they insisted it was a bad dream? Insisted she was still alive? What if they made her walk and talk and go to school and eat, when really she was dead? (Bass, 1988, p. 89)

Until she feels safe and in control, she may not be able to relinquish her shame. So, while some of the survivor's parts may be comforted by the "You are not bad" message, and the therapists around the world should go on sending that message, additional exploration is needed to successfully relieve *all* parts of the burden of shame.

"The Molester Was Bad, and You Are Good"

A victim of incest may bear the burden of badness as a means of making Daddy a good parent (McCann, 1991). Indeed, the survivor "will go to any lengths to construct an explanation for her fate that absolves her parents of all blame and responsibility" (Herman, 1992, p. 101). Rieker and Carmen (1986) point out that therapists can easily be confused by clients who insist on maintaining loyalty to, and relationships with, their abusers.

Therapists are faced with contradictions between their clients' feelings towards the abusive parents and the details of abuse recounted by the clients: "Therapists' attempts to intervene in these enmeshed relationships through interpretations of objective reality are often frustrated by the strong resistance of their patients. These interpretations challenge the patient's 'desperate need to hold on to the promise of the good and loving parent'" (p. 367).

Survivors "commonly cling tenaciously to representations of parents formed before sexual abuse began and to hopeful representations of parents as being yet capable of giving them love, empathy, and acceptance" (Herman, 1992, p. 105). In this manner, survivors can preserve the relationships with their abusers. Until survivors are ready to give this up, "they may vigorously defend representations of parents against rage" (Ellenson, 1989, p. 593). A survivor fears that blaming Dad for the incest means abandoning all hope that he will love and redeem her. Ironically, survivors may be confused by the fact that sometimes—perhaps often—they *did* experience love from the offender. This further entrenches her belief that she is bad, because if Dad is capable of love, he certainly would have loved her all the time—if she had been worthy of that love. Or worse, if the abuser was *all* bad, then perhaps even that small bit of love she received was a farce. Herman (1992) explains:

> The child must construct some system of meaning that justifies [the abuse]. Inevitably the child concludes that her innate badness is the cause. The child seizes upon this explanation early and clings to it tenaciously, for it *enables her to preserve a sense of meaning, hope, and power* [italics added]. If she is bad, then her parents are good. If she is bad, then she can try to be good. If, somehow, she has brought this fate upon herself, then somehow *she has the power to change it* [italics added]. If she has driven her parents to mistreat her, then, if only she tries hard enough, she may some day *earn their forgiveness* [italics added] and finally win the protection and care she so desperately needs. (p. 103)

Putnam (1989) writes that particularly "severe and chronic child abuse can produce a strange bonding between abused and abuser. . . . One patient described how incredibly angry she became at me when I suggested that her incestuous father had abused her. How dare I accuse her father of being a child abuser!" (p. 177). This bonding is especially tenacious for the parts who have no memory of the abuse—the parts who "served as a respite from continual terror and allowed the child to make use of whatever nurturing and love the abuser was able to provide" (p. 178).

But the bonding may go even deeper. The perpetrator may rape or threaten, then grant a plea for no rape or even for life itself. "The goal of the perpetrator is to instill in his victim not only fear of death but also gratitude for being allowed to live. . . . After several cycles of reprieve from certain death, the victim may come to view the perpetrator, paradoxically, as her savior" (Herman, 1992, p. 77). These intermittent rewards of love or simply reprieve eventually bind the victim and perpetrator by the "intensity of his possessive attention" (p. 79). As a consequence of this cycle, the "victim will be racked by the question, 'Is there life without father and mother?' That is the central issue of these therapies" (Shengold, 1989, p. 315). Therapists "must respect the inherent sense of loyalty and trust survivors maintain toward their families-of-origin and recognize that survivors may prefer to terminate therapy rather than betray these fundamental loyalties" (Siegel & Romig, 1990, pp. 247–48).

Managerial parts are most helpful in masking this inner sense of badness by making "persistent attempts to be good. In the effort to placate her abusers, the child victim often becomes a superb performer," perhaps by becoming a great caretaker, housekeeper, or academic achiever (Herman, 1992, p. 105). But the managers and other parts know the performance is not real; the survivor's core still reeks of evil and badness. Nevertheless, the performance buys protection because it: convinces other people that the survivor is normal; does not draw attention to the survivor as being different or peculiar; and makes the survivor worthwhile in some small way.

Survivors also fear that if they relinquish their own guilt and place the blame on their abusers, they (the abusers) may be able to "strike back at them somehow. (Abusers are often seen as having super-human knowledge of the victims' thoughts, feelings, and whereabouts)" (Swink & Leveille, 1986, p. 134).

Another reason the child must view the abusive parent as good is that the child's most basic physical needs require the parent's intercession. The very young child's food, water, and sleep all depend on the parent's willingness to open the refrigerator, turn on the water faucet, and leave the child undisturbed for a night. And if the child falls down, cuts her finger with a knife, burns her arm with hot water, or bleeds, it is the parent who provides the Band-Aid, medicine, or doctor: "The little girl kicked by her mother cannot turn to the mother for physical or psychological rescue. Yet to whom else can she turn? How can she deal by herself with the pain, fear, humiliation and above all the rage?" (Shengold, 1989, p. 24).

By uttering a kind word periodically, the abuser addicts the child to even the most meager indication of affection. By offering a gentle touch now and then, he sentences her to a lifelong search for gentleness. The child becomes addicted to the search for this relief, hoping to get another ounce of affection which will lift the burden momentarily, allowing her to breathe freely, without fear of annihilation. These fleeting moments of relief coalesce into the good parent image, to which the child—and later the adult—clings tenaciously:

> Only the mental image of a good parent who will rescue can help the child
> deal with the terrifying intensity of fear and rage that is the effect of the

tormenting experiences. . . . So the bad has to be registered as good. . . . To survive, such children must keep in some compartment of their minds the delusion of good parents and the delusive promise that all the terror, pain, and hate will be transformed into love. . . . The mysterious compulsion to repeat traumatic experiences . . . can be understood partly as the child's need to affirm in action that the next time the contact will bring love instead of hate. (Shengold, 1989, p. 26)

SUCCESSFUL TECHNIQUES

We go on, then, to look at some techniques that help release survivors from the burdens of shame and worthlessness.

Focusing on the Survivor's Value

It is more helpful to focus on the survivor's value than it is to explore her bottomless feelings of badness. Under IFS principles, instead of trying to convince the survivor that she is not bad, the therapist may ask one of the child-parts of the survivor what would it mean *if* it turned out that she was not bad. Ask: "Without giving up your feelings of being bad or worthless, what would it mean *if you were* a valuable human being?" Possible responses include:

- "Then I could take care of myself."
- "Finally, other people would want to share my life, even without being tricked. I would no longer have to be alone."
- "Even if I lapsed into my worthless feelings, my Self could assure me that the feeling was without basis in reality. Imagine!"
- "My conduct in the past does not mean I am condemned forever. I would understand now why I did those things."

It may seem odd to give the survivor permission to *keep* her feeling of worthlessness — but it is only while she considers what it would be like to be a valuable person. Often parts have become quite attached to their burden of worthlessness, like a comfortable, familiar friend. Challenging them to relinquish that friendship only makes the parts frightened or angry. The therapist would hear responses like this:

- "If I'm not bad, then the abuser was bad, and I'm not willing to believe that."
- "If I'm not worthless, then I must live as though I am a valuable person; that is a much harder responsibility than sitting still like a reservoir of toxic materials."
- "If I'm not bad, why didn't someone rescue me? After all, other children get rescued from abusers."

- "If I were good, I would have blown the whistle on my abuser when I was a child. Other children tell without anything dreadful happening to them — in fact, they get saved!"

Therapists must understand that the sense of badness is like a complex web, threading its way throughout the survivor's internal system. Some parts quickly weave additional threads of shame while the therapist is busy focusing on snipping away one thread at a time in a different section of the web.

Consequently, there must be *alliances* of parts who are willing to dissolve whole sections of the web at a time. For example, at one point in Lorene's therapy, Alexandra, Nicholas, and Victor agreed that they would try living under the premise that they were good. They recognized that instead of providing a safety net, their web of shame had now trapped them, leaving them no room to explore preferred roles. They wanted to enjoy life and pursue their own interests, but they could not do so when their energy was constantly being drained into maintaining or trying to become unstuck from the web of shame. Once this agreement was in place, the portion of the web where these three parts lived simply dissolved. The parts knew they could rebuild the web, reinstating their feelings of shame, but they chose not to when they saw how much freedom they enjoyed. Without the sense of badness, a myriad of choices opened up for these parts.

Thus, we believe that the therapist can delay challenging the belief that the survivor is a bad person; in time, when they are ready, the parts will let go of that burden. The therapist need not become combative, trying to force the parts to believe they are good. It is better to allow the parts to explore their relationships with feelings of shame and badness, identify the source (the abuser? other parts? the part's own reasoning?), and then help the parts imagine how it would be to experience life without shame.

Focusing on the Abuser's Parts

Shengold (1989) notes how threatening it is for the incest survivor to concede that her father was bad: "The desperate need to hold on to the *promise* of the good and loving parent is the source of the greatest resistance to the therapist's efforts to undo the delusion" (p. 26). Much of the good parent/bad child dichotomy can be relieved if the frightened parts of the survivor realize that it is not necessary to wall off the "bad" memories of Dad; it is not necessary to avoid "bringing the contradictory pictures together" (p. 30). The good parent/bad child sequence changes when each part of the survivor understands that the abuser, too, had extreme parts — that he was *both* the good parent and the bad parent. It also changes when the survivor's parts believe that she does not *need* the abuser to love her or take care of her, because she now has access to her Self, and her Self will ensure her safety and ensure that she will receive the love and support that all people need. Lorene recorded this in her journal:

Lorene's Self: *What if I tell you that even if Dad had lived, he never would have shown me love, that parts of him simply would not allow it?*
Jennifer: *Then I can't be loved.*
Self: *Is it enough that my sister loves you? That I love you? That I have friends who love us?*
Jennifer: *Can they replace Dad's love?*
Self: *Jenny, you need love—but you don't need one particular person's love.*
Jennifer: *It feels like I do.*
Self: *I know. Do you remember how upset Alex was when I was a teenager and my boyfriend Al said he was breaking up with me? Alex was sure that I (we) couldn't go on without Al's love. It didn't matter that there would be other boys to date, or other boys to love. It was Al or no one, according to Alex. I know that you wish you had one father who never hurt you. But many, many children grow up without a father's love. You must trust me when I tell you that just as Alex could survive without Al's love, so can you survive without Dad's love.*

Under the IFS view, then, the abusive father (or uncle, neighbor, teacher) can be *both good and bad*, depending on which of his parts are activated. It is an extraordinary turning point for many survivors to realize that their abusers had extreme parts that caused them to molest and injure. The survivor learns that an extreme part of her father caused the abuse, not anything *inside of her*. The survivor also knows that she can be angry at Part A of her abuser and still love Part B. This permits the woman who was molested by her father to feel love for him and know that his love for her was not a sham, superseded by his abuse. She is finally free to say, "Part of him *does* love me!" This is especially hard for the parts of a survivor who hate the abuser and cannot believe she would further betray her parts by pardoning the abuser's crimes. Seeing the abuser through the lens of multiplicity, however, does not pardon his acts or diminish the fact that the survivor is entitled to her rage.

A survivor's parts are usually shocked and relieved to find that their abuser was also a person with extreme parts and no leader to guide them. Lorene's parts depict this:

Self: *How would you describe Dad?*
Nicholas: *An ogre, a monster, a despicable child molester.*

Jennifer: *He was my Daddy and he paid a lot of attention to me.*

Self: *Would each of you consider the idea that he had some ogre parts and some lovable Daddy parts?*

Nicholas: *That's hard to believe; the guy did really horrifying things.*

Jennifer: *I only remember that he loved me.*

Self: *Nicholas, do you remember anything good he did? And Jenny, do you remember anything bad?*

Nicholas: *No, nothing.*

Jennifer: *He was very kind and gentle.*

Self: *You're both right. Parts of him were cold and mean, and parts of him were generous and loving. But for reasons that had nothing to do with me, his parts were extreme and lived in inner chaos.*

Nicholas: *If what you're saying is true, well . . . I guess you're saying he had parts who were like me — tough guys capable of acting, cold, and uncaring, willing to steal intimacy in the most expedient way possible. Well — uh, I'm starting to get the picture.*

Jennifer: *If I believe parts like Nicholas who say Daddy did bad, wrong things to me, I don't have to be afraid to cry about it.*

Self: *What do you mean?*

Jennifer: *If I looked at the sad things Daddy did, I would cry and then it would feel like he really didn't love me at all.*

Self: *He loved me (and therefore all of you) very much, but he had no Self to lead him, and his parts fought constantly about how to behave in the family. The parts who were not extreme and could see past the chaos showed me love. But other parts suffered terribly and could not see beyond their own pain.*

Nicholas: *I'd really like to get my hands on those parts who liked molesting little kids.*

Self: *It's okay to be angry with Dad for the things he did. But it's also okay to want to send him Father's Day cards and thank him for being a good dad (sometimes) to you.*

Jennifer: *It doesn't make a lot of sense, but it feels a lot better to me.*

REDEMPTION — OR COMPASSION?

Ultimately most survivors understand that neither redemption nor absolution hold the key to healing. They finally learn to seek "not absolution but fairness, compassion, and the willingness to share the guilty knowledge of what happens to people in extremity" (Herman, 1992, p. 69). They learn that they do not need redemption because they are inherently valuable, and each part is highly valued by the Self. The burden of worthlessness was given to them by their abuser, and they can now free themselves of it. Lorene's parts each struggled through the maze of identifying who (if anyone) should be held accountable for the abuse. They asked over and over: Was it my fault? His fault? Fate? Each part, from his or her own perspective, explored concepts of right and wrong, vulnerability and strength, good and evil, retribution and compensation.

Vincent, for example, often reflected about good and evil. He concluded that no ultimate truth existed but that he now had the *choice* to define his own goodness. Super-She often thought of retribution and compensation. She decided that there was no punishment and no compensation that could match the damage caused by the abuse, so that continuing to seek either one would be futile and non-productive. Alexandra focused on vulnerability and strength. She concluded that there was no way to be all of the first (vulnerable) and none of the latter (strong). She learned to appreciate the fragile beauty of vulnerability and was rarely frightened by it after she learned to trust Lorene's Self for protection.

Jenny also struggled with thoughts of right and wrong. She decided quite simply that hurting someone was wrong, and not hurting someone was right. Victor clung to the idea that compassion was useless and that only a violent purging or cleansing of badness from Lorene would lead to redemption. With time, he grew to understand that any *new* sense of badness growing in Lorene was being reproduced by Victor himself in his attempt to locate and destroy her inner badness. Victor was only able to back away from his badness-buster job by completely relinquishing the role. Like an ex-drinker or ex-smoker, he found he could not tolerate even a little bit of participation in accusations or identification of badness in Lorene, or he would immediately be consumed by the issue again.

And so each part learned that showing compassion for each other, and letting Lorene's Self show compassion for all of them, was satisfying and healthy. Ultimately this helped them achieve their preferred goals on a day-to-day basis, rather than centering their lives around issues of badness and redemption.

CHAPTER 17

Inability to Feel

He lived his life as if he were an actor on stage. Only at
rare moments was he responsible for his feelings.

—*Leonard Shengold, 1989*

SURVIVORS OFTEN DESCRIBE a horrible emptiness, a residing sense of nothingness which wraps their souls in thick insulation. Abused children
quickly learn that engulfing their entire personality in numbness may
offer the only available protection against the intense emotions and bodily
sensations they experience. This uncanny ability allows the child to move
into another state of reality. Lacking connection with her own feelings,
with safe people, or with safe places, an abused child is forced to create an
alternate reality where the child can continue functioning despite the
horrors she experiences during the abuse itself and during the periods
when she tries to anticipate the abuse. Despite the survivor's being an
adult, her parts still believe that blocking emotions continues to serve
useful functions. Selective amnesia ("How can I suffer if I can't even
remember?") targets both memories and emotions.

The purposes behind shutting off feelings vary with managers, firefighters, and exiles, all of whom incorporate different methods of achieving
numbness into the adult survivor's daily experience of life: being too busy
with work, children, community activities, or taking care of others; substance abuse, self-mutilation, eating disorders; or something as seemingly
benign as excessive reading, television watching, or shopping. Here we
explore how the three groups of parts differ in their methods of shutting
off the ability to feel emotions or experience bodily sensations.

EMERGENCY SHUTDOWN TRIGGERED
BY FIREFIGHTERS

Firefighters execute automatic, emergency shutdowns. When an abusive event floods a child with physical and emotional sensations, this auto-

matic shutdown of feeling is necessary because the sensations push the small child past her biological and emotional limitations. The child's only hope is to attain a state of living deadness. Shengold (1989) explains that "what happens to the child . . . is so terrible, so overwhelming, and usually so recurrent that the child must not feel it and cannot register it, and resorts to a massive isolation of feelings, . . . [a] hypnotic living deadness, a state of existing 'as if' one were there" (p. 25). Consider the three-year-old who is suddenly awakened in the night by the shocking sensation of her father's penis pushed against her. The child's managerial parts have little or no time to react. The firefighters' response must be automatic. Comparable to a circuit breaker or fuse blowing, an instantaneous shutdown is effected to prevent further damage: The child immediately stops feeling either emotions or bodily sensations. Briere (1989b) refers to the child's "need to stop being" (p. 117), and Rieker and Carmen (1986) explain that experiencing affect can be "incompatible with survival" (p. 365). Shengold (1989) captures this experience of the abused child drowning in feelings: "The terrifying too-muchness requires massive and mind-distorting defensive operations for the child to continue to think and feel and live" (p. 24).

The ability to achieve shutdown continues into adult life. The firefighters become adept at stepping in and closing off all sensations and emotions in perceived emergency situations; for instance, when the survivor is in danger of feeling overwhelmed (her father stops by unexpectedly); when she is suddenly in a vulnerable position (her boss makes sexual advances); or when she flashes back to a scene from the childhood abuse (a passing stranger winks at her like her father often did). Lorene's firefighters would often disrupt therapy sessions by stepping in and immediately shutting down all feelings when they perceived impending danger. Lorene's Self explains:

Self: Sometimes Dick talks directly to Destiny. She is so straightforward about her fears and thoughts. Then suddenly she slips into a catatonic state. Dick asks a question and she just sits. No answer, no moving, no breathing. She retreats to a cold, hopeless place. Dick keeps probing gently, trying to bring her back. No sound, no response, just staring.

Destiny hides, but it's only at the prompting of her protector, Alex, who is my expert at freezing out all feelings. I have to try to convince Alex not to do this. She's interfering with Destiny's desire to feel her sadness and tell Dick about it. Destiny has never before had the opportunity to express herself. She's always been hidden. But she has such a fresh, vibrant quality to her, and I miss her when she is hidden from me. I need to work with Alex; otherwise I will rarely enjoy the experience of having Destiny in my daily life.

Briere (1989b) describes this catatonic shutdown during therapy sessions and also offers the encouraging observation that "most clients are not totally 'absent' during shutdown. There is often a part . . . that remains focused on the environment for protective purposes and thus is somewhat accessible to the therapist. The clinician may find it helpful to talk to this part, even though the survivor appears nonresponsive" (pp. 120–21).

Lorene provides another example of the confusing disruptions in therapy that occur when a firefighter blocks all feeling. The Self must work hard, often with the help of managerial parts, to uncover the firefighter who is busily performing her job:

Self [*blended with parts*]: *I can't understand what happened in therapy today. At first, I was almost able to feel Dashiell's tremendously powerful sadness, but then I couldn't feel any connection with Dashiell—or even with Dick. Maybe Dick doesn't like Dashiell, or is afraid of him, so Dick withdrew?*

Vincent: *It was you who retreated, not Dick.*

Self: *Me? But Dick seemed so far away all of a sudden.*

Vincent: *You ask Dick for honesty and caring and guidance; yet you refuse to cry, to feel anything in his presence, to let him have access to parts who are sad. I watched today while you let parts freeze you. Whenever Dick said something kind, you just cut him off because it brought tears to your eyes so quickly.*

Self: *Are you saying the distance I felt from Dick was my fault because I retreated and let parts take over?*

Vincent: *Absolutely. I'm not sure what you were supposed to do, but you certainly weren't leading. Dick would catch a glimpse of Dashiell's pain, but he couldn't get near it. For example, twice you told him Dashiell's fear that at the doctor's, they make people disappear. As your Self, you know damn well that isn't true. Yet you block Dick's response to Dash by insisting it's true. There's no answer Dick can give to that. You won't let Dick comfort Dash by telling him (even through you) that doctors don't make people disappear. You become impenetrable because his assurance that the doctor's office is safe might make you start crying!*

Self: *What else?*

Vincent: *Nearly everything he suggests about Dash, you let parts block—even to the point of saying you can't protect Dash. For example, Dick suggests you talk to Dash, hold Dash, listen to his fears, and your immediate reaction is NO—it's too dangerous.*

Self: *I understand what you're saying, Vincent, and I agree with everything—except that it wasn't me. That couldn't be me as my Self. Who can immobilize me like that, freeze me? Alex, Alex, Alex. Do you make me forget the path to Dash, make me even forget what it is Dick wants me to ask Dash? When he says "go to Dash and ask him," my mind just goes blank. That's Alex. Even when Dick said I should tell Dash I would protect him, my mind went blank. It was empty. I could only say no, no,* *no, no. Filling my mind with that humming—no, no, no, no—so I couldn't think. Why, Alex? Why did you freeze everything today?*

Alexandra: *I'm so afraid of Dick.*

Self: *Of Dick? You're kidding!!*

Alex: *It isn't funny at all.*

Self: *I'm sorry, but it is funny. It's absurd.*

Alex: *Dick is jealous of Dashiell.*

Self: *What?!*

Alex: *He envies the zest for life and the ease with which Dashiell expresses that zest. Dick envies Dashiell's passion for life, his extraordinary ability to experience emotion directly, without first processing it through filters.*

Self: *Look, Alex, I have no idea what you're talking about. But you must stop "protecting" Dashiell from Dick.*

Alex: *If Dash cries, Dick will smother him—just to stop the crying.*

Self: *Do you think Dick has never cried?*

Alex: *Never.*

Self: *And he never saw other people cry?*

Alex: *Those people have disappeared.*

Self: *That's absurd. You're wasting my time and Dick's. There is work I could be doing with him and you're interfering. Ask Dashiell whether he needs your protection.*

Dashiell: *Alex, I'm okay. Dick has never hurt me. I really do care for him and he knows exactly what I'm talking about when I tell him how wonderful it is to be connected to my body's sensations, like when I'm outside and I feel the wind blow against me. He knows. No one can pretend that. Are you jealous of the relationship I've started to build with him?*

Alex: *Well, is he taking you away? Will you become so healthy you won't talk to me?*

Dashiell: *Impossible. You're more like me than anyone. Our relationship will only be enhanced by the work I do with Dick.*

Alex: *Maybe. Well, I guess I could try not to interfere by making her mind blank. I guess I could. Maybe. Just for a few minutes.*

IFS principles permit the therapist to work closely with firefighters like Alex to help them learn to trust both the client's Self and the therapist around the issue of experiencing feelings and giving up the outdated defense of numbing. When the firefighters are helped to not feel so frightened and extreme, they admit a yearning to let other parts—and themselves—directly experience their long-masked feelings. The firefighters' urge to experience a range of emotions shows up in the survivor's life in a number of ways. Firefighters may seek out adventures. Some find they can *only* feel something (avoid the automatic shutdown) if sudden trauma occurs, and thus they fill the survivor's life with emergencies and catastrophes. They may recognize intense feelings—like those triggered by the abuse—as the only type of feelings that are legitimate feelings. Later, they are surprised to learn that even "mild" emotions deserve respect and recognition.

Ultimately, firefighters are grateful to relinquish the numbness-related skills of forgetting, blocking memories, and selective amnesia. Firefighters are exhausted from watching managerial parts live as if they were actors on a stage, with the firefighters locked into the role of sentry—watching for any errant parts who forget their lines or try to step off the stage. Firefighters long for the release of anger and despair and for the chance to experience sheer joy. They will only permit such experiences, however, if they believe it is safe to step away from their job as living thermostats who remain ever on alert to shut off all feelings.

LONG-TERM SHUTDOWN
BY MANAGERS

A second type of numbness develops as a result of a conscious, decided plan by managers to impose a long-term shutdown of emotions to protect the young exiles from feeling the aloneness and betrayal accompanying the abuse. Because of this ability to sustain numbness for extensive periods of time, managers are key to breaking through to a survivor's feelings. The managers empathize with the child-like parts who feel "helpless, inadequate and guilty in a world [they] never made" (Shengold, 1989, p. 69). The managers' intense isolation of affect predominantly takes the form of a carefully executed "defensive autohypnosis" (p. 109). In the belief that terror and rage will be overwhelming, the managers alter the survivor's consciousness to a "state of detached calm, in which terror, rage and pain dissolve" (Herman, 1992, p. 42).

In the firefighters' emergency shutdown, the survivor instantaneously feels as though she has stopped existing. In contrast, the managers' shutdown of all emotions is effected through a gradual but thorough makeover of the survivor, who now wears the disguise of a "normal" person, concealing her heartfelt belief that she is abnormal, vulnerable, and grotesque. The managers convince other parts that to reveal their "true" nature would invite disaster. In *You Don't Love Yourself* (Sarraute, 1990), the parts of the narrator experience great inner turmoil as the narrator talks to a man whom the narrator's parts fear might see the narrator's true (and secret) nature. The managers frantically send out one part ("delegate") after another as they try to appear invisible, not noticeable. Finally, however, the managerial parts achieve their goal: "We're recovering our transparency... other people's looks go through us..." (p. 116). They sigh with relief: "So here we are, once again wearing our precious cap... The magic cap that makes people invisible in fairy stories" (p. 117). Remaining invisible is a remarkable talent survivors learn in conjunction with their skills at being numb to all physiological and emotional sensation. Survivors not only manage to be invisible to other people ("Oh, was Lorene at that party? I didn't notice her"), but can also be invisible to internal parts ("Alex isn't real; Vincent isn't real; Lorene isn't real; I don't exist").

In keeping with this ability to numb, survivors magnify normal social distancing and make it an art. For example, many adults ward off an unkind remark from a parent ("Do you always have to dress like that?" "Can't you get a better job?") by simply brushing it off. The adult survivor, however, has taken this ability to brush off pain and extended it to encompass her entire life. In the adult survivor, the managerial parts are proficient at living "as if" lives. Shengold (1989) describes one woman who remarked, "'I certainly act as if I love my husband and children, but I can't really feel it'" (p. 108). Another man described a part of him that was "wrapped in cellophane," unable to feel (p. 110). Alice Miller (1981) listened to a patient report: "'I no longer have a feeling of myself. How could it happen that I should lose myself again? I have no connection with what is within me'" (p. 52).

Unlike firefighters, managers do not release terror or rage by action; they usually resort to *inaction*. They impose a variety of constrictions, including a "feeling of indifference, emotional detachment, and profound passivity in which the person relinquishes all initiative and struggle" (Herman, 1992, p. 43). This passivity extends to physical sensations. For example, headaches are ignored; orgasms are stopped as soon as they start; physical activities that produce erratic exhilaration (skiing, roller coasters) are avoided; and doctors are dodged for years despite chronic and potentially serious medical problems. The managers confine the survivor to "just going through the motions of living" (p. 48). Although managers still interact with their immediate environment, they impose severe restrictions that narrow the survivor's emotional focus to the immediate present. Ignore the past, ignore the future—except to worry. Managers also rob survivors of the ability to "take initiative, carry out plans, and exercise independent judgment" (p. 166), outside of superficial achievements that act as window-dressing for the benefit of the outside world. The poet Pessoa (1991) described this passivity in his diary as "apocalyptic sentiment":

> Thinking that each new step in my life meant contact with the horror of the New, and that each new person I met was a new, living fragment of the unknown . . . I decided to abstain from everything, to refrain from advancing toward anything, to reduce action to a minimum, to avoid insofar as it was possible being found out either by men or events, to refine my abstinence and make my abdication byzantine. To that extent does living frighten and torture me. (p. 251)

The managerial parts work hard to prevent the other parts from experiencing their intense emotions for a number of reasons: the experience may be overwhelming and open them to more vulnerability, it may cause them to remember the abuse, or it may drain much needed energy from their task of acting "as if" everything is normal. Dashiell, one of Lorene's managerial parts, expressed the sense of paralyzing lethargy: "There is so little in me that feels real. I feel like I am a walking bag of flesh, just pretending to be a person."

In keeping with their function of insulating the survivor from intense emotion or bodily sensations, managers frequently impose a "no crying" rule on survivors (see Terr, 1990). "Many victims will resist tears to avoid contact with the reservoirs of pain and sadness within them" (Agosta & Loring, 1989, p. 128). The survivor fears that "if she begins to cry, her tears will take over and again she will lose that delicate, fragile balance within her" (p. 120). This "no crying" rule forces the exiles to leak their sadness in surreptitious ways. For example, the survivor who cannot shed a tear for the pain of her molestation may easily sob over a television show, even becoming so overwrought with sadness about the show that she feels compelled to hide at home in bed for days. The protective parts fear that crying about a real sadness will release a torrent of uncontrollable emotions and memories. They insist that if one doesn't let a single teardrop form, the torrent will remain forever withheld. One of Lorene's managers, Super-She, connects the enforcement of the "no crying" rule to overwhelming sexual sensations.

Super-She: *We learned not to cry when Dad hurt the body. The crying made him more excited. Now I believe that crying is like an orgasm. Your head fills up with tears, you beg someone to stop doing something to you, while simultaneously the other end of your body is being pounded with vibrations and sensations (whether painful or pleasurable does not matter), which are completely foreign to your everyday existence. You are helpless to stop what is happening to you; the gasping continues. All boundaries between you and the other person disappear.*

Dick tells young parts like Jenny that it is okay to cry, but he ignores the obvious and inevitable results: the exposure of a brittle despair that can crush us all. Stay away! I will never, never allow this to happen. When you invite tears and sadness, you invite the rape that accompanies it. Reassuring parts that they should feel "free to express pain in therapy" is absurd. Much too dangerous.

Super-She and several other of Lorene's parts insisted that the "no crying" rule was based on the principle that nothing was to enter Lorene's body, and nothing should come out of the body. The effect on the way

Lorene lived, of course, was extensive, hampering her eating, health, sexual relations, and ability to express any emotion.

Like the firefighters, however, the managers yearn for the ability to directly experience feelings. They are acutely aware that draining all their energy into the numbing defense robs them of the energy needed to experience love, to be creative, to explore themselves, and to participate in life. The managers are exhausted from acting, always smiling, always pretending. There may even be a manager or two who have experimented with feeling their emotions, but ultimately they fail because they have too many other duties and cannot maintain the feeling state. Again, however, managers will only agree to attempt to feel if they believe it is safe.

EXILED CHILD-PARTS ARE EMPTIED BY THE ABUSER

A third type of numbing results from the abuser indirectly or directly teaching the child to believe that she is hollow, emptied of her own beingness, valuable only as a tool to satisfy his desires. Sarraute (1990) offers a penetrating description of this lack of self-ness: "By his mere existence, there, in front of us, he dispossessed us... He completely invaded us, occupied us... Nothing, anywhere, belongs to us any longer. Everything belongs to him. He is the absolute master, everywhere he does whatever he likes..." (p. 187). Closely related to this experience of being nothing is the survivor's ability to focus all her energy on "reading" the abuser. In effect, she says to him: "I am what you say I am; I am what you want me to be." Briere (1989b) describes this other-directedness where the survivor lives exclusively in terms of what others think and desire:

> The victim of sexual or physical abuse quickly learns that "safety" is predicated on hypervigilance. He or she may become expert at reading the slightest nuance in the abuser, since rapid and correct assessment of the perpetrator's psychological state may allow the victim either to (a) avoid or forestall an abuse incident by escaping in some manner or (b) placate or fulfill the abuser's needs before a more aversive consequence ensues. (pp. 40–41)

Other-directedness benefits the child by giving her some control. Perhaps she can fulfill the perpetrator's needs without getting hurt too badly or even escape an oncoming attack, if she reads him well enough. Ironically, she also benefits by feeling connected to the abuser through her hyper-vigilance. As an adult, the survivor still has parts (especially exiles) who feel hollow and she still uses other-directedness to link herself to others. Alice Miller (1981) describes the emptiness of functioning in this manner as an "as if" personality:

This person develops in such a way that he reveals only what is expected of him, and fuses so completely with what he reveals that—until he comes to analysis—one could scarcely have guessed how much more there is to him, behind this "masked view of himself." He cannot develop and differentiate his "true self," because he is unable to live it. It remains in a "state of noncommunication," as Winnicott has expressed it. Understandably, these patients complain of a sense of emptiness, futility, or homelessness, for the emptiness is real. A process of emptying, impoverishment, and partial killing of his potential actually took place when all that was alive and spontaneous in him was cut off. (pp. 12–13)

The IFS model directs the client and therapist to communicate with the parts who are still ordering one or more child-parts to remain empty and other-directed. Frequently the culprit is a manager trying to protect the younger parts. If young exiles feel nothing and hope for nothing, then the managers have successfully protected them from pain. But the managers know full well that the deadness is a camouflage, and that a torrent of emotions, memories, and experiences still exists beneath the surface image that serves as the survivor's false exterior.

RECLAIMING A FULL RANGE OF FEELINGS

Before a survivor can learn to feel again, she must first recognize the absence of feeling. Some survivors do not know whether or not they are truly *feeling* their emotions. Their attitude is, "Of course, anyone would feel sad about what Dad did to me, and so I probably do feel sad, I think." The therapist can easily identify numbness when the client recites violent and horrific stories of abuse in a deadened manner. She may seem to be in "suspended animation . . . and although the client makes eye contact, the eyes are not expressive or responsive (they look but do not see)" (Cornell & Olio, 1991, p. 64). The lights are on (she smiles, talks, answers questions), but nobody is home.

In learning to recognize her own numbness, the survivor can learn to look for body clues. For example, if she is refusing to cry despite powerful sadness, it means that she has imposed physical restraints on any bodily release of emotion. The "no crying" rule drains a tremendous amount of energy and the survivor can look for that drained feeling in her body. Other clues of numbness include ignoring signals from her body, such as eating too little or too much, not going to the bathroom, running a chronic fever, ignoring physical discomfort, and sleeping either too much or too little (Cornell & Olio, 1991, p. 64). Also ask if the survivor feels afraid to move—if she spends a significant amount of time sitting still, talking quietly, taking only shallow breaths, and restricting movement to bare necessities.

While many survivors have been told to try various types of body work (massage, dance, yoga), often they can tolerate nothing more than a simple act like taking deep breaths. When Lorene first tried breathing deeply (though silently) with the therapist, her protective parts were furious; they brutally chastised Lorene for exposing her body's vulnerability to another person, and accused her of being promiscuous because it was too intimate to breathe with a man. They demanded that Lorene walk out of the session, quit therapy, and punish herself with self-mutilation. How *dare* she blatantly expose herself to physical danger? Surely she knew that her parts had worked incessantly to disguise the fact that she had a body—she didn't cry in front of people, would rather suffer great discomfort than admit to someone that she needed to go to the bathroom, and didn't even eat, blow her nose, or cough in front of people if she could help it. Other parts simply pretended Lorene's body was someone else's. She could smoke, drink, take drugs, and have abusive sex because these parts had no connection to bodily sensations and refused to take responsibility for the body's existence and welfare. Both groups of parts ("I must hide and disguise *my* body"; "It's not my body") were on constant alert for anything that might try to shake them from their position. Taking deep breaths—especially in the presence of the therapist—was activating all these parts. Herman (1992) describes the physiological reactions seen in survivors like Lorene:

> Threat initially arouses the sympathetic nervous system, causing the person in danger to feel an adrenalin rush and go into a state of alert. Threat also concentrates a person's attention on the immediate situation. In addition, threat may alter ordinary perceptions: people in danger are often able to disregard hunger, fatigue, or pain. . . . The human system of self-preservation seems to go onto permanent alert, as if the danger might return at any moment. Physiological arousal continues unabated. (pp. 34–35)

As time passed, and as Lorene's Self worked cautiously with her parts, they learned to use her body as a tool to verify whether or not they were connecting with any emotions felt in the present. Lorene called them Self-exercises because they helped ensure that she was leading with her Self in her body, and had not been taken over by extreme parts. She might focus on breathing, or eye movement, or the weight of her arm's muscles and the texture of its skin. This in turn helped her parts focus on the immediate, present-day, emotional context of Lorene's life and separate it from feelings they carried because of events that had occurred in the past. Once the absence of feeling is acknowledged, each part can choose to have just one small feeling about one limited experience. Lorene describes one such moment:

Self: *What happened in therapy today?*

Alex: *Dick said I was sad. He used a soft voice. He knew I was sad that he was leaving on a trip—and he didn't get mad at me!*

Self: *What would he be mad about?*

Alex: *Sad is raw, exposed, repulsive. Crying is dangerous. If you pour acid on a raw areas, then the rawness is burned away and only anger and hate are left.*

Self: *What did Dick do today that made you trust him more?*

Alex: *He asked if I was sad because he was leaving on a trip and I just said yes! Just like that—yes! I accused him of abandoning me. He listened, we talked, and then we moved on. It was so simple. When he knew that I was sad because he's leaving, he had the chance to pour acid on that raw sadness. But he didn't. Maybe he won't ever hurt me when I tell him how I feel—?*

Each part must learn slowly to experience his or her feelings. The therapist and the survivor's Self must repeatedly communicate to the parts that it is safe to feel, that the need-to-be-frozen rule has changed. Parts don't have to *do* anything to release the feeling, or expect someone to do something *to* them in retaliation for their having felt something. They just feel; nothing more has to happen.

Therapists are sometimes surprised to discover that the survivor's process of learning to feel may even include such basics as wondering how to cry: Are tissues always needed? Is crying usually noisy or is it muffled? Do tears always come? How often do most people cry? A part learning to feel might also ask about anger: Does anger always involve yelling? How do I tell the difference between irritation, anger, and rage? Can I safely say I'm angry without being attacked by another person? Does anger always require me to *act*—to do something to myself or to someone else?

The same types of questions may be raised about sexual feelings: Should arousal always be either crushed or satiated? If a man acts sexually interested in me, do I have to comply? Did I purposely cause his arousal? Does everyone have violent fantasies? If I want someone to hurt me, does it mean that is the only way I will ever enjoy sex? Is it possible to simply eliminate sex from my life so that I never have to deal with it again? If I have sexual feelings, do I have to act on them? The therapist may find such questions startlingly naive and become impatient with their repetition, but should discuss them patiently and not fear making personal disclosures, when appropriate and comfortable, about how he or she experiences feelings of sadness, anger, or sexuality.

Learning to feel after so many years of shutdown is like learning to walk again after being paralyzed. Survivors may be voraciously interested in every aspect of it, in essence wanting the therapist to describe "how to

feel" in slow motion, to lessen the fear of what to expect. They may begin
to recall "normal" feelings they have had in the past or they might have
daydreams about how they could express spontaneous feelings in the present. In this way, survivors reestablish "automatic, natural contact with
[their] own emotions" (A. Miller, 1981, p. 33) and discover the "authentic-
ity of [their] own feelings" (p. 39).

The therapist and the client's Self should reassure parts about the pain
which often accompanies feelings. The release of genuine feelings is not
"immediately followed by visible relief, but by a period full of mourning
and tears" (A. Miller, 1981, p. 58). Initially it may frighten the part, who
desperately wonders what is going to happen to him or her. Lorene's part,
Victor, protests:

> **Victor:** *I hated seeing Dick today. I don't want him to be nice or make me
> feel safe, because then I'll see where I am stuck in time. He uncovered
> feelings that are related to bodies, and then I see bodies. It's not his
> fault I'm in this body-of-horrors place, but he's the one who makes me
> see it. I'm furious and terrified. I left Dick's office shaking and fright-
> ened and feeling my body being hurt all over. I don't want to see Dick
> again. He'll keep telling me it's okay to have feelings in my body—I
> don't want to—please.*

A part like Victor must learn that he need not see details of the childhood abuse. Moreover, being told it's okay to feel does not mean the parts
are being *ordered* to feel—or else the therapist will abandon them. Instead,
parts like Victor, who are trying out their "feeling legs," should be reassured that the pace is completely under their control. At first, all the part
might do is report on an isolated event in the present: "I felt sad today
when my friend fell and hurt her leg"; or "I felt content when I took a hot
bath yesterday." Later, the safety and familiarity of having feelings will
allow parts to tell their stories, releasing the emotions they have harbored
for so long. But these stories only come with time. Learning to ride a bike
with training wheels—even if you're 35 years old—is just fine. No need for
ten-speed racers.

Throughout this process of learning to feel again, the Self must gently
prod parts out of their comfortable numbness and repeatedly assure them
that it is safe to feel. Lorene's Self reports:

> **Self:** *Today Jenny believed she was on the basement floor and that Dad
> came and raped her. I didn't tell her it wasn't happening now, that it
> wasn't real. I went to her and sat on the cement floor and held her while
> she cried and she talked about it. I didn't try to clean off the blood or
> tell her to stop crying or talking. I just let her talk and feel. I think that
> if Jen can only survive abuse memories in a trance, she will never be*

well. She must feel it and make her own choice about leaving the basement.

This kind of communication assures a part like Jenny, and the managers and firefighters who wish to interfere and protect her, that the Self is capable of caring for and protecting her. In turn, the protective parts are encouraged to disclose and deal with their own feelings and vulnerability.

The parts who are learning to feel show great courage; other parts watch carefully. Ultimately, each feels tremendous excitement at the possibility of ending the numbness and the exhausting need to act "as if." Acting "as if" you're sad, because it seems the safest way to act, differs considerably from spontaneously, genuinely feeling sadness; the childhood abandonment is not just described but deeply acknowledged and experienced. The reward is the survivor's unfettered access to a full range of spontaneous feelings. In Alice Miller's (1981) words, "The true opposite of depression is not gaiety or absence of pain, but vitality; the freedom to experience spontaneous feelings. It is part of the kaleidoscope of life that these feelings are not only cheerful, 'beautiful,' and 'good'; they also can display the whole scale of human experience, including envy, jealousy, rage, disgust, greed, despair, and mourning" (p. 57).

"AS IF" THERAPY SESSIONS

When a survivor acts "as if" she were in therapy, it frustrates both the therapist and the survivor. Both may observe the survivor work hard in therapy, only to discover later that parts of her merely acted as if they were participating. Alice Miller (1981) writes that the client "can do anything that is expected of him" (p. 23). Indeed, in some cases, the client carefully "presents material that fits his analyst's knowledge, concepts, and skills, and therefore also his expectations" (p. 24). She also reports: "An analytically talented patient, one with 'antennae' for his analyst's unconscious, reacts promptly. He will present the analyst with . . . all the affects and insights [that] are required. The only disadvantage is that we then have to deal with an 'as-if' . . . a defense against the patient's real feelings" (p. 23). Breire (1989b) also describes the "as if" defense in therapy:

This defense is perhaps the most sophisticated form of dissociation found among sexual abuse survivors. Deployment of this protective mechanism in therapy can result in a client who appears to be present during treatment, who engages in spontaneous, "real"-appearing affect (*e.g.*, tears, anger), but who never seems to improve or gain emotional insight into his or her experience. . . . Careful examination of such individuals, however, may reveal that their participation is "too good to be true," and that there is a subtle sense of unconscious "playacting" about their presentation. It may appear, for example, that the survivor is an excellent performer of a script that requires one to act "as if" they were a client, with all the attendant emotions and behaviors that the role requires. (pp. 115–116)

Briere (1989b) goes on to describe the thoughts in a survivor's mind during "as if" therapy: "I will play the part of myself being in therapy; I will get angry, cry, remember things and report on them, but it won't be me—it will be me playing the part of me. The difference between these two states is enough to keep me safe and to keep me in control" (p. 116). Shengold (1989) also warns that initially, the therapeutic relationship may be a sham because the abuse victim only *seems* to develop a meaningful alliance with the therapist, when in fact "these people are likely to behave in 'as if' fashion, to possess a facade of relatedness" (p. 312).

Lorene's part Super-She is the most likely managerial part to pretend (with the best of intentions) that she is performing in precisely the way she believes the therapist wants her to perform. Super-She explains her sincere efforts to participate in therapy:

Super-She: *I'm very committed to therapy. I will candidly tell Dick about my clearly neurotic inability to remember anything from my childhood; keep a journal faithfully; be on time for all sessions; work hard; and sincerely describe all feelings I think would be relevant to either the few vague memories I might have access to or current events in my life now. When I talk about my father molesting me, I'll candidly report that it left me with a sense of betrayal and general fear of men and intimacy. When I tell him I cut my arm yesterday after talking to Dad on the phone, I'll be honest and say that perhaps a firefighter part took over briefly because Dad evoked feelings of self-disgust in me. I'll explain that it's like in that sex abuse book I read—that I'm just trying to take control of the abuse by recreating it and causing it myself.*

In fact, I think it would be best if I organized all these thoughts and drafted an outline so I can make the best possible use of the one-hour session and do an overall excellent job.

If Lorene (while blended with Super-She) believed the therapist wanted her to feel anger, to please him she would access just enough of a firefighter like Nicholas to produce real anger. If she thought that the therapist wanted her to gain insight, she would access Vincent just enough to reveal some reasonable-sounding understanding of her behavior. If she believed the therapist wanted her to expose fears and memories, she would report disconnected pieces of memories without actually feeling anything. If the therapist even hinted that expressing sadness would be helpful, Lorene would glance at a sad part, feel tears come to her eyes—and then stop them with a concerted burst of control before things got out of hand.

Initially it can be difficult to identify which part is acting "as if." The therapist should look for the absence of affect in combination with a healthy-sounding, rational, inquiring part who gently probes for information about the process and rules of therapy, the progressive timetable for getting "cured," and the key signs of being "cured." An abuse survivor will do a lot to make the therapist proud of her. ("Just explain what recovery stage I should be in, what behavior is appropriate after six months of therapy. I promise I can do it.") But the therapist has little to be proud of at this point, for he or she has never actually reached beyond the facade of protection, carefully constructed and maintained by the well-meaning managerial part who was elected by a committee of other parts to the pretend-you're-in-therapy role. The managerial part who decides the therapist has come too close to bursting the dam of repressed memories and emotions might feel compelled to announce, with true sincerity, her instantaneous healing. She happily discovered the miraculous recovery shortly after the last session, when the therapist spoke with a young exiled part at length. The triumphant, cured managerial part wholeheartedly compliments the therapist on his or her fine work. Such a client, Putnam (1989) writes, may also suddenly disavow any multiplicity and all abuse, confessing that he or she "made it all up" (p. 214).

This type of compliance, in which the survivor's parts truly believe they are performing deep emotional work, seriously impairs therapeutic progress. When the therapist senses this happening, she should ask to speak with the part and work intensively with that part about its fears. Given time, the survivor realizes that the dependable, non-punitive presence of the therapist "continues to be there, undestroyed and undestroying," and from this base of therapeutic continuity, the abuse victim learns to feel true emotions in therapy (Shengold, 1989, p. 312).

Superficial compliance in therapy might also be the work of protector parts who are attempting to redirect the therapist away from a raging exile and toward a needy (but relatively benign) child-part, who will reveal only as much as the protectors allow. As the child-part expresses fear, sadness, and a sense of abandonment, the therapist warms to her, offering support and comfort. In the meantime, the therapist (hopefully) forgets about the survivor's other parts. Putnam (1989) aptly describes this form of resistance, whereby the client "[keeps] the therapist preoccupied with 'babysitting' rather than psychotherapeutic work. In many instances these infant or child personalities are sent out by the system to thwart uncovering work" (pp. 213–14).

A word of caution: Therapists viewing a client working with young, frightened parts may confuse the client's absence of affect with the numbness and inability to feel discussed in this chapter. ("If I can't *see* her abreacting, how do I know what we're doing is real and will really work?") Two points to remember: You can ask the Self about this, talk to the young part directly, or ask if other parts are uncomfortable having the young part show her feelings in front of you. Second, retrieving a young part who is stuck in the past does not mean the young part will feel her emotions *before* leaving the past; she may not want to explore or expose those feelings until she knows she is safe in the present.

So, survivors come to therapy for help, but desperately try not to feel, instead acting "as if" they are in therapy. Only by working with a survivor's Self, separated from parts who shut down her entire being or launch "as if" behavior, will she learn to feel again. With time, each part learns that feeling bad does not mean that something bad will happen; feeling terrified does not mean that something terrifying will happen; and feeling the pain of having been abandoned does not mean that a new abandonment threatens her.

PART IV

Survivor-Therapist Relationship Issues

CHAPTER 18

Sexual Issues in the Therapeutic Relationship

Most multiples will have an alter who will try to seduce the therapist; in fact, the therapist can virtually count on this. I think that therapists who get into trouble at this point do so because they have already violated many other treatment boundaries and believe that the rules do not apply to them.

—Frank Putnam, 1989

A SURVIVOR OF SEXUAL abuse excels at allowing herself to be exploited. She is an accomplished victim; it is a familiar role that she has often played successfully. Even if she does not actively seek out abuse, she attracts it; wounded parts will trade anything for a little caring and friendship. Consequently, sexual abuse victims are a high-risk group for victimization or exploitation by therapists—they have what Kluft (1989) calls the "sitting duck syndrome." Although exploring the cause of such exploitation by therapists is beyond the scope of this book, awareness of the potential for this abusive behavior is important for any therapist-client relationship, particularly when the work revolves around child sexual abuse.

ABUSE INFLICTED BY THERAPISTS

The "power imbalance in the therapeutic relationship . . . render[s] all patients vulnerable to exploitation" (Herman, 1992, p. 135). This includes women therapists exploiting or abusing women clients. "Given the right set of circumstances, any mental health professional could become abusive" (Gartrell & Sanderson, 1994, p. 41). In fact, a woman-woman therapeutic relationship may expose even greater vulnerability in survivors because of "the greater trust women clients place in female caregivers" (p. 52).

Exploitation by therapists can take many forms. In some relationships it is limited to the violation of the therapist's implied "promise to abstain from using her power over the patient to gratify her personal needs" (Herman, 1992, p. 135). In other cases, in violation of all applicable laws and codes of ethics, some therapists convince themselves and their clients that it is healthy to reenact the molestation in the therapy relationship in order to gain control of the abusive memories.

The most obvious exploitation, of course, is to engage in a sexual relationship with the client. "Sexualized countertransference is a common experience, particularly for male therapists working with female patients who have been subjected to sexual violence" (Herman, 1992, p. 145). Therapists may act with sincere feelings of caring and closeness, or may become aroused from hearing either sexually explicit or sexually taboo information. Even if therapists do not *act* on the sexual feelings, the client may be aware of their "voyeuristic excitement, fascination, and even sexual arousal" (p. 145).

Therapists' exploitation may also take non-sexual forms, such as using the client to reinforce their view of themselves as great rescuers or to exercise their need to be powerful, directing, and in charge of as many people's lives as possible. Therapists may also ask clients to comfort them when personal problems arise in their lives, to offer assurance that they are skilled therapists who have saved their clients' lives, or to console them when they have had a bad week. Therapists might also use clients as personal counselors, disclosing furtive secrets, and exploring their own confusion or pain.

It is disheartening to know that in one recent study (Armsworth, 1989), 46% of incest survivors who sought help were sexually victimized or exploited during the 113 contacts with therapists. These professionals included psychologists, social workers, psychiatrists, and priests. Reasons given by the professionals for becoming sexually involved with clients included: priest fell in love with the survivor; client needed to get in touch with her sexuality in a "loving context"; client needed to re-experience feelings; client "sent by God" to help minister; and client needed to reenact the incest to permit her to experience sexual feelings. Others have reported varying appalling statistics and similar justifications — both ethically inadequate and legally deficient — for engaging in sexual relations with clients. Whatever justification is used to legitimize the abusive relationship, the "consequences of therapist-patient sexual exploitation are nearly universally negative" (Kluft, 1989, p. 489).

The incest victims in Armsworth's study (1989) identified additional exploitative practices or conditions that either were of little help or caused them harm. These included: therapists did not believe their clients and told them that they had fantasized the childhood abuse; the disclosed incest was ignored by therapists; therapists told clients the abuse was not important (e.g., since no intercourse occurred); clients were blamed for incest and told they must have enjoyed it since they stayed; therapists responded with shock or disgust; and therapists responded by overprescribing drugs.

Even beyond the ethical and legal violations of exploiting clients, therapists who victimize survivors of abuse can crush their chances of ever becoming strong, healthy human beings. Clinicians overwhelmingly agree that few transgressions bring as much pain as therapists' exploitation of abuse victims (Armsworth, 1989; Briere, 1989b; Courtois, 1988; Kluft, 1989). The destruction caused by a therapist's exploitation rivals that caused by the original abuse itself and makes it many times harder for the survivor to trust any therapist in the future.

Although clients hopefully will learn through sources other than an abusing therapist to recognize exploitation, ultimately the burden should rest upon therapists to ensure that their clients are never exposed to exploitation in therapy. If they fail to meet that burden, the criminal and civil legal sanctions, and the resultant professional consequences, are appropriately severe. Nevertheless, such sanctions rarely compensate a client for the harm caused by the fact that her "assumption that [she] is entering a benign and helping environment has been shattered" (Kluft, 1989, p. 490).

GENDER ISSUES

Both therapists and clients should be aware of the possible issues that gender raises. Briere (1989b), Courtois (1988), McCann (1991), and others offer excellent discussions of gender-related issues. The purpose here is to highlight how the IFS model permits therapists and clients to work on these issues without recrimination or blame.

Some survivors feel more comfortable with a therapist who is the opposite sex of the perpetrator. A female survivor may prefer facing a woman when discussing her body, the sexual abuse details, or her rage at men. Frequently, however, she finds herself with a male therapist. If this is by choice, it may be relevant to explore whether the client dislikes women, perhaps thinking they are weak and vulnerable. Herman (1981) discusses the fact that ironically, "in spite of repeated mistreatment, the majority of the incest victims did not express a great deal of hostility toward men" (p. 102). Instead, many "seemed to regard all women, including themselves, with contempt . . . [that] masked a deeper longing for a relationship with a caring woman. This longing was rarely expressed" (p. 103). At some point, then, a female survivor may find it helpful to see a woman therapist, or to supplement individual sessions with group therapy led by a woman and comprised of all female group members. On the other hand, some female survivors prefer working with a male therapist in order to explore and resolve fears of being involved in a trusting relationship with a man.

Similarly, male survivors who were abused by a woman may prefer to discuss intimacy and sexual issues with a male therapist. Some men have learned to always please a woman in authority and will have difficulty not being compliant and overly-giving to a woman therapist. Other men will benefit greatly from a female therapist if it is their first experience trusting a woman.

A multitude of other gender-related issues are possible in the complex interactions between survivors and therapists. For example, "female survivors may unconsciously attempt to sexually stimulate the male therapist as a way of both recapitulating the incest experience as well as testing out whether the therapist will respect her boundaries" (McCann, 1991, p. 7). Also, some male therapists treating female sexual abuse survivors "report feeling ashamed and afraid of becoming sexually stimulated by their clients' disclosures" (p. 7). In addition, male therapists may find they have parts who "crave the attention of or, conversely, fear being rejected by attractive young women" (Schwartz, 1995, p. 161). Similarly, female therapists may find their more maternal parts want to re-parent survivors of either sex, or may encounter parts who want to please their male clients.

When gender-related problems originate in the therapist, he or she should remember that it is only a *part* who feels that gender (perhaps the therapist's attraction to the client, or the therapist's irritation with the client's mistrust of all people of the abuser's sex) is negatively impacting the relationship. The concerns raised by the feelings or behavior of the therapist's part must be addressed by the therapist, either by working on maintaining Self leadership or by asking for the help of another clinician. Even though clients may sense a problem, the issue need not be directly discussed in therapy—assuming the therapist's part has not *acted* on the problematic feelings.

If a client's parts raise gender-related problems, the issue should be discussed directly instead of the part throwing wild insults and accusations at the therapist. A therapist should make sure his or her Self is in a leadership position when answering the client's questions. He must work to prevent his own parts from interfering ("I'm tired of being called untrustworthy scum just because I'm male"). If, after discussion, the client continues to indicate as his or her Self a preference for a therapist of a different sex, respect that choice.

SEXUAL BEHAVIOR BY CLIENTS

Sexual issues inevitably arise in a therapy relationship with a sexual abuse survivor. Jehu (1988) writes that survivors have a "tendency to over-sexualize all relationships" (p. 25). Often, seduction enters the picture because the abusive setting resembles the dynamics of the therapy relationship. For example, both relationships include a power imbalance, an authority figure, and exposure of the client's vulnerability (Armsworth, 1989; Jehu, 1988; Rieker & Carmen, 1986). It is frightening for the survivor to voluntarily submit herself "to an unequal relationship in which the therapist has superior status and power" (Herman, 1992, p. 134). However, the survivor's parts can play varying roles in leading the relationship to the door of seduction.

A survivor may seek a sexual relationship with the therapist because parts (especially exiles) assume that the therapist *wants* the survivor to offer sex, and that an authority figure's wishes must always be met. Jehu (1988) found that 48% of female survivors surveyed believed: "I don't have the right to deny my body to any man who demands it" (p. 48).

Parts of the survivor (again, especially exiles) may also feel that if the therapist truly cares, the therapist *must* express this caring through sex. ("When someone really loves you—like Dad loved me—sex must be part of the relationship.") In his study Jehu (1988) found that 86% of the survivors believed: "No man could care for me without a sexual relationship." If all people important to the survivor have demanded sex in exchange for attention, why would the therapist be different? Alexandra expresses this point explicitly in the following example:

Alexandra: I was so embarrassed and scared when Nicholas told Dick about secret sexual feelings, secret masturbating, secret fantasies. Dick will know I'm real. My body is real. I always pretended I didn't have a body—I thought I had convinced Dick of this. I could pretend I had no sexual feelings at all.

Vincent: I think Lorene has it under control. She and Dick will handle this.

Nicholas: I can talk about whatever I want to with Dick.

Alex: You're trying to ruin everything. Tonight is a good night to die. The worst thing has happened.

Vincent: What is the worst thing?

Alex: Dick knows I have a body, that I'm sexual.

Vincent: What do you think he believed?

Nicholas: Well he was obviously too stupid to even think about it. He believed she was asexual!

Vincent: What's the big deal? They've talked about sex 100 times.

Nicholas: That was about past sex. I was smart enough to let him in on present sexual feelings in this secret world.

Alex: Shut up. You've ruined all our safety. Secrets make things safe.

Vincent: Dick says you should trust him not to judge you, trust him not to stop caring.

Alex: Well, I figured if he had a sex monster in him—like Nicholas—it could make him do anything, even break all his rules. You see, if a man really loves you, even when he's not supposed to love you, he'll break all the rules. It proves his love.

Sexual advances by a client may also be used, especially by a firefighter part, as a dramatic means to punish either the client (by setting up a rejection scenario) or the therapist. It may be "a way of castrating the therapist and/or rejecting the therapy" (Kluft, 1989, p. 488). A punishment aimed at the therapist might include a protective part's repeated accusations that the therapist is sexually aroused by the relationship. By manipulating the therapist into either admitting or denying having these sexual feelings for the client, parts of the client accomplish a great coup. Now it is the abuse victim who becomes powerful (in a negative way).

Sexual advances may also be a wonderful distraction from painful or frightening therapy-related issues. A survivor's protective managerial or firefighter parts may try to (casually) trap the therapist into admitting the existence of sexual feelings for the client; then they watch with glee as sexual innuendo bounces around the therapist's office:

Vincent: You promised we would always be honest, so tell me if you feel sexual arousal when you are with Lorene, or when you think of her.
Therapist: It isn't really an issue with me.
Alexandra: Ha! I thought so! I'm so repulsive and disgusting that you're afraid touching me would make you physically sick.
Therapist: That's not true.
Vincent: Then you do harbor sexual feelings for Lorene!

Thus, parts use various routes to bring the therapist and client to these sexual issues. It is critical for the survivor to learn that she has more to offer than sex; she must be helped to explore her own intrinsic worth, her value absent the dispensing of sexual favors. The therapist can facilitate this exploration without embarrassing the client or allowing managerial parts to punish the client for offering sexuality as a trade for caring. The therapist can gently decline any advances by not responding in a sexual manner, and can respectfully talk about the issue directly with any part who raises it (perhaps in the form of a sexual invitation or as an accusation that the therapist is "lusting after" the client).

Most importantly, therapists should remember that the survivor's parts often know of no better way of communicating, of offering her trust, of saying thank you. Without sexualizing the interaction, the therapist should acknowledge an acceptance of, and an appreciation for the deep value of the survivor's desire to communicate, to trust, or to show appreciation. It can be extraordinary for a survivor to experience a trusting relationship in which she is valued and cared for without any expectation that she must pay dues with sexual favors.

CHAPTER 19

Reactions of Therapist's Parts to Work with Survivors

When you can, in your own time, turn and face that deep chasm within. Let go. Grieve, rage, shed tears.

—*Kathy Steele, 1991*

A THERAPIST'S PARTS also join the therapy relationship. How could a person *not* react to tales of horror, incredible anguish, brutal attacks by angry parts, self-mutilation, and memories of sexual feats rivaling the strongest pornography available? Survivors often rouse complex responses from therapists. To ignore these responses can be fatal to the therapeutic relationship. Putnam's (1989) experience with MPD clients applies to all types of abuse survivors: A therapist "may simultaneously be aware of hostility toward one alter, sexual feelings toward another, and a wish to hold and nurture a third alter. A therapist may feel pulled one way and then another throughout a session with a [patient], struggling to identify what is going on in the patient as well as within himself or herself" (p. 187).

Agosta and Loring (1989) advise therapists that it is important to understand their own reactions and processes related to working with victims of child sexual abuse: "Knowing yourself and knowing when you are in over your head is an important part of this process" (p. 121). Steele (1991) discusses the post-traumatic stress disorder therapists can experience in response to working with survivors of severe abuse. For example, therapists may develop symptoms such as disturbed sleep, poor appetite, anxiety, numbing, preoccupation with the content of the abuse, questioning their own safety, or even uncovering their own history of abuse. Steele also describes the rage and desire for revenge against the perpetrator that a therapist might experience.

The IFS model encourages therapists to *not* remain aloof or distant from the survivor. Instead, it emphasizes the importance of the therapist-client relationship. Schwartz (1995) found that the more experience he gained with IFS therapy, the more the importance of the therapist-client relationship became evident, particularly with clients who suffered severe abuse. Moreover, it is difficult to elicit the client's Self if the therapist cannot elicit his or her own Self and control any parts activated by the therapy process. "We find that most therapists do not need to learn techniques for 'joining' with people; instead they need to work on themselves, to the point where they can keep their parts from interfering with therapy" (p. 156). Schwartz also notes that the "therapists who are the most effective with this model are those who understand it intuitively because they know their own internal family" (p. 160).

Therapists need not banish their parts from therapy sessions; in fact, parts breathe life into each session and enrich the therapists' experience. In addition, therapists' parts give valuable feedback and act as role models in demonstrating how to control extreme feelings and resolve polarizations with other parts. But Schwartz (1995) warns that the therapist bears the responsibility for curbing extreme parts during therapy sessions:

> Before speaking for a part, however, a therapist must try to determine whether [his or her] part is extreme and distorting in its perceptions; if unsure as to whether it is, he or she should report this uncertainty to the client. It is therapists' responsibility to work with their own parts outside of sessions, to keep them from distorting and interfering, and to maintain the compassion and respect of Self-leadership. (p. 89)

Inevitably, therapists' extreme parts nudge their way into sessions. Anger, sadness, frustration, or aloofness may abound. When a therapist's extreme parts interfere, the therapist should tell the client. The effect on the client is powerful, because it demonstrates how another person deals effectively with an extreme part by not blending with the part and by not being ashamed of the part's feelings. More importantly, the acknowledgment shows great respect for the client. With Lorene, the therapist's honesty about his parts often immediately alleviated a potential disruption in a session. Lorene, as her Self, recorded in her journal:

Self: *Dick was upset today when he worked with Nicholas. He seemed so cranky. I almost left. Then he finally told me it was because he lost a lot of material from his hard disk. Oddly enough, it immediately calmed Nicky.*

Revealing information about reactions from the therapist's parts also communicates to the survivor that she has an impact on the therapist—she is, in fact, significant—and that the therapist is human, too—not so different from the survivor after all. Also, survivors are used to having their experiences invalidated—if the therapist acknowledges that her parts can also be extreme, the survivor feels validated and more trusting of both her own perceptions and those of the therapist. In the rest of this chapter, we explore common reactions from therapists' parts who get activated when working with survivors.

"HER PARTS ACCUSE ME OF INCOMPETENCE EVERY CHANCE THEY GET"

Every therapist working with survivors of abuse will find comfort in the familiarity of Putnam's (1989) discovery that MPD clients have "a way of pumping up [a therapist's] vanity—and then pricking it with a pin" (p. 193). They will try to set up the therapist in order to demonstrate "once again that all important figures in the patient's life are really frauds and are not to be trusted" (p. 194). The "demeaning of the therapist is one of the inevitable dynamics of multiplicity. Whenever there are strong positive feelings on the part of one or more personalities, there will be a counterweight of negative feeling" (p. 194).

The therapist may have to answer hundreds of "test" questions, including challenge after challenge to the therapist's commitment and abilities. Lorene wrote about interactions between herself and her therapist during one session:

Nicky walked out on Dick twice during today's session, but Dick coaxed him back each time. Dick promised to tell Nicky if any of the "secrets" Nicky revealed made parts of Dick back off. Dick is supposed to say, "It's really hard for part of me to listen to this." Nicky told Dick that he didn't want to see that goddamned part of Dick who put up a wall to protect Dick from feeling too overwhelmed. Very important to Nicky. Vincent tried to quiz Dick about whether he was really qualified to recognize the signs of true pathology. Dick said yes. I hope he's right.

Schwartz (1992) wrote about one survivor who challenged his competence and personality at every turn:

My protectors, as well as the client's, can make the situation worse; part of me hates surprise attacks on my competence and personal qualities, and can feel coldly defensive and businesslike in the face of [an attack]. "It's not your life, it's hers," this cold subself would say to me. "There's nothing more you can give, it's pointless to keep trying, she doesn't appreciate all you've done for her, she's trying to manipulate you, she doesn't really *want* to get better, and you can't force her." (p. 37)

Schwartz (1992) found it imperative that he work with his own parts, particularly his "cold subself [who was] protecting my insecure selves" and who would "withdraw my compassion from the client." When he failed to work with his own parts, the client and he ended up "facing each other warily from the thorny barricades of our mutual defensiveness" (p. 37).

The survivor's managers and firefighters inevitably challenge the therapist's competence. The therapist should answer questions raised by the client's parts, but insist that the questions be phrased with some respect. The questions or remarks from the client's parts should also directly address that part's concerns instead of merely distracting the therapist by trying to infuriate his or her parts.

"CAN'T SHE SEE THAT I HAVE A BAD COLD?"

When the therapist suffers from a bad cold, the flu, or a headache, chaos strikes as turmoil erupts throughout the survivor's internal system. Some parts are certain that the therapist will die; some believe the therapist got sick on purpose to avoid the survivor; and others become overwhelmed with empathy for any suffering the therapist experiences. Lorene's part, Nicholas, explains his interpretation of the meaning behind the therapist's bad cold:

Nicholas: I went there ready to be open with him, but he acted mean and not real.
Self: Nicholas, Dick told you he had a bad cold and felt sick.
Nicholas: Then he should have canceled the appointment.
Self: Oh, sure. You wouldn't have been upset about that, right?
Nicholas: Why does Dick have to be mean?
Self: He wasn't mean, he was just quiet.

When illness strikes, the easiest approach is to be honest with the client. The survivor's protective parts will be activated immediately if the therapist just sits there, head back, eyes glazed, rubbing her temples. They will quickly move in for the kill, accusing the therapist of being too tired to perform the job adequately; too aloof to care about the client; or generally worthless as a human being. In contrast, if the therapist states from the outset that she feels a bit under the weather and might sound or look different than usual, the parts of the client usually respond with understanding, even eliciting the Self's guidance to compensate for the less animated therapist. Lorene described another session when her therapist was sick with a virus, and she kept her Self in the lead to prevent parts from attacking:

Dick "moved" Victor out of the past today. I was so surprised that Victor decided he'd come to the present! It actually helped that Dick was so sick. It was strange to see Victor feel compassion for Dick, but it really helped Victor control his urge to attack Dick. Victor actually experienced having a Self separate from extreme feelings. Victor was also surprised he could be close to Dick without Bonnie interfering—he was always so sure that she'd interfere by flirting.

The parts of a survivor who are frightened by a therapist's illness need specific information. For example, the therapist can tell the client that she won't talk as much because it triggers coughing fits, or that she may seem listless because of an aching body and swollen tonsils. The survivor too easily concludes that since last week's session the entire relationship has changed for the worse. Assurance that the therapist is the same person— that despite the blurry eyes, raspy voice, and pasty complexion, she still cares, is still committed, and will be back to normal in a week or so—goes a long way in calming the client's agitated parts.

Therapists should also attend to their own parts who might insist, for example, that the client is being a "big baby," that the therapist should have stayed home in bed, or that physical exhaustion is a valid excuse for ignoring the client's accusations, so why not just withdraw and hope the session ends soon. When illness inevitably intercedes, it may also be advisable to cancel any appointments that would not cause clients undue trauma. Another alternative is to stay in bed, eyes closed, with cold remedies near at hand, and speak with some clients on the telephone instead of meeting with them.

In addition, when a therapist (or anyone) is ill, it also may be wise to check with parts to see if any *prefer* to remain sick, perhaps to force the therapist to slow down, lighten a hectic schedule, or find someone to take care of the therapist for a change. There's nothing unusual about these responses. They don't mean that *all* of the therapist wants to get out of the business of mental health, or to drop two committees, the teaching position, or half of the private practice. It only means that these parts need some attention. Sometimes a promise to sleep late on Thursdays and to buy fresh orange juice every day comforts them sufficiently. Sometimes it requires a negotiation among parts in which the result might be putting aside one of many research, writing, or speaking projects, or not taking new clients for six months.

"NO MATTER WHAT I DO, SHE INTERPRETS IT AS REJECTION"

Survivors, like the MPD patients described by Putnam (1989), are "exquisitely sensitive to any form of rejection and will often perceive it where none is intended" (p. 172). Responses to this perceived rejection may include self-mutilation, suicide attempts, fugue episodes, and missed sessions. The reason for this sensitivity is no mystery: "[To] be an abused child is to be profoundly rejected by the people who are supposed to love and care for the child. . . . It would be difficult to overestimate the feelings of rejection and abandonment that these patients have experienced in childhood" (p. 172).

In addition, all parts of the survivor may desperately yearn for a rescuer. Only the most powerful rescuer can match the total sense of rejection and abandonment the survivor has carried since childhood. Herman (1992) notes:

> At the moment of trauma the victim is utterly helpless. Unable to defend herself, she cries for help, but no one comes to her aid. She feels totally abandoned. The memory of this experience pervades all subsequent relationships. The greater the patient's emotional conviction of helplessness and abandonment, the more desperately she feels the need for an omnipotent rescuer. Often she casts the therapist in this role. (p. 137)

Problems arise when the therapist fails to live up to the survivor's expectations of the almighty rescuer. She becomes enraged, accusing the therapist of abandonment. "Because the patient feels as though her life depends upon her rescuer, she cannot afford to be tolerant; there is no room for human error" (Herman, 1992, p. 137). Inevitably, the abuse survivor's parts will manufacture experiences of rejection during the course of treatment. Consider Lorene's part, Nicholas, and his blow-up over the fact that the therapist came into the session a little out of breath:

Self: *Nicholas, you were upset with Dick from the beginning of the session — why?*

Nicholas: *Because he came in out of breath, said he'd rushed there to be on time. Why?? I'm not worth it! How embarrassing! I don't want him to do anything for me.*

Self: *So you got mad?*

Nicholas: *He tricked me into coming there with my guard down. He said last time I was there that I had begun to believe I was human, not some type of evil entity. I didn't want to — couldn't — listen. I remember I cried last time, and I don't want to ever mention that because I don't want to know if he noticed.*

Self: *Why?*

Nicholas: *What difference does it make? He's not real anyway. The only thing real is this body of Lorene's and it must die. I don't have a body and her body is evil and nothing else exists. The End!*

Self: *Your reasoning is a little hard to follow. Be more direct, just for a minute.*

Nicholas: *I want Dick to prove to me that his world is stronger and more real than mine. But today I frustrated him, drained him, and then I left.*
Self: *Why couldn't you just tell him that?*
Nicholas: *Look, I admit that I'm very difficult to deal with, but I can't pretend I'm you or Alex or Dashiell. I can't pretend to be cheerful and cooperative and rattle on about intellectual nonsense like you do. I've had a lot more responsibility for danger-guarding than you.*
Self: *So what do we have to do in order to work with you?*
Nicholas: *First, realize that I am completely unsure about what is real and what is not. That's just the way I am. So I ask more questions and test more than other parts—maybe I do it on their behalf! In fact, if someone gave me a lie detector test, you'd see that sometimes I really believe that Dick is not real; that I am horrible; that I deserve to die; that Dad still comes and does sexual things to me. (Dick told me once that I have a choice about all that—said that I know those things aren't true. He's wrong.)*

Second, realize that I am filled with self-hatred and I have no room for someone's pretend-caring. Finally, remember that I keep buried all the memories that trigger my sense of abandonment, mistrust, betrayal and anger. So I'm not exactly a relaxed, happy-go-lucky guy.
Self: *Why don't you just refuse to work with Dick?*
Nicholas: *Because I think he's my best shot at leaving my crazy, dark world.*

Frightened parts easily blow things out of proportion, attack the therapist with accusations, or simply become cold and withdraw. Of course, the best thing would be if Lorene's Self had stepped in and acknowledged Nicholas' fear of rejection *before* Nicholas had a chance to decimate the therapist. Instead, Lorene's Self and the therapist both sat stunned while Nicholas successfully transformed the session into a circus. Barring intervention by Lorene's Self, it became necessary for her to wait until after the session, when Lorene's Self returned, for her to discover why Nicholas behaved as he did.

In addition, if the therapist dreads being blamed for rejecting the client when the blame belongs to the abuser, it is important for the therapist to remember that it is just a part of the client who holds that view. The client may be torn between an exiled child-part who is desperate for the therapist's approval and another protector part who anticipates rejection and consequently pushes away the therapist. Therapists should not work with the young, exiled parts until the therapist can maintain Self-leadership and prevent her own parts from interfering. When exiles finally reach out, tentatively searching for someone to listen to their stories, but suddenly encounter an aloof, business-like part of the therapist, the sense of rejection can feel devastating. Unless the therapist is certain that her parts won't display rejection, she should never assure the client that she will not be repulsed or become distanced. The issue of abandonment by the therapist will arise repeatedly since each part needs to experience and resolve the issue separately with the therapist.

Finally, in order to prevent unconsidered counterattacks, therapists should carefully monitor their own parts' feelings of rejection. When the client opens the session by challenging the therapist's competence, and then ten minutes later whispers, "I'm afraid you don't like me," it doesn't mean the therapist's hurt parts should take the opportunity to slam the client by coolly replying, "Well, it's difficult to deal with patients who are so resistant." A therapist who feels caught in this predicament should refrain from responding until her Self is back in charge.

"THEY WANT TOO MUCH FROM ME"

Survivors ask a great deal of therapists; they can easily drain therapists with their demands for more time, more energy, and more commitment. Therapists may feel impatient or burdened by these clients. Although his comments do not involve working with abuse survivors, Johnson (1986) provides a wonderful description of working with the parts of himself who fought against patients' monopolizing his time:

> When I first became an analytical psychologist, I often had to work in the evening. . . . For some reason I resented it bitterly. Some inner part of me was used to having my evenings free for me. . . . This childish part of me was furious. And the unconscious, irrational resentment found its way into my practical life. I was irritable toward my patients. I almost forgot appointments. These are the kinds of things that happen when someone in the unconscious is absolutely opposed to what the ego has set up. . . . I looked for that part of me that was angry at my work schedule. The image that came up was a spoiled adolescent. . . . So I set up a long conversation with him. I explained and explained. . . . At first he wouldn't budge. . . . There was general chaos because such a large part of me was in rebellion against my work.
>
> Finally I got this fellow by the throat—in my imagination, of course, and up against the wall, and I said: "You have got to listen, or we are in bad trouble. Now, what kind of a deal can we make?"
>
> So the following horse-trade developed: He agreed that if I would go to a drive-in at 10:00 every night and have a nice meal and take him to a movie a couple of times a week after the patients were gone, then he would keep off my back the rest of the time and let me work in peace with my patients. For many months it worked that way. . . . But if I missed one evening of our meal out, this juvenile would be irritable the next day. He would make me resentful and forgetful in my work. It was incredible to me that this character had so much power over my moods and my functioning. But he did.
>
> I never admitted until many years later that I had been forced to make such a sordid, mercantile, back-room deal with my self-indulgent inner child.

... But in retrospect I have come to respect these kinds of dialogues, these negotiations, these compromises between warring factions. (pp. 201–203)

The negotiation Johnson made with his part demonstrates the type of internal work a therapist must often do when working with survivors (although grabbing the parts "by the throat" is not always advised). The "horse-trading" may also involve the therapist educating clients about the time and energy concerns raised by the therapist's parts.

The first step is to identify the source of the overburdened feeling. If the burden originates in the client (e.g., the therapist feels that the client isn't helping enough by trying to lead with her Self), this should be discussed openly, showing the client respect and understanding, but emphasizing that she must recognize her own strengths, too. If the burden originates in the therapist (e.g., an overwhelming caseload, speaking engagements, professional duties and personal chaos), then these indications that parts feel overburdened should be heeded by the therapist.

"SHE SAYS I'M MAKING HER WORSE!"

Putnam (1989) observes that clients may "blame the therapist or accuse him or her of compounding their suffering when therapeutic exploration triggers an abreaction" (p. 191). Lorene's parts were quite proficient at hurling accusations. Alexandra, for example, ranted her complaints:

Alex: *I think Dick's heading us down a path that will eventually force us to relive all the torture and betrayal. Why is he doing this? He's making us worse! Is this some weird experiment? He doesn't know what the hell he's doing? He cares about me but doesn't realize the drastic consequences of what he's doing? He thinks he's so great that he can fix anything? He's in over his head but doesn't realize it? He doesn't recognize true psychopathology when he sees it?*

Therapists should answer questions like Alex's directly, but only after they move aside their own parts who cringe with fury when blatant accusations challenge their professional expertise and their personal qualities. Once the therapist's Self is free to answer the questions without interference from extreme parts, the client's part, like Alex, will calm down, which permits the therapist's protective parts to relax. Schwartz (1995) writes of being "exposed to all types of provocation, accusation, or expectation" and finds:

It helps to remember that only a part of such a client has temporarily taken over and is relating to me this way—a part that is frozen at a time when there were good reasons to relate to authority figures in these extreme ways.

If I can maintain Self-leadership in the face of such activation, gradually the [client's] part will realize that I am different from the person it has me confused with. (p. 88)

Therapists should also be aware that some parts of the survivor *want* the therapist to be hurtful and abusive towards her. Notably, the part does not want to feel pain as much as she wants to feel purged, or perhaps wants some attention, and thinks she has to be hurt to get it. In many ways this is a reenactment of the original abuse when the perpetrator/rescuer "loved" the child by inflicting pain. Herman (1992) notes:

The patient may imagine a kind of sadomasochistic orgy, in which she will scream, cry, vomit, bleed, die, and be reborn cleansed of the trauma. The therapist's role in this reenactment comes uncomfortably close to that of the perpetrator, for she is invited to rescue the patient by inflicting pain. (p. 172)

"HER PARTS CATCH EVERY ERROR I MAKE"

It's not easy to face a survivor's ever-vigilant parts who have elected themselves the therapist's supervisor. Survivors are "extraordinarily sensitive to a therapist's errors" and have a "highly sensitized, extraordinarily vigilant perceptual system" by which they "pick up and react and/or abreact to many apparently innocuous experiences" (Putnam, 1989, p. 186). Lorene's part, Victor, like Alex, has much to say on the topic of the therapist's competence — or lack thereof:

Victor: *I'm not going to see Dick this week. Look what a terrible job you both did last week—leaving abandoned, bleeding bodies of little child-parts lying around.*

Self: *We forgot to check on Andy. So what am I supposed to do?*

Victor: *Clean up your mess. Return things to normal. Send Andy back to the past.*

Self: *No. That means I'll have no body, no physical boundaries. I'll blend with parts and be scared all the time. No.*

Victor: *So instead of being scared, now you're petrified. Great. And stop thinking you can count on Dick! He doesn't know what he's doing. He keeps babbling about time—going to the past, etc. That is a useless concept. It doesn't help anybody; it simply makes Dick feel superior because he thinks he knows something.*

Dick tries to get the seven-year-old part to tell him secrets. He asks her what she sees, who is there ("nothing but the facts, ma'am"), and thinks then she'll be magically cured and ready to "leave the past." What crap! I'm sick of it! It has nothing to do with the seven-year-old's feel-

ings. She describes the screaming, moaning, tormented part (Andy), and so Dick says to move that part away so she doesn't blend with it. You can't go around moving half-dead, half-psychotic bodies! Stop! Both of you, stop! And tell Dick to stop going away on trips, too.

A therapist's parts silently scream, "Will she *ever* trust me? What more can I possibly do?" Frustration is not surprising; the months and months of painstaking work and unrelenting commitment now seem futile. Again and again, the survivor's protective parts accuse the therapist of not being worthy of trust. However, if the therapist's Self communicates directly with the client's Self, the therapist's fear that "trust will never happen" eventually disappears.

Therapists faced with such hostility must remember that for survivors the fear of re-abandonment far outweighs the fear of repeated physical or sexual assault. Thus, while assurances of physical safety are important, trusting in the unfailing support of the therapist is even more important. Herman (1992) notes:

> The survivor who is often in terror of being left alone craves the simple presence of a sympathetic person. Having once experienced the sense of total isolation, the survivor is intensely aware of the fragility of all human connections in the face of danger. She needs clear and explicit assurances that she will not be abandoned once again. (pp. 61–62)

Survivors in their hyper-vigilance can interpret even the most innocuous behavior as abandonment. Therapists who fear committing errors will stop actively participating in sessions. To a survivor, this passivity feels like abandonment. Therapists *will* make mistakes (e.g., accessing an exile without the managers' permission, forgetting an appointment, avoiding horrendous details of the abuse, confusing the parts of two different clients). And survivors will inevitably zero in on the mistake. Therapists can handle the mistakes by calming their own parts and by being honest with clients. Be embarrassed, perhaps, but honest. Survivors' managers especially need to know that nothing dangerous occurs when someone who cares about them makes a mistake.

"WE'RE BACK TO SQUARE ONE"

Therapists may have parts who feel defeated when the survivor arrives for a session with self-inflicted, fresh cuts on her face, a blank stare in her eyes, and reports that she had returned to an ex-boyfriend who had previously raped her. While the last session was trusting and congenial, the survivor now hurls criticisms at the therapist. The therapist, opening the door with a greeting smile, is slapped in the face by the client's torn face and caustic remarks. The therapist quickly sinks into an awed state of confusion and disappointment. (What happened to her since last week? Did I screw up? I have nothing left in my bag of tricks to help her!) The survivor, though busy attacking, senses the disappointment of the therapist. Lorene's Self reports:

Self: *I think today Dick was experiencing something I've seen in him before—first surprise, then disappointment (and a certain level of defeat?) because he'd thought I was doing better.*

Working with an abuse survivor's extreme parts who repeatedly initiated surprise attacks, Schwartz discovered, triggered his own parts, who despaired that therapy with this client was failing. Schwartz had to reassure his parts that the client's parts were frightened and that, with all due respect for his parts' wisdom, his *Self* would remain in charge of determining whether or not therapy was going well. Schwartz (1992) describes this insight: "Now I know that these sudden ambushes by clients reflect fear, generated not by therapy's failure but by the real danger in our enterprise. If I can lead with my Self in the face of these scared [parts] of clients, I eventually reassure [my] managers and we get back on track" (p. 37). Schwartz also noticed that as soon as his "ambitious, competitive selves became impatient with [the survivor's] pace, her managers sensed my frustration and convinced her that I was about to abandon her. She would distance, and I would become more frustrated" (p. 37). The repetition of common pitfalls faced by therapists working with survivors is similar to the pattern that Putnam (1989) described in his work with MPD patients:

> Every improvement is followed by a relapse. Hostile alters threaten suicide, internal or external homicide, and assorted other catastrophes. . . . It is important to remain calm and unruffled by much of this chaos. . . . It is important not to overreact to [quasi-psychotic] symptoms, but rather to explore who and what is responsible. . . . The therapist can often sidestep the pathology by engaging the personality system to find out who is responsible for these symptoms. [Often it is merely an attempt] to divert the therapist away from painful areas. (pp. 160–161)

It is important, then, for therapists to reassure their parts when they worry that things aren't going well. A therapist's Self should listen and evaluate the validity of her parts' concerns. Their advice may be invaluable and should be treated with respect, even if the parts' opinions sometimes prove to be unfounded.

"MY PARTS? INTERFERING? BUT I'M THE THERAPIST . . . "

Survivors have developed incredibly powerful—and accurate—internal lie detectors. Inevitably, they will sense when therapists experience a strong reaction or are distracted by some internal or external event in their own lives. Agosta and Loring (1989) note how important it is for therapists to be direct and honest if they feel angry, either because of something that took place during the day or because of something that occurred within the therapy session itself.

> The survivor of child sexual abuse will be astonished that you are angry with her [yet] do not wish her harm. She may defend herself mightily or collapse in tears, but she probably believes that you are leaving (anger and abandonment are closely intertwined in her experience), and she is bracing herself for the pain of losing you, as well as ruing the day she first trusted you. (p. 128)

Given the survivor's tendency to perceive rejection, danger, and abandonment everywhere, the IFS model promotes the therapist's honesty, no matter how trivial or unimportant the disclosure may sound. When therapists realize that their parts are interfering, they should tell the client. "It seems to be helpful to my clients to know that I, too, am actively involved in this work, and to have their perception that I was not my Self confirmed" (Schwartz, 1995, p. 117). Moreover, "if the therapist tries to cover up during or after a time when a part has taken over, the client's parts will sense this coverup and will trust the therapist less" (p. 124). Lorene's Self is quite articulate on this point:

I always feel better when Dick admits it was a part of him speaking. Then I'm just mad at part of him and not at all of him. Today I got the part of him that acts like, "Well, it's not my fault that you won't let me help you . . . " Destiny and Bonnie immediately think that I have somehow lost Dick by disappointing him. When my Self steps in and confronts Dick, usually his Self returns immediately. Then Destiny and Bonnie calm down, too.

It is a very powerful experience for survivors to have their parts' perceptions (that the therapist is not leading with his or her Self) validated rather than denied. Schwartz (1995) advises that the therapist be aware of when his or her parts are becoming extreme and interfering during sessions, and either "get those parts to step back and trust the Self, or, when that is not possible, to acknowledge to the client that a part is interfering. . . . The therapist need not and cannot always be a model of Self-leadership, but he or she can model taking responsibility for times when parts interfere and trying to prevent that" (pp. 87–88).

"I CAN'T EVEN TAKE A SIMPLE VACATION"

Vacations and business trips trigger tremendously powerful responses in some of the survivor's parts, particularly those who are angry about feeling any dependency on the therapist. While the therapist should not eliminate vacations and business trips, it helps to understand the survivor's terror that the therapist will not return, that she never even existed, and that all hope is lost. Lorene's Self poignantly describes her seven-year-old part's feelings in response to the therapist's upcoming absence:

I told Dick about my seven-year-old part's perception of the world. She sees the world filled with vulnerable human bodies. A mass of human meat. To believe everything remains the same means the childhood tor-ture that she still lives in could continue forever. So she believes nothing is constant. The world is horribly unpredictable. She wouldn't be surprised if suddenly gravity or sunshine were eliminated, or if each day no longer lasted 24 hours.

So, whether Dick will come back from trips, whether he exists during the week between sessions, whether he's real at all, and other similar problems permeate my seven-year-old's perception of life. Nothing can be counted on to stay the same. Knowing this helps me to understand her better and to not blend with her.

With this kind of understanding of the survivors' internal terror and confusion, a therapist can help the client's Self learn how to comfort and care for these scared parts in the therapist's absence. It also helps if thera-pists cover several points before leaving: (1) Explain the reason for the absence—e.g., to rest or to share information with colleagues at a con-ference. (2) Assure the client that the therapist will return, her caring and commitment unaltered. (3) Encourage the survivor's parts to permit the Self to continue to practice leading. (4) Explain to the client's scared parts that encouraging Self-leadership in the client does not mean the therapist has decided to stop interacting with the parts when sessions begin again.

Some therapists also find that a telephone call to a client in crisis is helpful while the therapist is on a business trip or vacation; others will only make such calls while on a business trip, but not on a vacation. Some therapists send a letter or postcard to a client in crisis, or allow the client to keep a physical token of the therapist, like a photograph or an item from the office. If any of these techniques is comfortable and does not feel invasive to the therapist, it will often help the survivor a great deal.

"I LIKE SOME OF HER PARTS BETTER THAN OTHERS"

Being human, therapists struggle with personal likes and dislikes of their clients' parts. Putnam (1989) warns that there will be "intense sibling-like rivalry [among alters] for the affections of the therapist" (p. 159) and that there may be "increased competition for therapy time" (p. 157). This rivalry is complicated by compassionate responses from parts of the therapist, who may want to reparent the struggling young parts. Putnam (1989) notes that clients "may elicit strong parental feelings. Multiples will push the reparenting process to an extreme" (p. 193). Beahrs (1982) agrees: "The cry of help from a desperate and confused primary personality can be like seeing an abandoned baby lying in the street" (p. 138). The therapist's managerial parts may clamor to rescue the survivor's frightened parts by reparenting them or trying to fulfill their seemingly insatiable needs.

For example, Lorene's young part, Andy, looked up to the therapist with such trust and adoration that it was easy for other parts to accuse the therapist of preferring Andy to the biting, snarling Nicholas or the pathetically frail, bleeding Jennifer. (Or the opposite—they might direct the therapist to Andy to keep him away from another part or from themselves.)

Self: Dick worked with Andy today. Andy was direct with him, revealing a lot of his personality that I'd never seen before and that helped me to understand and like him better. Dick didn't sidestep Andy's hard questions. When Andy asked him about sexual things (e.g., could sex ever include love?), Dick remained straightforward and consistent with his answers. The most incredible result of today's session is that Andy has felt connected to his body the entire day. He still looks for danger, but hasn't seen any.

Andy: I have been watching, and there have been no weapons or naked bodies or mean faces. But I really don't know much about how it feels to be in my body because I just sit very still and watch. I don't move at all. I'm afraid Dick is going to abandon me here in this body. He might think I'm okay just because I'm in a body. I'll write him a letter:

Dear Dick,

Hi. I'm Andy, remember me? We talked this morning and you promised you'd talk to me again. Well, you had me go into my body, which was okay but, well, it seemed like you wanted me to be brave. What I was wondering is, how brave do you think I have to be? You might think I should be strong and try this body thing by myself. You might say, "Well, I care about Andy and want what's best for him, so I'm going to leave him all alone in that body of his."

What I'm asking is, please don't leave me alone. Could you stay with me until I get used to this? I promise I'll try my hardest. I'll keep learning to breathe with my lungs, walk with my feet, etc., and you keep saying, "You're doing fine, Andy." After I take a short walk, I'll come back and sit next to you again, and you'll say, "That was just fine, next time will be easier."

Of course you won't really be there, but maybe you could let me pretend you're there. I'm not really mean or rude, although I do hide a lot, which can be a pain. Well, think about it.

Thanks for being so nice to me today. Sometimes I think about our talk and I get chills, because it makes me excited to think there's a chance that I can have a body, be safe, and not be lonely. Amazing!

Thanks for answering my questions about sex, too. I'm not sure you're right about some things, but I appreciate your trying so hard.

Sometimes I hurt so much I don't think I can live. Do you think if someone loves you and puts their arms around you, then they will kill you?

I know this is a pretty childish letter, but I hope you don't mind too much.

From your new friend,

Andy

Notwithstanding Andy's appealing character, the therapist must monitor his own parts in the event that those parts persistently steer him toward some of Lorene's parts and away from others. In general, therapists must be aware of their approval-seeking managerial parts who enjoy having clients depend on or worship them, or who worry about not being liked or seen as a failure if the client doesn't leave a session smiling and filled with praise for the therapist.

"IT'S A STANDOFF"

Putnam (1989) makes two important points about struggles between therapists and MPD alters, which apply equally to any struggle between a therapist and client's part: First, the parts' "claims of total power are greatly exaggerated"; second, if the therapist struggles for control over the patient, "the therapist will lose" (p. 171). Putnam also reminds therapists that the parts who proclaim their power the loudest are functioning as protectors as best they can. The therapist should "preemptively concede all control over the ultimate fate of the patient to the patient as a whole in the early stages of therapy. Struggles for control serve to divert the therapist away from dealing with real-life issues and exploration of past trauma. The malevolent alters are often simply performing in their larger role of protecting the patient" (p. 171). A survivor's protective parts who act obstinate may face off with a therapist's critical and punitive parts. Lorene's Self recorded the following transaction:

Self: Vincent was somewhat overwhelmed by being so close to the seven-year-old part's feelings today, afraid they'd bury him alive. He was disappointed that Dick didn't talk to the seven-year-old and establish a better relationship with her. Vincent's exhausted; he's protected the seven-year-old for so long. He wants Dick to take over any responsibility for exploring who the seven-year-old part is and what she wants. Instead of telling Dick that, Vincent just started ripping into Dick.

Vincent accused Dick of veering away from younger girl parts. Even when we had 15 minutes left today, (Vincent says) Dick preferred to get ready to leave rather than touch base with her. He accuses Dick of (over)worrying that he'll cause irreparable damage to these young parts—especially the girls. He'll insist on talking to other parts having trouble.

Anyhow, Vincent was scared to leave Dick and was mad at him, too. He accused Dick of being the most unfair he'd ever seen him; of refusing to be him Self; and of refusing to "fix" Vincent.

Dick responded by slipping into conflicting defensive postures from various parts of his, who seemed to imply:

—"I screwed up."

—"I absolutely didn't screw up and if Vincent wants more time, then he damn well better ask for it, since I already have enormous time demands from family, colleagues, clients, and friends."

—"Business is business, and time is up and Vincent's jacking me around, and I won't play."

—"I did the best I could."

The more brittle and unbending Vincent became—insisting that the feelings in him were unacceptable—the more distant Dick became. Dick goes into "automatic pilot" at times like that. As him Self, Dick knows that 15 seconds of reassurance would calm Vincent. But once Dick's protective parts step in, that possibility is temporarily gone. This in turn scares my extreme parts more, because they're convinced that Dick has magically disappeared.

Later, I explained much of this to Vincent. He's mad and insists that, if Dick were competent, he could "fix" Vincent's feelings. (I think that means neutralize them.)

I'm sorry that parts of Dick were either scared ("She'll never get better"), felt guilty ("I screwed up"), or angry ("If you've going to demand more of my time, you'll have to stand in line!"). And I'm sorry that Vincent is struggling with wanting to be with Dick, wanting to be alone, and being suffocated by his direct encounter with the seven-year-old's strong feelings. Dick and Vincent need to resolve their power struggle.

This example demonstrates the quandary that can be created when both the therapist's and survivor's parts become extreme. Typically the problem can be relieved by following basic rules, such as being direct with each other, acknowledging to each other when parts are interfering, and trying to return the Selves of both therapist and client to their leadership positions. Failing that, following this type of pervasive clash between two internal systems, a short telephone call initiated by either the therapist's Self or the client's Self often preempts a week-long sense of frustration and failure and makes it unnecessary for either the therapist or the client to enter the next session with mistrustful parts in charge.

"HER PARTS MANIPULATE ME!"

Therapists who treat survivors of sexual abuse may feel manipulated at times. Herman (1992) writes that therapists "often complain of feeling threatened, manipulated, exploited, or duped" (p. 147). Managerial parts are especially likely to purposely seek to worry therapists, to get extra time or attention in some way, or to induce guilt by accusing the therapist of not making the survivor "well" more quickly. At such trying times, it is helpful to remember that parts of survivors often believe that no rational person would voluntarily give them anything, so they must be tricked into giving something. A husband may be tricked into acting kind if his wife trades him sex for affection. A teacher may be tricked into helping a student with a difficult subject if the student feigns interest in the teacher's research project. And a therapist may be tricked into scheduling an extra session if the client cuts up her arm.

This doesn't mean an extra session wouldn't be beneficial. But it is far better if the part who needs that extra time can be direct and simply ask for it, explaining why the extra time is necessary. Then the therapist doesn't feel manipulated, and the problem can be resolved quickly. The part may simply mistrust the ability of the client's Self to care for the part between sessions. The client, as her Self, may not even want an extra session and may feel confused by the manipulative behavior. In one session, Lorene's part, Nicholas, ended the hour by making all sorts of demands of the therapist and then storming out:

Self: Why were you so upset at the end of the session this week?

Nicholas: You and Jennifer were talking about memories. I was being brave and taking charge, organizing things to be bearable.

Self: Did it help to call Dick later and tell him what you were feeling?

Nicholas: No. He wasn't super friendly. He acted a little colder than usual. Sometimes I say, "I am not coming next week," and he says, "You must be having a hard time." This time he didn't say that. He just said, "Well, I'll be here at the usual time and I hope you come."

Self: Nicholas, you have to realize that you're very difficult to deal with when you aren't being direct.

Nicholas: Well, I still think I'm at least a little bit right. Do I have to apologize to him?

Self: It might help your relationship.

Nicholas: Will he apologize to me?

Self: Ask him yourself.

Nicholas: *I'd rather hide behind you.*
Self: *No more hiding. That's not what I'm here for, Nicholas.*
Nicholas: *Well, okay. I'll ask him.*

Before concluding that a client's behavior is manipulative, the therapist should spend some time exploring both her own parts' reactions and the underlying reasons behind the conduct of the client's parts.

"SHE WANTS ME TO SAY (OUT LOUD!) THAT I CARE ABOUT HER"

A survivor's parts may labor long and hard to elicit an I-care-about-you response from the apprehensive therapist. Sometimes, *all* of the survivor's parts will do anything to gain a sense of acceptance and caring. Survivors of abuse search endlessly for signs that someone cares about them. They will accuse the therapist of just doing a job so she can rake in more money. They might rant on and on about how repulsive and unlovable they are, repeating self-denigrations over and over. What they really hope is that the therapist will simply say, "No, you aren't repulsive, and I like you. It is my job, but I also care about you."

Many therapists, however, are afraid to tell clients they like or care about them. Schwartz (1995) advises that, with many clients, the most important therapeutic touchstone is to "express what might be called 'tenacious caring'—caring in the face of sometimes constant provocation" (p. 89). He also explains:

> Many therapists are trained to deflect these requests and to remain opaque regarding their feelings. Such opaqueness only heightens the clients' distrust and prolongs the process. Instead, I find ways to reassure clients that I do care about them, including telling them so. . . .
> The opaque position is based on the fear that a therapist's direct expressions of caring promote unrealistic or inappropriate fantasies in clients or take away the pressure to explore the need to be cared for. The IFS model helps with these concerns as well, because both therapist and client know that only the young parts of the client need the reassurance and may have fantasies. Also, the client has a Self who can help these young parts with their needs and fantasies, and who, with the therapist, can encourage these parts to show where they are frozen in time—how they became so scared and needy. Thus, I can reassure a client that I care about him or her, and can also ask the client to find the parts that are so worried about that. Then I can help those parts see that they can also look to the client's Self for that reassurance. (p. 102)

The therapist might resent a client's manipulations, preferring to be asked directly, "Do you like me?" or "Do you care about what happens to me?" Such direct questioning is difficult because a survivor's wary, protective parts are rarely ready to risk the horrendous rejection they would feel if the therapist were to act aloof, hiding under a professional cloak. Therapists should assure their own parts that it is appropriate to offer survivors professional but tenacious caring. But the therapist must be sincere. If this feeling of caring is not present, the therapist should not pretend otherwise. The client will recognize it as a false claim of caring, even if the therapist understands that her own parts are interfering with her Self's ability to experience a sense of caring.

"SOME CLIENTS ARE JUST TOO NEEDY"

Anderson (1986) describes the patient who hides an "inner self which is a repository of neediness, cravings, and loneliness," warning that as "the therapist comes into contact with the patient's inner neediness, he or she can easily become frightened by its intensity" (p. 69). The survivor's parts will immediately latch onto the therapist's fear or aloofness: "Many patients are acutely sensitive even to subtle signs of discomfort and disapproval on the therapist's part, and they respond either by retreating . . . or by becoming panicked at the prospect that their needs never will be met" (p. 69). As the survivor learns to trust and rely upon the therapist, she will learn that she has parts who desperately want a very basic human need, simple caring in a safe environment. Most people had this need fulfilled in childhood, but survivors wait through long, barren years without fulfillment. The basic need grows and intensifies, finally becoming neediness, which might trigger parts of the therapist who feel forced into giving too much, and are reminded of their own unfulfilled needs. Schwartz (1992) discovered that turning away from the neediness of survivors often was caused by disdain for his own needy parts:

> I had reacted to my clients' pain, insecurity and neediness in the same way I reacted to my own, by changing the subject, making a joke, shifting to a problem-solving mode, or becoming coldly businesslike. Over the years, however, I have learned not to back off from these feelings in myself or clients, and not to assume they can be willed away. Now I realize that when the client and I can help our compassionate, differentiated Selves stay with the parts of us that feel pain, desperation, fear, shame or hopelessness, these child-selves become normal little boys and girls with a full range of feelings that we can enjoy. These formerly despised exiles can enrich our lives. (p. 36)

Finally, what therapists perceive as smothering neediness may be survivors' attempts to blend or fuse with them, leaving little room for the therapists to breathe and causing great anxiety in their parts. Survivors' managerial parts may believe the merging will allow them to continuously please their therapists, thereby permanently avoiding betrayal and rejection. Fusion with the therapist may also give the survivor a protective "cover" by an authority figure and a type of pseudo-nurturing that relieves the managers of duty and provides the exiles with a superficial sense of safety and sustenance.

Firefighter parts in particular may feel they deserve some type of compensation for the trauma the survivor has suffered. This quest for compensation, though often legitimate, also presents a potential trap: survivors may turn to their therapists for that compensation, resenting limitations placed on the therapy relationship, and insisting on "some form of special dispensation" (Herman, 1992, pp. 190–91). The attempted fusion may also be an attempt by the young exiled parts to "reassure one's self that the therapist is not separate and cannot be lost" (Kluft, 1989, p. 488). Young parts' fears of losing the therapist can be staggering; these parts may believe that "only the boundless love of the therapist, or some other magical personage, can undo the damage of the trauma" (Herman, 1992, p. 191). Therapists may be tempted to try to fulfill the role of the great savior — after all, "it is flattering to be invested with grandiose healing powers and only too tempting to seek a magical cure in the laying on of hands" (p. 192). Inevitably, however, disappointment reigns, since the type of compensation and "boundless love" extreme parts seek can never be attained.

"SHE IS MUCH SICKER THAN I THOUGHT"

The parts of abuse survivors with highly polarized internal systems don't sit still for long. At first, they may gently reach out to the therapist; but then attack; then freeze or regress with amazing speed. Herman (1992) writes that therapists working with traumatized clients may "feel completely bewildered by the rapid fluctuations in the patient's moods or style of relating," feeling a "sense of unreality [and] strange and incongruous combinations of emotional responses" to the client (pp. 146–47). Putnam (1989) notes that the therapist should watch for his or her "own fears of multiplicity and of frightening alters who might emerge, wishes that the patient would stabilize and stop ceaselessly changing, [and] confusion as to 'who' is the real patient" (p. 171).

Schwartz (1992) also struggled with abrupt changes in survivors: "I found these apparent reversals utterly dismaying, taking them as evidence that the therapy was turning to ashes, we were getting nowhere, my client was much sicker than my overly optimistic model had let me realize" (p. 37). It was only as he worked with his own parts, with his Self in the lead, that Schwartz understood that the survivor's parts believed that the survivor was involved in a highly dangerous escapade — therapy. Schwartz learned that "these flashes of fury and denial, these stinging setbacks, meant that some of the parts interfering with therapy might be mine as well as theirs" (p. 37).

"SHE'S A BOTTOMLESS PIT OF PARTS, PAIN, AND CRISES"

Putnam (1989) notes that, as new parts keep surfacing, therapists sometimes feel that the client has a "bottomless pit." Therapists, worn out and even overwhelmed by new personalities creating new crises, may show visible signs of wear and tear. When Lorene arrived at a session to find the therapist exhausted, Victor angrily decided to spring a new part on him, yet prevent the therapist from learning anything helpful about the new part. The therapist valiantly tried to work with the new mysterious and frightened "seven-year-old" part, but Victor interfered again and again, leaving the therapist frustrated and disappointed. Later, Victor reported his experience in Lorene's journal:

Victor: *So he met the seven-year-old. Big deal. She tried to explain about being all curled up, screaming and moaning in the basement. Dick pretended to "move" the seven-year-old to Dashiell's spot outside. What bunk! What total idiocy to believe that these little "imaginings" have any significance! It changes nothing! Dick will lose at this game; I will win. He can't just go around stirring up new parts and grabbing at their shabby secrets.*

The therapist's power to withstand such assaults will necessarily ebb and flow. "It is not uncommon for experienced therapists to feel suddenly incompetent and hopeless in the face of a traumatized patient" (Herman, 1992, p. 141). Therapists must explore what is happening with their own parts, listen to their parts' complaints about the session, and then reassure their parts that the client's Self has the ability to provide strength and direction to the client. In this way, therapists need not despair about new parts appearing, new protectors denigrating them, and new disasters suddenly leaping out at them.

"I KNOW SHE HAS A SELF IN THERE SOMEWHERE"

In using the IFS model, one of the most important agreements made is that the survivor will assist in therapy by trying to keep her Self differentiated from her extreme parts. Therapists can become frustrated quickly when left holding the bag of extreme parts, while the client's Self trundles off to some safe internal hideaway. In response to Schwartz's comment on her choice of a boyfriend, Lorene describes why her Self abdicated its leadership role, letting her parts take over and causing her to break a promise not to walk out in the middle of a session:

Nicholas: *I'm furious with Dick for thinking I'm not able to tell the difference between a man who is safe and a man who is abusive to me. Does he think I'm blind? An idiot?*

Vincent: *I feel hurt that he wouldn't even consider the possibility that I'm right.*

Destiny: *I've disappointed him. He still thinks I don't know how to pick a boyfriend!*

Self: *Why did I walk out? Too many different parts activated. I felt furious, hurt, scared I'd disappointed him, afraid he'd spend an hour telling me I'd failed him; I was just too tired to argue.*

Alexandra: *I wondered if things would only go from bad to worse if I stayed. Nicky jumped at the chance. I've never been so mad at Dick. Even now, 12 hours later, I'm still furious.*

Vincent: *I'm furious that Dick isn't just exploring the issue—he's challenging me! He says I'm wrong and that he "should have asked me about this before." He even accused me of not letting the Self lead! He said I'm pretending to be the Self! Dick was being mean and cold. It's not like him to be closed to other possibilities. He felt like a stranger. So I left.*

Dashiell: *Well, I agree, overall. But there was one other variable involved in the session today. Super-She wanted to leave, otherwise she'd be late for an important meeting at work this morning.*

Self: *Well, it would be fair if you told Dick that little piece of information. He didn't know what was going on. It's nice that I can be so angry at Dick (I think some of the parts have a valid point) and not be overwhelmed by Destiny's or Bonnie's fears that I've disappointed Dick and he'll abandon me. I can feel little pieces of those feelings, but they are not overwhelming me. They're activated, but not in control.*

I feel quite bad, however, that I walked out in the middle of a session when I had promised not to. I think it's Nicholas who gets me to shut out any sense of respect or manners. The non-feeling state or sense of cold righteousness is usually Victor or Nicholas. And I blend right into it.

Unfortunately, Dick has his own part who, like Nicholas, kicks in and probably would like to say: "I've had enough of this crap. I shouldn't have to leap up and beg clients to stay in a session when I could have slept later or taken care of a thousand other things waiting for me."

Also, the fact that Dick sounded so black-or-white in his reasoning should have immediately signaled me that he was not him Self, in which case I should have given him a break.

It is incumbent on therapists to repeatedly encourage, even insist, that the client's Self participate in the relationship. While the Self may not return immediately, it does hear the message, usually returning later in that session, or in the next one.

"AM I A POTENTIAL VICTIM OR PERPETRATOR?"

Every therapist has experienced some level of victimization in life, even if slight, and some level of being abusive to another human being. Therapists inevitably confront their own internal wounded parts as well as their "own capacity for evil" (Herman, 1992, p. 145). Therapists who treat survivors must develop "an appreciation of their own potential, both to become victims of violence and to become violent and abusive themselves. Each of us has the capacity to hurt and be hurt" (Agosta & Loring, 1989, p. 122). Steele (1991) warns that the therapist might have to face his own "Shadow self that is mirrored in the Abuser" (p. 13). Herman (1992) writes that while the "emotions of identification with the victim may be extremely painful for the therapist, those of identification with the perpetrator may be more horrifying to her, for they represent a profound challenge to her identity as a caring person" (p. 144).

Therapists may feel wary, irritated, or disdainful in the presence of the extreme type of weakness or vulnerability that survivors' parts often show. Schwartz (1992) describes feeling the "fear and contempt of my own internal managers for the sad, vulnerable, insecure little selves within me" (p. 36). He discovered that it was not enough to tell his parts (and, indirectly, the client's parts) to "quit sniveling." Such an attitude never eliminated their pain, but merely abandoned it. He learned that it was vital to look into his own disliked and feared exiles as well.

The internal parts that a therapist confronts within herself while working with survivors may frighten her. Rather than abandoning those parts, she should welcome the opportunity to meet them. Inevitably, the therapist's exploration of her internal system's potential victims and perpetrators benefits both the therapist and the survivors she works with each day.

"I CAN'T LISTEN TO THIS HORROR—IT JUST GETS WORSE AND WORSE!"

It is difficult to sit down at the family dinner table, or to coach your daughter's baseball game, after a session watching a client writhe in agony as she describes her abuser inserting a snake into her vagina, or her mother helping force her father's penis into her rectum. Cornell and Olio (1991) note that in treating survivors of severe physical and sexual abuse, the "emergence of strong, sometimes uncontrollable, affect during treatment can be deeply disturbing and disorienting to both client and therapist" (p. 59). Putnam (1989) describes the difficulty some therapists experience when listening to graphic details of the abuse.

> The details of these events may activate within the therapist countertrans-ference feelings of anxiety, rage, revulsion, and an existential fear of death. There may be accompanying strong feelings of concern, sympathy, and a sense of helplessness. Empathic reactions . . . can be powerful. The therapist may find that the explicit details of the abuse activate sadistic, punitive, or voyeuristic impulses within him or her that may be disturbing to acknowl-edge. (p. 191)

Therapists may even attempt to stop clients from relating the details of the abuse, "reluctant to follow up hints or clues left by patients about the existence of undisclosed trauma" (p. 191).

Still, therapists must protect their own parts who cringe with pain at hearing survivors talk about particularly bizarre, sadistic torture. It is vital, therefore, that the therapist not passively or stoically absorb the survivor's pain and the details of the abuse. The therapist must work closely with his own parts—those who overidentify with the client's pain, those who are frightened, those who are disgusted (perhaps in fear of encountering their own pain), and those who desperately want to rescue the client from her pain. Both the therapist and the client will benefit tremendously by the therapist's ability to acknowledge when parts of him are upset and his ability to restore his Self to a position of leadership.

Schwartz (1992) has found himself reacting to survivors' pain by chang-ing the subject, joking around, or becoming aloof and distant. Steele (1991) agrees that the therapist may "try the standard protective maneu-vers. We deny. We close our eyes and ears, we deftly change the subject without knowing it ourselves. We do not look too closely at their eyes so that we cannot see the searing pain. We call them psychotic. We disbe-lieve" (pp. 13–14). In reporting details of the abuse, survivors may be testing whether the therapist can contain and tolerate intense affects and painful traumatic imagery. For example, a client might "pour out graphic traumatic material that is associated with shame and self-loathing, uncon-sciously looking for subtle indications of shock, dismay, disgust" (p. 6).

But therapists must be able to share the survivors' stories. "A patient will know if the therapist is unable to tolerate hearing what has happened" (Putnam, 1989, p. 191). Survivors are quick to point out that the details are repulsive and to conclude that they themselves must be repulsive or "bad." In contrast, "a client's disclosure of the victimization secret to a therapist who remains calm, matter of fact, accepting, supportive, and therapeutically constructive is likely to reduce the client's feelings of isola-tion, rejection, and hopelessness" (Jehu et al., 1985–1986, p. 66). Herman

(1992) wisely notes that "working with victimized people requires a committed moral stance. The therapist is called upon to bear witness to a crime" (p. 135). It is the therapist's Self who must validate the horrible injustice the survivor faced alone as a child. (Sadly, even as adults, survivors may not recognize the injustice of what they suffered.) Survivors acutely observe therapists' reactions to details, especially horrific ones. If there is such a thing as a "best reaction" to survivors' stories, it is one of sincere horror, compassion, and sadness, but not one of being overwhelmed or repulsed.

"IT CAN'T BE REAL—I USED TO BELIEVE THE WORLD WAS JUST, AND PEOPLE WERE GOOD"

Can people really terrorize and rape children in the ways my clients have described? Is our world truly saturated with such horror? Will watching my clients travel a path of terror and betrayal expose me to pure malevolence, as I accompany them through heinous sights and sounds and smells?

Therapists working with survivors face deep, troubling questions about the world in which we live. Herman (1992) warns that "repeated exposure to stories of human rapacity and cruelty inevitably challenges the therapist's basic faith" (p. 141). Cornell and Olio (1991) write that therapy with survivors often reveals that these patients "endured some of the most threatening and terrorizing experiences imaginable. . . . It typically presents the therapist with many challenges to their values and personal conceptions of a just and decent world" (p. 60).

Sometimes therapists deny or ignore clients' stories just so they won't have to give up their safe view of the world. This is especially true of therapists working with survivors of satanic cults. It is imperative that therapists believe in some level of intrinsic goodness in all people, no matter what level of destruction they have suffered (or inflicted). Beahrs (1982) emphasizes that in the therapy relationship, the most critical factor is faith—"a trust in the Okness of all that is, which embraces the therapist and patient and all of their parts" (p. 139). He concludes that "conveying confidence that the basic being of all parts is OK lightens the load of anxiety and enables the patient to mobilize his own resources more fully" (p. 140).

The therapist's presuppositions about human nature permeate the manner in which the therapeutic services are delivered. The IFS model rejects a deficit-based view of human nature and instead rests upon the belief that everyone, at the core, is good. But how can that be, considering what some people do to others? The IFS model suggests that those who hurt children are dominated by rageful, wounded parts who carry burdens from their abusers. Both offenders and victims still have a Self, even though initially it may be extremely difficult to access.

CHAPTER 20

Epilogue

IN THIS BOOK WE HAVE tried to show how the IFS model works with adults who suffered severe abuse as children. We hope that it is clear to the reader that this process is intense, emotional, and often frustrating for both therapist and client—but ultimately fulfilling and rewarding. As disparate, extreme, and polarized parts are gradually released from their fear-bound roles and, as a result of this liberation, learn to harmonize with one another, it is like the many pieces of a shattered mind being arranged to form a beautiful mosaic. It is one picture; yet each piece still has a separate existence and plays a crucial role in creating the whole.

When Lorene stopped therapy, her mosaic was still emerging. She felt that many of the pieces were in place and that she could keep helping those that were not quite there. She was free to return at any time and we agreed that she should return for brief periods when problems arose (she returned twice for a few sessions). In this final chapter, we describe some of the general changes in her approach to life, as well as the changes in her individual parts during the last year of therapy.

Lorene gradually found herself growing less terrified of strangers, of new situations, and of her own emotions. Her migraines disappeared, as did episodes of self-mutilation. Lorene remarried and had a second child. The support of her new extended family helped Lorene continue to avoid contact with her mother—a relationship permeated by a sense of loss and betrayal.

Most significantly, Lorene was able to make choices about how to spend each day and how to direct her life. She could choose to go to the gas station without fearing the attendants; choose to go to a movie without fearing other people sitting with her in the dark theater; and choose to have conversations and relationships with new people or to renew relationships with old friends. Lorene no longer had to stay home and hide; she no longer missed a great deal of work, social gatherings, and favorite community events; this change greatly pleased her most active part, Super-She. Lorene became active in community organizations, which the gregarious Nicholas enjoyed. Vincent was pleased that Lorene began teaching economics part-time. Dashiell and Alex enjoyed Lorene's newfound friendship with her body, and particularly enjoyed biking and tennis. Her younger parts, Jenny and Andy, were happy to have time to just relax and play.

Lorene's Self established strong, enduring relationships with each of her parts during therapy. The parts, in turn, responded with enthusiasm to their new roles:

Dashiell. After polarizations involving Dashiell and other parts were resolved, Dashiell became very strong, lean, and brown. Now he spends most of his time outside. He maintains a deep connection to the physical world of nature and has intense sensory experiences; for example, he is exhilarated by the ocean, the wind, or simply the sunlight. He is very content, at last free of torment. He is aware of communicating with other parts, but spends little time with them. Despite this solitariness, he has a strong position within the system and can affect the others a great deal.

Super-She. After Super-She was relieved of protector duties, it was surprising to find that she enjoys art and music. She remains very managerial, but is now free to explore her own interests in addition to her work in accounting and economics.

Vincent. Vincent eventually relinquished the protector role. He still offers wisdom and help to Lorene's Self, but he no longer feels ultimately responsible for decisions. This leaves him free to pursue the philosophical explorations he loves so much.

Nicholas. Working with Nicky in therapy revealed his hidden anguish and desolation. He had a deep longing for a safe connection with others and for freedom from guilt and shame. It is now apparent that Nicky is rich in vitality and passion. He can abandon himself with complete commitment to any goal, and he offers unconditional loyalty to those he chooses as friends. Nicky also has a strong imagination and an agile, complex mind.

Alex. Alex now displays a vibrant, intuitive intelligence and has intense powers of concentration. She carries the intellectual side of Dashiell's almost sensory love for being alive. She has a deep sense of commitment and loyalty to many of the parts, but has learned to tame much of her destructive protectiveness. Alex often seems to be at the center of the action.

Victor. Ultimately, Victor revealed an intense yearning to give up his "evilness." He felt heavily burdened by this role and was grateful to relinquish it. Victor now tends to show up with Dashiell, using him as a mentor to explore what his new role and interests will be.

The "seven-year-old" part. Although she still rarely initiates conversations, she is immensely grateful when Lorene's Self seeks her out. She is slowly learning to relax, to read, to play, and to be seven years old.

Bonnie. Bonnie learned in therapy that it was not necessary to offer her body as a sacrifice; that it was okay to have a girl's body; that no one could invade or use the body without Lorene's permission; and that Lorene was now able to be responsible for her body.

Destiny. After releasing Destiny from the hold of her protector, Nicholas, Lorene found that she was very lighthearted, full of energy, and delighted to have the freedom to explore the world.

Jennifer. While Jenny's sadness, isolation, and betrayal were profound, working with her also revealed extraordinary strength, which surprised many of the parts. Jenny consistently and courageously exhibited an intense desire to survive and to be happy. Because so many parts felt a connection to Jenny, moving her out of the past, where she had felt "frozen in time," and into the present had a very positive effect on the rest of the internal family. A great deal of her energy goes toward sensing other people's feelings, desires, or pain. Originally a skill used to "read" the abuser, it now enables her to connect with other parts and people.

Andy. Moving Andy from the past was extremely difficult. It was only after much work with Victor and Nicholas that Andy was freed from the past. He now spends time with Jennifer, but he appears to be growing up while she remains the same age.

Bridgette. Bridgette is rarely involved in polarizations, unless her loyalty to Destiny compels her to take sides. One of her unique abilities is to form a bridge of communication between the parts or between Lorene and other people.

Lorene returned twice during the year following the termination of therapy. Both times she asked for help in working through relationship problems with the man she eventually married. The work went smoothly and quickly because Lorene had become adept at maintaining her Self in a leadership position, and she was able to recognize when parts were so extreme that they interfered with her life.

Now, two years after this therapy (which lasted for three years, twice a week), these improvements have expanded, and Lorene is thriving. She continues to work with her parts on her own but finds that, rather than having to engage in long, reassuring conversations, she now has to merely remind the parts that they can trust her, and they quickly calm down.

Lorene's appears to be a happy ending. And the IFS model? We believe that the contents of this and an earlier book (Schwartz, 1995) represent only the first small steps toward an ecology of mind. Many topics remain to be explored through the IFS lens, including connections between mind and body, the nature of delayed memories, spiritual aspects of the model, parallels between internal and external systems, and the techniques of unburdening and retrieval. In addition, the surface has only been scratched regarding the application of the model to other modes of therapy (such as group, couples, family), and to other treatment populations (such as sex offenders, eating disorders, or children and adolescents). The connections in theory to other models, like object relations, psychosynthesis, and narrative theory, are also relatively unexplored as are the methods for incorporating techniques from other models (e.g., psychodrama, hypnosis, Hakomi). Miles to go, but for now we rest.

References

Agosta, C., & Loring, M. (1989). Understanding and treating the adult retrospective victim of child sexual abuse. In S. M. Sgroi (Ed.), *Vulnerable populations: Sexual abuse treatment for children, offenders, and persons with mental retardation*, Vol. 2 (pp. 115–135). Lexington, MA: Lexington Books.

Anderson, J. W. (1986). Finding the concealed Self in the selfless patient. *Psychotherapy Patient, 2*(2), 59–70.

Armsworth, M. W. (1989). Therapy of incest survivors: Abuse or support? *Child Abuse and Neglect, 13*(4), 549–562.

Assagioli, R. (1965). *Psychosynthesis: A manual of principles and techniques.* New York: Penguin Books.

Barall, V. (1994). Thanks for the memories: Criminal law and the psychology of memory. *Brooklyn Law Review, 59,* 1473–1493.

Bass, E., & Davis, L. (1988). *The courage to heal.* New York: Harper & Row.

Beahrs, J. O. (1982). *Unity and multiplicity: Multilevel consciousness of self in hypnosis, psychiatric disorder and mental health.* New York: Brunner/Mazel.

Begley, S., & Brant, M. (1994). You must remember this, *Newsweek* (September 26), p. 68.

Benner, D. G., & Evans, C. S. (1984). Unity and multiplicity in hypnosis, commissurotomy, and multiple personality disorder. *Journal of Mind and Behavior, 5*(4), 423–432.

Bierman, J. (1992). Pieces of the night sky: My body's legacy. In L. Wisechild (Ed.), *She who was lost is remembered* (pp. 189–194). Seattle, WA: Seal Press.

Bird, S. (1992). Emotion goddesses. In L. Wisechild (Ed.), *She who was lost is remembered* (pp. 222–227). Seattle, WA: Seal Press.

Blake-White, J., & Kline, C. M. (1985). Treating the dissociative process in adult victims of childhood incest. *Social Casework, 66,* 394–402.

Bogart, V. (1994). Transcending the dichotomy of either "subpersonalities" or "an integrated unitary self." *Journal of Humanistic Psychology, 34*(2), 82–89.

Booth, T. Y. (1990). A suggested analogy for the elusive self. *Journal of Analytical Psychology, 35,* 335–337, 341–42.

Braun, B. G. (1989). Psychotherapy of the survivor of incest with a dissociative disorder. In R. P. Kluft (Ed.), *The Psychiatric Clinics of North America: Treatment of victims of sexual abuse, 12*(2), 307–324. Philadelphia: Saunders.

Breunlin, D. C., Schwartz, R. C., & Mac Kune-Karrer, B. (1992). *Metaframeworks: Transcending the models of family therapy.* San Francisco: Jossey-Bass.

Briere, J. (1989a, September). *Psychotherapy with the survivor of severe sexual abuse*. Paper presented at the Midwest Conference on Child Sexual Abuse and Incest, Madison, WI.

Briere, J. (1989b). *Therapy for adults molested as children: Beyond survival*. New York: Springer.

Briere, J. (1992). Methodological issues in the study of sexual abuse effects. *Journal of Consulting and Clinical Psychology*, 60(2), 193–203.

Briere, J., & Conte, J. (1993). Self-reported amnesia for abuse in adults molested as children. *Journal of Traumatic Stress*, 6, 21–31.

Calof, D. L. (1994a). From traumatic dissociation to repression: Historical origins of the "False Memory Syndrome" hypothesis. *Treating Abuse Today*, 4(4), 24–35.

Calof, D. L. (1994b). A conversation with Michael D. Yapko, Ph.D., Part I. *Treating Abuse Today*, 4(5), 24–40.

Calof, D. L. (1993). A conversation with Pamela Freyd, Ph.D., Executive Director and Co-founder of the False Memory Syndrome Foundation, Inc. *Treating Abuse Today*, 3(3), 25–39; 3(4), 26–33.

Campbell, J., & Moyers, B. (1988). *The power of myth*. New York: Doubleday.

Childers, J. H. (1988). Parts processing: A therapeutic technique for facilitating adolescent identity. *TACD Journal*, 16(1), 17–27.

Cornell, W. F., & Olio, K. A. (1991). Integrating affect in treatment with adult survivors of physical and sexual abuse. *American Journal of Orthopsychiatry*, 61(1), 59–69.

Courtois, C. A. (1988). *Healing the incest wound: Adult survivors in therapy*. New York: Norton.

Courtois, C. A. (1992). The memory retrieval process in incest survivor therapy. *Journal of Child Sexual Abuse*, 1(1), 15–31.

Csikszentmihalyi, M. (1990). *Flow: The psychology of optimal experience*. New York: HarperCollins.

Dawes, R. M. (1992, July). *Why believe that for which there is no good evidence?* Paper presented at the Convention of the American Psychological Society, San Diego, CA.

DeBerry, S. (1989). Schizoid phenomena, psychobiology, and psychiatric paradigms: A proposed integrative model. *Journal of Contemporary Psychotherapy*, 19(2), 81–107.

Dolan, Y. M. (1991). *Resolving sexual abuse: Solution-focused therapy and Ericksonian hypnosis for adult survivors*. New York: Norton.

Ellenson, G. S. (1989). Horror, rage and defenses in the symptoms of female sexual abuse survivors. *Social Casework*, 70(10), 589–596.

Ellis, J. (1990). The therapeutic journey: A guide for travelers. In T. A. Laidlaw & C. Malmo (Eds.), *Healing voices: Feminist approaches to therapy with women* (pp. 243–271). San Francisco: Jossey-Bass.

Engel, B. (1982). *The right to innocence: Healing the trauma of childhood sexual abuse*. Lexington, MA: Lexington Books.

Ernsdorff, G. M., & Loftus, E. F. (1993). Let sleeping memories lie? Words of caution about tolling the statute of limitations in cases of memory repression. *Journal of Criminal Law & Criminology*, 84, 129–174.

Ewing, K. P. (1990). The illusion of wholeness: Culture, self and the experience of inconsistency. *Ethos*, 18(3), 251–278.

Fadiman, J. (1993). Who's minding the store? A comment on Frick's defense of unitary personality. *Journal of Humanistic Psychology*, 33(2), 129–133.

Feinauer, L. (1989). Relationship of treatment to adjustment in women sexually abused as children. *American Journal of Family Therapy*, 17(4), 326–334.

Feinberg-Moss, B., & Oatley, K. (1990). Guided imagery in brief psychodynamic therapy: Outcome and process. *British Journal of Medical Psychology, 63*(2), 117–129.

Fine, C. G. (1990). The cognitive sequelae of incest. In R. P. Kluft (Ed.), *Incest related syndromes of adult psychopathology* (pp. 161–182). Washington: American Psychiatric Press, Inc.

Finkelhor, D., & Browne, A. (1985). The traumatic impact of child sexual abuse: A conceptualization. *American Journal of Orthopsychiatry, 55*(4), 530–541.

Freyd, J. J. (1993, August). *Theoretical and personal perspectives on the delayed memory debate.* Paper presented at the Center for Mental Health at Foote Hospital's Continuing Education Conference: Controversies around recovered memories of incest and ritualistic abuse, Ann Arbor, MI.

Frick, W. B. (1993). Subpersonalities: Who conducts the orchestra? *Journal of Humanistic Psychology, 33*(2), 122–128.

Friedrich, W. N. (1990). *Psychotherapy of sexually abused children and their families.* New York: Norton.

Gainer, J., & Torem, M. (1993). Ego-state therapy for self-injurious behavior. *American Journal of Clinical Hypnosis, 5*(4), 257–266.

Gannon, J. P. (1989). *Soul survivors.* New York: Prentice-Hall.

Gartrell, N. K., & Sanderson, B. E. (1994). Sexual abuse of women by women in psychotherapy: Counseling and advocacy. *Women and Therapy, 15*(1), 39–54.

Gazzaniga, M. S. (1985). *The social brain.* New York: Basic Books.

Gazzaniga, M. S. (1989). Organization of the human brain. *Science, 245*(4921), 947–952.

Gelinas, D. J. (1983). The persisting negative effects of incest. *Psychiatry, 46*(4), 312–332.

Gergen, K. (1972). Multiple identity: The healthy, happy human being wears many masks, *Psychology Today, 5*(12), 31–35, 64–66.

Gil, E. (1990). *Treatment of adult survivors of childhood abuse* (2nd ed.). Walnut Creek, CA: Launch Press.

Gilligan, S. G., & Kennedy, C. M. (1989). Solutions and resolutions: Ericksonian hypnotherapy with incest survivor groups. *Journal of Strategic and Systemic Therapies, 8*(4), 9–17.

Glass, J. M. (1993). *Shattered selves: Multiple personality in a postmodern world.* Ithaca, NY: Cornell University Press.

Haller, O. L., & Alter-Reid, K. (1986). Secretiveness and guardedness: A comparison of two incest-survivor samples. *American Journal of Psychotherapy, 40*(4), 554–563.

Herman, J. L. (1981). *Father-daughter incest.* Cambridge, MA: Harvard University Press.

Herman, J. L. (1992). *Trauma and recovery: The aftermath of violence — from domestic abuse to political terror.* New York: Basic Books.

Herman, J. L. (1987). Recovery and verification of memories of childhood sexual trauma. *Psychoanalytic Psychology, 4*(1), 1–14.

Herman, J. L., Perry, C., & van der Kolk, B. A. (1989). Childhood trauma in borderline personality disorder. *American Journal of Psychiatry, 146*(4), 490–495.

Herman, J. L., Russell, D., & Trocki, K. (1986). Long term effects of incestuous abuse in childhood. *American Journal of Psychiatry, 143*(10), 1293–1296.

Hilgard, E. R. (1986). *Divided consciousness: Multiple controls in human thought and action* (rev. ed.). New York: Wiley.

Hillman, J. (1975). *Revisioning psychology.* New York: Harper & Row.

Hochman, J. (1994, January 10). Buried memories challenge the law. *National Law Journal, 16*(17), 17.

Horn, M. (1993, November). Memories lost and found. *U.S. News & World Report,* *115*(21), 52–63.

Hymer, S. (1984). The self in victimization: Conflict and developmental perspectives. *Victimology: An International Journal, 9,* 142–150.

Ingerman, S. (1989). Welcoming our selves back home: The application of shamanic soul-retrieval techniques in the treatment of trauma cases. *Shaman's Drum,* Mid-summer, 25–29.

James, W. (1890). *The principles of psychology.* New York: Holt.

Jehu, D. (1988). *Beyond sexual abuse: Therapy with women who were childhood victims.* New York: Wiley.

Jehu, D., Klassen, C., & Gazan, M. (1985–86). Cognitive restructuring of distorted beliefs associated with childhood sexual abuse. *Journal of Social Work and Human Sexuality, 4*(1–2), 46–69.

Johnson, R. A. (1986). *Inner work: Using dreams and active imagination for personal growth.* San Francisco: Harper & Row.

Jung, C. G. (1921/1971). Definitions. *The collected works of C. G. Jung, vol. 6. A psychological theory of types* (R. F. C. Hull, Trans.). Bollingen Series XX. Princeton, NJ: Princeton University Press.

Jung, C. G. (1917/1926/1936/1943/1966). On the psychology of the unconscious. In *The collected works of C. G. Jung, vol. 7. Two essays on analytical psychology* (R. F. C. Hull, Trans.). (2nd ed.) Bollingen Series XX. Princeton, NJ: Princeton University Press.

Jung, C. G. (1934/1969). A review of the complex theory. In *The collected works of C. G. Jung, vol. 8, pt. I. The structure and dynamics of the psyche* (R. F. C. Hull, Trans.). (2nd ed.) Bollingen Series XX. Princeton, NJ: Princeton University Press.

Jung, C. G. (1939/1968). Conscious, unconscious, and individuation. In *The collected works of C. G. Jung, vol. 9, pt. I. The archetypes and the collective unconscious* (R. F. C. Hull, Trans.). (2nd ed.) Bollingen Series XX. Princeton, NJ: Princeton University Press.

Jung, C. G. (1955/1968). Mandalas. In *The collected works of C. G. Jung, vol. 9, pt. I. The archetypes and the collective unconscious* (R. F. C. Hull, Trans.). (2nd ed.) Bollingen Series XX. Princeton, NJ: Princeton University Press.

Jung, C. G. (1957/1964). The undiscovered self (present & future). In *The collected works of C. G. Jung, vol. 10. Civilization in transition* (R. F. C. Hull, Trans.). (2nd ed.) Bollingen Series XX. New York: Pantheon Books.

Jung, C. G. (1958/1964). Flying saucers: A modern myth of things seen in the skies. In *The collected works of C. G. Jung, vol. 10. Civilization in transition* (R. F. C. Hull, Trans.). (2nd ed.) Bollingen Series XX. New York: Pantheon Books.

Jung, C. G. (1938/1940/1969). Psychology and religion (the Terry lectures). In *The collected works of C. G. Jung, vol. 11. Psychology and religion: West and east* (R. F. C. Hull, Trans.). Bollingen Series XX. New York: Pantheon Books.

Jung, C. G. (1934/1966). The practical use of dream analysis. In *The collected works of C. G. Jung, vol. 16. The practice of psychotherapy* (R. F. C. Hull, Trans.). (2nd ed., rev.) Bollingen Series XX. Princeton, NJ: Princeton University Press.

Jung, C. G. (1935/1976). The Tavistock lectures. In *The collected works of C. G. Jung, vol. 18. The symbolic life* (R. F. C. Hull, Trans.). Bollingen Series XX. Princeton, NJ: Princeton University Press.

Kane, E. (1989). *Recovering from incest: Imagination and the healing process.* Boston: Sigo Press.

Kanovitz, J. (1992). Hypnotic memories and civil sexual abuse trials. *Vanderbilt Law Review, 45,* 1185–1262.

Kernberg, O., Selzer, M. A., Koenigsberg, H., Carr., A. C., & Appelbaum, A. H. (1989). *Psychodynamic psychotherapy of borderline patients.* New York: Basic Books.

Kilgore, L. C. (1988). Effect of early childhood sexual abuse on self and ego development. *Social Casework, 69,* 224–230.

Kluft, R. P. (Ed.). (1989). *The Psychiatric Clinics of North America: Treatment of victims of sexual abuse, 12*(2), Philadelphia: Saunders.

Kluft, R. P. (Ed.). (1990). *Incest related syndromes of adult psychopathology.* Washington: American Psychiatric Press, Inc.

Kluft, R. P. (1985). *Childhood antecedents of multiple personality disorder.* Washington: American Psychiatric Press, Inc.

Knowles, E. S., & Sibicky, M. E. (1990). Continuity and diversity in the stream of selves: Metaphorical resolution of William James's one-in-many-selves paradox. *Personality and Social Psychology Bulletin, 16*(4), 676–687.

Lancaster, B. (1991). *Mind, brain and human potential: The quest for an understanding of self.* Rockport, MA: Element, Inc.

Larsen, S. (1990). Our inner cast of characters. *Humanistic Psychologist, 18*(2), 176–187.

Lepine, D. (1990). Ending the cycle of violence: Overcoming guilt in incest survivors, In T. A. Laidlaw & C. Malmo (Eds.), *Healing voices: Feminist approaches to therapy with women* (pp. 272–287). San Francisco: Jossey-Bass.

Lister, E. (1982). Forced silence: A neglected dimension of trauma. *American Journal of Psychiatry, 139,* 872–76.

Loftus, E. F. (1993). The reality of repressed memories. *American Psychologist, 48*(5), 518–537.

Loftus, E. F., & Ketcham, K. (1994). *The myth of repressed memory: False memories and allegations of sexual abuse.* New York: St. Martin's Press.

Loftus, E. F., & Rosenwald, L. A. (1993). Buried Memories, shattered lives, *American Bar Association Journal* (Nov.), 70–73.

Lynn, S. J., & Nash, M. R. (1994). Truth in memory: Ramifications for psychotherapy and hypnotherapy. *American Journal of Clinical Hypnosis, 36*(3), 194–208.

Maclean, H. N. (1993). *Once upon a time: A true story of memory, murder, and the law.* New York: HarperCollins.

Malmo, C. (1990). Recreating equality: A feminist approach to ego-state therapy. In T. A. Laidlaw & C. Malmo (Eds.), *Healing voices: Feminist approaches to therapy with women* (pp. 288–319). San Francisco: Jossey-Bass.

Malz, W., & Halman, B. (1987). *Incest and sexuality: A guide to understanding and healing.* Lexington, MA: Lexington Books.

Matousek, M. (1991, March/April). America's darkest secret. *Common Boundary,* 16–25.

McCann, I. L. (1991). A combined approach to taking a trauma history. *Treating Abuse Today, 1*(1), 3–8.

McCann, I. L., & Pearlman, L. A. (1990). *Psychological trauma and the adult survivor: Theory, therapy, and transformation.* New York: Brunner/Mazel.

McCann, I. L., Pearlman, L. A., Sakheim, D. K., & Abrahamson, D. J. (1988). Assessment and treatment of the adult survivor of childhood sexual abuse within a schema framework. In S. M. Sgroi (Ed.), *Vulnerable populations: Evaluation and treatment of sexually abused children and survivors, vol. 1* (pp. 77–101). Lexington, MA: Lexington Books.

McCann, I. L., Sakheim, D. K., & Abrahamson, D. J. (1988). Trauma and victimization: A model of psychological adaptation. *The Counseling Psychologist, 16*(4), 531–594.

McHugh, C. (1993, September 22). Suits claiming childhood sex abuse on rise;

lawyers, experts question recovered memories. *Chicago Daily Law Bulletin*, p. 1.

McKee, M. (1994, June 1). Erasing the memory of *Molien*. *The Recorder*, p. 1.

Meiselman, K. C. (1978). *Incest: A psychological study of causes and effects with treatment recommendations*. San Francisco: Jossey-Bass.

Meiselman, K. C. (1990). *Resolving the trauma of incest: Reintegration therapy with survivors*. San Francisco: Jossey-Bass.

Miller, A. (1981). *The drama of the gifted child* (R. Ward, Trans.). New York: Basic Books.

Miller, A. (1984). *Thou shalt not be aware: Society's betrayal of the child* (H. & H. Hannum, Trans.). New York: New American Library.

Miller, A. (1986). Hypnotherapy in a case of dissociated incest. *International Journal of Clinical and Experimental Hypnosis, 34*(1) 13–28.

Miller, D. L. (1974). *The new polytheism: Rebirth of the gods and goddesses*. New York: Harper & Row.

Miller, D. (1994). *Women who hurt themselves: A book of hope and understanding*. New York: Basic Books.

Morrison, T. (1970). *The bluest eye*. New York: Holt, Rinehart and Winston.

Napier, N. (1993). *Getting through the day: Strategies for adults hurt as children*. New York: Norton.

Nash, M. R. (1992, August). *Retrieval of childhood memories in psychotherapy: Clinical utility and historical verifiability are not the same thing*. Paper presented at the annual convention of the American Psychological Association, Washington, DC.

Nathan, D. (1992, October). Cry incest. *Playboy*, p. 84.

Nathanson, D. L. (1992). *Shame and pride: Affect, sex, and the birth of the self*. New York: Norton.

Newall, K. (1992). My body's language. In L. Wisechild (Ed.), *She who was lost is remembered* (pp. 1–8). Seattle, WA: Seal Press.

Nichols, M. P., & Schwartz, R. C. (1991). *Family therapy: Concepts and methods* (2d ed.). Boston: Allyn & Bacon.

Nichols, M. P., & Schwartz, R. C. (1994). *Family therapy: Concepts and methods* (3d ed.). Boston: Allyn & Bacon.

Ofshe, R., & Watters, E. (1994). *Making monsters: False memory, psychotherapy and sexual hysteria*. New York: Scribner.

Oksana, C. (1994). *Safe passage to healing: A guide for survivors of ritual abuse*. New York: HarperCollins.

Ornstein, R. (1987). *Multimind: A new way to look at human behavior*. New York: Houghton Mifflin.

Pessoa, F. (1991). *The book of disquiet* (A. MacAdam, Trans.). New York: Pantheon.

Putnam, F. W. (1989). *Diagnosis and treatment of multiple personality disorder*. New York: Guilford.

Putnam, F. W. (1990). Disturbances of "self" in victims of childhood sexual abuse. In R. P. Kluft (Ed.), *Incest related syndromes of adult psychopathology* (pp. 113–131). Washington: American Psychiatric Press, Inc.

Redfearn, J. W. T. (1985). *Myself, my many selves*. London: Academic Press.

Redfearn, J. W. T. (1990). Comment on "A suggested analogy for the elusive self." *Journal of Analytical Psychology, 35*(3), 339–340.

Rieker, P. P., & Carmen, E. H. (1986). The victim-to-patient process: The disconfirmation and transformation of abuse. *American Journal of Orthopsychiatry, 56*(3), 360–370.

Rilke, R. M. (1918). The quest.

Roberts, S. C. (1992, May/June). Multiple realities: How MPD is shaking up our notions of the self, the body and even the origins of evil. *Common Boundary,* 25–31.

Russell, D. E. H. (1986). *The secret trauma: Incest in the lives of girls and women.* New York: Basic Books.

Samuels, A. (1989). *The plural psyche: Personality, morality and the father.* New York: Routledge.

Sargent, N. M. (1989). Spirituality and adult survivors of child sexual abuse: Some treatment issues. In S. M. Sgroi (Ed.), *Vulnerable populations: Sexual abuse treatment for children, offenders, and persons with mental retardation,* vol. 2 (pp. 167–202). Lexington, MA: Lexington Books.

Sarraute, N. (1990). *You don't love yourself* (B. Wright, Trans.). New York: George Braziller, Inc.

Satir, V. (1978). *Your many faces.* Berkeley, CA: Celestial Arts.

Saunders, D. (1994, September 13). The coffee's hot, stupid! A proud nation of pioneers has become a land of whining plaintiffs. *Atlanta Journal and Constitution,* section A, p. 6.

Schetky, D. H. (1990). A review of the literature on the long-term effects of childhood sexual abuse. In R. P. Kluft (Ed.), *Incest related syndromes of adult psychopathology* (pp. 35–54). Washington: American Psychiatric Press, Inc.

Schwartz, R. C. (1987, March/April). Our multiple selves: Applying systems thinking to the inner family. *Family Therapy Networker, 11,* 25–31, 80–83.

Schwartz, R. C. (1988). Know thy selves. *Family Therapy Networker, 12,* 21–29.

Schwartz, R. C. (1992, May/June). Rescuing the exiles. *Family Therapy Networker, 16,* 33–37, 75.

Schwartz, R. C. (1993, Winter). Constructionism, sex abuse and the self. *American Family Therapy Academy Newsletter, 50,* 6–10, 24–27.

Schwartz, R. C. (1995). *Internal family systems therapy.* New York: Guilford Press.

Sgroi, S. M. (Ed.). (1988). *Vulnerable populations: Evaluation and treatment of sexually abused children and adult survivors,* vol. 1. Lexington, MA: Lexington Books.

Sgroi, S. M. (Ed.). (1989). *Vulnerable populations: Sexual abuse treatment for children, offenders, and persons with mental retardation,* vol. 2. Lexington, MA: Lexington Books.

Sgroi, S. M., & Bunk, B. S. (1988). A clinical approach to adult survivors of child sexual abuse. In S. M. Sgroi (Ed.), *Vulnerable populations: Evaluation and treatment of sexually abused children and adult survivors,* vol. 1 (pp. 137–186). Lexington, MA: Lexington Books.

Shengold, L. (1989). *Soul murder: The effects of childhood abuse and deprivation.* New York: Ballantine Books.

Sheridan, R. (1994, September 26). Power of belief over truth: "Repressed memories" may be falsehoods made believable through the power of suggestion. *The Recorder,* p. 7.

Siegel, D. R., & Romig, C. A. (1988). Treatment of adult survivors of childhood sexual assault: Imagery within a systemic framework. *American Journal of Family Therapy, 16*(3), 229–242.

Sisk, S. L., & Hoffman, C. F. (1987). *Inside scars: Incest recovery as told by a survivor and her therapist.* Madison, AL: Pandora Press.

Spiegel, D. (1989). Hypnosis in the treatment of victims of sexual abuse. In R. P. Kluft (Ed.), *The Psychiatric Clinics of North America: Treatment of victims of sexual abuse, 12*(2), 295–305. Philadelphia: Saunders.

Spiegel, D. (1990). Trauma, dissociation, and hypnosis. In R. P. Kluft (Ed.), *Incest related syndromes of adult psychopathology* (pp. 247–261). Washington: American Psychiatric Press, Inc.

Steele, K. (1991). Sitting with the shattered soul. *Treating Abuse Today*, 12–15.

Steele, K. (1988). The healing pool. *Voices*, 74–79.

Stone, H., & Winkelman, S. (1985). *Embracing our selves: The voice dialogue manual*. Marina del Rey, CA: DeVorss & Co.

Storr, A. (1983). *The essential Jung*. Princeton, NJ: Princeton University Press.

Summit, R. C. (1983). The child sexual abuse accommodation syndrome. *Child Abuse and Neglect, 7*, 177–193.

Summit, R. C. (1989). The centrality of victimization: Regaining the focal point of recovery for survivors of child sexual abuse. In R. P. Kluft (Ed.), *The Psychiatric Clinics of North America: Treatment of victims of sexual abuse, 12*(2), 413–430. Philadelphia: Saunders.

Summit, R. C. (1992a). Misplaced attention to delayed memory. *The Advisor, 5*(3), 21–26.

Summit, R. C. (1992b). Abuse of the child sexual abuse accommodation syndrome. *Journal of Child Sexual Abuse, 1*(4), 153–163.

Summit, R. C. (1992c). The rehabilitation of the child sexual abuse accommodation syndrome in trial courts in Kentucky: Commentary. *Journal of Child Sexual Abuse, 1*(4), 147–151.

Summit, R. (1994). Digging for the truth: The McMartin tunnel project versus trenchant disbelief. *Treating Abuse Today, 4*(4), 5–13.

Swink, K. K., & Leveille, A. E. (1986). From victim to survivor: A new look at the issues and recovery process for adult incest survivors. *Women and Therapy, 5*, 119–141.

Tavris, C. (1993, January 3). Beware the incest-survivor machine. *New York Times Book Review*, p. 1.

Terr, L. (1994). *Unchained memories: True stories of traumatic memories, lost and found*. New York: Basic Books.

Terr, L. (1990). *Too scared to cry*. New York: Basic Books.

Utain, M., & Oliver, B. (1989). *Scream louder: Through hell and healing with an incest survivor and her therapist*, Deerfield Beach, FL: Health Communications.

van der Kolk, B. A., Perry, J. C., & Herman, J. L. (1991). Childhood origins of self-destructive behavior. *American Journal of Psychiatry, 148*, 1665–1671.

Wakefield, H., & Underwager, R. (1992). Recovered memories of alleged sexual abuse: Lawsuits against parents. *Behavioral Sciences and the Law, 10*, 483–507.

Watanabe, S. K. (1986). Cast of characters work: Systemically exploring the naturally organized personality. *Contemporary Family Therapy, 8*(1), 75–83.

Watkins, J. G., & Johnson, R. J. (1982). *We, the divided self*. New York: Irvington Publishers.

Watkins, J. G., & Watkins, H. H. (1979). Ego states and hidden observers. *Journal of Altered States of Consciousness, 5*, 3–18.

Watkins, J. G., & Watkins, H. H. (1981). Ego-state therapy. In R. J. Corsini (Ed.), *Handbook of innovative psychotherapies* (pp. 252–270). New York: Wiley.

Watkins, J. G., & Watkins, H. H. (1988). The management of malevolent ego states in multiple personality disorder. *Dissociation, 1*(1), 67–72.

Watkins, J. G., & Watkins, H. H. (1979). The theory and practice of ego-state therapy. In H. Grayson (Ed.), *Short-term approaches to psychotherapy* (pp. 176–220). New York: Human Sciences Press.

Watkins, M. (1986). *Invisible guests: The development of imaginal dialogues*. Hillsdale, NJ: Analytic Press.

Watkins, M. (1976). *Waking dreams*. Dallas, TX: Spring Publications.

Watzlawick, P., Weakland, J. H., & Fisch, R. (1974). *Change: Principles of problem formation and problem resolution*. New York: Norton.

Williams, M. J. (1991). *Healing hidden memories: Recovery for adult survivors of childhood abuse.* Deerfield Beach, FL: Health Communications.

Williams, W. J. (1992). *Aristoi.* New York: Tom Doherty Associates.

Wisechild, L. M. (1988). *The obsidian mirror: An adult healing from incest.* Seattle, WA: Seal Press.

Wisechild, L. M. (Ed.). (1992). *She who was lost is remembered: Healing from incest through creativity.* Seattle, WA: Seal Press.

Wisechild, L. M. (1994). *The mother I carry: A memoir of healing from emotional abuse.* Seattle, WA: Seal Press.

Wright, J. (1994, August 5). Recalling or fabricating past abuse? *Los Angeles Times,* part E, page 1.

Wyatt, G. E., & Newcomb, M. D. (1990). Internal and external mediators of women's sexual abuse in childhood. *Journal of Consulting and Clinical Psychology, 58*(6), 758–767.

Wyatt, G. E., & Powell, G. J. (Eds.). (1988). *Lasting effects of child sexual abuse.* Newbury Park, CA: Sage Publications.

Yapko, M. D. (1994). *Suggestions of abuse: True and false memories of childhood sexual trauma.* New York: Simon & Schuster.

Yates, M., & Pawley, K. (1987). Utilizing imagery and the unconscious to explore and resolve the trauma of sexual abuse. *Art Therapy, 3,* 36–41.

Zalaquett, C. (1989). The internal parts model: Parts, polarities and dichotomies. *Journal of Integrative and Eclectic Psychotherapy, 8*(4), 329–343.

Zohar, D. (1990). *The quantum self: Human nature and consciousness defined by the new physics.* New York: Morrow.

Zohar, D., & Marshall, I. (1994). *The quantum society: Mind, physics, and a new social vision.* New York: Morrow.

Index

NAMES